Household Safety
Safety
SOURCEBOOK

Health Reference Series

First Edition

Household Safety
SOURCEBOOK

*Basic Consumer Health Information about
Household Safety, Including Information
about Poisons, Chemicals, Fire, and Water
Hazards in the Home*

*Along with Advice about the Safe Use of Home
Maintenance Equipment, Choosing Toys and
Nursery Furniture, Holiday and Recreation
Safety, a Glossary, and Resources for Further
Help and Information*

Edited by
Dawn D. Matthews

615 Griswold Street • Detroit, MI 48226

Bibliographic Note

Because this page cannot legibly accommodate all the copyright notices, the Bibliographic Note portion of the Preface constitutes an extension of the copyright notice.

Each new volume of the *Health Reference Series* is individually titled and called a "First Edition." Subsequent updates will carry sequential edition numbers. To help avoid confusion and to provide maximum flexibility in our ability to respond to informational needs, the practice of consecutively numbering each volume has been discontinued.

Edited by Dawn D. Matthews

Health Reference Series

Karen Bellenir, *Managing Editor*
David A. Cooke, MD, *Medical Consultant*
Maria Franklin, *Permissions Assistant*
Joan Margeson, *Research Associate*
Dawn Matthews, *Verification Assistant*
Carol Munson, *Permissions Assistant*

Omnigraphics, Inc.

Matthew P. Barbour, *Vice President, Operations*
Laurie Lanzen Harris, *Vice President, Editorial Director*
Kevin Hayes, *Production Coordinator*
Thomas J. Murphy, *Vice President, Finance and Controller*
Peter E. Ruffner, *Senior Vice President*
Jane J. Steele, *Marketing Coordinator*

Frederick G. Ruffner, Jr., *Publisher*

© 2002, Omnigraphics, Inc.

Library of Congress Cataloging-in-Publication Data

Household safety sourcebook / edited by Dawn D. Matthews.-- 1st ed.
   p. c.m. -- (Health reference series)
   "Basic consumer health information about household safety, including information about poisons, chemicals, fire, and water hazards in the home; along with advice about the safe use of home maintenance equipment, choosing toys and nursery furniture, holiday and recreation safety, a glossary, and resources for further help and information"
   Includes bibliographical references and index.
   ISBN 0-7808-0338-8
   1. Home accidents--Handbooks, manuals, etc. 2. Product safety--Handbooks, manuals, etc. I. Matthews, Dawn D. II. Series.
TX150 .H68 2001
613.6--dc21
2001052380

∞

This book is printed on acid-free paper meeting the ANSI Z39.48 Standard. The infinity symbol that appears above indicates that the paper in this book meets that standard.

Printed in the United States

Table of Contents

v

Part III: Burn Hazards

Part IV: Water Hazards

Part V: Choking, Strangulation, and Suffocation Hazards

Part VI: Other Household Hazards

Part VII: Indoor Air Quality

Part VIII: Nurseries, Toys, Playgrounds, and Other Equipment

Part IX: Home Maintenance Equipment

Part X: Holiday and Recreation Safety

Part XI: Additional Help and Information

Preface

About This Book

About 2.5 million children are injured or killed by hazards in the home each year. Many of these incidents could be prevented by using simple child safety devices. Many other needless household accidents, including falls, burns, poisonings, and drownings, occur when lack of knowledge about risks results in dangerous conditions. Safety is best accomplished through accident prevention, and the first step toward a safer home is identifying household hazards.

Household Safety Sourcebook contains information about common household hazards and injury prevention strategies, including safety concerns regarding poisons, chemicals, fire, water, electricity, indoor air quality, toys, playgrounds, lawnmowers, and other home equipment. Guidelines for holiday and recreation safety are also provided, along with a glossary and resources for further help and information.

How to Use This Book

This book is divided into parts and chapters. Parts focus on broad areas of interest. Chapters are devoted to single topics within a part.

Part I: Introduction to Household Safety provides information about making the home environment safer for children and older adults. It offers suggestions for parents, babysitters, and other caregivers.

Part II: Poison and Chemical Hazards describes poison prevention strategies and risks associated with lead, pesticides, household plants, and household chemicals.

Part III: Burn Hazards provides information about avoiding burns and scalds associated with cooking, tap water, fireplaces, space heaters, generators, and other household appliances and devices. Information about using electricity safely is also included.

Part IV: Water Hazards offers suggestions for keeping children and others safe from drowning hazards, including home pools, spas, and hot tubs. A separate chapter offers tips for flood victims.

Part V: Choking, Strangulation, and Suffocation Hazards includes facts about identifying toys and other household objects that can accidentally cut off a victim's air supply.

Part VI: Other Household Hazards provides information about risks associated with cordless telephones, windows, recliner chairs, and folding tables.

Part VII: Indoor Air Quality includes information about risks associated with airborne chemical and biological pollutants, including carbon monoxide, asbestos, formaldehyde, and methylene chloride.

Part VIII: Nurseries, Toys, Playgrounds, and Other Equipment describes safety guidelines associated with such items as cribs, bunk beds, walkers, toys, playground equipment, and home exercise paraphernalia.

Part IX: Home Maintenance Equipment provides facts about the safe use of lawnmowers, weed trimmers, chain saws, pressure washers, and garage door openers.

Part X: Holiday and Recreation Safety offers tips about safe Christmas, Halloween, and Fourth of July celebrations. It also offers safety suggestions for commonly used recreational items, such as bicycles, skates and skateboards, all-terrain vehicles, and showmobiles.

Part XI: Additional Help and Information includes a glossary and information about various agencies able to answer questions about different aspects of household safety.

Bibliographic Note

This volume contains documents and excerpts from publications issued by the following government agencies: Centers for Disease Control and Prevention (CDC); Consumer Product Safety Commission (CPSC); and the U.S. Environmental Protection Agency (EPA).

In addition, this volume contains copyrighted articles from Alberta Agriculture, Food and Rural Development; American Association of Poison Control Centers; King County, Washington; and Parasol EMT Pty. Limited.

Full citation information is provided on the first page of each chapter. Every effort has been made to secure all necessary rights to reprint the copyrighted material. If any omissions have been made, please contact Omnigraphics to make corrections for future editions.

Acknowledgements

Thanks go to Karen Bellenir for her help and patience during this process, and to Carol Munson for her work on this book.

Note from the Editor

This book is part of Omnigraphics' *Health Reference Series*. The *Series* provides basic information about a broad range of medical concerns. It is not intended to serve as a tool for diagnosing illness, in prescribing treatments, or as a substitute for the physician/patient relationship. All persons concerned about medical symptoms or the possibility of disease are encouraged to seek professional care from an appropriate health care provider.

Our Advisory Board

The *Health Reference Series* is reviewed by an Advisory Board comprised of librarians from public, academic, and medical libraries. We would like to thank the following board members for providing guidance to the development of this series:

Dr. Lynda Baker,
Associate Professor of Library and Information Science,
Wayne State University, Detroit, MI

Nancy Bulgarelli,
William Beaumont Hospital Library, Royal Oak, MI

Karen Imarasio,
Bloomfield Township Public Library, Bloomfield Township, MI

Karen Morgan,
Mardigian Library, University of Michigan-Dearborn,
Dearborn, MI

Rosemary Orlando,
St. Clair Shores Public Library, St. Clair Shores, MI

Medical Consultant

Medical consultation services are provided to the *Health Reference Series* editors by David A. Cooke, MD. Dr. Cooke is a graduate of Brandeis University. He received his M.D. degree from the University of Michigan and completed residency training at the University of Wisconsin Hospital and Clinics. He is board-certified in Internal Medicine. Dr. Cooke currently works as part of the University of Michigan Health System and practices in Brighton, MI. In his free time, he enjoys writing, science fiction, and spending time with his family.

Health Reference Series *Update Policy*

The inaugural book in the *Health Reference Series* was the first edition of *Cancer Sourcebook* published in 1992. Since then, the *Series* has been enthusiastically received by librarians and in the medical community. In order to maintain the standard of providing high-quality health information for the layperson the editorial staff at Omnigraphics felt it was necessary to implement a policy of updating volumes when warranted.

Medical researchers have been making tremendous strides, and it is the purpose of the *Health Reference Series* to stay current with the most recent advances. Each decision to update a volume will be made on an individual basis. Some of the considerations will include how much new information is available and the feedback we receive from people who use the books. If there is a topic you would like to see added to the update list, or an area of medical concern you feel has not been adequately addressed, please write to:

Editor
Health Reference Series
Omnigraphics, Inc.
615 Griswold
Detroit, MI 48226

The commitment to providing on-going coverage of important medical developments has also led to some format changes in the *Health Reference Series*. Each new volume on a topic is individually titled and called a "First Edition." Subsequent updates will carry sequential edition numbers. To help avoid confusion and to provide maximum flexibility in our ability to respond to informational needs, the practice of consecutively numbering each volume has been discontinued.

Part One

Introduction to Household Safety

Chapter 1

Protect Your Child

Each year, more children die in home accidents than from all childhood diseases combined. Watch your children as they play—nothing can substitute for careful supervision.

The Consumer Product Safety Commission (CPSC) has released several studies examining injury and death data across a range of children's products.

CPSC data show that nursery product-related injuries and crib-related deaths have declined, injuries to children on scooters and trampolines have increased, and injuries involving toys have stayed about the same over recent years.

Household Dangers

Know where the "danger" items are—medicines, toxic bleaches, oven and drain cleaners, paint solvents, polishes, and waxes. Look for items packaged in child-resistant containers. Don't leave them under a sink or in plain view in a garage—lock them away in a secure place, out of your child's sight and reach.

Keep all thin plastic wrapping materials, such as dry cleaning, produce, or trash bags away from children. Never use thin plastic

"Protect Your Child," an undated fact sheet produced by the Consumer Product Safety Commission, available online at http://www.cpsc.gov/cpscpub/pubs/241.html; cited July 2001; and "Preventing Childhood Falls," an undated fact sheet produced by Centers for Disease Control and Prevention; cited August 2001.

material to cover mattresses or pillows—the plastic film can cling to a child's face causing suffocation.

Guard against electrical shocks. Cover unused outlets with safety caps. Disconnect electric rollers or hairdryers when not in use; some children have been electrocuted when hairdryers that were left plugged-in fell into bathroom sinks or tubs.

Keep children away from open windows to prevent falls. Don't depend on screens to keep the child from falling out of the window. They are designed to keep insects out, not children in. Avoid placing furniture near windows to keep children from climbing to a window seat or sill.

Nursery Equipment

Many nursery products have a long life and may be stored in anticipation of future use. When choosing used or new nursery equipment, check for sturdy construction and stability. Avoid exposed screws, bolts, or fasteners with sharp edges or points; avoid scissor-like mechanisms which could crush fingers; and avoid cutout designs that could entrap a child's head.

Safety straps on high chairs and strollers are a must. Look for straps that are easy to fasten and unfasten so that you will be sure to use them properly each time.

Mesh playpens and portable cribs should never be used with a side left down. They can pose a serious hazard to newborns and infants because the mesh forms a loose pocket into which an infant can roll and suffocate.

Use baby walkers only on smooth surfaces. Edges of carpets, throw rugs, or raised thresholds can cause a walker to tip over. Remove throw rugs when a walker is in use, and block the tops of stairways. Children have fallen down stairs in walkers.

If cribs or playpens are placed near a window, make sure there are no drapery or Venetian blind cords hanging within your baby's reach. Don't hang objects with strings or elastics (toys or laundry bags, for example) around cribs or playpens where your child might become entangled and choke to death.

When children begin to climb and explore, they can become caught in small or narrow openings. Some have been strangled when they caught their heads or necks in the open "V" shapes atop expandable wooden gates or enclosures, or in decorative cutouts in cribs.

Never tie pacifiers or other items around your baby's neck. Cords and ribbons can become tightly twisted, or can catch on crib cornerposts or other protrusions, causing strangulation.

4

Toys, Toy Chests and Labeling

Keep small objects out of your child's reach. Tiny toys, and toys with small, removable parts can be swallowed or become lodged in a child's windpipe, ears, or nose. Check to see that toys have not broken or come apart at the seams, exposing small pellets that might be swallowed or inhaled. Even such common items as coins, pins, buttons, or small batteries can choke a child.

When choosing toys, look for labels that give age recommendations such as "Recommended for Children Three to Five Years Old." Some toys or games which are safe for older children may contain small parts which are hazardous in a younger child's hands.

If a toy chest, trunk or other container for storing toys has a freefalling lid, remove the lid. A lid can drop on a child's head or neck, and some children have been killed or seriously injured. Look for a chest which has supports to hold the lid open in any position, or choose one with sliding panels or a lightweight, removable lid.

Preventing Childhood Falls

Childhood falls account for an estimated 2 million Emergency Department visits each year and in 1997, fall-related injuries claimed the lives of 87 children under age 9. The majority of childhood fall-related injuries occur at home, particularly among younger children.

Adult supervision, home modification, and informed product selection can help reduce the likelihood of childhood falls and fall-related injuries. To help protect your children from fall-related injuries, follow these safety tips from the American Academy of Pediatrics, National Safety Council, HUD, and the Lowe's Home Safety Council. (Note: If your child falls and acts abnormally in any way, call your pediatrician immediately.)

Infants

Babies are particularly vulnerable to falls and need to be closely supervised at all times.

- Never leave babies alone on any furniture, including beds, tables, sofas, or cribs and changing tables with the guard rails down—even if they have never rolled over before. In just a few seconds, babies can wiggle or roll off furniture and potentially hurt themselves. Instead, put babies on the floor or in a crib with secured guard rails.

5

- When changing a baby's diaper in a crib or on a changing table, be sure the guard rails are up and latched securely. Some changing tables also come with safety straps that you can use to secure your baby. When you do not have access to a crib or changing table with guard rails or safety straps, be sure to keep at least one hand on your baby at all times.

Choosing Safe Baby Products

When purchasing baby products, buy items and equipment that meet current safety standards and be sure to follow instructions and use the equipment properly (e.g., use the straps on highchairs, strollers, and changing tables). Be particularly cautious when buying used cribs or furniture as certain safety standards or regulations may have changed since the time they were built. Refer to some of the safety resources listed below for more specific information about current standards and features.

Highchairs

- In one year, approximately 7,000 children were sent to the hospital for falls from highchairs.

- Buy a highchair that has important safety features like a wide base, a locking tray, and a restraining belt or safety strap. Look for a label on the chair certifying that it meets current safety standards.

- Always use safety straps to restrain children in their high chairs.

Cribs

When buying a crib, look for the following features:

- Certification that it meets safety standards.

- Corner posts that do not stick up more than 1/16 of an inch.

- Rail slats that are spaced less than 2 3/8 inches apart (to prevent strangulation from children getting their heads caught between the slats). If a soda can fits through the openings between slats, the slats are too wide.

- A snug-fitting mattress.

- As the baby gets older and learns to sit and pull himself up to a standing position, lower the mattress in the crib. You should stop using the crib as soon as the top rails are less than 3/4 of the child's height.

- Do not put toys or pillows in the crib that she could stand on or use to crawl out of the crib. (The Consumer Product Safety Commission recommends that you avoid putting any toys or soft bedding in infants' cribs as they may contribute to suffocation.)

- When your child switches to a toddler bed, be sure to install guard rails on both sides of the bed. Check to make sure the mattress fits snugly into the frame.

- You might also consider installing soft flooring around your child's crib or bed to lessen the severity of a fall-related injury. Examples of such flooring include thick carpeting, a pad, or a gym mat.

Baby Walkers

According to the American Academy of Pediatrics, baby walkers should not be used. In 1997, baby walker-related injuries resulted in more than 16,000 children receiving treatment in hospital emergency rooms. Most of the injuries occur when children in baby walkers fall down stairs (80%) or tip over (5%). And falls down stairs are associated with the most severe injuries and are more likely to result in head injury and hospitalization. Supervision is not enough to make these products safe—nearly 80% of the baby walker-related injuries occurred while infants were being supervised. Baby walkers enable children to be more mobile than they are ready to be developmentally. And baby walkers make it easier for infants to reach dangerous things on tables—things they would not be able to reach if they were crawling.

A safer alternative to a baby walker is a "stationary walker"—a play table that has a turning seat.

Infants, Toddlers, and Older Children

Constant supervision is extremely important in preventing falls among children. Children are active, energetic, and fast moving and serious falls can occur in a matter of seconds. There are some steps you can take, however, to modify your home and reduce the likelihood of a fall occurring.

Modify Your Home to Make It Child-Friendly

- Crawl through each room and look at your house from a child's perspective. Look under the sofa cushions, cabinets, throw rugs, etc.

- Arrange furniture in such a way that you can see children from all parts of the room.

- Install padding on sharp corners to lessen the severity of fall-related injuries against them.

- Pay special attention to coffee tables, file cabinets, and other items that may be low to the ground.

- Lock doors and block access to any dangerous areas. Hide the keys from your children.

Floors

Look closely at your floor surfaces. Modify slippery surfaces and remove hazards whenever possible.

- Secure area rugs and throw rugs by using a nonskid backing (foam carpet backing, double-sided tape, and rubber pads can be found at many carpet and department stores.)

- If you have hard floors (e.g., wood, tile, linoleum), clean up spills immediately to avoid slipping. Avoid over-waxing.

- Use rubber mats or slip-resistant stickers on bathroom tiles and in the bathtub to prevent slips and falls. And never leave children alone in the tub—if they slip and fall, they may not be able to call for help.

- To prevent tripping on wires, route electrical and other cords behind furniture or along the walls, and tape or tack them down.

- Remove clutter from the floor—pick up toys, books, clothing, and any other items that may be on the floor.

- Make your stairs safer by keeping them well-lit and free of clutter. You can also install non-skid stair runners.

Safety Gates

- Use safety gates to prevent infants and toddlers from falling down stairs or entering dangerous rooms or areas (i.e., rooms with furniture that babies might climb on or hard edges against which they might fall).

- Properly install gates at the top and bottom of all staircases.

- Teach members of the family, including older children, to consistently latch the gate whenever they use it.

- Look for gates with vertical slats that are no more than 2 3/8 inches apart. If the gate has diamond-shaped openings, they should be less than 12 inches wide.

- Do not use accordion gates with large openings as a child's neck can get trapped.

Windows

- Install window guards on all windows above the first floor (excluding those that serve as fire emergency exits). Window guards that can be forcefully dislodged from the inside in case of fire are safest.

- When using double-hung windows, or windows that can open at the top or the bottom, open them from the top to prevent children from falling out. Install locks on all other types of windows.

- Keep furniture away from windows to prevent children from climbing out.

- Do not rely on insect screens to prevent falls. They are designed to keep insects out and are not strong enough to keep children in. Keep children away from all open windows—with or without screens.

Monitor Outdoor Play

- Select play equipment that is safe for children. For example, select tricycle models that keep children low to the ground.

- Discourage active play on outdoor decks, balconies, fire escapes, high porches, and roofs. When possible, remove climbing aids in yards or on balconies (e.g., woodpiles, tree branches, furniture near deck railings).

- Cover window wells to prevent children from falling in.

9

- Buy your children shoes that will reduce their chances of falling. A good example would be low-cut sneakers with rough, rubber soles.

Falls affect everyone. For younger children and older adults, however, falls are a special concern and fall-related injuries can be extremely serious. In 1997, 87 children age 9 and younger and 9,023 adults age 65 and older died as a result of fall-related injuries. Falls are also the most common cause of injury visits to the emergency department for young children and older adults. Each year, approximately 3,125,000 children visit emergency departments for fall-related injuries. Falls are responsible for more open wounds, fractures, and brain injuries than any other cause of injury.

Chapter 2

Childproofing Your Home

About 2½ million children are injured or killed by hazards in the home each year. The good news is that many of these incidents can be prevented by using simple child safety devices on the market today.

Any safety device you buy should be sturdy enough to prevent injury to your child, yet easy for you to use. It's important to follow installation instructions carefully. In addition, if you have older children in the house, be sure they re-secure safety devices. Remember, too, that no device is completely childproof; determined youngsters have been known to disable them.

You can childproof your home for a fraction of what it would cost to have a professional do it. And safety devices are easy to find. You can buy them at hardware stores, baby equipment shops, supermarkets, drug stores, home and linen stores, and through mail order catalogues.

Following are some child safety devices that can help prevent many injuries to young children.

- Use *Safety Latches and Locks* for cabinets and drawers in kitchens, bathrooms, and other areas to help prevent poisonings and

"Childproofing Your Home," an undated fact sheet produced by the Consumer Product Safety Commission, available online at http://www.cpsc.gov/cpscpub/pubs/grand/12steps/12steps.html; cited July 2001; and "Baby Safety Shower How-to Kit," an undated fact sheet produced by the Consumer Product Safety Commission; cited August 2001.

other injuries. Safety latches and locks on cabinets and drawers can help prevent children from gaining access to medicines and household cleaners, as well as knives and other sharp objects.

Look for safety latches and locks that adults can easily install and use, but are sturdy enough to withstand pulls and tugs from children. Safety latches are not a guarantee of protection, but they can make it more difficult for children to reach dangerous substances. Even products with child-resistant packaging should be locked away, out of reach; this packaging is not childproof.

Typical cost of a safety latch or lock: less than $2.

- Use *Safety Gates* to help prevent falls down stairs and to keep children away from dangerous areas. Safety gates can help keep children away from stairs or rooms that have hazards in them. Look for safety gates that children cannot dislodge easily, but that adults can open and close without difficulty. For the top of stairs, gates that screw to the wall are more secure than "pressure gates."

New safety gates that meet safety standards display a certification seal from the Juvenile Products Manufacturers Association (JPMA). If you have an older safety gate, be sure it doesn't have "V" shapes that are large enough for a child's head and neck to fit into.

Typical cost of a safety gate: $13 to $40.

- Use *Door Knob Covers and Door Locks* to help prevent children from entering rooms and other areas with possible dangers. Door knob covers and door locks can help keep children away from places with hazards, including swimming pools.

Be sure the door knob cover is sturdy enough not to break, but allows a door to be opened quickly by an adult in case of emergency. By restricting access to potentially hazardous rooms in the home, door knob covers could help prevent many kinds of injuries. To prevent access to swimming pools, door locks should be placed high out of reach of young children. Locks should be used in addition to fences and door alarms. Sliding glass doors, with locks that must be re-secured after each use, are often not an effective barrier to pools.

Typical cost of a door knob cover: $1 and door lock: $5 and up.

- Use *Anti-Scald Devices* for faucets and shower heads and set your water heater temperature to 120 degrees Fahrenheit to help prevent burns from hot water. Anti-scald devices for regulating water temperature can help prevent burns.

  Consider using anti-scald devices for faucets and showerheads. A plumber may need to install these. In addition, if you live in your own home, set water heater temperature to 120 degrees Fahrenheit to help prevent burns from hot water.

  Typical cost of an anti-scald device: $6 to $30.

- Use *Smoke Detectors* on every level of your home and near bedrooms to alert you to fires. Smoke detectors are essential safety devices for protection against fire deaths and injuries. Check smoke detectors once a month to make sure they're working.

  If detectors are battery-operated, change batteries at least once a year or consider using 10-year batteries.

  Typical cost of a smoke detector: less than $10.

- Use *Window Guards and Safety Netting* to help prevent falls from windows, balconies, decks, and landings. Window guards and safety netting for balconies and decks can help prevent serious falls.

  Check these safety devices frequently to make sure they are secure and properly installed and maintained. There should be no more than four inches between the bars of the window guard. If you have window guards, be sure at least one window in each room can be easily used for escape in a fire. Window screens are not effective for preventing children from falling out of windows.

  Typical cost of a window guard or safety netting: $8 to $16.

- Use *Corner and Edge Bumpers* to help prevent injuries from falls against sharp edges of furniture and fireplaces. Corner and edge bumpers can be used with furniture and fireplace hearths to help prevent injuries from falls or to soften falls against sharp or rough edges.

  Be sure to look for bumpers that stay securely on furniture or hearth edges.

  Typical cost of a corner and edge bumper: $1 and up.

- Use *Outlet Covers and Outlet Plates* to help prevent electrocution. Outlet covers and outlet plates can help protect children from electrical shock and possible electrocution.

  Be sure the outlet protectors cannot be easily removed by children and are large enough so that children cannot choke on them.

  Typical cost of an outlet cover: less than $2.

- Use a *Carbon Monoxide (CO) Detector* outside bedrooms to help prevent CO poisoning. A carbon monoxide (CO) detector can help prevent CO poisoning. Consumers should install CO detectors near sleeping areas in their homes. Households that should use CO detectors include those with gas or oil heat or with attached garages.

  Typical cost of a carbon monoxide (CO) detector: $30 to $70.

- *Cut Window Blind Cords and use Safety Tassels* to help prevent children from strangling in blind cord loops. Window blind cord safety tassels on miniblinds and tension devices on vertical blinds and drapery cords can help prevent deaths and injuries from strangulation in the loops of cords.

  For older miniblinds, cut the cord loop, remove the buckle, and put safety tassels on each cord. Be sure that older vertical blinds and drapery cords have tension or tie-down devices to hold the cords tight. When buying new miniblinds, verticals, and draperies, ask for safety features to prevent child strangulation.

  You can get window blind cord safety tassels free by calling 1-800-506-4636.

- Use *Door Stops and Door Holders* to help prevent injuries to fingers and hands. Door stops and door holders on doors and door hinges can help prevent small fingers and hands from being pinched or crushed in doors and door hinges.

  Be sure any safety device for doors is easy to use and is not likely to break into small parts, which could be a choking hazard for young children.

  Typical cost of a door stop and door holder: less than $4.

14

- 12 Use a *Cordless Phone* to make it easier to continuously watch young children, especially when they're in bathtubs, swimming pools, or other potentially dangerous areas.

Cordless phones help you watch your child continuously, without leaving the vicinity to answer a phone call. Cordless phones are especially helpful when children are in or near water, whether it's the bathtub, the swimming pool, or the beach.

Typical cost of a cordless phone: $30 and up.

How to Give a "Baby Safety Shower"

If you're looking for ways to help parents take better care of their children, consider organizing a baby safety shower.

A baby safety shower is a learning party where all the activities revolve around home safety themes. Parents and caregivers have fun—and leave with new ideas about keeping their babies safe at home.

Baby safety showers have been organized in all kinds of communities—for all kinds of audiences. These showers are an especially good way to reach young, low-income, low-literacy, or non-English speaking parents and parents-to-be with important safety information.

You can arrange a baby safety shower for any number of people—from 20 to 200. At larger baby safety showers, parents can visit a variety of exhibits where volunteers illustrate important home safety information with games, puzzles, songs, prizes, and other activities. At smaller showers, a few volunteers can lead the group in safety games.

Your theme can focus, like the material included here, on childproofing one's home—or on additional issues, like nutrition and health.

Baby safety showers are also a good way to create and promote public-private partnerships among many different organizations. By offering, for example, to distribute donated baby products or health information, you can enhance your ties with the local business community and build your relationships with local health and social service organizations. All this creates community goodwill—and provides your invited parents with welcome information, products, and services.

The materials you'll need to get started are included here. Take special note of the Baby Safety Checklist, in both English and Spanish, which provides 12 important home safety tips that all parents should know.

Use your imagination to create a baby safety shower for your specific situation. The key to success is providing important safety information in a festive and inviting setting. So, roll up your sleeves — and have fun!

Getting Organized

A baby safety shower should be fun for all involved. But it's important to be well organized.

As your first task, put together a planning committee to help you. The more assistance you get, the easier your job will be. Recruit representatives from groups and organizations who are interested in baby safety issues and can do the job well. Discuss early on:

- Who and how many people you want to invite to your baby safety shower.
- Where you can hold the shower.
- Who in the community — volunteers, organizations, businesses — can help you.
- How you will cover any costs.
- What theme and safety messages you want to convey.
- What games and activities you can use to make learning fun.
- Whether you want to enhance your shower with food, exhibits, gifts, and publicity.
- How you will schedule the shower day.

Delegate responsibility for broad categories of shower-related activities (getting sponsors, publicity, food, program, decorations, etc.) to your committee members. Keep in touch with everyone regularly to ensure that everything gets done.

Think about how you can use contributions from many different sources. For example:

- Your partners can help you plan and organize the event — and form the core of your working committee.
- Your sponsors can contribute most of the goods and services for the event.
- Your volunteers — recruited from your organization and those of your partners and sponsors — can staff the actual event.

Start planning early — and enjoy yourself!

Following a Timetable

Planning and organization are key to the success of your baby safety shower. This timetable should help you.

16-18 weeks ahead:

- Recruit baby safety shower partners
- Form a planning committee
- Select tentative shower dates
- Decide whom to invite
- Select site and confirm exact date

14-16 weeks ahead:

- Choose shower theme, programs, activities, and workshops
- Recruit volunteers
- Recruit local businesses and organizations to donate shower goods, exhibits, and services
- Estimate costs
- Develop master "to-do" list
- Invite celebrity guests and public officials

12-14 weeks ahead:

- Develop activity, game workshop, and program materials
- Plan refreshments
- Plan site logistics with building management
- List needed equipment and supplies

10-12 weeks ahead:

- Print materials (e.g., signs, flyers, posters, invitations, games, checklist)
- Plan opening ceremony
- Plan schedule of shower activities
- Plan publicity
- Make transportation and parking arrangements

8-10 weeks ahead:

- Arrange babysitting or child care
- Recruit greeters, workshop leaders, food preparers, and servers
- Prepare invitation list

6-8 weeks ahead:

- Assign volunteers to shower activities
- Begin collecting donated items

4-6 weeks ahead:

- Confirm food arrangements
- Finalize activities and workshops
- Invite shower guests
- Publicize shower through flyers, posters, and local media

2-4 weeks ahead:

- Distribute news releases
- Finish collecting donated items
- Reconfirm shower arrangements with partners and sponsors
- Hold orientation sessions for volunteers

1 week to 1 day ahead:

- Check with volunteers to ensure that everything is on track
- Make final media arrangements
- Remind invited celebrities, partners, sponsors, public officials about the event
- Assemble workshop materials and equipment
- Reconfirm food arrangements
- Prepare gift bags for shower guests

Day of the event:

- Set up
- Enjoy the event!
- Clean up

1 week after:

- Thank everyone who helped
- Evaluate the event (what went well, what didn't, what you'd do differently next time)

Inviting Your Guests

Decide which group you want to reach with safety information. For example, you may want to work with teen mothers, parents-to-be, low-income parents, low-literacy parents, or non-English speaking parents. The shower activities work best if developed around the special needs of one group at a time.

Work with community organizations who serve this target population. They can help you decide who and how many to invite and plan an appropriate program for this group.

Determine how many people to invite. For example, you can hold a shower in someone's living room for 20 people or in your local high school gymnasium for 200.

Make your guests feel special by inviting each one personally—and encouraging them to RSVP. This will communicate that you really want them at the shower and will help you plan for the number of guests actually attending.

Choosing the Site

Choose a site for the shower that's familiar and convenient to your invited audience and offers a warm, friendly environment.

Depending on the size of your shower, the site could be a community center, public library conference room, church social hall, hospital or clinic reception area, school cafeteria, gymnasium, auditorium, or a similar space in a professional office building. Be sure that:

- The site is available at a convenient time for your invited guests.

- The space in the facility:

    can accommodate your audience for a variety of activities (greeting/reception area, opening session, game workshops, refreshments, and exhibits).

    has sufficient lighting and electrical outlets, a kitchen, conveniently located rest rooms, and telephones.

has building staff to assist you when needed (e.g., to unlock the kitchen or rest rooms or control lighting, heating/air conditioning).

- You can provide transportation for your guests, if needed. If your guests drive to the shower, be sure the site has free and safe parking. If your guests take public transportation, nearby bus or subway stops should be safe and convenient.

- The space in the facility can accommodate child care, if needed, during the shower.

- Any costs can be covered.

No matter where you hold your shower, keep a list of emergency or medical services telephone numbers handy, just in case you need them.

Recruiting and Working with Volunteers

You'll need plenty of volunteers to prepare for the shower and then help on the day of the event. Start recruiting early.

Decide how many volunteers you want and what they will do. Volunteers can head committees, solicit sponsors, collect donations, set up equipment, make decorations, greet guests, run game workshops, serve food, clean up, and much more. Plan to line up more people than you need, in case some drop out before the event.

To help volunteers, be very clear about what they must do. Provide orientation sessions. If needed, schedule a dry run close to the event so all involved feel comfortable about their assignment.

After the shower, be sure to thank everyone for making the event a success!

Working with Businesses and Organizations

Baby showers involve games, gifts, and edible goodies. Start early to enlist the help of interested health and safety organizations, local businesses, and volunteers. There are probably many in your community who would be eager to help you.

Good places to start:

- Trade groups, local manufacturers, or merchants (e.g., grocery, drug, or department stores): Contact the community relations

managers for possible donations of baby-related goods and services, refreshments, prizes, free advertising, etc.

- Community organizations (e.g., hospitals, auxiliary leagues, chambers of commerce, local print and broadcast media): Contact community relations or public affairs managers about speakers, medical support, or babysitting help.

- Government organizations (e.g., local CPSC office, state and local health departments, local offices servicing the community with federally sponsored health and safety programs for children): Contact public affairs or public relations offices to alert them and solicit help and support.

- Local elected officials (e.g., mayor, city or town council members): Invite celebrity guests with an important link to the community you're serving.

Tips for working with other organizations:

- Target organizations that have goods or services relevant to the health and safety of babies, young toddlers, or new parents.

- Provide the company or organization with an incentive for contributing to your event (e.g., good community public relations; potential new customers).

- When contacting a company or organization, describe the purpose of the shower and what valuable role this group can play.

- After an organization makes a commitment, write a letter to it spelling out your understanding of the agreement.

- Identify a contact person (and a backup individual) who can get you the needed goods or services in the time and quantities you require.

- Keep in touch with the contact people about how plans for your event are developing or changing.

- Try to arrange for these groups to deliver their goods to the event site.

- If an organization is providing an exhibit, get the name and phone number of the person staffing it at the shower.

- Make arrangements at the shower site to receive and store deliveries for the event.

- Make arrangements with either staff at the shower site or the organizations providing exhibit booths to have the materials and props removed or thrown away at the conclusion of the event.

- Following the shower, write or call to thank everyone involved. Let them know how important they were to the shower's success.

Covering Your Costs

A baby safety shower need not cost a lot, but you'll probably have some expenses. Your partners and sponsors may be able to donate most of the goods and services. Here is a list of possible expenses:

- Facility (electricity, janitorial services, tables, chairs, etc.)

- Game and program materials (game workshops, exhibits, etc.)

- Buying, printing, mailing invitations

- Transportation for shower guests

- Food (refreshments or meal)

- Decorations

- Prizes

- Audio-visuals (television and VCR, overhead or slide projector)

If you can't cover these costs or arrange for donations, you may need to modify the shower activities. For example, you can make your own invitations and hand-deliver them. You can ask volunteers to donate homemade food. You can design your own decorations. Be creative. What's most important is developing a warm and friendly atmosphere where your guests feel comfortable and motivated to learn.

Arranging Publicity

Publicizing your shower can have many benefits. It can announce details of your upcoming shower to your target audience.

It also can alert businesses, local elected officials, media celebrities, and other community leaders to your efforts and attract their support.

Notify the local media about your event. Follow up with personal calls to the news or community events director.

It helps if there is a celebrity or unique angle associated with your shower. You may want to invite some well-known V.I.P.'s, like the mayor or a local TV personality. Try enlisting a radio or television show or local newspaper as a sponsor of the shower. These organizations often are interested in supporting community efforts important to their audiences.

Don't forget the value of flyers posted in grocery stores, drugstores, libraries, bus stops—any public location where your targeted audience is likely to see it.

Shower Theme

Plan to select an overall theme for your baby safety shower. This guide is developed around the theme of keeping your baby safe at home. Integral to this program is the Baby Safety Checklist, which presents 12 tips for keeping babies safe in the bedroom, bathroom, kitchen, and other living areas.

While this is critical information for every new parent, you may want to include additional health and safety themes. Choosing quality child care, selecting safe toys and nursery equipment, ensuring immunizations and proper nutrition for infants and toddlers—all of these would work.

If you invite a small group, focus on one theme. If your group is larger and you have the space, consider broadening the scope. Bring in other partners to work with you. For example, get the health department or local hospital to offer an immunization clinic. Ask a local supermarket to sponsor a nutrition booth—with appropriate games and prizes.

Pick your theme early, so you can better plan your program and activities. Coordinate your work with all involved, so that everyone knows what to do to make each activity successful.

Baby Safety Checklist

In the bedroom:

- Put your baby to sleep on her back in a crib with a firm, flat mattress and no soft bedding underneath her. Follow this advice to reduce the risk of suffocation and Sudden Infant Death Syndrome (SIDS). To prevent suffocation, never put babies to sleep on adult beds.

- Make sure your baby's crib is sturdy and has no loose or missing hardware. This will prevent babies suffocating or strangling by becoming trapped between broken crib parts.

- Never place your baby's crib or furniture near window blind or curtain cords. This will prevent babies from strangling on the loop of the cord. To prevent falls, keep children away from windows.

In the bathroom:

- Keep medicines and cleaning products in containers with safety caps and locked away from children. This will prevent children from being poisoned.

- Always check bath water temperature with your wrist or elbow before putting your baby in to bathe. This will prevent burns to a baby's delicate skin.

- Never, ever, leave your child alone in the bathtub or near any water. This will prevent children from drowning. In addition, keep children away from all standing water, including water in toilets, 5-gallon buckets, and pools.

In the kitchen:

- Don't leave your baby alone in a highchair; always use all safety straps. This will prevent injuries and deaths from the baby climbing out, falling, or sliding under the tray. Be sure to use safety straps in strollers and baby swings.

- Use your stove's back burners and keep pot handles turned to the back of the stove. This will prevent deaths and injuries from burns. In addition, keep children away from tablecloths, so they can't pull down hot foods or liquids on themselves.

- Lock household cleaning products, knives, matches, and plastic bags away from children. This will prevent poisonings, bleeding injuries, burns, and suffocation.

In other living areas:

- Install smoke detectors on each floor of your home, especially near sleeping areas; change the batteries each year. This will prevent deaths and injuries from fires.

- Use safety gates to block stairways and safety plugs to cover electrical outlets. This will prevent injuries from falls and electric shocks.

- Keep all small objects, including tiny toys and balloons, away from young children. This will prevent choking and possible death.

Game Workshops

Games and other fun activities are an effective way to teach and reinforce safety and health messages. The games included here focus on the theme: keeping your baby safe at home.

These games are based on the safety messages found in the Baby Safety Checklist. There is one suggested game for each area of the home: bedroom, bathroom, kitchen, and other living areas.

Following is a brief description of each game.

Adapt these games to your needs or develop new ones. Be sure you have more than enough materials for every participant to play each game.

- *For the bedroom:* Can You Answer This? The game leader asks each team questions. The team that answers the most questions correctly wins the round.

- *For the bathroom:* Wheel of Safety. Each team calls out letters that spell a safety message. The team that first guesses the safety message wins.

- *For the kitchen:* Picture Safety. One person on each team draws an image based on the Baby Safety Checklist. The team that first identifies the image and tells why it's important wins the round.

- *For other living areas:* Safety Bingo. Each guest marks an answer to each question asked on her bingo card. The winner is the first to mark three answers in a row and call out bingo!"

Bedroom Safety Game: "Can You Answer This?"

Game Tips

- Before playing this game, review the relevant bedroom Baby Safety Checklist tips with shower participants.

- Decide whether your guests can peek at the Checklist for the answers during the game.

- After each game, review the Checklist again.

- Materials Needed: Flip chart, markers, two bells.

Game Rules

Participants are split into two teams. The moderator asks everyone on Team A for three answers to each game question. For each correct answer, Team A gets one point. If Team A is stumped, Team B gets a chance to answer. The moderator then asks Team B one game question—and so on.

When the four game questions are answered, the moderator simultaneously asks each team a bonus round question. The team that first rings the bell and answers the question correctly wins.

Game Questions (1 point for each correct answer)

- Q: What are the three possible sleep positions for your baby in a crib that are safe?

  A: (1) back (safe) (2) side (less safe) (3) stomach (unsafe)

- Q: Can you name three things that describe an unsafe crib?

  A: (1) missing hardware (2) not sturdy (3) loose hardware

  Also correct: mattress that doesn't fit snugly; corner posts; decorative cutouts in head or foot boards; crib slat spacing that is too wide

- Q: Can you name three examples of soft bedding?

  A: (1) pillows (2) soft, fluffy comforters (3) quilts Also correct: sheepskin

- Q: Can you name three things you should never place near a window with blind or curtain cords?

  A: (1) crib (2) playpen (3) highchair. Also correct: other children's furniture

Bonus Round Questions (2 points for each correct answer):

- Q: Can you name three small objects that are choking hazards for children under three years of age?

  A: Accept answers like: buttons, balloons, marbles; foods like grapes, peanuts, hard candy, cut-up hot dogs

- Q: What are three safety concerns to look for in and on your child's toy box or toy chest?

A: Accept answers like: toys with sharp edges or points; toys that are too small; toys with detachable small parts; hinged lid toy boxes without safety lid supports

- Q: What are three common hazards found on children's clothing?

  A: Accept answers like: loose buttons, drawstrings, loose snaps, small decorations that detach

Bathroom Safety Game: "Wheel of Safety"

Game Tips

- Before playing this game, review the relevant bathroom Baby Safety Checklist tips with shower participants.
- Decide whether your guests can peek at the Checklist for the answers during the game.
- After each game, review the Checklist again.
- Materials Needed: Flip chart, marking pens, two bells.

Game Rules

Option 1: Flip Chart

Participants are split into two teams. On the flip chart, draw the number of blank lines (similar to the game of hangman) corresponding to the number of letters and spaces in the safety phrase. Each team takes a turn to call out a letter in the safety phrase. Correct letters are written in the appropriate blank(s). When one team thinks it knows the phrase, it rings the bell and calls out the phrase. The team correctly guessing the most safety phrases wins.

Option 2: Wheel

The game can be played with a homemade wheel with game points around the edge from 1-9. Team A guesses a letter for the safety phrase. If Team A guesses correctly, the moderator writes the letter in the appropriate blank, spins the wheel, and awards Team A the points on the wheel. Then, Team B guesses a letter—and so on. The first team to ring the bell and guess the correct safety phrase wins 10 points. The team with the most points wins.

Safety Phrases:

- Keep baby safe
- Use child-safety caps
- Keep medicines locked up
- Babies and water don't mix
- Never leave children alone in water
- Check bath water with wrist or elbow

Kitchen Safety Game: "Picture Safety"

Game Tips

- Before playing this game, review the relevant kitchen Baby Safety Checklist tips with shower participants.
- Decide whether your guests can peek at the Checklist for the answers during the game.
- After each game, review the Checklist again.
- Materials Needed: Two flip charts on easels, markers, 3" x 5" cards (for safety clues).

Game Rules

Participants are split into two teams. The teams sit or stand facing each other. The flip charts are positioned back to back between the teams. The moderator selects a safety clue card and shows it to one person from each team. When the moderator says "go", these two people draw a picture of the safety clue on their team's flip chart. The first team to guess the picture wins 5 points. The team can win 5 more points if it correctly describes how the clue is safety-related. The team with the most points wins.

Safety Clue Cards and Safety or Hazard Issue

- Cabinet Safety Latch—Prevents children from getting into cabinets where harmful household products are kept.
- Dish Detergents—Can be harmful if children swallow them.
- Highchair with Safety Straps—Prevents children from climbing or falling out and getting injured.

- Pot and Pans on Stoves—Can burn children if they can reach handles and spill hot liquid or food on themselves

- Knives—Can injure children if they can reach them and cut themselves

- Plastic Trash Bags—Can cause children to suffocate if the bag gets over their noses and mouths.

- Matches—Can burn and start fires.

Other Living Areas Safety Game: "Safety Bingo"

Game Tips

- Before playing this game, review the relevant Baby Safety Checklist tips with shower participants.

- Let your guests peek at the Checklist for the answers during the game.

- After each game, review the Checklist again.

- Materials Needed: bingo game cards and several "chips" or buttons for each participant.

Game Rules

This game is similar to bingo. Each participant is given a game card with pictures in each box. The moderator reads a safety clue aloud, and each participant marks the appropriate picture. The winners are those who first correctly mark all the boxes on their card in a row across, down, or diagonally and call out "bingo." This game can be played many times, with the questions read in different order.

Safety Clues

- Q: One of these should be on every level of the home for protection.
  A: Smoke detector.

- Q: One of these will prevent children from falling down stairs.
  A: Safety gate.

- Q: Stops children from poking fingers and inserting objects into electrical outlets.
  A: Safety plugs.

- Q: This child's game poses a choking hazard to young children.

  A: Small toy ball and jacks set.

- Q: If burst or uninflated, these can be a choking hazard to young children.

  A: Balloons.

- Q: These may look like candy to small children. Keep in container with safety cap.

  A: Medicine pills in bottles with safety caps.

- Q: This is the best position for babies to sleep.

  A: On their back.

- Q: Stops children from opening cabinet or cupboard doors where cleaning products or medicines are stored.

  A: Cabinet lock.

- Q: In a smoke detector, change this every year.

  A: Battery.

Putting Your Shower Together

Equipment and Supplies

Plan far ahead for all the materials, equipment, and supplies you'll use at the shower. Your own list of needed materials will reflect the specific activities planned for your shower. Here are some suggestions:

- Reception area: welcome signs, tables, chairs, name tags, markers, and information packets/bags for guests.

- Opening session: chairs and podium for VIP guests, microphones, and colored posters illustrating shower themes.

- Game workshops/exhibits: tables, chairs, table coverings, signs and posters for exhibit booths, tabletop displays with props and literature, lighting, decorations, TV monitor/VCR, colored markers, and game materials.

Food

No party is complete without food! Whether you serve snacks or a full luncheon, make it a festive and sociable part of the shower. What you serve depends on the time of day, your resources, and the generosity of your sponsors. Here are some basics.

Table/food center: Be sure you have ample food preparation and serving space and a place to seat your guests. You also may need a refrigerator for storage; a coffee maker or a stove for hot goods; plastic trash bags/cans for clean-up; tables, tablecloths, napkins, plates, cups, utensils, trays, serving dishes, utensils, and ice.

- Healthy snacks: Fruit and juice reinforce good nutrition messages.

- Box or bag lunches: Get a local supermarket to contribute food such as sandwiches, drinks, and fruit.

- Decorations: Baby-related centerpieces enliven any party.

Exhibits

If your shower includes exhibits displaying health and safety information or baby-related products and services, be sure your facility can accommodate this. Provide each exhibitor with this list:

- Set-up and take-down times.

- Space dimensions.

- Table dimensions allowable (whether provided by facility or by exhibitor).

- Dimensions of backdrop allowable (whether provided by site or by exhibitor) and if items can be hung from it.

- The number of items (literature, samples, etc.) they should plan to offer based on the number of guests expected.

Gifts and Prizes

Everyone loves receiving gifts, and your shower guests are no exception.

Supermarkets, drug stores, baby stores, or specialty shops are great places to ask for contributions of gifts and prizes. Remember that your invited guests are potential customers—and merchants are always looking for ways to establish a good reputation in the community.

Try to get some donated items related to baby safety, such as cabinet locks or electric socket plugs. Include also products every parent can use: baby bath items, disposable diapers, baby food, toys, and baby clothing. Moms, for example, also may welcome special treats for themselves—like a makeover or gift certificates from local stores.

Have enough gifts so everyone can take home something. A "goody bag" filled with product samples, discount coupons, gift certificates—and safety literature—will delight all your guests.

Save your best and biggest prizes for a raffle or door prize. Finish off your shower with an exciting finale!

Shower Day Schedule

Whether you plan a two-hour or an all-day event, develop a realistic schedule for the day. Make arrangements ahead of time with the building management to reserve the room, tables, chairs, partitions, kitchen, and other facilities or equipment at the site. Allow sufficient time before and after the shower for setup and cleanup.

Room Setup (1-1/2 hours)

Make sure volunteers help set up the room. Consider traffic flow around room entrances, game workshops, exhibits, food tables, and child-are area. Room arrangements may include:

- Registration table. Have chairs for volunteers helping with registration. Have paper and pens for signing in and name tags. Keep "goody" bags of prizes, products, and other materials here.

- Refreshment table. Use simple table decorations that reflect the shower theme.

- Game workshops. Make sure there are enough chairs, tables, and materials for each game area.

- Exhibit booths. Arrange enough floor space for each booth.

- Signs. If needed, post signs to designate game workshops, exhibits, and rest room locations.

- Audio-visual equipment. If used, make sure all equipment works before the day of the shower. Provide extension cords and duct tape. Tape loose cords to the floor to prevent tripping.

Registration and Welcoming Activities (1/2 hour)

Register each guest, hand out name tags, and provide materials about the day's event. Consider including refreshments and entertainment as ice breakers.

Opening Remarks (15 minutes)

The primary organizer welcomes the guests, sets the theme, and reviews the overall shower program. Consider asking a parent to relate a human interest story based on the importance of child safety in the home.

Game Workshops (1 hour)

At the start of the shower, each guest is assigned to a game workshop focusing on one topic or room area. Throughout the hour, guests rotate to each of the other game workshops. Or, if your group is not too large, you might hold one session where all the games are played.

Closing Remarks (15 minutes)

The primary organizer summarizes the game workshop messages, encourages guests to use the products and materials given out, and thanks all the sponsors and organizations who contributed to the event.

Meal (1/2 – 1 hour)

If time and resources permit, serve a meal, like lunch. This allows time for further exchange of information with your guests.

Exhibits (1/2 – 1 hour)

Schedule time for guests to visit exhibits for additional health and safety information. This can be done during the lunch hour or after the program's closing remarks.

Cleanup (1 hour)

After the guests leave, clean up! Make arrangements with the building management for janitorial services or tell your volunteers ahead of time what they need to do before leaving the facility. A simple checklist might include such duties as packing up unused workshop materials, sweeping the room, cleaning kitchen facilities, and removing trash. Be sure to leave the facility in clean condition.

Chapter 3

Back-to-School Safety Checklist

When you drop off your child at school, use this checklist to make sure these hidden hazards aren't waiting to cause injury or death.

1. *Drawstrings on Jackets and Sweatshirts*—There should be no drawstrings on hoods or around the neck. Drawstrings at the waist or bottom of jackets should extend no more than 3 inches to prevent catching in car and school bus doors or getting caught on playground equipment.

2. *Loops on Window Blind Cords*—Cut the loop and attach separate tassels to prevent entanglement and strangulation in window blind cords. One child a month strangles and dies in the loop of a window blind cord.

3. *Bike Helmets*—Buy a helmet that meets one of the safety standards (U.S. CPSC, Snell, ANSI, ASTM, or Canadian), and insist that your children wear the helmet each time they ride their bike. About 900 people, including more than 200 children, are killed annually in bicycle-related incidents, and about 60 percent of these deaths involve a head injury. More than 500,000 people are treated annually in U.S. hospital

"Back-to-School Safety Checklist," an undated fact sheet produced by the Consumer Product Safety Commission, available online at http://www.cpsc.gov/cpscpub/pubs/btscheck.html;cited July 2001.

emergency rooms for bicycle-related injuries. Research indicates that a helmet can reduce the risk of head injury by up to 85 percent.

4. *Soccer Goals*—Make sure that the athletic director or the custodian anchors the soccer goals into the ground so that the soccer goal will not tip over and crush a child.

5. *Playgrounds*—Check the surfaces around playground equipment at schools and parks to make sure there is a 12-inch depth of wood chips, mulch, sand, or pea gravel, or mats made of safety-tested rubber or fiber material to prevent head injury when a child falls. Each year, more than 200,000 children go to U.S. hospital emergency rooms with injuries associated with playground equipment. Most injuries occur when a child falls from the equipment onto the ground.

6. *Recalled Products*—Make sure your child's school has up-to-date information on recalled toys and children's products. Schools, daycare providers, and parents can receive recall information by FAX, e-mail, or in the regular mail free of charge by calling the CPSC hotline at (800) 638-2772, or writing to the U.S. Consumer Product Safety Commission, Washington, D.C. 20207.

Chapter 4

Home Safety Tips for the Babysitter

The Super Sitter

Babysitting can be a super way for you to earn money. And, it's a good way for you to learn a lot about children, about families, about having a job, about managing money ... and about product safety. Every job has certain guidelines. Babysitting is no exception. There are certain things that will be expected of you as a sitter and things that you should expect of the parents. The chapter will help you become more aware of some of these things, particularly:

- the need for constant observation and alertness to the child's environment
- selecting toys for children that are not dangerous
- the importance of children playing with toys in the proper manner
- the need for keeping children's products in good condition so they don't become dangerous for them to use

What Is Expected of the Sitter

There are certain do's and don'ts. In addition to "sitting" with the children, these are a few of the things you should know and remember as a Safe Sitter.

"The Super Sitter," an undated fact sheet produced by the Consumer Product Safety Commission, available online at http://www.cpsc.gov/cpscpub/pubs/243.html; cited July 2001.

- Before the parents leave, get the names and phone numbers suggested in the Super Sitter's Very Important Phone Numbers List.

- Have the parents show you through the house or apartment and point out where the items you will need are located, such as the children's clothing or playthings.

- Always know where the emergency exits are located. In case of fire don't stop to try to put it out by yourself! Get the children out of the house without stopping to phone. Take them to a neighbor. Call the fire department, and then call the parents to let them know where you and the children are.

- Keep the youngsters safe by preventing accidents. Know where the potential hazards are, such as electrical outlets, appliances, and exposed heating elements. Also ask the parents if all medicine, bleaches and household cleaners are securely locked up.

- Stairs can be dangerous for youngsters. Keep a curious toddler from playing on or around them. Running or horseplay on them can lead to falls, particularly if the youngsters are wearing socks or other "slippery" footwear. Remember, too, that stairs are not meant to be a storage area. Anything placed on the stairs can become an obstacle to fall over.

- If there is a gate across the stairway, make sure it is kept latched. Babies in carriages, walkers or strollers should never be left unattended, especially in an area around stairs or ramps—whether indoors or out. A malfunction of the carriage's safety brake or a sudden movement by the child could put it right over the edge. If a gate is not provided, place a barrier of some kind in front of the stairway that a child cannot climb over. Accordion-style gates with large V-shaped or diamond-shaped openings should not be used since they can entrap a child's head, causing strangulation. A gate with a straight top or small V's and diamond-shaped openings is safer. Make sure pressure gates are firmly in place and can't be dislodged by the child.

- Caution the child about the dangers of glass doors or windows. A child running or riding on a trike or bike could easily go through the glass. Be sure you keep toys, scatter rugs and other articles that could cause someone to slip or trip away from these areas. If you are caring for a particularly active child, place a large chair or other piece of furniture in front of the glass area for safety's sake. You also can suggest to the parents that large, colorful decals at eye level for both children and adults can make glass doors safer.

- Unless specifically instructed by the parents, do not bathe the baby. A clean facecloth in lukewarm water will suffice in most cases for cleaning the skin. Bathing a baby calls for utmost care and supervision; aside from the risk of hot water scalds, there is always the danger of drowning. While you may want to be of help to the parents, bathing the infant is not recommended.

- If you are changing the baby's diapers, plan on having everything within immediate reach so you won't have to step away from the infant even for a second. If you are not constantly watching them, babies can roll over and fall from changing tables or other high places. Have diapers, pins, etc., next to you so the baby is under constant supervision.

- Infants may choke on small items which they put in their mouths. Small pieces of food, coins, pins and other non-toy items could lodge in the baby's throat and cause choking or asphyxiation. It could also occur with small toys or parts of toys intended for older children. Watch the baby carefully to make sure these objects are not within reach. In the event of accidental choking, apply first aid measures to clear the child's airway. Also call the rescue squad. (If you don't know first aid, contact your local American Red Cross office or an approved community agency for instruction.)

- A "super sitter" will look for hazards before they surface. Loose, baggy clothing can be dangerous if it gets caught on furniture, cribs, playpens, etc., as children climb, play or scamper about the room. Clothing can also be a problem if it becomes tightly wound around the baby. Be on the alert for hazards such as these, and adjust the clothing so that it cannot become tangled.

- To prevent accidental injuries, keep doors and windows locked at all times. Remember that children, though under your supervision, can at times just "seem to disappear" from your watchful eye.

- Never open the door to strangers. If there is a question about someone at the door, call the parents to check with them.

- In case of accident or illness, don't try to be doctor or nurse except for minor cuts and bruises. Call the parents for instructions. If they cannot be reached, call your own parents or go to a neighbor for help. The sick or hurt child may require a doctor or emergency care.

Where the Child Is ...

With several children—particularly toddlers (2 and 3 year olds)—you won't be doing much "sitting." You'll be playing with them and supervising their play activities. Just a reminder that whether you're actually playing with the children or supervising them, keep them within safe play areas, preferably within your sight. Keep them away from potential danger areas in the home such as the kitchen, bathroom, workshop and storage areas. They move fast, so you will have to be able to move even faster!

The Playpen

You should be aware of hazards to a child left alone in a playpen. A string of toys across the top or even to one side of the playpen could be a strangulation risk. Dropside mesh playpens and portable mesh cribs, used with a side left down, can pose a serious hazard to newborns and infants.

When the side is down, the mesh forms a loose pocket into which an infant can fall or roll and suffocate. Dropsides should ALWAYS be up and locked securely in position when a child is in the playpen or crib. Don't put any toys in the playpen that a child can climb on to get out. And little fingers can get caught in hinges.

Baby Walkers ... The Baby Hot Rod!

Baby walkers seem fun to scoot around in, but they also can scoot down a flight of stairs, into a hot stove, against a table edge or into a glass door. They offer limited balance to a child not yet completely able to stand or walk. If unstable, walkers can easily tip over. Stay with the child when he or she is in the walker, and assist it over thresholds or carpeting.

High Chairs

A child in a high chair requires almost constant attention. Babies can slip out of a high chair in an instant if not properly strapped in. An unstable high chair can tip over ... with the baby in it!

Make sure that any safety belts or straps on the high chair are securely fastened and that the tray is properly secured. Don't let the child stand up while in the chair, and keep other children from climbing on it. Keep the chair away from "traffic lanes," doorways, refrigerator and stove, and far enough away from tables and walls so that the child can't push the chair over.

The Crib

If baby is to sleep safely, make sure that the crib is as safe as you can make it. If there is too much room (more than two fingers width) between the mattress and the side of the crib, an infant's head could get caught in between and the infant could suffocate. Roll up a couple of large bath towels and place them in the space. If the slats are more than 2-3/8 inches apart, the baby's body can slide between the slats and the baby can suffocate.

If the child is old enough to stand up, the parents should set the mattress at its lowest position, with the side rail at its highest position. Check the mattress support frequently to make sure it hasn't become unhooked from the end panels. Any toys you leave in the crib should never be ones that could be used to help in climbing out. Also, do not use crib toys that may have strings or elastic attached to them—these can strangle or choke! Cribs with decorative knobs on the cornerposts can be a strangulation hazard. Children's clothing and strings or necklaces can catch on the protrusions, especially if the child is trying to climb out. Crib gyms should be removed from the crib when the baby is five months old or can push up on hands and knees, otherwise the baby can get his/her chin across the crib gym or catch clothing on it and strangle.

Toys They Play with ...

Teach children to play safely by showing them how to use their toys in a safe manner and by teaching them to put their toys away after play.

Be particularly aware of safe and unsafe toys. These are some toy dangers you should be aware of:

41

1. **Small Parts.** Tiny toys and toys with small removable parts can be swallowed or become lodged in a child's throat, windpipe, ears or nose. The seams of poorly constructed stuffed dolls or animals can break open and release small pellets that can be swallowed or inhaled.

2. **Sharp Edges.** Toys of brittle plastic or glass can be broken easily, leaving dangerous, sharp, cutting edges. Metal and plastic toys sometimes have sharp edges due to poor construction.

3. **Sharp Points.** Broken toys can expose dangerous prongs and knifelike sharp points. Pins and staples on dolls' clothes, hair and accessories can easily puncture an unsuspecting child.

4. **Loud Noises.** Toy caps and some noise-making guns and other toys can produce sounds at noise levels that can damage hearing. Do not allow children to fire cap guns closer than one foot to the ear; also, do not use indoors.

5. **Propelled Objects.** Projectiles—guided missiles and similar flying toys—can be turned into weapons and can injure eyes in particular. Children should never be permitted to play with adult lawn darts or other hobby or sporting equipment that have sharp points. Arrows or darts used by children should have soft cork tips, rubber suction cups or other protective tips intended to prevent injury. Teach children that these toys should never be aimed at people or pets.

6. **Electric Toys.** Electric toys that are improperly constructed, wired or used can shock or burn. Electric toys with heating elements are only recommended for children over eight years old. Children should be taught to use electric toys cautiously and under adult supervision.

7. **Wrong Toy for the Wrong Age.** Toys that may be safe for older children—like a chemistry or hobby set or games with small pieces—can be extremely dangerous in the hands of little ones.

8. **Cords and Strings.** Toys with long strings or cords may be dangerous for infants and very young children. The cords may become wrapped around an infant's neck, causing strangulation.

Never hang toys with long strings, cords, loops or ribbons in cribs or playpens. Pacifiers should never be attached to strings or ribbons around a baby's neck.

Super Sitter's Surprise Box

To overcome any outbursts from the children when the parents are leaving, you may want to have your own *Super Sitter's Surprise Box.* This can be anything in the way of toys or treasures for them to play with, to stimulate curiosity and to take away fear of being left "forever."

The box can be of your own design. It can be as complicated and complex as an overnight case filled with colorful, new, exciting and safe toys you buy (or borrow from a younger sister or brother). It can be as simple as a shoe box filled with toys you have made. It will help ease those first difficult moments and many more besides.

Here's How You Can Make Your Super Sitter's Surprise Box

A variety of colors of "sticky-back" tape and a medium sized box with a lid or an old overnight case are all you need. Cut the tape into strips, squares, triangles and circles and tape them on to the box or case. Besides being attractive and eye-catching, the shapes can be educational. Fill the Surprise Box with any of the "surprises" below:

- rubber animals
- plastic or wooden animals with smooth edges
- soft plastic or cloth covered books
- plastic or wooden toy cars or trucks with no small detachable parts
- large rubber ball
- playing cards
- set of measuring cups
- different colored bandage strips to use as "puppets" on your fingers, or on the baby's fingers.

Try to put a surprise or two—a book, coloring book, game, puzzle or some item of amusement into your box for an older brother or sister.

When making your Surprise Box, remember to use only safe toys! Check to see that they don't have any of the toy dangers. Make your Super Sitter's Surprise Box a safe surprise!

Playing Outdoors

Some of your daytime sitting may include playing outdoors with the children. Outdoor play equipment—swings, seesaws and slides—can be fun, but can be dangerous too. Play safety can be taught to even the youngest toddlers.

Children often do the unexpected on playground equipment. They are naturally and normally curious and adventuresome. Standing in a swing is "bigger and better" than sitting in one. Climbing to the top, sitting or swinging on it shows great daring. Little ones are unaware of risk ... often jumping off or in front of swings, seesaws or gliders. They may walk in front or in back of a moving swing. In an atmosphere of "the more the merrier," they may overload any one piece of equipment and tip the entire structure. Hanging "rings" are particularly dangerous to small children whose heads may be small enough to go through the ring, turning it into a hanging "noose."

All children should be supervised when playing on this kind of equipment. They should be told to sit in the center of a swing. Explain the following hazards: walking in front or in back of a swing; pushing other children off of the swing; swinging empty seats; twisting the swing chains; and, climbing up the front of the slide. Roughhousing, overloading equipment and misuse can be curbed from the start if you're there supervising their play.

Older children can be taught certain safety rules and why they are important. Asking them to assist you in supervising the younger ones will help them to understand these rules better. Dangerous roughhousing, stunts, overloading, abuse and misuse of equipment and showing off are unacceptable.

Pool Safety

Daytime sitting can also include time in or around a swimming pool, wading pool or spa. Children are naturally attracted to water, therefore, a "super sitter" must take precautions at all times to prevent accidents from happening. Drowning is the third leading cause of accidental death nationwide to children under five years of age. In addition, some 3,000 youngsters in the same age group are treated each year in hospital emergency rooms as a result of near-drownings;

some of these children are hospitalized for life as a result of near-drowning.

Drowning is a silent killer. When a child drowns, a babysitter won't hear a cry or even a splash. Drownings can happen very quickly.

How Do Children Drown? How Can You Prevent a Tragedy from Happening?

- Seconds count. In seconds, a child can leave the house and walk to the edge of the pool. In seconds, a child can drown in only a few inches of water. A child can drown in the few seconds taken to answer a telephone in the house.

- Eyes on the child at all times is your best bet. There is no substitute for constant supervision of the child.

- Children should be supervised and accompanied at all times, even though the parents previously instructed the children not to go near the water.

- Make sure gates leading to the pool are closed and locked. Lock all doors leading from the house to the pool area. Locks should always be out of reach of children.

- Don't consider a child to be water-safe even if the youngster has had swimming lessons or water-familiarity class.

- Don't assume a pool to be safe, even one with a pool cover or a fence.

- Don't allow children to play on the apron surrounding the pool.

- If the pool is above-ground, remove the ladder to prevent access by anyone.

- Learn how to perform cardiopulmonary resuscitation (CPR) on infants and young children. Contact your local chapter of the American Heart Association or American Red Cross about registering for classes.

- If for any reason you discover the child to be missing, check the pool, wading pool, spa or hot tub first.

- Know the telephone numbers to call for emergency medical service. In some locations you dial 911, in others a seven-digit number. As a "super sitter" you can teach the children that safe play can still be fun play!

Poison: Food for Thought Only!

What You Should Know about It...

Not everything that goes into a child's mouth falls into the category of food. Too often, what ends up in mouths and stomachs may be deadly! Growing children are curious about things that glitter and shine, pretty colored pills, bottles and containers of all kinds, and what's in them. Children under the age of five are in stages of growth where they are constantly exploring and investigating. This is how they learn. Unfortunately, what children see and reach for, they put into their mouths and swallow.

Every year thousands of youngsters across the country receive emergency hospital or doctor's care because of accidental poisoning. These are chiefly children under five who have ingested some common household item which suddenly becomes poison in the wrong hands (and mouths). These include medicines, cleaning products and preparations, insect sprays, lighter fluid and kerosene, turpentine and paints.

You can help prevent accidental poisonings, while babysitting and in your own home too. Here are some things you should remember:

- All household products and medicines should be stored out of sight and reach of young children—preferably locked up! (If you are sitting where household cleaning agents are stored under the sink and you are in charge of a "crawler"—or the medicine cabinet is accessible to a "climber"—you can put protective tape across the front of the cabinet as an extra precaution.)

- As a babysitter you should not be expected to give any medication. But in certain circumstances, you may be asked to give a medication during the time the parents are away. If it is absolutely necessary that you do this, have the parents leave explicit, written instructions for you.

Some General Points to Remember about Medications Are:

1. Read the label on the container carefully as well as the instructions from the parents.

2. Never leave the child alone with the medication. If the phone rings take the medication with you.

3. Return the medication to its safe storage place with the safety closure on securely.

4. Do not call the medication candy.

5. Do not give the medication in the dark.

6. Do not take any medication yourself in the presence of the child.

7. Be careful of what you might be bringing into the house.

Children are normally curious and can get into a pocketbook, brief-case or overnight case of a guest which could contain medications. An otherwise "poison-proof" household can become the scene of an accidental poisoning incident.

What You Should Know to Do If There Is a Poisoning Accident:

1. DON'T WAIT to see what effect it may have. If you think the child has swallowed medicine or a household product, call a Poison Control Center, doctor, or hospital IMMEDIATELY! (These should be emergency numbers on your list.) Describe what was taken and how much, giving as much information as you can. Describe the condition of the child—vomiting, drowsiness, change of color, coldness of skin. In the event no medical instructions are available, check the label on the container for emergency procedures and directions, if any.

   DO NOT INDUCE VOMITING UNLESS INSTRUCTED BY MEDICAL PERSONNEL OR THE LABEL GIVES SUCH INSTRUCTIONS. IF INSTRUCTED TO INDUCE VOMITING, GIVE SYRUP OF IPECAC. (NOTE: PARENTS SHOULD KEEP ON HAND A ONE-OUNCE BOTTLE OF SYRUP OF IPECAC FOR EACH CHILD IN THE HOME).

2. Call in a neighbor who can help you take care of this emergency; get the child medical aid, or help take care of other children in the family. At this point, don't try to take on all of the care and responsibility yourself.

3. Call the parents. Explain what has happened, what has already been done and what is yet to be done. If the child is to be taken to a hospital or doctor's office, it may be more expedient to get the child there and have the parents go there immediately rather than come home first. Speed, of course, is

important. But equally important is the way you handle the situation. Try to keep control. A frightened and sick child will become more frightened if you are excited or show panic.

Accidental poisoning is a frightening experience, but if you know preventive measures, you will be able to handle the situation when it happens. (Tell the parents about child resistant safety packaging which can help prevent these kinds of accidents.)

Time to Leave!

Before you realize it, the parents have arrived to find you and their children safe and sound, and to see you home safely. During your first sitting experience, you may have been nervous, but with each new one, you will gain confidence, especially if you remember the Super Sitter Tips we have discussed. Here is a summary of those tips which you should keep foremost in your mind until you are confident that you know them:

- Know what to do in emergencies by being prepared for one, knowing what could happen and how to react to it. Take first aid instructions.

- Always know where the emergency exits are located.

- Keep doors and windows locked for the safety of both yourself and the children.

- Know where the "danger" items are—medicines, bleaches, household cleaners and electrical appliances. Keep them out of children's reach if the parents have not locked them away in a secure place.

- In case of accident or illness, don't try to be a doctor or nurse except for minor cuts and bruises.

- Keep your emergency telephone list handy—use these numbers when you need them.

- Depend on the parents or a neighbor in any emergency situation that you are not sure how to handle yourself.

- Prevent play accidents by keeping the youngsters safe—supervise where they play, what they play with and teach them safe play. Keep these safety tips in mind ... they will make your babysitting experience both safe and fun for you and the children. They will make you a SUPER SAFE SITTER.

The Super Sitter's Very Important Phone Numbers

Post these names and phone numbers by the telephone. Then you'll have them when and if you need them.

Where parents will be:

Nearby friend:

Nearby relative:

Nearby neighbor:

Children's doctor:

Fire Department:

Police Department:

Poison Control Center:

Hospital:

Chapter 5

Home Safety for Older Consumers

Each year, many older Americans are injured in and around their homes. CPSC believes that many of these injuries result from hazards that are easy to overlook, but also easy to fix. By spotting these hazards and taking some simple steps to correct them, many injuries might be prevented.

Use this checklist to spot possible safety problems which may be present in your home. Use it as a reminder of safe practices, and use it periodically to re-check your home.

This checklist is organized by areas in the home. However, there are some potential hazards that need to be checked in more than just one area of your home.

All Areas of the Home

In all areas of your home, check all electrical and telephone cords; rugs, runners and mats; telephone areas; smoke detectors; electrical outlets and switches; light bulbs; space heaters; woodburning stoves; and your emergency exit plan.

"Safety for Older Consumers Home safety Checklist," an undated fact sheet produced by the Consumer Product Safety Commission, available online at http://www.cpsc.gov/cpscpub/pubs/701.html; cited July 2001; and "A Grandparents' Guide for Family Nurturing and Safety," available online at http://www.cpsc.gov/cpscpub/pubs/grand/704.html; cited August 2001.

Check All Cords

Are lamp, extension, and telephone cords placed out of the flow of traffic?

Cords stretched across walkways may cause someone to trip.

- Arrange furniture so that outlets are available for lamps and appliances without the use of extension cords.
- If you must use an extension cord, place it on the floor against a wall where people can not trip over it.
- Move the phone so that telephone cords will not lie where people walk.

Are cords out from beneath furniture and rugs or carpeting?

Furniture resting on cords can damage them, creating fire and shock hazards. Electric cords which run under carpeting may cause a fire.

- Remove cords from under furniture or carpeting.
- Replace damaged or frayed cords.

Are cords attached to the walls, baseboards, etc., with nails or staples?

Nails or staples can damage cords, presenting fire and shock hazards.

- Remove nails, staples, etc.
- Check wiring for damage.
- Use tape to attach cords to walls or floors.

Are electrical cords in good condition, not frayed or cracked?

Damaged cords may cause a shock or fire.

- Replace frayed or cracked cords.

Do extension cords carry more than their proper load, as indicated by the ratings labeled on the cord and the appliance?

Overloaded extension cords may cause fires. Standard 18 gauge extension cords can carry 1250 watts.

- If the rating on the cord is exceeded because of the power requirements of one or more appliances being used on the cord, change the cord to a higher rated one or unplug some appliances.

- If an extension cord is needed, use one having a sufficient amp or wattage rating.

Check All Rugs, Runners and Mats

Are all small rugs and runners slip-resistant?

- Remove rugs and runners that tend to slide.

- Apply double-faced adhesive carpet tape or rubber matting to the backs of rugs and runners.

- Purchase rugs with slip-resistant backing.

- Check rugs and mats periodically to see if backing needs to be replaced.

- Place rubber matting under rugs. (Rubber matting that can be cut to size is available.)

- Purchase new rugs with slip-resistant backing.

Over time, adhesive on tape can wear away. Rugs with slip-resistant backing also become less effective as they are washed. Periodically, check rugs and mats to see if new tape or backing is needed.

Are emergency numbers posted on or near the telephone?

In case of emergency, telephone numbers for the Police, Fire Department, and local Poison Control Center, along with a neighbor's number, should be readily available.

- Write the numbers in large print and tape them to the phone, or place them near the phone where they can be seen easily.

Do you have access to a telephone if you fall (or experience some other emergency which prevents you from standing and reaching a wall phone)?

- Have at least one telephone located where it would be accessible in the event of an accident which leaves you unable to stand.

Check Smoke Detectors

Are smoke detectors properly located?

At least one smoke detector should be placed on every floor of your home.

- Read the instructions that come with the smoke detector for advice on the best place to install it.
- Make sure detectors are placed near bedrooms, either on the ceiling or 6-12 inches below the ceiling on the wall.
- Locate smoke detectors away from air vents.

Do you have properly working smoke detectors?

Many home fire injuries and deaths are caused by smoke and toxic gases, rather than the fire itself. Smoke detectors provide an early warning and can wake you in the event of a fire.

- Purchase a smoke detector if you do not have one.
- Check and replace batteries and bulbs according to the manufacturer's instructions.
- Vacuum the grillwork of your smoke detector.
- Replace any smoke detectors which can not be repaired.

Some fire departments or local governments will provide assistance in acquiring or installing smoke detectors.

Check Electrical Outlets and Switches

Are any outlets and switches unusually warm or hot to the touch?

Unusually warm or hot outlets or switches may indicate that an unsafe wiring condition exists.

- Unplug cords from outlets and do not use the switches.
- Have an electrician check the wiring as soon as possible.

Do all outlets and switches have cover plates, so that no wiring is exposed?

Exposed wiring presents a shock hazard.

- Add a cover plate.

Are light bulbs the appropriate size and type for the lamp or fixture?

A bulb of too high wattage or the wrong type may lead to fire through overheating. Ceiling fixtures, recessed lights, and "hooded" lamps will trap heat.

- Replace with a bulb of the correct type and wattage. (If you do not know the correct wattage, use a bulb no larger than 60 watts.)

Check Space Heaters

Are heaters which come with a 3-prong plug being used in a 3-hole outlet or with a properly attached adapter?

The grounding feature provided by a 3-hole receptacle or an adapter for a 2-hole receptacle is a safety feature designed to lessen the risk of shock.

- Never defeat the grounding feature.
- If you do not have a 3-hole outlet, use an adapter to connect the heater's 3-prong plug. Make sure the adapter ground wire or tab is attached to the outlet.

Are small stoves and heaters placed where they can not be knocked over, and away from furnishings and flammable materials, such as curtains or rugs?

Heaters can cause fires or serious burns if they cause you to trip or if they are knocked over.

- Relocate heaters away from passageways and flammable materials such as curtains, rugs, furniture, etc.

If your home has space heating equipment, such as a kerosene heater, a gas heater or an LP gas heater, do you understand the installation and operating instructions thoroughly?

Unvented heaters should be used with room doors open or window slightly open to provide ventilation. The correct fuel, as recommended by the manufacturer, should always be used. Vented heaters should have proper venting, and the venting system should be checked frequently. Improper venting is the most frequent cause of carbon monoxide poisoning, and older consumers are at special risk.

- Review the installation and operating instructions.
- Call your local fire department if you have additional questions.

Check Woodburning Heating Equipment

Is woodburning equipment installed properly?

Woodburning stoves should be installed by a qualified person according to local building codes.

- Local building code officials or fire marshals can provide requirements and recommendations for installation.

Some insurance companies will not cover fire losses if wood stoves are not installed according to local codes.

Check the Emergency Exit Plan

Do you have an emergency exit plan and an alternate emergency exit plan in case of a fire?

Once a fire starts, it spreads rapidly. Since you may not have much time to get out and there may be a lot of confusion, it is important that everyone knows what to do.

- Develop an emergency exit plan.
- Choose a meeting place outside your home so you can be sure that everyone is capable of escape quickly and safely.
- Practice the plan from time to time to make sure everyone is capable of escape quickly and safely.

Kitchen

In the kitchen, check the range area, all electrical cords, lighting, the stool, all throw rugs and mats, and the telephone area.

Are towels, curtains, and other things that might catch fire located away from the range?

Placing or storing non-cooking equipment like potholders, dish towels, or plastic utensils on or near the range man result in fires or burns.

- Store flammable and combustible items away from range and oven.

- Remove any towels hanging on oven handles. If towels hang close to a burner, change the location of the towel rack.

- If necessary, shorten or remove curtains which could brush against heat sources.

Do you wear clothing with short or close-fitting sleeves while you are cooking?

CPSC estimates that 70% of all people who die from clothing fires are over 65 years of age. Long sleeves are more likely to catch fire than are short sleeves. Long sleeves are also more apt to catch on pot handles, overturning pots and pans and causing scalds.

- Roll back long, loose sleeves or fasten them with pins or elastic bands while you are cooking.

Are kitchen ventilation systems or range exhausts functioning properly and are they in use while you are cooking?

Indoor air pollutants may accumulate to unhealthful levels in a kitchen where gas or kerosene-fire appliances are in use.

- Use ventilation systems or open windows to clear air of vapors and smoke.

Are all extension cords and appliance cords located away from the sink or range areas?

Electrical appliances and power cords can cause shock or electrocution if they come in contact with water. Cords can also be damaged by excess heat.

- Move cords and appliances away from sink areas and hot surfaces.

- Move appliances closer to wall outlets or to different outlets so you won't need extension cords.

- If extension cords must be used, install wiring guides so that cords will not hang near sink, range, or working areas.

- Consider adding new outlets for convenience and safety; ask your electrician to install outlets equipped with ground fault circuit interrupters (GFCIs) to protect against electric shock. A GFCI is a shock-protection device that will detect electrical fault and shut off electricity before serious injury or death occurs.

Does good, even lighting exist over the stove, sink, and countertop work areas, especially where food is sliced or cut?

Low lighting and glare can contribute to burns or cuts. Improve lighting by:

- Opening curtains and blinds (unless this causes to much glare).
- Using the maximum wattage bulb allowed by the fixture. (If you do not know the correct wattage for the fixture, use a bulb no larger than 60 watts.)
- Reducing glare by using frosted bulbs, indirect lighting, shades or globes on light fixtures, or partially closing the blinds or curtains.
- Installing additional light fixtures, e.g. under cabinet/over countertop lighting. (Make sure that the bulbs you use are the right type and wattage for the light fixture.)

Do you have a step stool which is stable and in good repair?

Standing on chairs, boxes, or other makeshift items to reach high shelves can result in falls.

- If you don't have a step stool, consider buying one. Choose one with a handrail that you can hold onto while standing on the top step.
- Before climbing on any step stool, make sure it is fully opened and stable.
- Tighten screws and braces on the step stool.
- Discard step stools with broken parts.

Living Room/Family Room

In the living room/family room, check all rugs and runners, electrical and telephone cords, lighting, the fireplace and chimney, the telephone area, and all passageways.

Are chimneys clear from accumulations of leaves, and other debris that can clog them?

A clogged chimney can cause a poorly burning fire to result in poisonous fumes and smoke coming back into the house.

- Do not use the chimney until the blockage has been removed.
- Have the chimney checked and cleaned by a registered or licensed professional.

Has the chimney been cleaned within the past year?

Burning wood can cause a build up of a tarry substance (creosote) inside the chimney. This material can ignite and result in a serious chimney fire.

- Have the chimney checked and cleaned by a registered or licensed professional.

Are hallways, passageways between rooms, and other heavy traffic areas well lit?

Shadowed or dark areas can hide tripping hazards.

- Use the maximum wattage bulb allowed by the fixture. (If you do not know the correct wattage, use a bulb no larger than 60 watts.)
- Install night lights.
- Reduce glare by using frosted bulbs, indirect lighting, shades or globes on light fixtures, or partially closing blinds or curtains.
- Consider using additional lamps or light fixtures. Make sure that the bulbs you use are the right type and wattage for the light fixture.

Are exits and passageways kept clear?

Furniture, boxes, or other items could be an obstruction or tripping hazard, especially in the event of an emergency or fire.

- Rearrange furniture to open passageways and walkways.
- Remove boxes and clutter.

Bathroom

In the bathroom, check bathtub and shower areas, water temperature, rugs and mats, lighting, small electrical appliances, and storage areas for medications.

Are bathtubs and showers equipped with non-skid mats, abrasive strips, or surfaces that are not slippery?

Wet soapy tile or porcelain surfaces are especially slippery and may contribute to falls.

- Apply textured strips or appliqués on the floors of tubs and showers.

- Use non-skid mats in the tub and shower, and on the bathroom floor.

Do bathtubs and showers have at least one (preferably two) grab bars?

Grab bars can help you get into and out of your tub or shower, and can help prevent falls.

- Check existing bars for strength and stability, and repair if necessary.

- Attach grab bars, through the tile, to structural supports in the wall, or install bars specifically designed to attach to the sides of the bathtub. If you are not sure how it is done, get someone who is qualified to assist you.

Is the water temperature 120 degrees or lower?

Water temperature above 120 degrees can cause tap water scalds.

- Lower the setting on your hot water heater to "Low" or 120 degrees. If you are unfamiliar with the controls of your water heater, ask a qualified person to adjust it for you. If your hot water system is controlled by the landlord, ask the landlord to consider lowering the setting.

    NOTE: If the water heater does not have a temperature setting, you can use a thermometer to check the temperature of the water at the tap.

- Always check water temperature by hand before entering bath or shower.

- Taking baths, rather than showers, reduces the risk of a scald from suddenly changing water temperatures.

Is a light switch located near the entrance to the bathroom?

A light switch near the door will prevent you from walking through a dark area.

- Install a night light. Inexpensive lights that plug into outlets are available.

- Consider replacing the existing switch with a "glow switch" that can be seen in the dark.

Are small electrical appliances such as hair dryers, shavers, curling irons, etc., unplugged when not in use?

Even an appliance that is not turned on, such as a hairdryer, can be potentially hazardous if it is left plugged in. If it falls into water in a sink or bathtub while plugged in, it could cause a lethal shock.

- Unplug all small appliances when not in use.

- Never reach into water to retrieve an appliance that has fallen in without being sure the appliance is unplugged.

- Install a ground fault circuit interrupter (GFCI) in your bathroom outlet to protect against electric shock.

Are all medicines stored in the containers that they came in and are they clearly marked?

Medications that are not clearly and accurately labeled can be easily mixed up. Taking he wrong medicine or missing a dosage of medicine you need can be dangerous.

- Be sure that all containers are clearly marked with the contents, doctor's instructions, expiration date, and patient's name.

- Dispose of outdated medicines properly.

- Request non-child-resistant closures from your pharmacist only when you cannot use child-resistant closures.

NOTE: Many poisonings occur when children visiting grand-parents go through the medicine cabinet or grandmother's purse. In homes where grandchildren or other youngsters are frequent visitors, medicines should be purchased in containers with child-resistant caps, and the caps properly closed after each use. Store medicines beyond the reach of children.

Bedrooms

In the bedroom, check all rugs and runners, electrical and tele-phone cords, and areas around beds.

Are lamps or light switches within reach of each bed?

Lamps or switches located close to each bed will enable people get-ting up at night to see where they are going.

- Rearrange furniture closer to switches or move lamps closer to beds.
- Install night lights.

Are ash trays, smoking materials, or other fire sources (heaters, hot plates, teapots, etc.) located away from beds or bedding?

Burns are a leading cause of accidental death among seniors. Smoking in bed is a major contributor to this problem.

- Remove sources of heat or flame from areas around beds.
- Don't smoke in bed.

Is anything covering your electric blanket when in use?

"Tucking in" electric blankets, or placing additional coverings on top of them can cause excessive heat buildup which can start a fire.

Do you avoid "tucking in" the sides or ends of your electric blanket?

- Use electric blankets according to the manufacturer's instruc-tions.

- Don't allow anything on top of the blanket while it is in use. (This includes other blankets or comforters, even pets sleeping on top of the blanket.)
- Don't set electric blankets so high that they could burn someone who falls asleep while they are on.

Do you ever go to sleep with a heating pad which is turned on?

Never go to sleep with a heating pad if it is turned on because it can cause serious burns even at relatively low settings.

Is there a telephone close to your bed?

In case of an emergency, it is important to be able to reach the telephone without getting out of bed.

Basement/Garage/Workshop/Storage Areas

In the basement, garage, workshop, and storage areas, check lighting, fuse boxes or circuit breakers, appliances and power tools, electrical cords, and flammable liquids.

Are work areas, especially areas where power tools are used, well lit?

Good lighting can reduce the chance that you will accidentally cut your finger.

- Either install additional light, or avoid working with power tools in the area.

Can you turn on the lights without first having to walk through a dark area?

Basement, garages, and storage areas can contain many tripping hazards and sharp or pointed tools that can make a fall even more hazardous.

- Keep an operating flashlight handy.
- Have an electrician install switches at each entrance to a dark area.

If fuses are used, are they the correct size for the circuit?

Replacing a correct size fuse with a larger size fuse can present a serious fire hazard. If the fuse in the box is rater higher than that intended for the circuit, excessive current will be allowed to flow and possibly overload the outlet and house wiring to the point that a fire can begin.

- Be certain that correct-size fuses are used. (If you do not know the correct sizes, consider having an electrician identify and label the sizes to be used.)

  NOTE: If all, or nearly all, fuses used are 30-amp fuses, there is a chance that some of the fuses are rated too high for the circuit.

Are power tools equipped with a 3-prong plug or marked to show that they are double insulated?

These safety features reduce the risk of an electric shock.

- Use a properly connected 3-prong adapter for connecting a 3-prong plug to a 2-hole receptacle.

- Consider replacing old tools that have neither a 3-prong plug nor are double insulated.

Are power tools guards in place?

Power tools used with guards removed pose a serious risk of injury from sharp edges or moving parts.

- Replace guards that have been removed from power tools.

Has the grounding feature on any 3-prong plug been defeated by removal of the grounding pin or by improperly using an adapter?

Improperly grounded appliances can lead to electric shock.

- Check with your service person or an electrician if you are in doubt.

Are containers of volatile liquids tightly capped?

If not tightly closed, vapors may escape that may be toxic when inhaled.

- Check containers periodically to make sure they are tightly closed.

NOTE: CPSC has reports of several cases in which gasoline, stored as much as 10 feet from a gas water heater, exploded. Many people are unaware that gas fumes can travel that far.

Are gasoline, paints, solvents, or other products that give off vapors or fumes stored away from ignition sources?

Gasoline, kerosene, and other flammable liquids should be stored out of living areas in properly labeled, non-glass safety containers.

- Remove these products from the areas near heat or flame such as heaters, furnaces, water heaters, ranges, and other gas appliances.

Stairs

For all stairways, check lighting, handrails, and the condition of the steps and coverings.

Are stairs well lighted?

Stairs should be lighted so that each step, particularly the step edges, can be clearly seen while going up and down stairs. The lighting should not produce glare or shadows along the stairway.

- Use the maximum wattage bulb allowed by the light fixture. (If you do not know the correct wattage, use a bulb no larger than 60 watts.)

- Reduce glare by using frosted bulbs, indirect lighting, shades or globes on light fixtures, or partially closing blinds and curtains.

- Have a qualified person add additional light fixtures. Make sure that the bulbs you use are the right type and wattage for the light fixture.

Are light switches located at both the top and bottom of the stairs?

Even if you are very familiar with the stairs, lighting is an important factor in preventing falls. You should be able to turn on the lights before you use the stairway from either end.

- If no other light is available, keep an operating flashlight in a convenient location at the top and bottom of the stairs.

- Install night lights at nearby outlets.

- Consider installing switches at the top and bottom of the stairs.

Do the steps allow secure footing?

Worn treads or worn or loose carpeting can lead to insecure footing, resulting in slips or falls.

- Try to avoid wearing only socks or smooth-soled shoes or slippers when using stairs.

- Make certain the carpet is firmly attached to the steps all along the stairs.

- Consider refinishing or replacing worn treads, or replacing worn carpeting.

- Paint outside steps with paint that has a rough texture, or use abrasive strips.

Are steps even and of the same size and height?

Even a small difference in step surfaces or riser heights can lead to falls.

- Mark any steps which are especially narrow or have risers that are higher or lower than the others. Be especially careful of these steps when using the stairs.

Are the coverings on the steps in good condition?

Worn or torn coverings or nails sticking out from coverings could snag your foot or cause you to trip.

- Repair coverings.
- Remove coverings.
- Replace coverings.

Can you clearly see the edges of the steps?

Falls may occur if the edges of the steps are blurred or hard to see.

- Paint edges of outdoor steps white to see them better at night.

- Add extra lighting.

- If you plan to carpet your stairs, avoid deep pile carpeting or patterned or dark colored carpeting that can make it difficult to see the edges of the steps clearly.

Is anything stored on the stairway, even temporarily?

People can trip over objects left on stairs, particularly in the event of an emergency or fire.

- Remove all objects from the stairway.

REMEMBER PERIODICALLY TO RE-CHECK YOUR HOME.

Family Nurturing & Safety

The most exciting thing about being a grandparent is watching your own child become nurturing. The miracle of a new baby is overwhelming, but to watch your son or daughter becoming a parent is just as miraculous. We watch with awe, pride and, sometimes, trepidation as our sons and daughters do their best to raise strong and healthy offspring. We know how demanding a job that is. We want to help. We should help. And we do.

We want to keep our grandchildren safe and sound. We want to make our homes and theirs safe havens where nothing bad can happen to them. We want to share with our own children the lessons we learned—and learn a few new tips ourselves.

The contributions grandparents make to their families are extraordinary. Some, like babysitting or giving them safe cribs or strollers, are tangible. Others, like providing a role model for grandchildren, are intangible but just as powerful and real. We do know that virtually every study of child development shows that youngsters lucky enough to have loving grandparents are destined to be winners. All research on single parents shows that the future of the children is correlated with support from grandparents.

We also know that grandparents can make their children's job of parenting a lot easier. When you lend a sympathetic ear to an upset parent you provide a safe outlet for often difficult emotions. When you give your children a night off by babysitting, you give them and your grandchild a much-needed break from the inevitable strains of the nuclear family. When your children know that, in a pinch, there is someone to step in to love their children and keep them safe, you give them the most valuable kind of support.

More and more, we see grandparents providing reliable and dedicated child care. In fact, the U.S. Census Bureau estimates that about 1.3 million children are entrusted to their grandparents every day. That same 1994 study says another 2.4 million children live in households headed by a grandparent. It means that numbers of grandparents make it possible for the young ones to grow up in stable homes and communities.

But it's the daily acknowledgment that we get from our children and grandchildren that inspires us to develop and maintain those loving connections. What fun to watch their eyes widen and sparkle when you tell your grandchildren about how their mommy was as a small child! We know it's not always easy, that it takes thought, finesse and devotion. It requires us to be emotionally flexible and nurturing. We have to be vigilant and make our homes safe for children.

We need to take our role modeling seriously—for our children and grandchildren. We hope we can help. Because when grandparenting works, there's nothing better.

Making your home safe for your grandchildren is an ongoing project that changes with each stage of his or her development. What works for a newborn isn't going to be enough for a crawling, alert 8-month-old, and certainly not for an inquisitive toddler. Daunting as it seems now, I can assure you, it'll seem less so as you grow along with your grandchild. It's an effort that will make you, your grandchildren and their parents feel relaxed and secure.

Maintain an "emergency procedure" that allows you to quickly contact your grandchild's doctor, hospital emergency room and poison control center. Keep these phone numbers by every phone in the house when your grandchild is visiting.

One way that will help you see potential hazards to your grandchildren is to get down on your hands and knees and see a room from their perspective.

Never underestimate your grandchild's ability to climb, explore or move furniture to reach something high up. Follow the U.S. Consumer Product Safety Commission's Grandchild Safety Checklist to ensure your home will be safe for your grandchild.

It's important to keep in close touch with your children and respect the way they raise their own children. While you have considerably more experience in child-rearing, there are still things your children can teach you. For example, when I was a young mother, I thought I was keeping my daughters safe by putting them to sleep on their stomachs.

Well, parents today are putting infants to sleep on their backs—which has dramatically reduced the risk of Sudden Infant Death Syndrome (SIDS). We've also learned that putting babies to sleep on top of comforters or pillows, no matter how beautiful, may be associated with infant suffocation. Even that special old crib you've kept for your long-awaited grandchild may be dangerous because it doesn't meet current safety standards. As grandparents, then, it's important for us to be attuned to changes in child-rearing and safety practices.

Grandchild Safety Checklist

Young Infants

Young infants follow objects with their eyes. They explore with their hands, feet and mouths. They begin sitting and crawling.

Put your grandchild to sleep on his or her back in a crib with a firm, flat mattress and no soft bedding underneath.

Make sure your crib is sturdy, with no loose or missing hardware; used cribs may not meet current safety standards.

Don't give grandchildren toys or other items with small parts, or tie toys around their necks.

In a car, always buckle your grandchild in a child safety seat on the back seat.

Older Infants

Older infants crawl and learn to walk. They enjoy bath play and explore objects by banging and poking.

Never leave your grandchild alone for a moment near any water or in the bathtub, even with a bath seat; check bath water with your wrist or elbow to be sure it is not too hot.

Don't leave a baby unattended on a changing table or other nursery equipment; always use all safety straps.

If you use a baby walker for your grandchild, make sure it has special safety features to prevent falls down stairs, or use a stationary activity center instead.

Keep window blind and curtain cords out of reach of grandchildren; dress grandchildren in clothing without drawstrings.

Toddlers

Toddlers have lots of energy and curiosity. They like exploring, climbing and playing with small objects.

Keep all medicines in containers with safety caps; be sure medicines, cleaning products, and other household chemicals are out of reach and locked away from children.

Use safety gates for stairs, safety plugs for electrical outlets, and safety latches for drawers and cabinets.

Buy toys labeled for children under age 3; these are often safety recommendations, not measures of a child's skill or ability.

Never leave your grandchildren alone in or near swimming pools.

Preschoolers

Preschoolers are very active. They run, jump and climb.

Keep children—and furniture they can climb on—away from windows.

At playgrounds, look for protective surfacing under equipment.

Be sure your grandchildren wear helmets when riding tricycles or bicycles.

At all ages, make sure your smoke detectors work; keep matches and lighters away from children.

Chapter 6

First Aid Kits

Principles of First Aid

First aid is the initial care of the injured or sick. It is the care administered by a concerned person as soon as possible after an accident or illness. It is this prompt care and attention prior to the arrival of the ambulance, that sometimes means the difference between life and death, or between a full or partial recovery.

First aid has limitations, as not everybody is a paramedic or doctor, but it is an essential and vital element of the total medical system. FIRST AID SAVES LIVES! ...ask any person who works in the emergency medical field.

Immediate Action

As in most endeavors, the principle to be adopted in first aid is immediate action. Bystanders or relatives not knowing what to do, or being too timid to try, have unwittingly contributed to unnecessary deaths and chronic injuries. If a person is sick or injured, then they need help—and they need it immediately.

It is important that any action taken by the first aid provider is commenced as quickly as possible. Quick action is necessary to preserve

Text in this chapter is excerpted from "Principles of First Aid," from http://www.parasolemt.com.au/afa/afa1.html, and "Recommended Contents of a First Aid Kit," from http://www.parasolemt.com.au.afa/fakits.html, © 2000 Parasol EMT Pty., Limited; reprinted with permission.

life and limb. A casualty who is not breathing effectively, or is bleeding copiously, requires immediate intervention. If quick effective first aid is provided, then the casualty has a much better chance of a good recovery.

It should be remembered though that any action undertaken is to be deliberate, and panic by the first aid provider and bystanders will not be beneficial to the casualty. Try to remain calm and think your actions through. A calm and controlled first aider will give everyone confidence that the event is being handled efficiently and effectively.

Will I Harm the Casualty?

It is unlikely that the casualty being treated by a trained first aid provider will come to any additional harm, provided that the care and treatment is rendered in accordance with the provider's level of training. Many horror stories abound of well meaning first aiders causing irreversible injuries to their casualties, but these are usually just that—stories! If first aid is administered quickly, effectively, and with due care, then the casualty will not suffer any additional harm.

How Do I Get Help?

To get expert medical assistance, call an 911 as early as possible. If you are attending a casualty, get a bystander to telephone for help. If you are on your own then you may have to leave the casualty momentarily to make a call. It's common sense; the decision is yours!

"Medical Alert"

Some individuals suffer from certain medical conditions that may cause them to present with serious signs and symptoms at any time. As a form of assistance and notification, these people may wear a form of medical identification, usually a special bracelet, or less commonly, a necklace.

These devices are commonly referred to as "Medical Alert" bracelets, but other types are available, such as "Vial of Life".

They are imprinted with the person's identity, the relevant medical condition, and other details which may include allergies, drugs required, or specialized medical contact. Medical conditions that may be notified vary from specific heart diseases, to diabetes, epilepsy, asthma, and serious allergies.

First Aid Kits

Possession of a personal first aid kit will equip you to provide emergency assistance if required. First aid kits can contain different contents, depending on your requirements. Personal first aid kits should be stored in a clean and dry area that is childproof. A periodic check of contents is essential to ensure that the contents are present, in date, and in good condition.

Recommended Contents of a Personal First Aid Kit

- Adhesive Strips (Bandaids)—10
- Hand Towels—3
- Adhesive Tape—1
- Non-Adhesive Dressing—2
- Alcohol Swab—3
- Plastic Bag for Amputations—1
- Combine Dressing (Large)—1
- Safety Pins—5
- Crepe Bandage (cm 1)—5
- Scissors (Blunt/Sharp)—1
- Crepe Bandage (7.5 cm)—1
- Eye Pad (Sterile)—1
- Sterile Eye Wash Solution (10ml)—2
- First Aid Pamphlet—1
- Triangular Bandage—2
- Gauze Swab—3
- Wound Dressing—1
- Gloves Disposable—2

Part Two

Poison and Chemical Hazards

Chapter 7

Poison Prevention Questions and Answers

Parents must always be watchful when household chemicals or drugs are being used. Many incidents happen when adults are using a product but are distracted (for example, by the telephone or the doorbell) for a few moments. Children act fast, and adults must make sure that household chemicals and medicines are stored away from children at all times.

If my child eats or drinks a substance that might be a poison, where can I find information on treatment?

If you think someone has been poisoned from a medicine or household chemical, call your Poison Control Center immediately. Its phone number can be found on the inside cover of the yellow or white pages of the telephone directory. Keep the number on your phone. There are currently some 100 Poison Control Centers in the United States that maintain information for the doctor or the public on recommended treatment for the ingestion of household products and medicines. They are familiar with the toxicity (how poisonous it is) of most substances found in the home or know how to find this information.

"National Poison Prevention Week," an undated fact sheet produced by the Consumer Product Safety Commission, available online at http://www.cpsc.gov/cpscpub/pubs/386.html; cited July 2000.

If I find my youngster playing with a bottle of medicine or some household product, how can I tell if he or she has swallowed some and what should I do?

Reactions vary, depending on the product. Sometimes the child may vomit; or he or she may appear to be drowsy or sluggish. Some of the substance may remain around the child's mouth and teeth. There may be burns around the lips or mouth from corrosive items; or you may be able to smell the product on the child's breath. Some products cause no immediate symptoms. If a household chemical has been ingested, call the Poison Control Center or follow the first aid instructions on the label. Even if you suspect, but don't know for sure, that your child has ingested a potentially hazardous product, call your Poison Control Center, emergency department, or doctor. Keep these telephone numbers on your phone.

Are there some first aid measures I can take when an ingestion takes place?

Remain calm. Not all medicines and household chemicals are poisonous, and not all exposures necessarily result in poisoning. For medicines, call the Poison Control Center or doctor immediately. For household chemical products, call the Poison Control Center or follow the first aid instructions on the label. If unable to contact them, call your local emergency number (911 in most areas) or the operator. Keep emergency numbers listed near the phone before an emergency arises. When you contact the Poison Control Center or other emergency personnel, be prepared to give the facts to the expert on the other end of the phone. Have the label ready when you call the expert. The label provides information concerning the product's contents and advice on what immediate first aid to perform. This will be useful when giving first aid and when you call the Poison Control Center. Tell the expert:

- The victim's age.
- The victim's weight.
- Existing health conditions or problems.
- The substance involved and how it contacted the child. For example, was it swallowed, inhaled, absorbed through skin contact, or splashed into the eyes?
- Any first aid which may have been given.

- If the person has vomited.

- Your location, and how long it will take you to get to the hospital.

If medicine has been swallowed, do not give anything by mouth until advised by the Poison Control Center. If chemicals or household products have been swallowed, call the Poison Control Center or follow the first aid instructions on the label. Always keep on hand at home a one-ounce bottle of syrup of ipecac for each child or grandchild under age 5 in the home. Use only on advice of the Poison Control Center, emergency department, or doctor.

Why are so many poisonings related to children under 5 years of age?

Children under the age of 5 are in stages of growth and development in which they are constantly exploring and investigating the world around them. This is the way they learn. It is a normal characteristic and should not be discouraged. Unfortunately, what children see and reach for they usually put in their mouths. It is this behavior to which parents must be alerted. As the youngsters' mobility, ingenuity, and capabilities increase, they can reach medicines and household chemicals wherever stored. For instance, when children are crawling, they can find such products as drain cleaners stored under the kitchen sink and on the floor. As soon as they are able to stand, they can reach such products as furniture polish on low-lying tables, as well as medications in purses on beds. When they start to climb, they can reach medicine on countertops or open the medicine cabinet and get to the medicine. These products should be locked up where possible, out of the child's reach—even when safety packaging is used. Adults should never leave a medicine or household chemical product unattended while in use; children act fast and can get hold of a product and swallow it during the short time while the adult is answering the telephone or doorbell. Advise the caregiver to take the child (or product) with them to answer the phone or doorbell.

Why do we need child-resistant packaging?

Although labeling requirements and educational programs have had some effect in reducing the number of childhood ingestions, significant numbers of children are still being poisoned by ingesting household products that can be hazardous, such as medicines (sometimes brought into the child's home by grandparents or other visitors or accessed by a child visiting a home), cleaning products, and solvents. Child-resistant packaging, if used properly, provides an additional barrier to help prevent ingestions.

As a parent, how certain can I be regarding the effectiveness of this kind of packaging?

While child-resistant packaging provides an increased element of protection, children are going to investigate several different ways of opening a container. If their fingers won't work, their teeth might. It would be impossible to manufacture a package or a closure that would prevent every single child from getting into the contents under all possible circumstances. Therefore, the Poison Prevention Packaging Act requires that packages be difficult for children under 5 years of age to open and obtain a toxic amount within a reasonable time. For example, U.S. Consumer Product Safety Commission (CPSC) regulations require that aspirin, and other products, be packaged in special containers that would prevent at least 80% of those children tested from opening the container during a 10-minute test. This requirement means that some children may still be able to open a container or otherwise obtain a toxic amount. So, keep poisonous substances locked up.

How can I use child-resistant packaging properly?

Remember these steps:

1. Read the instructions to make it easier to open the packaging.

2. Be sure to resecure the closure tightly. Never transfer the contents to other containers.

3. Do not leave loose pills anywhere.

4. Keep medicines and household products (even those with safety caps) locked up and out of sight. Use locks or child-resistant latches to secure storage areas. The pharmacist or merchant from whom the product was purchased can teach you how to open and close the packaging, if you have difficulty. Opening and closing becomes easier with practice. While it may take a few additional seconds of your time, those few seconds may save the life of a child who is very dear to you.

What kind of products can I expect to find in child-resistant packaging?

Aspirin and aspirin-substitutes (acetaminophen), oral dosage prescription drugs, iron-containing drugs and dietary supplements, over-the-counter ibuprofen, loperamide (an anti-diarrhea medicine), over-the-counter preparations containing lidocaine and dibucaine (anesthetic medicines), mouthwash containing 3 grams or more of ethanol (alcohol), over-the-counter naproxen, ketoprofen, certain types of liquid furniture polish, oil of wintergreen, drain cleaners, oven cleaners, lighter fluids, turpentine, paint solvents, windshield washer solutions, automobile antifreeze, fluoride-based rust removers, over-the-counter minoxidil, and methacrylic acid are among the substances required to be in child-resistant packaging. The U.S. Consumer Product Safety Commission is considering child-resistant packaging for the classes of products containing hydrocarbons. The Environmental Protection Agency requires that most pesticides be in child-resistant packaging.

There are no small children in my home. Do I have to use child-resistant packaging?

In general, all adults should use child-resistant packaging because young children may visit the adult's home. To benefit people who are elderly or handicapped, the Poison Prevention Packaging Act allows a manufacturer to offer a regulated non-prescription product in one size or package that does not comply with the safety packaging standard and that bears the label statement "This package for households without young children," if that manufacturer also offers the same product in child-resistant packages. Additionally, if a prescription is involved, the purchaser or prescribing physician can request regular, non-child-resistant packaging. However, such requests should be kept to a minimum, since they increase the danger of childhood poisonings.

Poisonings have happened when youngsters have visited homes where no children live. Little ones have been poisoned after finding medicine containers left in purses or on bedside tables. Poisonings have happened when older persons carried medicines into homes that have small children. A study conducted for the U.S. Consumer Product Safety Commission (CPSC) by the American Association of Poison Control Centers found that 23% of the oral prescription drugs that were ingested by children under 5 belonged to someone who did not live with the child. Overall, 17% of the medicines ingested belonged to a grandparent or great-grandparent. This percentage varied from city to city: in Salt Lake City, 9% of the medicines ingested belonged to a grandparent, but in Shreveport, Louisiana, 24% of the medicines ingested belonged to a grandparent. The data suggest that grandparents—and all adults—need to use child-resistant packaging and keep medicines properly secured, away from young children.

CPSC requires that child-resistant packaging be "adult-friendly" so that adults can open it more easily. This will encourage adults of all ages to keep their medicines in their original child-resistant packaging and not be tempted to leave the tops off medicine.

Table 7.1. Deaths of Children under Age 5 Involving Household Products (Source: National Center for Health Statistics)

Deaths from All Medicines and Household Chemicals		Deaths from Aspirin	
Year	Number of Deaths	Year	Number of Deaths
1972	216	1972	46
1973	149	1973	26
1974	135	1974	24
1975	114	1975	17
1976	105	1976	25
1977	94	1977	11
1978	81	1978	13
1980	73	1980	12
1981	55	1981	6
1982	67	1982	5
1983	55	1983	7
1984	64	1984	7
1985	56	1985	0
1986	59	1986	2
1987	31	1987	3
1988	42	1988	3
1989	55	1989	2
1990	49	1990	1
1991	50	1991	2
1992	42	1992	0
1993	50	1993	2
1994	34	1994	1
1995	29	1995	1
1996	47	1996	1
1997	22		

Is there any evidence that deaths from child poisonings have decreased since child-resistant packaging began to be used?

Yes. The staff of the U.S. Consumer Product Safety Commission (CPSC) estimates that child-resistant packaging for aspirin and oral prescription medicine has saved the lives of about 800 children since the requirements went into effect in the early 1970s. CPSC staff analyzed child fatality data for unintentional ingestions of aspirin and oral prescription medicines. The death rate for these medicines declined even after taking account of the overall decline in the unintentional child death rate from all causes and changes in per capita product consumption. The CPSC staff study showed that child-resistant packaging for aspirin and oral prescription drugs reduced the child death rate by over 2 deaths per million children under age 5. This represents a fatality rate reduction of up to 45 percent from levels that would have been projected in the absence of child-resistant packaging requirements. The estimate of about 800 lives saved relates to aspirin and oral prescription medicines only and does not include additional lives that may have been saved by child-resistant packaging on other products.

There has been a reduction in deaths with all household chemicals and with aspirin products in particular since 1972 (when aspirin was first required to be in child-resistant packaging).

However, the number of ingestions or exposures to household medicines and chemicals continues to be high. The American Association of Poison Control Centers reports that in 1999 there were 1,111,198 children age 5 and under exposed to potentially poisonous substances.

Why is it dangerous to use cups or soft-drink bottles to hold paint thinner, turpentine, gasoline, or other household chemicals?

Children associate cups, soft-drink bottles, and drinking glasses with food and drink. For example, fatalities have been reported when lighter fluid intended for outdoor barbecue fires was poured into such containers and subsequently swallowed by children.

Are there any good housekeeping rules I can use to prevent poisonings?

1.   Use child-resistant packaging properly by closing the container securely after use.

2. Keep all chemicals and medicines locked up and out of sight.

3. Call the poison center immediately in case of poisoning. Keep on hand a bottle of "syrup of ipecac" but use it only if the poison center instructs you to induce vomiting.

4. When products are in use, never let young children out of your sight, even if you must take them along when answering the phone or doorbell.

5. Keep items in original containers.

6. Leave the original labels on all products, and read the label before using.

7. Do not put decorative lamps and candles that contain lamp oil where children can reach them.

8. Always leave the light on when giving or taking medicine. Check the dosage every time.

9. Avoid taking medicine in front of children. Refer to medicine as "medicine," not "candy."

10. Clean out the medicine cabinet periodically, and safely dispose of unneeded medicines when the illness for which they were prescribed is over. Pour contents down drain or toilet, and rinse container before discarding.

Is the poinsettia still considered to be extremely toxic?

The poinsettia was blamed for a death in 1919; however, recent studies indicate that the plant is not as highly toxic as was thought at that time. It is unlikely that ingestion of a poinsettia would be fatal, although it may cause some gastric irritation and burning in the mouth. Many other plants are toxic also. If any indoor or outdoor plants are ingested, Poison Control Center or medical advice should be sought.

Is lead in paint a serious problem if a child should ingest it?

In the past, paints could—and did—contain much higher levels of lead than they do now. Since 1971, however, the permissible amount of lead in consumer paint products has been reduced through a series of federal laws and regulations. This reduction also applies to paints or coatings on toys or articles intended for use by children. Children can still, however, become lead poisoned from ingesting chips or breathing dust from old, heavily leaded paint that is still present on walls and other surfaces in old houses and buildings. Workers and entire families face the same hazard when older homes and buildings are rehabilitated and sanding raises dust as leaded paint is removed from walls, floors, and ceilings.

Can miniature "button" batteries present a risk of childhood poisoning?

These tiny batteries (used in watches, calculators, cameras, and hearing aids) usually pass through the person without any problem. However, miniature batteries may cause poisoning if swallowed and they can cause internal burns if they become lodged in the esophagus or intestinal tract. If a miniature battery is swallowed, you should contact your Poison Control Center. In order to prevent ingestion of miniature batteries, consumers should keep the batteries out of children's reach and throw away old batteries, securely wrapped, after they have been removed from the appliance.

Are adults also at risk when they swallow medicines and household chemicals?

Yes, poisonings happen to adults—especially older people—who cannot read labels or who fail to follow instructions. Some people may confuse one medicine for another, especially if the light is not on when they reach for a medicine at night. Others may take too much of a medicine or may mix medicine with alcohol or other substances. Adults should take precautions to avoid poisonings:

1. Turn on a light at night and put on your glasses to read the label when you need to take a medicine.

2. Always read the label and follow instructions when taking medicines. If any questions arise, consult your physician.

3. Never mix medicines and alcohol, and never take more than the prescribed amount of medicine.

4. Never "borrow" a friend's medicine or take old medicines.

5. Tell your doctor what other medicines you are taking so you can avoid adverse drug interactions.

What can consumers do to protect themselves and their families from medicines that have been tampered with?

Although most medicines are packaged in tamper-evident packaging, they are not tamper-proof. Each consumer must be alert for the packaging to be protective. Here's how you can help protect yourself and your family:

1. Read the label. Over-the-counter medicines with safety closures tell you on the label what tamper-evident features you should look for on the package.

2. Inspect the outer packaging. Look before you buy!

3. Inspect the product itself when you open the package. Look again before you take it! If it looks suspicious, be suspicious.

4. Look for tablets or capsules that are different in any way from others in the package.

5. Don't use any medicine from a package that shows cuts, slices, tears, or other imperfections.

6. Never take medicine in the dark.

7. Read the label and look at the medicine every time you take a dose.

8. Whenever you suspect something wrong with a medicine or it's packaging, take it to the store manager.

9. Tamper-evident packaging can help protect you if you are alert!

What can consumers do to protect children from pesticide-related poisonings?

A recent survey by the U.S. Environmental Protection Agency regarding pesticide use in and around the home revealed that almost half (47%) of all households with children under the age of 5 had at least one pesticide stored in an unlocked cabinet, and less than 4 feet off the ground (i.e., within reach of children). The survey also found that 75% of households without children under the age of 5 also stored one pesticide within reach of children. This number is especially significant because 13% of all pesticide poisonings occur in homes other than the child's home. Adults should take the following steps to safeguard children from exposures to pesticides:

1. Always store pesticides away from children's reach, in a locked cabinet or garden shed.

2. Read the label first and follow the directions to the letter, including all precautions and restrictions.

3. Before applying pesticides (indoors and outdoors), remove children and their toys from the area and keep them away until it is dry or as recommended by the label.

4. Never leave pesticides unattended when you are using them— not even for a few minutes.

5. Never transfer pesticides to other containers—children may associate certain containers with food or drink.

6. Use child-resistant packaging properly by closing the container tightly after use.

7. Alert others to the potential hazard, especially grandparents and caregivers.

Chapter 8

Poison Lookout Checklist

The home areas listed below are the most common site of accidental poisonings. Follow this checklist to learn how to correct situations that may lead to poisonings. If you answer "No" to any questions, fix the situation quickly. Your goal is to have all your answers "Yes."

The Kitchen

Do all harmful products in the cabinets have child-resistant caps?

Products like furniture polishes, drain cleaners and some oven cleaners should have safety packaging to keep little children from accidentally opening the packages.

Are all potentially harmful products in their original containers?

There are two dangers if products aren't stored in their original containers. Labels on the original containers often give first aid information if someone should swallow the product. And if products are stored in containers like drinking glasses or pop bottles, someone may think it is food and swallow it.

"Poison Lookout Checklist," an undated fact sheet produced by the Consumer Product Safety Commission, available online at http://www.cpsc.gov/cpscpub/pubs/383.html; cited July 2001.

Are harmful products stored away from food?

If harmful products are placed next to food, someone may acciden-tally get a food and a poison mixed up and swallow the poison.

Have all potentially harmful products been put up high and out of reach of children?

The best way to prevent poisoning is making sure that it's impos-sible to find and get at the poisons. Locking all cabinets that hold dangerous products is the best poison prevention.

The Bathroom

Did you ever stop to think that medicines could poison if used improperly?

Many children are poisoned each year by overdoses of aspirin. If aspirin can poison, just think of how many other poisons might be in your medicine cabinet.

Do your aspirins and other potentially harmful products have child-resistant closures?

Aspirins and most prescription drugs come with child-resistant caps. Check to see yours have them, and that they are properly se-cured. Check your prescriptions before leaving the pharmacy to make sure the medicines are in child-resistant packaging. These caps have been shown to save the lives of children.

Have you thrown out all out-of-date prescriptions?

As medicines get older, the chemicals inside them can change. So what was once a good medicine may now be a dangerous poison. Flush all old drugs down the toilet. Rinse the container well, then discard it.

Are all medicines in their original containers with the original labels?

Prescription medicines may or may not list ingredients. The pre-scription number on the label will, however, allow rapid identifica-tion by the pharmacist of the ingredients should they not be listed.

Without the original label and container, you can't be sure of what you're taking. After all, aspirin looks a lot like poisonous roach tablets.

If your vitamins or vitamin/mineral supplements contain iron, are they in child-resistant packaging?

Most people think of vitamins and minerals as foods and, therefore, nontoxic, but a few iron pills can kill a child.

The Garage or Storage Area

Did you know that many things in your garage or storage area that can be swallowed are terrible poisons?

Death may occur when people swallow such everyday substances as charcoal lighter, paint thinner and remover, antifreeze and turpentine.

Do all these poisons have child-resistant caps? Are they stored in the containers? Are the original labels on the containers? Have you made sure that no poisons are stored in drinking glasses or pop bottles? Are all these harmful products locked up and out of sight and reach?

When all your answers are "Yes," then continue this level of poison protection by making sure that, whenever you buy potentially harmful products, they have child-resistant closures and are kept out of sight and reach. Post the number of the Poison Control Center near your telephone.

Chapter 9

Safe Storage of Medicines and Household Substances

Young Children Will Eat and Drink Almost Anything!

Keep all liquids and solids that may be poisonous out of their reach. Use child-resistant packaging to help prevent poisonings with medicines and household chemicals. Each year poison control centers report nearly one million children under the age of five are exposed to potentially poisonous medicines and household chemicals.

Medicines (especially iron pills and food supplements containing iron), household substances, insect sprays, kerosene, lighter fluid, some furniture polishes, turpentine, points, solvents, and products containing lye and acids are most frequently the cause of accidental poisoning among children.

Always Return to Safe Storage Immediately (Locked Up—Away From Children)

Never leave a bottle of aspirin or other pills where children can reach it Return it to a safe place immediately after using.

Medicines

Medicines are often swallowed by young children who find medicines where their grandparents have left them. Grandparents—and

"Locked Up Poisons," an undated fact sheet produced by the Consumer Product Safety Commission, available online at http://www.cpsc.gov/cpscpub/pubs/382.html; cited July 2001.

all adults—should use child-resistant closures whenever young children are around. Keep medicines out of reach—and out of sight—of all children.

Household Products

Read labels before using any household product and follow the directions carefully. Store these products so that children cannot reach them.

Always re-secure child-resistant packaging.

Keep All Products in Original Containers

Never place kerosene, anti-freeze, paints, or solvents in cups, glasses, milk or soft-drink bottles, or other utensils customarily used for food or drinks.

Never transfer products to a bottle without a child-resistant closure.

Destroy Old Medications

Pour contents down drain or toilet, and rinse container before discarding. Do not put container with its contents into trash.

Keep Foods and Household Products Separated

Cleaning fluids, detergents, lye, soap powders, insecticides, and other everyday household products should be stored away from food and medications Death could be the result of a mistaken identity.

Never Call Medicine "Candy"

Children should not be deceived by having flavored medicines called "candy." When left alone, they may locate the bottle and eat or drink its contents.

Growing Children Are Curious

Things that glitter, pretty colored pills, bottles and containers of all kinds arouse their natural curiosity. If a child is in the crawling stage, arrange to keep household products in places other than below the kitchen sink unless the cabinet is locked or secured with child safety latches.

If the child is walking, be certain that bottles and boxes containing medicines or household products are put away before answering the telephone or doorbell.

If he is able to climb, find a shelf that is completely beyond his ability to reach, or, better yet, lock these products in a cabinet or closet.

After using a product, always re-secure the child-resistant closure.

To reduce the risk of poisoning:

1. Keep household products and medicines out of reach and out of sight of children, preferably in a locked cabinet or closet. Even if you must leave the room for only an instant, put the container in a safe spot.

2. Store medicines and dietary supplements (especially iron pills) separately from other household products and keep these items in their original containers—never in cups or soft-drink bottles.

3. Be sure that all products are properly labeled, and read the label before using.

4. Always turn the light on when giving or taking medicine to be sure you have the right medicine and the correct measure or count of the dosage.

5. Since children tend to imitate adults—avoid taking medications in their presence. Avoid drinking medicine from the bottle.

6. Refer to medicines by their proper names. They are not candies.

7. Clean out your medicine cabinet periodically. Get rid of old medicines by flushing them down the drain or toilet, rinsing the container in wafer, and then discarding it.

8. Ask for and use household products which are available in child resistant packaging. Insist on safety packaging for prescription medicines. Re-secure safety feature carefully after using Safety packaging gives extra protection to your children.

If there is a poisoning incident:

- Call the Poison Control Center
- Call a Doctor, or
- Call a Hospital

Chapter 10

Child Resistant Packaging

The Consumer Product Safety Commission (CPSC) analyzed child fatality data for accidental ingestions of aspirin and oral prescription medicines. The death rates for aspirin and oral prescription medicines declined even after taking account of the overall decline in the accidental child death rate from all causes. The study also accounted for changes in per capita product consumption and reductions in the aspirin fatality rate associated with therapeutic overdose.

The CPSC study showed that child-resistant packaging reduced the aspirin-related child death rate by up to 0.88 deaths per million children under age five. The results also showed that special packaging reduced the oral prescription medicine-related death rate by up to 1.27 deaths per million children under age five. This represents a fatality rate reduction of up to 45 percent from levels that would have been projected in the absence of child-resistant packaging requirements.

The lower fatality rate represents a total reduction of about 700 child deaths since the requirements for child-resistant packaging on these products went into effect in the early 1970's.

The estimate of about 700 lives saved relates to aspirin and oral prescription medicines only and does not include additional lives that

"Child Resistant Packaging Saves Lives," an undated fact sheet produced by the Consumer Product Safety Commission, available online at http://www.cpsc.gov/cpscpub/pubs/5019.html; and "Child-Resistant closures and Veterinary Drugs Dispensed by Veterinarians to the Consumer," an undated fact sheet produced by the Consumer Product Safety Commission, available on line at http://www.cpsc.gov/cpscpub/pubs/5104.html; both cited July 2001.

may have been saved by child-resistant packaging on other products. Therefore, the CPSC's staff concludes that child-resistant packaging saves lives.

Consumers should use child-resistant packaging to help prevent accidental poisonings with medicines and household chemicals.

Child-Resistant Closures and Veterinary Drugs Dispensed by Veterinarians to the Consumer

In the U S. there are about 36 million households that own at least one dog; 24 million households with at least one cat; and 15 million households owning (in decreasing order of frequency) fish, birds, rodents, and reptiles.

The American Veterinary Medical Association has long been on record as favoring the use of child-resistant packaging by dispensing veterinarians.

The U.S. Consumer Product Safety Commission strongly urges all veterinary medical practitioners to adopt the practice of routinely using child-resistant packaging, particularly when dispensing some of the more toxic agents available for veterinary use.

Early attempts to reduce accidental poisonings by household substances relied on labeling of hazardous substances and efforts to educate parents about the hazards associated with the use and storage of hazardous substances in the home. These efforts prevented many accidents; however, they were only partially effective for the most frequently involved group, children under the age of five.

The Poison Prevention Packaging Act (PPPA) of 1970, authorizes the establishment of mandatory safety packaging standards for categories of products which, because of the nature of the hazard to children, require child-resistant packaging to prevent death or serious injury or illness in children under the age of five.

Sixteen categories of substances have been regulated to date. These include caustics such as sodium and/or potassium hydroxide drain cleaners, various petroleum distillate-containing household cleaning products, solvents and' fuels, several over-the-counter drugs, and oral human prescription drugs as well as controlled drugs.

A manufacturer of a non-prescription product regulated under the PPPA may market a single size of that product In a conventional package, provided that the package is labeled to Indicate that it is for households without young children and provided that the manufacturer also markets the product in packages which comply with the regulation. On the other hand, those regulated substances which may be sold only on the order of a licensed medical practitioner must be dispensed in child-resistant (CR) packaging unless requested otherwise by the purchaser or the prescribing medical practitioner.

Therefore, unless requested otherwise, human oral prescription drugs are required to be in child-resistant packaging when they are dispensed by pharmacists. However, veterinary prescription drugs, which are often both prescribed and dispensed by veterinarians, are not required to be In child-resistant packaging.

In studies by the U.S. Consumer Product Safety Commission, a number of facts were revealed about veterinary prescription drugs and their dispensing patterns:

- The majority of veterinary drugs prescribed for small animals were generic equivalents of orally administered human prescription drugs.

- Approximately 95 percent of all veterinary drug prescriptions were for small animals kept in or around the home.

- A high percentage of veterinary drugs (more than 90 percent) are dispensed by veterinarians, the balance (generally controlled drugs) are dispensed by pharmacists.

Many toxic prescription drugs are consequently available in the home in conventional packaging when prescribed for the family pet, while they would be in protective safety packaging when prescribed for a family member. While not all prescription drugs are so classed on the basis of toxicity, a potential for childhood injury exists anytime one of the more toxic prescription items enters the home in a non-safety package. Therefore, CPSC urges all veterinary medical practitioners to use child-resistant packaging.

Chapter 11

Lead Hazards in the Home

Lead-Based Paint Is Hazardous to Your Health

Lead-based paint is a major source of lead poisoning for children and can also affect adults. In children, lead poisoning can cause irreversible brain damage and can impair mental functioning. It can retard mental and physical development and reduce attention span. It can also retard fetal development even at extremely low levels of lead. In adults, it can cause irritability, poor muscle coordination, and nerve damage to the sense organs and nerves controlling the body. Lead poisoning may also cause problems with reproduction (such as a decreased sperm count). It may also increase blood pressure. Thus, young children, fetuses, infants, and adults with high blood pressure are the most vulnerable to the effects of lead.

Children Should Be Screened for Lead Poisoning

In communities where the houses are old and deteriorating, take advantage of available screening programs offered by local health

Text in this chapter is from " What You Should Know about Lead Based Paint in Your Home: Safety Alert," "CPSC Warns about Hazards of "Do It Yourself" Removal of Lead Based Paint: Safety Alert," "Don't Use Solder that Contains Lead for Work on Drinking Water Systems: Safety Alert," undated fact sheets, produced by the U.S. Consumer Product Safety Commission (CPSC), and "Protect Your Family from Lead in Your Home," 1995, Consumer Product Safety Commission (CPSC), and "CPSC Releases Lead and Cadmium Test Results on Vinyl Products," 1997, Consumer Product Safety Commission (CPSC).

departments and have children checked regularly to see if they are suffering from lead poisoning. Because the early symptoms of lead poisoning are easy to confuse with other illnesses, it is difficult to diagnose lead poisoning without medical testing. Early symptoms may include persistent tiredness, irritability, loss of appetite, stomach discomfort, reduced attention span, insomnia, and constipation. Failure to treat children in the early stages can cause long-term or permanent health damage.

The current blood lead level which defines lead poisoning is 10 micrograms of lead per deciliter of blood. However, since poisoning may occur at lower levels than previously thought, various federal agencies are considering whether this level should be lowered further so that lead poisoning prevention programs will have the latest information on testing children for lead poisoning.

Consumers Can Be Exposed to Lead from Paint

Eating paint chips is one way young children are exposed to lead. It is not the most common way that consumers, in general, are exposed to lead. Ingesting and inhaling lead dust that is created as lead-based paint "chalks," chips, or peels from deteriorated surfaces can expose consumers to lead. Walking on small paint chips found on the floor, or opening and closing a painted frame window, can also create lead dust. Other sources of lead include deposits that may be present in homes after years of use of leaded gasoline and from industrial sources like smelting. Consumers can also generate lead dust by sanding lead-based paint or by scraping or heating lead-based paint.

Lead dust can settle on floors, walls, and furniture. Under these conditions, children can ingest lead dust from hand-to-mouth contact or in food. Settled lead dust can re-enter the air through cleaning, such as sweeping or vacuuming, or by movement of people throughout the house.

Older Homes May Contain Lead Based Paint

Lead was used as a pigment and drying agent in "alkyd" oil based paint. "Latex" water based paints generally have not contained lead. About two-thirds of the homes built before 1940 and one-half of the homes built from 1940 to 1960 contain heavily leaded paint. Some homes built after 1960 also contain heavily leaded paint. It may be on any interior or exterior surface, particularly on woodwork, doors, and windows. In 1978, the U.S. Consumer Product Safety Commission lowered the legal maximum lead content in most kinds of paint to 0.06% (a trace amount). Consider having the paint in homes constructed before the 1980s tested for lead before renovating or if the paint or underlying surface is deteriorating. This is particularly important if infants, children, or pregnant women are present.

Consumers Can Have Paint Tested for Lead

There are do-it-yourself kits available. However, the U.S. Consumer Product Safety Commission has not evaluated any of these kits. One home test kit uses sodium sulfide solution. This procedure requires you to place a drop of sodium sulfide solution on a paint chip. The paint chip slowly turns darker if lead is present. There are problems with this test, however. Other metals may cause false positive results, and resins in the paint may prevent the sulfide from causing the paint chip to change color. Thus, the presence of lead may not be correctly indicated. In addition the darkening may be detected only on very light-colored paint.

Another in-home test requires a trained professional who can operate the equipment safely. This test uses X-ray fluorescence to determine if the paint contains lead. Although the test can be done in your home, it should be done only by professionals trained by the equipment manufacturer or who have passed a state or local government training course, since the equipment contains radioactive materials. In addition, in some tests, the method has not been reliable.

Consumers may choose to have a testing laboratory test a paint sample for lead. Lab testing is considered more reliable than other methods. Lab tests may cost from $20 to $50 per sample. To have the lab test for lead paint, consumers may:

- Get sample containers from the lab or use resealable plastic bags. Label the containers or bags with the consumer's name and the location in the house from which each paint sample was taken. Several samples should be taken from each affected room.

- Use a sharp knife to cut through the edges of the sample paint. The lab should tell you the size of the sample needed. It will probably be about 2 inches by 2 inches.

- Lift off the paint with a clean putty knife and put it into the container. Be sure to take a sample of all layers of paint, since only the lower layers may contain lead. Do not include any of the underlying wood, plaster, metal, and brick.

- Wipe the surface and any paint dust with a wet cloth or paper towel and discard the cloth or towel.

The U.S. Department of Housing and Urban Development (HUD) recommends that action to reduce exposure should be taken when the lead in paint is greater than 0.5% by lab testing or greater than 1.0 milligrams per square centimeter by X-ray fluorescence. Action is especially important when paint is deteriorating or when infants, children, or pregnant women are present. Consumers can reduce exposure to lead-based paint.

If you have lead-based paint, you should take steps to reduce your exposure to lead. You can:

1. Have the painted item replaced.

    You can replace a door or other easily removed item if you can do it without creating lead dust. Items that are difficult to remove should be replaced by professionals who will control and contain lead dust.

2. Cover the lead-based paint.

    You can spray the surface with a sealant or cover it with gypsum wallboard. However, painting over lead-based paint with non-lead paint is not a long-term solution. Even though the lead-based paint may be covered by non-lead paint, the lead-based paint may continue to loosen from the surface below and create lead dust. The new paint may also partially mix with the lead-based paint, and lead dust will be released when the new paint begins to deteriorate.

3. Have the lead-based paint removed.

    Have professionals trained in removing lead-based paint do this work. Each of the paint-removal methods (sandpaper, scrapers, chemicals, sandblasters, and torches or heat guns) can produce lead fumes or dust. Fumes or dust can become airborne and be inhaled or ingested. Wet methods help reduce the amount of lead dust. Removing moldings, trim, windowsills, and other painted surfaces for professional paint stripping outside the home may also create dust. Be sure the professionals contain the lead dust. Wet-wipe all surfaces to remove any dust or paint chips. Wet-clean the area before re-entry.

You can remove a small amount of lead-based paint if you can avoid creating any dust. Make sure the surface is less than about one square foot (such as a window sill). Any job larger than about one square foot should be done by professionals. Make sure you can use a wet method (such as a liquid paint stripper).

4. Reduce lead dust exposure.

You can periodically wet mop and wipe surfaces and floors with a high phosphorous (at least 5%) cleaning solution. Wear waterproof gloves to prevent skin irritation. Avoid activities that will disturb or damage lead based paint and create dust. This is a preventive measure and is not an alternative to replacement or removal.

Professionals are available to remove, replace, or cover lead-based paint.

Contact your state and local health departments lead poisoning prevention programs and housing authorities for information about testing labs and contractors who can safely remove lead-based paint.

The U.S. Department of Housing and Urban Development (HUD) prepared guidelines for removing lead-based paint which were published in the Federal Register, April 18, 1990, page 1455614614. Ask contractors about their qualifications, experience removing lead-based paint, and plans to follow these guidelines.

- Consumers should keep children and other occupants (especially infants, pregnant women, and adults with high blood pressure) out of the work area until the job is completed.

- Consumers should remove all food and eating utensils from the work area.

- Contractors should remove all furniture, carpets, and drapes and seal the work area from the rest of the house. The contractor also should cover and seal the floor unless lead paint is to be removed from the floor.

- Contractors should assure that workers wear respirators designed to avoid inhaling lead.

- Contractors should not allow eating or drinking in the work area. Contractors should cover and seal all cabinets and food contact surfaces.

- Contractors should dispose of clothing worn in the room after working. Workers should not wear work clothing in other areas of the house. The contractor should launder work clothes separately.

- Contractors should clean up debris using special vacuum cleaners with HEPA (high efficiency particulate air) filters and should use a wet mop after vacuuming.

- Contractors should dispose of lead-based paint waste and contaminated materials in accordance with state and local regulations.

Government officials and health professionals continue to develop advice about removing lead-based paint. Watch for future publications by government agencies, health departments, and other groups concerned with lead-paint removal and prevention of lead poisoning.

Simple Steps to Protect Your Family from Lead Hazards

If you think your home has high levels of lead:

- Get your young children tested for lead, even if they seem healthy.
- Wash children's hands, bottles, pacifiers, and toys often.
- Make sure children eat healthy, low-fat foods.
- Get your home checked for lead hazards.
- Regularly clean floors, windowsills, and other surfaces.
- Wipe soil off shoes before entering house.
- Talk to your landlord about fixing surfaces with peeling or chipping paint.
- Don't use a belt-sander, propane torch, dry scraper, or dry sandpaper on painted surfaces that may contain lead.
- Don't try to remove lead-based paint yourself.

Are You Planning to Buy, Rent, or Renovate a Home Built Before 1978?

Many houses and apartments built before 1978 have paint that contains lead (called lead-based paint). Lead from paint, chips, and dust can pose serious health hazards if not taken care of properly. Federal law will requires that individuals receive certain information before renting, buying, or renovating pre-1978 housing:

- LANDLORDS have to disclose known information on lead-based paint hazards before leases take effect. Leases should include a federal form about lead-based paint.

- SELLERS have to disclose known information on lead-based paint hazards before selling a house. Sales contracts should include a federal form about lead-based paint in the building. Buyers will have up to 10 days to check for lead hazards.

Important!

Lead from Paint, Dust, and Soil Can Be Dangerous If Not Managed Properly

- Lead exposure can harm young children and babies even before they are born.

- Even children that seem healthy can have high levels of lead in their bodies.

- People can get lead in their bodies by breathing or swallowing lead dust, or by eating soil or paint chips with lead in them.

- People have many options for reducing lead hazards. In most cases, lead-based paint that is in good condition is not a hazard.

- Removing lead-based paint improperly can increase the danger to your family.

If you think your home might have lead hazards, read this section to learn some simple steps to protect your family.

Lead Gets in the Body in Many Ways

One out of every 11 children in the United States has dangerous levels of lead in the bloodstream. Even children who appear healthy can have dangerous levels of lead.

People can get lead in their body if they:

- Put their hands or other objects covered with lead dust in their mouths.

- Eat paint chips or soil that contain lead.
- Breathe in lead dust (especially during renovations that disturb painted surfaces).

Lead is even more dangerous to children than adults because:

- Babies and young children often put their hands and other objects in their mouths. These objects can have lead dust on them.
- Children's growing bodies absorb more lead.
- Children's brains and nervous systems are more sensitive to the damaging effects of lead.

Lead's Effects

If not detected early, children with high levels of lead in their bodies can suffer from:

- Damage to the brain and nervous system
- Behavior and learning problems (such as hyperactivity)
- Slowed growth
- Hearing problems
- Headaches

Lead is also harmful to adults. Adults can suffer from:

- Difficulties during pregnancy
- Other reproductive problems (in both men and women)
- High blood pressure
- Digestive problems
- Nerve disorders
- Memory and concentration problems
- Muscle and joint pain

Lead affects the body in many ways.

Checking Your Family for Lead

Get your children tested if you think your home has high levels of lead.

A simple blood test can detect high levels of lead. Blood tests are important for:

- Children who are 6 months to 1 year old (6 months if you live in an older home that might have lead in the paint).

- Family members that you think might have high levels of lead.

- If your child is older than 1 year, talk to your doctor about whether your child needs testing.

Your doctor or health center can do blood tests. They are inexpensive and sometimes free. Your doctor will explain what the test results mean. Treatment can range from changes in your diet to medication or a hospital stay.

Where Lead-Based Paint Is Found

In general, the older your home, the more likely it has lead-based paint.

Many homes built before 1978 have lead-based paint. In 1978, the federal government banned lead-based paint from housing. Lead can be found:

- In homes in the city, country, or suburbs.

- In apartments, single-family homes, and both private and public housing.

- Inside and outside of the house.

- In soil around a home. (Soil can pick up lead from exterior paint, or other sources such as past use of leaded gas in cars.)

Where Lead Is Likely to Be a Hazard

Lead from paint chips, which you can see, and lead dust, which you can't always see, can both be serious hazards.

Lead-based paint that is in good condition is usually not a hazard.

Peeling, chipping, chalking, or cracking lead-based paint is a hazard and needs immediate attention.

Lead-based paint may also be a hazard when found on surfaces that children can chew or that get a lot of wear-and-tear. These areas include:

- Windows and windowsills.

- Doors and door frames.
- Stairs, railings, and banisters.
- Porches and fences.

Lead dust can form when lead-based paint is dry scraped, dry sanded, or heated. Dust also forms when painted surfaces bump or rub together. Lead chips and dust can get on surfaces and objects that people touch. Settled lead dust can reenter the air when people vacuum, sweep, or walk through it.

Lead in soil can be a hazard when children play in bare soil or when people bring soil into the house on their shoes. Call your state agency to find out about soil testing for lead.

Checking Your Home for Lead Hazards

Just knowing that a home has lead-based paint may not tell you if there is a hazard.

You can get your home checked for lead hazards in one of two ways, or both:

- A paint inspection tells you the lead content of every painted surface in your home. It won't tell you whether the paint is a hazard or how you should deal with it.

- A risk assessment tells you if there are any sources of serious lead exposure (such as peeling paint and lead dust). It also tells you what actions to take to address these hazards.

Have qualified professionals do the work. The federal government is writing standards for inspectors and risk assessors. Some states might already have standards in place. Call your state agency for help with locating qualified professionals in your area.

Trained professionals use a range of methods when checking your home, including:

- Visual inspection of paint condition and location.
- Lab tests of paint samples.
- Surface dust tests.
- A portable x-ray fluorescence machine.

Home test kits for lead are available, but the federal government is still testing their reliability. These tests should not be the only method used before doing renovations or to assure safety.

What You Can Do Now to Protect Your Family

If you suspect that your house has lead hazards, you can take some immediate steps to reduce your family's risk:

- If you rent, notify your landlord of peeling or chipping paint.
- Clean up paint chips immediately.
- Clean floors, window frames, windowsills, and other surfaces weekly. Use a mop or sponge with warm water and a general all-purpose cleaner or a cleaner made specifically for lead.
  REMEMBER: NEVER MIX AMMONIA AND BLEACH PRODUCTS TOGETHER SINCE THEY CAN FORM A DANGEROUS GAS.
- Thoroughly rinse sponges and mop heads after cleaning dirty or dusty areas.
- Wash children's hands often, especially before they eat and before nap time and bed time.
- Keep play areas clean. Wash bottles, pacifiers, toys, and stuffed animals regularly.
- Keep children from chewing windowsills or other painted surfaces.
- Clean or remove shoes before entering your home to avoid tracking in lead from soil.
- Make sure children eat nutritious, low-fat meals high in iron and calcium, such as spinach and low-fat dairy products. Children with good diets absorb less lead.

How to Significantly Reduce Lead Hazards

Removing lead improperly can increase the hazard to your family by spreading even more lead dust around the house.

Always use a professional who is trained to remove lead hazards safely.

In addition to day-to-day cleaning and good nutrition:

- You can temporarily reduce lead hazards by taking actions like repairing damaged painted surfaces and planting grass to cover soil with high lead levels. These actions (called "interim controls") are not permanent solutions and will not eliminate all risks of exposure.

- To permanently remove lead hazards, you must hire a lead "abatement" contractor. Abatement (or permanent hazard elimination) methods include removing, sealing, or enclosing lead-based paint with special materials. Just painting over the hazard with regular paint is not enough.

Always hire a person with special training for correcting lead problems—someone who knows how to do this work safely and has the proper equipment to clean up thoroughly. If possible, hire a certified lead abatement contractor. Certified contractors will employ qualified workers and follow strict safety rules as set by their state or by the federal government.

Call your state agency for help with locating qualified contractors in your area and to see if financial assistance is available.

Remodeling or Renovating a Home with Lead-Based Paint

If not conducted properly, certain types of renovations can release lead from paint and dust into the air.

Take precautions before you begin remodeling or renovations that disturb painted surfaces (such as scraping off paint or tearing out walls):

- Have the area tested for lead-based paint.

- Do not use a dry scraper, belt-sander, propane torch, or heat gun to remove lead-based paint. These actions create large amounts of lead dust and fumes. Lead dust can remain in your home long after the work is done.

- Temporarily move your family (especially children and pregnant women) out of the apartment or house until the work is done and the area is properly cleaned. If you can't move your family, at least completely seal off the work area.

- Follow other safety measures to reduce lead hazards. You can find out about other safety measures by calling 1-800-424-5323.

Other Sources of Lead

While paint, dust, and soil are the most common lead hazards, other lead sources also exist.

- Drinking water—your home might have plumbing with lead or lead solder. Call your local health department or water supplier to find out about testing your water. You cannot see, smell, or taste lead, and boiling your water will not get rid of lead. If you think your plumbing might have lead in it:

    Use only cold water for drinking and cooking.

    Run water for 15 to 30 seconds before drinking it, especially if you have not used your water for a few hours.

- The job—if you work with lead, you could bring it home on your hands or clothes. Shower and change clothes before coming home. Launder your clothes separately from the rest of your family's.

- Old painted toys and furniture.

- Food and liquids stored in lead crystal or lead-glazed pottery or porcelain.

- Lead smelters or other industries that release lead into the air.

- Hobbies that use lead, such as making pottery or stained glass, or refinishing furniture.

- Folk remedies that contain lead, such as "greta" and "azarcon" used to treat an upset stomach.

For More Information

The National Lead Information Center
Tel: 800-LEAD-FYI (to learn how to protect children from lead poisoning)

The National Lead Information Center Clearinghouse
8601 Georgia Ave, Suite 503
Silver Spring, MD 20910
Tel: 800-424-LEAD
Fax: 301-585-7976
Internet: http://www.epa.gov/lead

EPA's Safe Drinking Water Hotline
Tel: 800-426-4791 (for information about lead in drinking water)

Consumer Product Safety Commission Hotline
Tel: 800-638-2772
TDD: 800-638-8270
Internet: http://www.cpsc.gov
To request information on lead in consumer products, or to report an
unsafe consumer product or a product-related injury.

Hazards of "Do It Yourself" Removal of Lead Based Paint

There is no completely safe method for "do-it-yourself" removal of
lead-based paint, according to the U.S. Consumer Product Safety
Commission. Each of the paint-removal methods—sandpaper, scrap-
ers, chemicals, and torches or heat guns—can produce lead fumes or
dust. Fumes or dust can become airborne and be inhaled. Further,
dust can settle on floors, walls, and tables, and can cause problems.
It can be ingested by children from hand-to-mouth contact. It can re-
enter the air through cleaning (such as sweeping or vacuuming) or
by movements of people throughout the house. Lead-based paint
should be removed only by professionals, trained in hazardous material removal, who follow detailed procedures to control and contain
lead dust.

Lead-based paint should be removed only by professionals trained
in hazardous material removal. Consumers should not attempt to
remove lead-based paint. Any attempt to remove lead-based paint may
create a serious hazard in the house. A trained professional must follow very detailed procedures to minimize, control and contain lead
dust generated by the removal process.

These procedures are included in the Department of Housing and
Urban Development (HUD) Interim Guidelines for Removal of Lead-
Based Paint. Homeowners should obtain the HUD interim guidelines
and assure that contractors use them. Homeowners should question
contractors about their familiarity with the following procedures:

- The room should be sealed from the rest of the house. All furniture, carpets and drapes should be removed.

- Workers should wear respirators designed to avoid inhaling lead.

- No eating or drinking should be allowed in the work area. All
  food and eating utensils should be removed from the room. All
  cabinets as well as food contact surfaces should be covered and
  sealed.

- Children and other occupants (especially infants, pregnant women, and adults with high blood pressure) should be kept out of the house until the job is completed.

- Clothing worn in the room should be disposed of after working. The work clothing should not be worn in other areas of the house.

- Debris should be cleaned up using special vacuum cleaners with HEPA (high efficiency particle absorption) filters. A wet mop should be used after vacuuming.

The U.S. Department of Housing and Urban Development (HUD) has evaluated methods for removal of lead-based paint. HUD has contracted out to develop for removal of lead-based paint.

Don't Use Solder that Contains Lead for Work on Drinking Water Systems

In the past, solder normally contained about 50 percent lead. (An example of the label marking would be: "ALLOY 50/50"). The use in drinking water systems of solder labeled like this is prohibited by federal law.

Now, there is solder on the market made from tin and antimony. (An example of the label marking would be: "95/TIN, 5/ANT.") Use this "lead-free" solder for plumbing in drinking water systems.

Consumers who do minor repairs of plumbing in drinking water systems should stop using solder that contains lead. Lead can leach from the solder and cause a health hazard when ingested.

Too much lead in the body can cause serious damage to the brain, kidneys, nervous system, and red blood cells. At greatest risk are young children and pregnant women. Amendments to the Safe Drinking Water Act (primarily administered by the U.S. Environmental Protection Agency) require the use of "lead-free" pipe, solder, and flux in the installation or repair of any public water system, or any plumbing In a residential or nonresidential facility connected to a public water system.

Do not use lead-containing solder for plumbing in drinking water systems. All solders that contain more than 0.2 percent lead must be labeled with this warning:

WARNING: Contains (more than 0.2 percent) LEAD. The use of this solder to make joints or fittings in any private or public potable water supply system is prohibited.

If your drinking water is contaminated with lead, or you suspect that it may be, EPA recommends two immediate steps:

- When the water in a particular faucet has not been used for six hours or longer, "flush" your cold water pipes by running the water until it becomes as cold as it will get.

- Use only water from the cold water tap for drinking, cooking, and especially for making baby formula. Hot water is likely to contain higher levels of lead.

Lead and Cadmium Test Results on Vinyl Products

Greenpeace released a study alleging that hazardous levels of lead and cadmium are present in many popular vinyl children's products. Testing by the U.S. Consumer Product Safety Commission (CPSC) does not support this conclusion.

CPSC takes action when it learns that products contain hazardous levels of lead. However, CPSC testing found that seven of the 11 vinyl products in which Greenpeace found high levels of lead had no or only trace levels of lead. CPSC conducted further analysis on the four other vinyl products and found two are not hazardous because exposure is not likely, and testing on two is incomplete. Children's health is at risk when they are exposed to hazardous levels of lead. This exposure occurs through ingestion or inhalation.

Of the 11 products, CPSC found eight had no or only trace levels of cadmium and one was not hazardous because exposure is not likely. Testing on two of the products is incomplete.

Using CPSC's experience with vinyl miniblinds, Greenpeace asserts that toxic dust will inevitably be released when vinyl products deteriorate. CPSC staff found that vinyl miniblinds do deteriorate when continuously exposed to sunlight and heat. However, CPSC experts do not believe that the vinyl products tested by Greenpeace will deteriorate because they are not exposed to the same extent of sunlight and heat as the vinyl miniblinds.

CPSC has most recently identified and taken actions to reduce or eliminate the risk of lead poisoning from a number of children's products and consumer products in which lead was accessible to children. These included imported crayons, imported non-glossy vinyl miniblinds, playground equipment and children's jewelry.

CPSC is continuing to evaluate the information provided by Greenpeace and will take action as appropriate.

Chapter 12

Pest Control and Pesticide Safety

Introduction

Sooner or later, we're all pestered by pests. Whether it's ants in the kitchen or weeds in the vegetable garden, pests can be annoying and bothersome. At the same time, many of us are concerned that the pesticides we use to control pests can cause problems too. How can pests be controlled safely? When and how should pesticides be used?

This chapter is intended to help answer these questions. The questions have no single right answer, there is information available to make informed decisions. You should be able to control pests without risking your family's health and without harming the environment.

Did you know that these common household products are pesticides?

- Cockroach sprays and baits.

- Insect sprays and wasp repellents for indoor use.

- Insect repellents for personal use.

- Termite control products.

- Rat and other rodent poisons.

- Flea and tick sprays, powders, and pet collars.

Excerpted from "Citizen's Guide to Pest Control and Pesticide Safety," United States Environmental Protection Agency (EPA), EPA 730-K-95-001, September 1995.

- Kitchen, laundry, and bath disinfectants and sanitizers, including bleach.

- Products to kill mold and mildew.

- Lawn and garden products such as weed killers.

- Swimming pool chemicals, including those that kill algae.

- Repellents that keep deer, raccoons, or rabbits away from your garden.

Pests, Pest Control, and Pesticides

Plants, insects, mold, mildew, rodents, bacteria, and other organisms are a natural part of the environment. They can benefit people in many ways. But they can also be pests. Apartments and houses are often hosts to common pests such as cockroaches, fleas, termites, ants, mice, rats, mold, or mildew. Weeds, hornworms, aphids, and grubs can be a nuisance outdoors when they get into your lawn, flowers, yard, vegetable garden, or fruit and shade trees. Pests can also be a health hazard to you, your family, and your pets. It's easy to understand why you may need and want to control them.

Nowadays, you can choose from many different methods as you plan your strategy for controlling pests. Sometimes a non-chemical method of control is as effective and convenient as a chemical alternative. For many pests, total elimination is almost impossible, but it is possible to control them. Knowing your options is the key to pest control. Methods available to you include pest prevention, non-chemical pest controls, and chemical pesticides.

Pest Management

The most effective strategy for controlling pests may be to combine methods in an approach known as integrated pest management (IPM) that emphasizes preventing pest damage. In IPM, information about pests and available pest control methods is used to manage pest damage by the most economical means and with the least possible hazard to people, property, and the environment.

Knowing a range of pest control methods gives you the ability to choose among them for an effective treatment. Knowing the options also gives you the choice of limiting your exposure to potentially harmful chemicals. No matter what option you choose, you should follow these steps to control your pest problem:

1. Identify the pest problem. This is the first and most important step in pest control—figuring out exactly what you're up against. Some pests (or signs of them) are unmistakable—most people recognize a cockroach or a mouse. Other signs that make you think "pest" can be misleading. For example, what may look like a plant "disease" may be, in fact, a sign of poor soil or lack of water.

    Use free sources to help identify your pest and to learn the most effective methods to control it. These sources include library reference books (such as insect field guides or gardening books) and pest specialists at your County Cooperative Extension Service or local plant nurseries. These resources are usually listed in the telephone book.

2. Decide how much pest control is necessary. Pest control is not the same as pest elimination. Insisting on getting rid of all pests inside and outside your home will lead you to make more extensive, repeated, and possibly hazardous chemical treatments than are necessary. Be reasonable. Ask yourself these questions:

    *   Does your lawn really need to be totally weed free?

    *   Recognizing that some insects are beneficial to your lawn, do you need to get rid of all of them?

    *   Do you need every type of fruit, vegetable, or flower you grow, or could you replace ones that are sensitive to pests with hardier substitutes?

    *   Can you tolerate some blemished fruits and vegetables from your garden?

    *   Is anyone in your home known to be particularly sensitive to chemicals?

3. Choose an effective option. Use the information gathered in Step 1, your answers to the questions in Step 2 to determine which option you want to choose. If you're still uncertain, get further advice from the free sources listed in Step 1.

4. Evaluate the results. Once a pest control method has been chosen and implemented, always allow time for it to work and then evaluate its effectiveness by taking the following steps:

- Compare pre-treatment and post-treatment conditions. Is there evidence of a clear reduction in the number of pests?

- Weigh the benefits of short-term chemical pesticide control against the benefits of long-term control using a variety of other treatments, including nonchemical methods.

It's easier to prevent pests than to control them. You may not need to worry about the four pest control steps just mentioned IF you make the effort to prevent pests in the first place.

Preventing Pests

Pests seek places to live that satisfy basic needs for air, moisture, food, and shelter. The best way to control pests is to try to prevent them from entering your home or garden in the first place. You can do this by removing the elements that they need to survive. Take the following preventive actions:

Indoor Prevention

- Remove water. All living things, including pests, need water for survival. Fix leaky plumbing, and do not let water accumulate anywhere in or around your home. For example, do not leave any water in trays under your houseplants, under your refrigerator, or in buckets overnight. Remove or dry out water damaged and wet materials. Even dampness or high humidity can attract pests.

- Remove food. Store your food in sealed glass or plastic containers, and keep your kitchen clean and free from cooking grease and oil. Do not leave food in pet bowls on the counter or floor for long periods of time. Put food scraps or refuse in tightly covered, animal-proof garbage cans, and empty your garbage frequently.

- Remove or block off indoor pest hiding places. Caulk cracks and crevices to control pest access. Bathe pets regularly and wash any mats or surfaces they lie on to control fleas. Avoid storing newspapers, paper bags, and boxes for long periods of time. Also, check for pests in packages or boxes before carrying them into your home.

- Block pest entryways. Install screens on all floor drains, windows, and doors to discourage crawling and flying pests from entering your home. Make sure any passageways through the floor are blocked. Place weatherstripping on doors and windows. Caulk and seal openings in walls. Keep doors shut when not in use.

Outdoor Prevention

- Remove or destroy outdoor pest hiding places. Remove piles of wood from under or around your home to avoid attracting termites and carpenter ants. Destroy diseased plants, tree prunings, and fallen fruit that may harbor pests. Rake fallen leaves. Keep vegetation, shrubs, and wood mulch at least 18 inches away from your house.

- Remove breeding sites. Clean up pet droppings from your yard; they attract flies that can spread bacteria. Do not accumulate litter or garbage; it draws mice, rats, and other rodents. Drain off or sweep away standing puddles of water; water is a breeding place for mosquitos and other pests. Make sure drain pipes and other water sources drain away from your house.

- Take proper care of all outdoor plants. These include flowers, fruit and shade trees, vegetable and other plants, and your lawn. Good plant health care reduces pest control needs—healthy plants resist pests better than do weak plants. Plant at the best time of year to promote healthy growth. Use mulch to reduce weeds and maintain even soil temperature and moisture. Water adequately. Native flowers, shrubs, and trees often are good choices because they adapt well to local conditions and require minimal care.

Gardening

- Select healthy seeds and seedlings that are known to resist diseases and are suited to the climate where you live. Strong seeds are likely to produce mature plants with little need for pesticides.

- If your garden is large, alternate rows of different kinds of plants. Pests that prefer one type of vegetable (carrots, for example) may not spread to every one of your carrot plants if other vegetables (not on the pests' diet) are planted in the neighboring rows.

121

- Don't plant the same crop in the same spot year after year. That way your plants are not as vulnerable to pests that survive the winter.

- Make sure your garden plot has good drainage. Raised beds will improve drainage, especially of clay soils. If a heavy clay soil becomes compacted, it does not allow air and water to get to the roots easily, and plants struggle to grow. To loosen compacted soil and create air spaces so that water and nutrients can reach the roots, buy or rent a tiller that breaks up the dirt and turns it over. Before planting, add sand and organic matter to enrich the soil mixture in your garden plot. Also, have the soil tested periodically to see whether you need to add more organic matter or adjust the pH (acidity/alkalinity) balance by adding lime or sulfur. Your County Cooperative Extension Service, listed in the telephone book, or local nursery should be able to tell you how to do this.

- Mulch your garden with leaves, hay, grass clippings, shredded/chipped bark, or seaweed. Do not use newspapers to keep down weeds or to fertilize plants. Newsprint may contain toxic metals such as lead and mercury.

Lawn Care

Tending a garden may not be your hobby; but if you rent or own a home, you might need to care for the lawn. You don't have to be an expert to grow a healthy lawn—the key is to work with nature. You need to create the right conditions for your grass to grow strong and stay healthy. A healthy lawn can resist damage from weeds, disease, and insect pests. Set realistic weed and pest control goals for your lawn.

Think of lawn care as a preventive health care program, like one you would follow to stay healthy yourself. The goal is to prevent problems from ever occurring.

Pesticides can be effective, but should not be relied on as the quick-fix solution to any lawn problem. Serious, ongoing pest problems are often a sign that your lawn is not getting what it needs to stay healthy. Pests may be a symptom of an underlying problem. You need to correct the underlying problem to reduce the chances of pests reappearing.

Make these six steps part of a preventive health care program for your lawn:

1. Develop healthy soil that has the right pH balance, key nutrients, and good texture. You can buy easy-to-use soil analysis kits at hardware stores or contact your local County Cooperative Extension Service for a soil analysis.

2. Choose a type of grass that grows well in your climate. For instance, if your area gets very little rain, don't plant a type of grass that needs a lot of water. Your local County Cooperative Extension Service can advise you on which grasses grow best in your area.

3. Mow high, mow often, and make sure the lawn mower blades are sharp. Grass that is slightly long makes a strong, healthy lawn with few pest problems. Weeds have a hard time taking root and growing when grass is fairly long (around 2 1/2 to 3 1/2 inches for most types of grass). A foot-high meadow isn't necessary; just adding an inch to the length of your grass will give most lawns a real boost.

4. Water deeply but not too often. The best rule is to water only when the lawn begins to wilt from dryness—when the color dulls and footprints stay in the grass for more than a few seconds. Avoid watering during the hottest part of the day because the water will evaporate too quickly.

5. Correct thatch buildup. Thatch is a layer of dead plant material between the grass blades and the soil. When thatch gets too thick (deeper than 3/4 of an inch), it prevents water and nutrients from getting into the soil and reaching the roots of the grass. Overusing synthetic fertilizer can create a heavy layer of thatch, and some kinds of grass are prone to thatch buildup.

    In a healthy lawn, earthworms, spiders, millipedes, and a variety of microorganisms help keep the thatch layer in balance by breaking it up and using it for food, which releases nutrients into the soil. You can get rid of excess thatch by raking the lawn using a dethatching rake or by using a machine that pulls plugs out of the grass and thatch layer to break it up. Sprinkle a thin layer of topsoil or compost over the lawn after dethatching or aerating it to speed up the process of decomposition.

6. Set realistic weed and pest control goals. It is almost impossible to get rid of all weeds and pests. However, even a lawn

that is 15 percent weeds can look almost weed-free to the casual observer. A healthy lawn will probably always have some weeds and some insect pests. But a healthy lawn will also have beneficial insects and other organisms like earthworms that keep pests under control. Improper use of pesticides can kill these beneficial organisms.

By following this preventive health care program for your lawn, you should be able to rely very little, if at all, on chemical pesticides for weed and insect pest control.

Using Non-Chemical Pest Controls

You've got pests, and you want to control them with a dependable pest control method that does not contain chemical pesticides. Non-chemical pest control methods really work, and they have many advantages. Compared to chemical treatments, non-chemical methods are generally effective for longer periods of time. They are less likely to create hardy pest populations that develop the ability to resist pesticides. And many non-chemical pest controls can be used with fewer safeguards, because they are generally thought to pose virtually no hazards to human health or the environment. Two examples of non-chemical pest control methods are biological and manual treatments.

Biological Controls

Did you know that pests themselves may be eaten or otherwise controlled by birds, insects, or other living organisms? You can use a pest's natural enemies (predators) to your advantage. These "biological controls," as they are called, take many forms:

- Beneficial predators such as purple martins and other birds eat insects; bats can eat thousands of insects in one night; lady beetles (ladybugs) and their larvae eat aphids, mealybugs, whiteflies, and mites. Other beneficial bugs include spiders, centipedes, ground beetles, lacewings, dragonflies, big-eyed bugs, and ants. You can install a purple martin house in your yard. You can also buy and release predatory insects. They are available from sources such as gardening catalogs and magazines. Contact your County Cooperative Extension Service, a nursery, or a garden association for information on how to attract and protect beneficial predators.

- Parasitoids such as miniature wasps lay their eggs inside the eggs or bodies of insect pests such as tomato hornworms. Once the eggs hatch, the offspring kill their insect hosts, making parasitoids highly effective pest controllers.

- Microscopic pathogens such as fungi, bacteria, and viruses control pests. An example is milky spore disease, which attacks Japanese beetles. A number of these biological pesticides are available commercially at hardware and garden stores.

- Biochemical pesticides include pheromones and juvenile insect hormones. Pheromones are chemical substances released by various organisms (including insects) as means of communicating with others of the same species, usually as an aid to mating. Pheromones lure pests inside a trap. Juvenile insect hormones interfere with an insect's normal growth and reproductive functions by mimicking the effects of compounds that occur naturally in the pest.

Manual Methods

- Spading and hoeing to cut up weeds.

- Hand-picking weeds from your lawn and pests from your plants, indoors or out.

- Using a flyswatter.

- Setting traps to control rats, mice, and some insects.

- Mulching to reduce weed growth.

One or a combination of several non-chemical treatments may be just what you need for your pest problem. You must be patient because results may not be immediate. And, you must work to prevent pests from entering your home or garden in the first place. Pheromone traps lure pests.

Using Chemical Pest Controls

If you decide that the best solution to your pest problem is chemical—by itself or, preferably, combined with non-chemical treatments— be aware that one of the greatest causes of pesticide exposure to humans is the use of pesticides in and around the home.

Anyone can buy a wide variety of "off the shelf" pesticide products to control weeds, unwanted insects, and other pests. No special training is required to use these pesticides. Yet many of the products can be hazardous to people, especially when stored, handled, applied, or disposed of improperly. The results achieved by using chemical pesticides are generally temporary, and repeated treatments may be required. Over time, some pests become pesticide-resistant, meaning they adapt to the chemical and are no longer harmed by it. This forces you to choose another product or method. If used incorrectly, home-use pesticide products can be poisonous to humans. As a result, it is extremely important for you to take responsibility for making sure that these products are used properly. The basic steps in reducing pesticide risks are:

- Choosing the right pesticide product.
- Reading the product label.
- Determining the right amount to purchase and use.
- Using the product safely and correctly.
- Storing and disposing of pesticides properly.

Choosing the Right Pesticide Product

Once you decide to use chemical pesticides, you must decide whether to do the job yourself or hire a professional pest control service. If you choose to tackle the job yourself, the next question is the most important. Which pesticide product is the best one for your situation?

Home-use pesticides come in many forms—including solutions, aerosols, dusts, granules, baits, and wettable powders. As the name implies, wettable powders are usually mixed with water and/or other liquids and then applied. Pesticide solutions are often diluted with water. Certain formulations work better for some pests and/or some target areas than others. Many pesticides also come in ready-to-use forms, such as aerosols and spray bottles, which are often more practical and easy to use because they don't require measuring or mixing.

Before you buy a product, read the label! Compare product labels, and learn as much as you can about the pesticide. Contact your County Cooperative Extension Service (listed in the telephone book), local pesticide dealers, the National Pesticide Telecommunications Network (NPTN) at 1-800-858-7378, or your state pesticide agency for assistance.

When you are ready to buy a pesticide product, follow these recommendations:

- First, be certain that you have identified the problem correctly. Then, choose the least toxic pesticide that will achieve the results you want and be the least toxic to you and the environment.

- When the words "broad-spectrum" appear on the label, this means the product is effective against a broad range of pests. If the label says "selective," the product is effective against one or a few pests.

- Find the signal word—either Danger-Poison, Danger, Warning, or Caution on the pesticide label. The signal word tells you how poisonous the product is to humans.

  Pesticide products labeled Danger-Poison are "Restricted Use" and are mainly used under the supervision of a certified applicator. For the most part, these products should not be available for sale to the consumer.

- Choose the form of pesticide (aerosol, dust, bait, or other) best suited to your target site and the pest you want to control.

Reading the Pesticide Label

The pesticide label is your best guide to using pesticides safely and effectively. The directions on the label are there primarily to help you achieve "maximum" benefits—the pest control that you desire—with "minimum" risk. Both depend on following label directions and correctly using the pesticide. Read the label. Read the label before buying the pesticide. Read the label before mixing or using the pesticide each time, and read the label before storing or disposing of the pesticide. Do not trust your memory. You may have forgotten part of the label instructions or they may have changed. Use of any pesticide in any way that is not consistent with label directions and precautions is illegal. It may also be ineffective and, even worse, dangerous.

The main sections of a pesticide label are described below:

1. *EPA Registration Number.* This number tells you that EPA has reviewed the product and determined that it can be used with minimal or low risk if you follow the directions on the label

properly. The number is not a stamp of approval or guarantee of effectiveness.

2. *Ingredients Statement or Active Ingredients.* Active ingredients are the chemicals in the pesticide that kill or control the target pest(s).

3. *Signal Words.* The signal words—Caution, Warning, or Danger—indicate the pesticide's potential for making you sick. The word CAUTION appears on pesticides that are the least harmful to you. A pesticide with the word WARNING is more poisonous than those with a Caution label. Pesticides with the word DANGER on the label are very poisonous or irritating. They should be used with extreme care because they can severely burn your skin and eyes.

4. *Precautionary Statements.* This part describes the protective clothing, such as gloves or goggles, that you should wear when using the pesticide. The section also tells you how to protect children or pets by keeping them away from areas treated with pesticides.

5. *Environmental Hazards.* This section tells you if the product can cause environmental damage—if it's harmful to wildlife, fish, endangered plants or animals, wetlands, or water.

6. *Directions for Use.* Make sure that the product is labeled for use against the pest(s) that you are trying to control. (For example, products labeled only for termites should not be used to control fleas.) Use only the amounts recommended, and follow the directions exactly.

7. *First Aid Instructions.* The label tells you what to do if someone is accidentally poisoned by the pesticide. Look for this information in the Statement of Practical Treatment section. The instructions are only first aid. ALWAYS call a doctor or your local poison control center. You may have to take the person to a hospital right away after giving first aid. Remember to take the pesticide label or container with you.

8. *Storage and Disposal.* Read carefully and follow all directions for safe storage and disposal of pesticide products. Always keep products in the original container and out of reach of children, in a locked cabinet or locked garden shed.

Determining the Correct Amount to Use

Many products can be bought in a convenient ready-to-use form, such as in spray cans or spray bottles, that won't require any mixing. However, if you buy a product that has to be measured out or mixed with water, prepare only the amount of pesticide that you need for the area where you plan to use the pesticide (target area). The label on a pesticide product contains much useful information, but there isn't always room to include examples of different dilutions for every home use. Thus, it is important to know how to measure volume and figure out the exact size of the area where you want to apply the pesticide. Determining the correct amount for your immediate use requires some careful calculations. Use the following example as an illustration of how to prepare only the amount of pesticide needed for your immediate pest control problem.

An example: The product label says, "For the control of aphids on tomatoes, mix 8 fluid ounces of pesticide into 1 gallon of water and spray until foliage is wet." You have only 6 tomato plants. From experience, you know that 1 gallon is too much, and that you really need only 1 quart of water to wet the leaves on these 6 plants. A quart is only 1/4 of a gallon. Because you want to use less water than the label says, you need less pesticide. You need only 1/4 of the pesticide amount listed on the label—only 2 fluid ounces. This makes the same strength spray recommended by the label, and is the appropriate amount for the 6 tomato plants.

In short, all you need to do is figure the amount of pesticide you need for the size of your target area, using good measurements and careful arithmetic.

Caution: When you use cups, teaspoons, or tablespoons to measure pesticides, use only level measures or level spoonfuls. NEVER use the same tools that you use for measuring pesticides—spoons, cups, bottles—to prepare food, even if you've washed them.

Using Pesticides Safely and Correctly

Once you have read the pesticide label and are familiar with all precautions, including first aid instructions, follow these recommendations to reduce your risks:

Before Using a Pesticide

- Wear the items of protective clothing the label requires: for example, long-sleeved shirts, long pants, overalls, nonabsorbent gloves (not leather or fabric), rubber footwear (not canvas or leather), a hat, goggles, or a dust-mist filter. If no specific clothing is listed, gloves, long-sleeved shirts and long pants, and closed shoes are recommended. You can buy protective clothing and equipment at hardware stores or building supply stores.

When Mixing or Applying a Pesticide

- Never smoke or eat while mixing or applying pesticides. You could easily carry traces of the pesticide from your hands to your mouth. Also, some pesticide products are flammable.

- Follow the use directions on the label carefully. Use only for the purpose listed. Use only the amount directed, at the time and under the conditions specified. Don't change the recommended amount. Don't think that twice the amount will do twice the job. It won't. You could harm yourself, others, or whatever you are trying to protect.

- If the directions on the label tell you to mix or dilute the pesticide, do so outdoors or in a well-ventilated area. Use the amount listed on the label and measure the pesticide carefully. (Never use the same measuring cups or spoons that you use in the kitchen.) Mix only the amount that you need for each application. Do not prepare larger amounts to store for possible future use.

- Keep children, pets (including birds and fish), and toys (including pet toys) away from areas where you mix and apply pesticides for at least the length of time required on the label.

- Never transfer pesticides to other containers, such as empty soft drink or milk bottles. Keep pesticides in their original containers—ones that clearly identify the contents. Refasten all childproof caps tightly.

- If a spill occurs, clean it up promptly. Don't wash it away. Instead, sprinkle the spill with sawdust, vermiculite, or kitty litter. Sweep it into a plastic garbage bag, and dispose of it as directed on the pesticide product label.

- Indoors or outdoors, never put bait for insects or rats, mice, and other rodents where small children or pets can reach it. When using traps, make sure the animal inside is dead before you touch or open the trap.

Indoor applications:

- Use pesticides indoors only when absolutely necessary, and use only very limited amounts.

- Provide adequate ventilation. If the label directions permit, leave all windows open and fans operating after the application is completed. If the pesticide product is only effective in an unventilated (sealed) room or house, do not stay there. Put all pets outdoors, and take yourself and your family away from treated areas for at least the length of time prescribed on the label.

- Apply most surface sprays only to limited areas such as cracks; don't treat entire floors, walls, or ceilings.

- Remove food, pots and pans, and dishes before treating kitchen cabinets. Don't let pesticides get on any surfaces that are used for food preparation. Wait until shelves dry before refilling them. Wash any surfaces that may have pesticide residues before placing food on them.

Outdoor applications:

- Never apply pesticides outdoors on a windy day (winds higher than 10 mph). Position yourself so that a light breeze does not blow pesticide spray or dust into your face.

- Before spraying, close the doors and windows of your home.

- Use coarse droplet nozzles on your sprayer to reduce misting, and spray as close to the target as possible.

- Keep pesticides away from plants and wildlife you do not want to treat. Do not apply any pesticide to blooming plants, especially if you see honeybees or other pollinating insects around them. Do not spray bird nests when treating trees.

- Follow label directions carefully to ensure that you don't apply too much pesticide to your lawn, shrubs, or garden. Never water your lawn after applying pesticides. Before using a pesticide outdoors, check the label or contact your EPA Regional Office or County Cooperative Extension Service to find out whether the pesticide is known or suspected to run off or seep into ground water. Ground water is the underground reservoir that supplies water to wells, springs, creeks, and the like. Excessive application of pesticides could cause the pesticide to run off or seep into water supplies and contaminate them. Excess spray may also leave harmful residues on your homegrown fruit and vegetables, and could affect other plants, wildlife, and fish.

- Never mix or apply a pesticide near a wellhead.

- If you have a well, be sure it extends downward to water sources that are below, and isolated from, surface water sources. Be sure the well shaft is tightly sealed.

- When using total release foggers to control pests, the most important precautions you can take are to use no more than the amount needed and to keep foggers away from ignition sources (ovens, stoves, air conditioners, space heaters, and water heaters, for example). Foggers should not be used in small, enclosed places such as closets and cabinets or under tables and counters.

After Applying a Pesticide, Indoors or Outdoors

- To remove pesticide residues, use a bucket to rinse tools or equipment three times, including any containers or utensils that you used when mixing the pesticide. Then pour the rinse water into the pesticide sprayer and reuse the solution by applying it according to the pesticide product label directions.

- Always wash your hands after applying any pesticide. Wash any other parts of your body that may have come in contact with the pesticide. To prevent tracking pesticides inside, remove or rinse your boots or shoes before entering your home. Wash any clothes that have been exposed to a lot of pesticide separately from your regular wash.

- Evaluate the results of your pesticide use. Consider using a different chemical, a non-chemical method, or a combination of non-chemical and chemical methods if the chemical treatment didn't work. Again, do not assume that using more pesticide than the label recommends will do a better job. It won't.

- Watch for negative effects on wildlife (birds, butterflies, and bees) in and near treated areas. If you see any unusual behavior, stop using that pesticide, and contact EPA's Pesticide Incident Response Officer.

Storing and Disposing of Pesticides Properly

Improper pesticide storage and disposal can be hazardous to human health and the environment. Follow these safety recommendations:

Safe Storage of Pesticides

- Don't stockpile. Reduce storage needs by buying only the amount of pesticide that you will need in the near future or during the current season when the pest is active.

- Follow all storage instructions on the pesticide label.

- Store pesticides high enough so that they are out of reach of children and pets. Keep all pesticides in a locked cabinet in a well-ventilated utility area or garden shed.

- Store flammable liquids outside your living area and far away from an ignition source such as a furnace, a car, an outdoor grill, or a power lawn mower.

- Never store pesticides in cabinets with or near food, animal feed, or medical supplies.

- Always store pesticides in their original containers, complete with labels that list ingredients, directions for use, and first aid steps in case of accidental poisoning.

- Never transfer pesticides to soft drink bottles or other containers. Children or others may mistake them for something to eat or drink.

- Use child-resistant packaging correctly—close the container tightly after using the product. Child resistant does not mean child proof, so you still must be extra careful to store properly— out of children's reach—those products that are sold in child resistant packaging.

- Do not store pesticides in places where flooding is possible or in places where they might spill or leak into wells, drains, ground water, or surface water.

- If you can't identify the contents of the container, or if you can't tell how old the contents are, follow the advice on safe disposal.

Safe Disposal of Pesticides

- The best way to dispose of small amounts of excess pesticides is to use them—apply them—according to the directions on the label. If you cannot use them, ask your neighbors whether they have a similar pest control problem and can use them.

- If all of the remaining pesticide cannot be properly used, check with your local solid waste management authority, environmental agency, or health department to find out whether your community has a household hazardous waste collection program or a similar program for getting rid of unwanted, leftover pesticides. These authorities can also inform you of any local requirements for pesticide waste disposal.

- State and local laws regarding pesticide disposal may be stricter than the Federal requirements on the label. Be sure to check with your state or local agencies before disposing of your pesticide containers.

- If no community program or guidance exists, follow the label directions for disposal. In general, to dispose of less than a full container of a liquid pesticide, leave it in the original container with the cap tightly in place to prevent spills or leaks. Wrap the container in several layers of newspaper and tie it securely. Put the package in a covered trash can for routine collection with municipal trash. If you do not have a regular trash collection service, take the package to a permitted landfill (unless your town has other requirements).

  Note: No more than 1 gallon of liquid pesticide at a time should be thrown out with the regular trash in this manner.

- Wrap individual packages of dry pesticides in several layers of newspaper (or place the pesticides in a tight carton or bag), and tape or tie the package closed. Put the package in a covered trash can for routine collection.

  Note: No more than 5 pounds of dry pesticide at a time should be thrown out with the regular trash in this manner.

- Do not pour leftover pesticides down the sink, into the toilet, or down a sewer or street drain. Pesticides may interfere with the operation of wastewater treatment systems or pollute waterways. Many municipal systems are not equipped to remove all pesticide residues. If pesticides reach waterways, they may harm fish, plants, and other living things.

- An empty pesticide container can be as hazardous as a full one because of residues left inside. Never reuse such a container. When empty, a pesticide container should be rinsed carefully three times and the rinse water thoroughly drained back into the sprayer or the container previously used to mix the pesticide. Use the rinse water as a pesticide, following label directions. Replace the cap or closure securely. Dispose of the container according to label instructions. Do not puncture or burn a pressurized container like an aerosol—it could explode. Do cut or puncture other empty pesticide containers made of metal or plastic to prevent someone from reusing them. Wrap the empty container and put it in the trash after you have rinsed it.

- Many communities have programs to recycle household waste such as empty bottles and cans. Do not recycle any pesticide containers, however, unless the label specifically states that the empty container may be recycled after cleaning.

Reducing Your Exposure When Others Use Pesticides

Even if you never use pesticides yourself, you can still be exposed to them—at home, school, work, or play—by being in treated areas, as a consumer of commodities that others have treated with pesticides, or through food, water, and air that may have been contaminated with pesticides.

If you know or suspect that you, or others close to you, are sensitive to chemicals, consult an expert who can help you develop a strategy for handling your potential exposure problems.

Exposure through Food

Commercial Food

To ensure a safe food supply, EPA regulates the safety of food by setting safety standards to limit the amount of pesticide residues that legally may remain in or on food or animal feed that is sold in the United States. Both domestic and imported foods are monitored by the Food and Drug Administration (FDA) and the U.S. Department of Agriculture (USDA) to ensure compliance with these safety standards.

Because most crops are treated with pesticides at least some of the time, foods you buy at the grocery store may contain small traces of pesticide residues. Pesticide levels tend to decline over time because the residues break down and because crops are usually washed and processed before reaching the marketplace. So, while we all consume small amounts of pesticides regularly, levels in our food generally are well below legal limits by the time the food reaches the grocery shelves.

Although EPA sets safety standards for the amount of pesticide residues allowed both in and on foods, you can take extra precautions to reduce the traces of pesticide residues you and your family consume in the food you buy. Follow these suggestions:

- Trim the fat from meat and poultry because residues of some pesticides concentrate in fat. Remove the skin from fish.

- Discard the fats and oils in broths and pan drippings.

- Rinse fruits and vegetables thoroughly with water. Scrub them with a brush and peel them, if possible. Taking these safety steps will remove most of the existing surface residues, along with any remaining dirt. Note that surface cleaning (rinsing and scrubbing) will not remove pesticide residues that are absorbed into the growing fruit or vegetable before harvest.

- Cook or bake foods to reduce residues of some pesticides even further.

Home-Grown Food

Growing your own food can be an enjoyable activity. It is also a way to reduce your exposure to pesticide residues in food—especially if you decide not to use chemical pesticides on your produce and you choose a garden site where drift or runoff from a neighbor's use of pesticides will not result in unintended residues on your food. If your house is regularly treated for pest prevention, don't plant your garden where the treatments are applied.

Food from the Wild

While it may seem that hunting your own game, catching your own fish, or gathering wild plant foods would reduce your overall exposure to pesticides, that isn't necessarily true. If you eat wild animals or plants from areas where pesticides are frequently used, this food may contain pesticide residues. In addition, birds such as ducks and geese may absorb pesticide residues if they have stopped to eat treated crops anywhere along their flight path.

If you eat food from the wild, you may want to take the following steps to reduce your exposure to pesticides:

- Do not fish in water bodies where contamination has occurred. Pay attention to posted signs that warn of contamination.

- Consult with fish and game officials or other appropriate officials where you plan to hunt or fish to determine whether there are any chemical problems associated with the area.

- Do not pick wild plants that are growing right next to a road, utility right-of-way, or hedgerow between farm fields. These areas may have been treated with pesticides.

- When preparing wild foods, trim fat from the meat. Discard the skin from fish.

Exposure through Water

When pesticides are applied to land, a certain amount may run off into streams and rivers. This runoff, together with industrial waste, may result in low-level contamination of surface water. In certain settings—for example, when sandy soil lies over a ground-water source that is near the surface—pesticides can seep down through the soil to the ground water.

To ensure a safe supply of drinking water, EPA's Office of Water sets standards for pesticides and other chemicals that may be found in drinking water. Municipal water systems test their water periodically and provide treatment or alternate supply sources if residue problems occur. Generally, private wells are not tested unless the well owner requests an analysis. If you get your drinking water from a private well:

- Contact your state or local health department if you have any questions about pesticide or other chemical residues in your well water.

- If your well water is analyzed and found to contain pesticide residue levels above established or recommended health standards, use an alternate water source such as bottled water for

137

drinking and cooking. The safest choice is distilled spring water in glass bottles. If you buy water from a local bottler, ask for the results of any recent pesticide analysis of the bottled water.

Exposure through Air

Outdoors

Air currents may carry pesticides that were applied on properties nearby. You can reduce your exposure outdoors to airborne pesticide residues, or drift, by following these recommendations:

- If a close neighbor or someone else is applying pesticides outdoors near your home, you may want to stay indoors with your children and pets. Keep windows and exterior doors closed.

- If you live near fields, parks, or other areas that receive regular pesticide treatment, consider planting a group of hardy, thick-branched trees or shrubs to help serve as a buffer zone and windbreak.

- Careless application can lead to drift or direct spraying of non-target sites. If your property is accidentally sprayed during an aerial pesticide application, you should call your local, state, or regional pesticide office. If you or someone in your family is accidentally sprayed, wash pesticide off immediately and change into clean clothes. Then call your local poison control center.

Some local governments require public notice before area—wide or broad—scale pesticide spraying activities take place. Affected residents are notified through newspaper announcements, fliers, letters, or signs posted in areas to be treated. Some communities have also enacted "right-to-know" ordinances that require public notice (usually through posting) of lawn treatments and other small-scale outdoor pesticide uses.

Indoors

The air you breathe may contain low levels of pesticide residues long after a pesticide has been applied to objects inside a building or to indoor surfaces and crawl spaces, or after it has been tracked in from outside. Pesticides break down and disappear more slowly indoors than outdoors. In addition, many homes have built-in energy efficiency features that reduce the exchange of indoor and outdoor air and thus aggravate the problem. To limit your exposure to indoor pesticide residues:

- Air out the building adequately after a pesticide is applied indoors. Open doors and windows, and run overhead, whole-house, or window fans to exchange indoor air for outdoor air rapidly and completely.

- If you suspect that the air in your building is contaminated, consult knowledgeable professionals in your local or state health department or EPA's pesticide hotline for advice on the appropriate steps to take.

Poisoned by Pesticides: Don't Let This Happen to Your Child!

A 5-year-old boy drinks from a bottle of bleach that he found under the bathroom sink.

A 3-year-old girl tries to spray her hair the way mommy does, but sprays an aerosol disinfectant in her eyes instead.

A baby who has just begun to crawl eats green pebbles from behind the sofa. They look like candy, but are really rat poison.

These accidents could happen to your children or to children visiting your home if you don't store pesticides out of their reach or if you don't read the label carefully before using the pesticide product.

The dangers are real. In 1993 alone, an estimated 80,000 children were exposed to or poisoned by a household pesticide product that was used or stored incorrectly.

Whether or not you have young children in your home, take the following precautions to protect all children from unintentional pesticide poisonings or exposures:

- Always store pesticides out of children's reach, in a locked cabinet or garden shed. Installing child-proof safety latches or padlocks on cupboards and cabinets is a good idea. Safety latches are available at your local hardware store or building supply warehouse.

- Before applying pesticides—indoors or outdoors—remove children and their toys, along with any pets and their toys, from the area. Keep them away from the area that has been treated until the pesticide has dried and for at least the length of time recommended on the pesticide label.

- If you are interrupted while applying a pesticide—by a phone call, for example—be sure to close the pesticide container properly and put it out of reach of any child who may come into the area while you are gone.

- Never remove labels from containers, and never transfer pesticides to other containers. Children may mistake them for food or drink.

- Never put rodent or insect baits where small children can find them, pick them up, and put them in their mouths.

- Make sure you close any container marked "child resistant" very tightly after you use the product. Check periodically to make sure the product is securely closed. Child resistant does not mean child proof, so you should still be careful with products that are sold in child-resistant packaging.

- Make sure others—specially babysitters, grandparents, and other caregivers—know about the potential hazards of pesticides.

- Teach children that "pesticides are poisons"—something they should never touch or eat.

- Keep the telephone number of your nearest poison control center near each phone. Have the pesticide container handy when you call.

- Always keep Syrup of Ipecac on hand (in your medicine cabinet) to use to induce vomiting. (Be sure the date is current.) But do not give it to your child until a physician or poison control center advises you to do so. The pesticide label may not recommend using Syrup of Ipecac.

Handling a Pesticide Emergency

- If the person is unconscious, having trouble breathing, or having convulsions . . . ACT FAST! Speed is crucial.

- Give needed first aid immediately. Call 911 or your local emergency service. If possible, have someone else call for emergency help while you give first aid.

- If the person is awake or conscious, not having trouble breathing, and not having convulsions . . . Read the label for first aid instructions.

- Call a doctor, a poison control center, a local emergency service (911), or the National Pesticide Telecommunications Network.

- Give first aid.

First Aid for Pesticide Poisoning

When you realize a pesticide poisoning has occurred or is occurring, try to determine what the victim was exposed to and what part of the body was affected before you take action—taking the right action is as important as taking immediate action. If the person is unconscious, having trouble breathing, or having convulsions, ACT FAST! Speed is crucial. Give needed first aid immediately. Call 911 or your local emergency service. If possible, have someone else call for emergency help while you give first aid. If the person is awake or conscious, not having trouble breathing, and not having convulsions, read the label for first aid instructions. Call a doctor, a poison control center, a local emergency service (911), or the National Pesticide Telecommunications Network. Give first aid.

Read the Statement of Practical Treatment section on the product label. The appropriate first aid treatment depends on the kind of poisoning that has occurred. Follow these general guidelines:

- *Swallowed poison*. A conscious victim should drink a small amount of water to dilute the pesticide. Always keep Syrup of Ipecac on hand (in your medicine cabinet) to use to induce vomiting. Be sure the date on the bottle is current. Induce vomiting only if a poison control center or physician advises you to do so, or if instructions on the pesticide label say so. If there is no label available to guide you, do not induce vomiting. Never induce vomiting if the victim is unconscious or is having convulsions.

- *Poison on skin*. Drench skin with water for at least 15 minutes. Remove contaminated clothing. Wash skin and hair thoroughly with soap and water. Dry victim and wrap in blanket. Later, discard contaminated clothing or thoroughly wash it separately from other laundry.

141

- *Chemical burn on skin.* Drench skin with water for at least 15 minutes. Remove contaminated clothing. Cover burned area immediately with loose, clean, soft cloth. Do not apply ointments, greases, powders, or other drugs. Later, discard contaminated clothing or thoroughly wash it separately from other laundry.

- *Poison in eye.* Hold eyelid open and wash eye quickly and gently with clean cool running water from the tap or a hose for 15 minutes or more. Use only water; do not use eye drops, chemicals, or drugs in the eye. Eye membranes absorb pesticides faster than any other external part of the body, and eye damage can occur in a few minutes with some types of pesticides.

- *Inhaled poison.* If the victim is outside, move or carry the victim away from the area where pesticides were recently applied. If the victim is inside, carry or move the victim to fresh air immediately. If you think you need protection like a respirator before helping the victim, call the Fire Department and wait for emergency equipment before entering the area. Loosen the victim's tight clothing. If the victim's skin is blue or the victim has stopped breathing, give artificial respiration (if you know how) and call 911 for help. Open doors and windows so no one else will be poisoned by fumes.

What to Do after First Aid

- First aid may precede but should not replace professional medical treatment. After giving first aid, call 911 or your local emergency service immediately. Have the pesticide label at hand when you call.

- Take the pesticide product container with its label to the doctor's office or emergency room where the victim will be treated. Carry the container in your trunk or flatbed away from the passengers in your vehicle. The doctor needs to know what active ingredient is in the pesticide before prescribing treatment. This information is on the label, which sometimes also includes a telephone number to call for additional treatment information.

To keep your pets from being poisoned, follow label directions on flea and tick products carefully. If you are concerned about the chemicals used in these products, consult your veterinarian.

How to Recognize Pesticide Poisoning

External irritants that contact skin may cause skin damage such as redness, itching, or pimples. External irritants may also cause an allergic skin reaction that produces redness, swelling, or blistering. The mucous membranes of the eyes, nose, mouth, and throat are also quite sensitive to chemicals. Pesticide exposure may cause stinging and swelling in these membranes.

Internal injuries also may occur if a pesticide is swallowed, inhaled, or absorbed through the skin. Symptoms vary from organ to organ. Lung injury may result in shortness of breath, drooling (heavy salivation), or rapid breathing. Direct injury to the stomach and intestines may produce nausea, vomiting, abdominal cramps, or diarrhea. Injury to the nervous system may cause excessive fatigue, sleepiness, headache, muscle twitching, and numbness. In general, different types of pesticides produce different sets of symptoms.

If someone develops symptoms after working with pesticides, seek medical help immediately to determine if the symptoms are pesticide related. In certain cases, blood or urine should be collected for analysis, or other specific exposure tests can be made. It is better to be too cautious than too late.

Avoid potential health problems by minimizing your exposure to pesticides.

Choosing a Pest Control Company

If you have a pest control problem that you do not want to handle on your own, you may decide to turn to a professional applicator. How can you be sure that the pest control company you hire will do a good job? Before you choose a company, get answers to these questions:

1. Is the company licensed?

Most state or local agencies issue state pest control licenses. Make sure the pest control operator's license is current if one is required in your state. Also, ask if the company's employees are bonded, meaning that the company reimburses you for any loss or damage caused by the employee.

You may want to contact your state pesticide agency to find out about its pesticide certification and training programs and to ask whether periodic recertification is required for pest control operators.

143

In addition, possession of a city license—where they are issued—is one more assurance that the company you are dealing with is reputable and responsible.

2. Is the company willing and able to discuss the treatment proposed for your home?

Selecting a pest control service is just as important as selecting other professional services. Look for the same high degree of competence you would expect from a doctor or lawyer. Any company, including those advertising themselves as "green," should inspect your premises and outline a recommended control program, including the:

- Pests to be controlled.

- Extent of the problem.

- Active ingredient(s) in the pesticide chosen.

- Potential adverse health effects and typical symptoms of poisoning associated with the active ingredient.

- Form of the pesticide and application techniques.

- Non-chemical alternatives available.

- Special instructions to reduce your exposure to the pesticide (such as vacating the house, emptying the cupboards, and removing pets).

- Steps to take to minimize your pest problems in the future.

3. Does the company have a good track record?

Don't rely on the company salesperson to answer this question. Research the answer yourself. Ask neighbors and friends if they have ever dealt with the company. Were they satisfied with the service they received? Call the Better Business Bureau or local consumer office and find out if they have received complaints about the company.

4. Does the company have appropriate insurance? Can the salesperson show proof on paper that the company is insured?

Most contractors carry general liability insurance, including insurance for sudden and accidental pollution. Their insurance gives you a certain degree of protection should an accident occur while pesticides are being applied in your home. Contractors may also carry workmen's compensation insurance, which can help protect you should one of their employees be injured while working in or around your apartment or house. Although most states do not require pest control companies to buy insurance, you should think twice before hiring a company that is not insured.

5. Does the company guarantee its work?

You should be skeptical about a company that does not guarantee its work. In addition, be sure to find out what you must do to keep your part of the bargain. For example, in the case of termite control treatments, the company's guarantee may become invalid if you make structural alterations to your home without giving prior notice to the pest control company.

6. Is the company affiliated with a professional pest control association?

Professional associations—national, state, or local—keep members informed of new developments in pest control methods, safety, training, research, and regulations. Members agree to honor a code of ethics. The fact that a company, small or large, chooses to join a professional association signals its concern for quality.

You and the company of your choice should develop the contract together. Your safety concerns should be noted and reflected in the choice of pesticides to be used. These concerns may include allergies, sensitivities, age of occupants (infants or elderly), resident pets, and treatment near wildlife and fish. Wise consumers get bids from two or three companies and look at value more than price. What appears to be a bargain may warrant a second look.

If you hire a pest control firm to do the job, ask the company to use the least toxic chemical method available that will do the job. Ask to see the label or Material Safety Data Sheet, which will show precautionary warnings.

Hiring a company to take care of your pest problem does not mean your job is over. You must evaluate the results. If you believe something has gone wrong with the pesticide application, contact the company and/or your state pesticide agency. Be a responsible, wise consumer and keep asking questions until your pests are under control.

145

Chapter 13

Poisonous House Plants

House plants have become an attractive and important part of home and office decor. In addition to adding both color and beauty to the home, they may also present a hazard, especially if there are young children in the home.

A poisonous plant is one that contains a chemical substance which produces a harmful reaction in the body of humans or animals when taken in small or moderate amounts. A harmful reaction could include allergic reactions, dermatitis or skin irritation, or internal poisoning. Allergic reactions are not always classified as poisoning and will not be treated as such here. This is because there is a wide range of plants that can cause allergic reactions, and sensitivity to a particular plant varies among individuals. There is also a range of tolerance among individuals to the toxins that cause dermatitis or internal poisoning. Not every person will react the same way when in contact with a poisoning agent.

We should all be aware of the potential problem that exists with certain house plants which have toxic properties. This does not imply that you should rid your of all of these plants but that you should realize some plants pose a potential danger. Often, large quantities of a plant classified as poisonous must be ingested before harmful effects occur.

"Poisonous House Plants," from http://www.agric.gov.ab.ca/crops/hort/houseplants/poisonous.html, ©1986 Her Majesty the Queen in the Right of Alberta; reprinted with permission. Reviewed and revised by David A. Cooke, M.D., May 2001.

It is your responsibility to know the identity and scientific name of the plants in your home that are potential hazards. Children should be taught at an early age to keep unknown plants and plant parts out of their mouths. They too should be made aware of the danger of poisonous plants.

It is a good idea to keep the number for your local Poison Control Center available. Poison Control Center staff are experts in identifying and treating poisoning, and have the most up-to-date information available to them. The Poison Control Center telephone number is listed prominently on the first or second page of nearly all telephone books.

If any of the house plants listed in this chapter are ingested and poisoning is suspected, phone your local Poison Control Center or call the nearest Emergency Room. Give all pertinent information, including the name of the plant (preferably the scientific name), the toxic agent, the quantity eaten and the symptoms. The more information you can give them, the better the help they can give you.

The following is a list of common poisonous house and garden plants and bushes. This is not a complete list, so if in doubt, always call for help.

*Azalea (*Rhododendron occidentale*)*
Toxic Agent: Andromedotoxin, Grayanotoxin, arbutin glucoside
Type of Poisoning: Internal poisoning
Poisonous Part: All parts, especially leaves.
Symptoms: Nausea, salivation, vomiting, weakness, dizziness, difficulty in breathing, loss of balance. Considerable variation in toxicity from species to species.

*Bird of Paradise (*Strelitzia reginae*) or (*Poinciana Gilliesii*); these are two completely different species but both are called Bird of Paradise*
Type of Poisoning: Internal poisoning
Poisonous Part: 3-angled capsule and seeds
Symptoms: Vomiting, diarrhea, dizziness and drowsiness. *Poinciana* species are more toxic than *Strelitzia* species

*Caladium (*Caladium hortulanum*)*
Toxic Agent: Calcium oxalate and asparagines
Type of Poisoning: Internal poisoning
Poisonous Part: All parts
Symptoms: Ingestion can cause severe irritation to the mouth and throat, may also be an irritant to stomach and intestines.

Calla Lily (**Zantedeschia aethiopica**)
Toxic Agent: Calcium oxalate
Type of Poisoning: Internal poisoning
Poisonous Part: Leaves and rhizome
Symptoms: Ingestion can cause burning and swelling of the mouth and throat. Vomiting.

Castor Bean (**Ricinus communis**)
Toxic Agent: Ricin
Type of Poisoning: Internal poisoning
Poisonous Part: Entire plant, especially seeds
Symptoms: Burning of the mouth and throat, nausea, vomiting, severe stomach pains, diarrhea, excessive thirst, prostration, dullness of vision, convulsions, uremia and death. Symptom onset may be delayed by several days. 1-3 seeds may be fatal to a child.

Crown of Thorns (**Euphorbia milii splendens**)
Toxic Agent: Unknown irritant in sap
Type of Poisoning Internal poisoning, and contact dermatitis
Poisonous Part: Sap
Symptoms: Contact causes skin and eye irritation. Ingestion of sap causes swelling of the tongue, mouth, and throat, vomiting.

Cyclamen (**Cyclamen persicum**)
Toxic Agent: Alkaloids
Type of Poisoning: Internal poisoning
Poisonous Part: Bulb is most toxic
Symptoms: Intense stomach cramps, vomiting and diarrhea.

Donkeytail (**Euphorbia Mysinites** *or* **Sedum morganianum;** *two different species both called donkeytail*)
Toxic Agent: Unidentified glucosides
Poisonous Part: All parts of Euphorbia; Sedum does not appear to be toxic.
Symptoms: Vomiting, diarrhea, weakness, respiratory depression.

Dumbcane (**Dieffenbachia sp.**)
Toxic Agent: Calcium oxalate and asparagines
Type of Poisoning: Internal poisoning
Poisonous Part: All parts

Symptoms: Biting or chewing rapidly produces irritation and burning of the surface of mouth, tongue and lips. The swelling may immobilize the tongue, interfere with swallowing and breathing and in severe cases cause choking. Symptoms can last for days.

Elephant Ear (Colocasia spp.)
Toxic Agent: Calcium oxalate Asparagine
Type of Poisoning: Internal poisoning
Poisonous Part: All parts
Symptoms: Burning of the mouth and throat with swelling, salivation, vomiting and diarrhea.

English Ivy (Hedera helix)
Toxic Agent: Saponic glycosine Hederagenin
Type of Poisoning: Internal poisoning
Poisonous Part: Leaves and berries; leaves are more toxic
Symptoms: Excitement, difficult breathing and coma.

Flamingo Flower or Flamingo Lilly (Anthurium spp.)
Toxic Agent: Calcium oxalate and asparagines
Type of Poisoning: Internal poisoning
Poisonous Part: All parts
Symptoms: Ingestion can cause severe irritation to the mouth and throat, may also irritate stomach and intestines.

Hyacinth (Hyacinth orientalis)
Toxic Agent: Alkaloid
Type of Poisoning: Internal poisoning
Poisonous: Part Bulb
Symptoms: Intense stomach cramps, vomiting and diarrhea.

Hydrangea (Hydrangea macrophylla)
Toxic Agent: Hydragin-cyanogenic glycoside
Type of Poisoning: Internal poisoning
Poisonous Part: Leaves and buds
Symptoms: Vomiting, diarrhea, gasping and rapid breathing.

Jerusalem Cherry (Solanum pseudocapsicum)
Toxic Agent: Solanine alkaloids
Type of Poisoning: Internal poisoning
Poisonous Part: All parts—highest concentrations in the unripened fruit and leaves

Symptoms: Stomach pains, paralysis, low temperature, dilated pupils, vomiting, diarrhea, circulatory and respiratory depression, loss of sensation and death.

Lantana or Yellow Sage or Red Sage (Lantana spp.)
Toxic Agent: Lantanin alkaloid or lantadene A
Type of Poisoning: Internal poisoning
Poisonous Part: Green berries most toxic; other parts possibly toxic
Symptoms: Stomach and intestinal irritation, muscular weakness, circulatory collapse and death. Acute symptoms resemble atropine poisoning.

Milk bush (Euphorbia trigona)
Toxic Agent: Unknown irritant in sap
Type of Poisoning: Dermatitis & Internal poisoning
Poisonous Part: Entire plant, especially sap
Symptoms: Skin and eye irritation, swelling of tongue, mouth and throat, vomiting.

Narcissus or Daffodil or Amaryllis (Narcissus spp.)
Toxic Agent: Alkaloids
Type of Poisoning: Internal Poisoning
Poisonous Part: Bulb
Symptoms: Nausea, vomiting, diarrhea, trembling, convulsions. May be fatal.

Oleander (Nerium oleander)
Toxic Agent: Oleandrin, Oleandroside, Nereoside
Type of Poisoning: Dermatitis and Internal poisoning
Poisonous Part: All parts—Green or dry
Symptoms: Extremely toxic—a single leaf is considered potentially lethal to humans. Symptoms begin several hours after ingestion, and include dizziness and drowsiness, increased pulse rate, cold extremities, abdominal pain, nausea, weakness and vomiting.

Philodendron (Philodendron spp.)
Toxic Agent: Calcium oxalate
Type of Poisoning: Internal poisoning
Poisonous Part: Leaves and stems
Symptoms: Burning of the mouth, vomiting and diarrhea.

*Poinsettia (*Euphorbia Pulcherrima*)*
Toxic Agent: Unknown toxin
Type of Poisoning: Internal poisoning
Symptoms: Stomach irritation. Probably not highly toxic.

*Sedum (*Sedum acre*)*
Toxic Agent: Unidentified glucosides
Poisonous Part: All parts
Symptoms: Vomiting, diarrhea, weakness, respiratory depression.

*Tulip (*Tulipa spp.*)*
Toxic Agent: Tulipene
Poisonous Part: Bulb. Flowers and leaves appear to be harmless.
Symptoms: Bulb can cause vomiting, diarrhea. Handling of bulbs can cause tingling sensation in fingers.

For More Information

If additional information is desired, there are several excellent books available on the subject of poisonous plants.

1. Creekmore, H. *Daffodils are Dangerous: The Poisonous Plants in Your Garden*. Walker and Co. N.Y. 1966.

2. Hardin, J.W. and J.M. Arena. *Human Poisoning from Native and Cultivated Plants*. Duke University Press. Durham, N.C. 1969.

3. Kingsbury, J.M. *Poisonous Plants of the United States and Canada*. Prentice Hall, Inc. Englewood Cliffs, N.J. 1964.

4. Kingsbury, J.M. *Deadly Harvest: A Guide to Common Poisonous Plants*. Holt Rinehart and Winston, N.Y. 1972.

Chapter 14

Household Hazardous Waste

What Is Household Hazardous Waste?

Some jobs around the home may require the use of products containing hazardous components. Such products may include certain paints, cleaners, stains and varnishes, car batteries, motor oil, and pesticides. The used of leftover contents of such consumer products are known as "household hazardous waste."

Americans generate 1.6 million tons of household hazardous waste per year. The average home can accumulate as much as 100 pounds of household hazardous waste in the basement or garage and in storage closets. When improperly disposed of, household hazardous waste can create a potential risk to people and the environment. This chapter describes steps that people can take to reduce the amount of household hazardous waste they generate and to ensure that those wastes are safely stored, handled and disposed of.

What Are the Dangers of Improper Disposal?

Household hazardous wastes are sometimes disposed of improperly by individuals pouring wastes down the drain, on the ground, into storm sewers, or putting them out with the trash. The dangers of such disposal methods may not be immediately obvious, but certain types of household hazardous waste have the potential to cause physical

United States Environmental Agency (EPA), Office of Solid Waste, an undated fact sheet; cited July 2001.

injury to sanitation workers; contaminate septic tanks or wastewater treatment systems if poured down drains or toilets; and present hazards to children and pets if left around the house. While households do not have to separate household hazardous waste from trash under federal law, some states have special requirements. Call local or state solid waste officials to learn what requirements apply to households or small businesses in your area.

Move to Reduce and Recycle

One way to reduce the potential concerns associated with household hazardous waste is to take actions that use nonhazardous or less hazardous components to accomplish the task at hand. Individuals can do this by reducing the amount and/or toxicity of products with hazardous components, use only the amount needed. Leftover materials can be shared with neighbors or donated to a business charity, or government agency, or given to a household hazardous waste program. Excess pesticide might be offered to a greenhouse or garden center, for example, and theater groups also need surplus paint. Some communities have even organized waste exchanges where household hazardous waste can be swapped or given away.

Recycling is an economical and environmentally sound way to handle some types of household hazardous waste, such as used automobile batteries and oil. Auto parts stores and service stations frequently accept used automobile batteries, and 80 percent of these batteries are currently recycled. In addition, hundreds of local governments working with civic organizations and private firms have implemented successful used oil recycling programs. Many service stations have begun collecting used oil as a service to their customers. Check with local solid waste officials to find out if a used oil recycling program is operating in your area.

Safe Management Methods

Because of the potential risks associated with household hazardous wastes, it is important that people always use, store, and dispose of materials containing hazardous substances safely:

- *Tip #1:* Use and store products containing hazardous substances carefully to prevent any accidents at home. Never store hazardous products in food containers. Keep products containing hazardous materials in their original containers and never remove the labels. Corroding containers, however, should be repackaged and clearly labeled. This will prevent accidental ingestion and also can help protect sanitation workers.

- *Tip #2:* When leftovers remain, never mix household hazardous waste with other products. Incompatibilities may react, ignite, or explode; contaminated household hazardous waste may become unrecyclable.

- *Tip #3:* Follow any instructions for disposal and use provided on the label.

- *Tip #4:* Take household hazardous waste to a local collection program, if available.

Household Hazardous Waste Collection Days

During the 1980s, many communities started special collection days or permanent collection sites for handling household hazardous waste. On collection days, qualified professionals collect hazardous wastes at a central location to ensure safe waste disposal. Over 3,000 collection programs have been undertaken in the United States. Check with the local chamber of commerce, county, or state environmental or solid waste agency to see if there is a household hazardous waste collection program in your area.

Additional Information

A wide assortment of information about the safe disposal and management of household waste is available on the Internet at http://www.epa.gov/osw.

Chapter 15

Safer Alternatives to Hazardous Household Products

Hazardous Household Product Safety

You can identify a hazardous product by reading the label. You can assume that a product is hazardous if its label bears one or more of the following signal words:

- **Poison** means highly toxic; toxicity is the primary hazard.

- **Danger** means extremely corrosive, flammable or reactive or highly toxic.

- **Warning** or **Caution** appear on all other hazardous substances. These signal words are followed by precautionary statements such as *"Keep out of reach of children."* When used on non-pesticide labels, Warning and Caution are used interchangeably; there is no distinction between hazard levels.

- For pesticides:

    Poison and **Danger** have the same meanings as above.

    Warning means moderately toxic; corrosive, flammable, or reactive.

    Caution signals slight toxicity; corrosive, flammable or reactive.

From KidsWeb Natural Resources Kids Page, http://www.metrokc.gov/dnr/ kidsweb/hhw/hhwsafety.htm, © 1999 King County, Washington; reprinted with permission.

157

Table 15.1. Characteristics of Hazardous Substances

Toxic/ Poisonous:

Capable of causing injury or death through ingestion (eating/ drinking), inhalation, or skin absorption.

Examples: Brake fluid, brass polish, fungicides, insecticides, fertilizers, rat and mouse poison, antifreeze, and medicines.

Corrosive:

Can eat away materials and living tissue by chemical action.

Examples: Oven, drain and toilet cleaners, chlorine bleach cleaners, scouring powders, some pool chemicals, car batteries, and silver polish.

Reactive:

Can react with air, water or other substances and result in explosions or the generation of toxic fumes.

Examples: Any products containing chlorine (bleach, automatic dishwasher detergent or pool chemicals) can produce a toxic gas when mixed with products containing ammonia.

Flammable/ Combustible:

Can undergo spontaneous combustion at relatively low temperatures, thereby presenting a significant fire hazard.

Examples: Paint thinners, some solvents, adhesives, rubber cement, hair spray, and furniture polishes.

Table 15.2. Reducing Exposure to Use Hazardous Products More Safely

Read and follow label instructions carefully

Use products in well-ventilated areas to avoid breathing fumes (for proper ventilation, you need to have the fumes blown out of the building. For instance, open two windows, and place a fan in the window next to your work space blowing out.)

Avoid use of aerosols (pressurized spray cans like spray paint)

Keep products out of reach of children and pets

Cleanup properly when you are finished using a product

Wear protective clothing

Never mix products

Use only the recommended amount

Keep products in their original containers

Buy only what you need

Use safer alternatives whenever possible

Table 15.3. Safer Alternatives to Hazardous Household Products

Potentially Hazardous Product	Safer Alternative
Aphid killer	Spray thoroughly with water. Repeat three times weekly.
Aerosol spray	Use non-aerosol, pump type sprays.
Ant control	Mix borax, sugar and water on a cotton ball.
Bathroom cleaner	Mix baking soda and castile soap. Scrub.
Bug spray	Place screens on windows and doors.
Chemical fertilizers	Use compost or coffee grounds, bone meal and wood ashes.
Copper cleaner	Scrub with vinegar and salt. Rinse well.
Deodorizers/Air fresheners	Simmer cinnamon and cloves.
Drain openers	Baking soda and vinegar, followed by boiling water. Or, use a plumber's snake.
Flea repellent	Use a flea comb. Bathe pet weekly. Feed pets Brewer's yeast, vitamin B or garlic cloves.
Floor cleaner	Vinegar and water.
Furniture polish	For unvarnished surfaces, mix lemon juice and vegetable oil.
Glass and window cleaners	Vinegar and water.
Laundry detergent	Use washing soda, or a non-phosphate concentrate.
Oven cleaners	Washing soda.
Oil or solvent based paint.	Water based or latex paints.
Rat and mouse poison.	Snap or live traps.
Rug and upholstery cleaners	Club soda.
Scouring powders.	Baking soda or borax. Rinse thoroughly.
Slug/snail bait.	Pan with beer or slug hotel.
Toilet bowl cleaner	Baking soda and castile soap.
Weed killer.	Pull by hand.

Part Three

Burn Hazards

Chapter 16

Home Fire Safety Checklist

Introduction

The United States has one of the highest fire death and injury rates in the world. Fire—in the form of flames and smoke—is the second leading cause of accidental death in the home.

More than 4,000 people die each year in home fires. Every year, there are more than 500,000 residential fires serious enough to be reported to fire departments. More than 90 percent of residential fire deaths and injuries result from fires in one and two family houses and apartments. Property losses exceed 4 billion dollars annually, and the long term emotional damage to victims and their loved ones is incalculable.

The U.S. Consumer Product Safety Commission (CPSC) has targeted the principal consumer products associated with fires namely home heating devices upholstered furniture, bedding, cigarette lighters, matches, and wearing apparel. The Commission is participating in a special Congressionally authorized study of cigarette-ignited fires, which cause more deaths than any other kind of fire. The Commission continues to push for extensive use of smoke detectors.

The CPSC is fulfilling its role to make products inherently more fire safe. We recognize that much more can be done to cut down on the needlessly high and tragic fire toll by an alert and informed public.

"Your Home Fire Safety Checklist," an undated factsheet produced by the Consumer Product Safety Commission, available online at http://www.cpsc.gov/cpscpub/pubs/556.html; cited July 2001.

Many of the injuries associated with flammable products result from hazards that are overlooked. Fire experts agree that one key to fewer fires is a greater awareness of how accidents can be prevented. By spotting these hazards and taking some simple precautions, many fires and fire-related injuries can be prevented.

Use this checklist as a safety guide to spot possible fire safety problems which may be present in your home. It is a first step in reducing the risk of fire. Answer YES or NO to each question. If you answer NO to any question, the potential hazard should be corrected to avoid the risk of injury or death.

How safe is your home from fire?

Sources of Fire

Supplemental Home Heating Equipment

The use of supplemental room heaters, such as wood and coal burning stoves, kerosene heaters, gas space heaters and electrical heaters, has decreased, along with the number of residential fires.

Even though there has been a decrease in fires associated with supplemental heaters, it is important to remember that about 120,000 residential fires still occur annually with the use of these heaters, or about 22 percent of all residential fires. These fires kill more than 600 people. Annually there are thousands of contact burn injuries and hundreds of carbon monoxide poisonings.

Wood Stoves

You should be able to respond "yes" to the following safety statements.

1. The wood stove or fireplace has been installed according to existing building codes and manufacturer's instructions.

2. The chimney and stovepipe are checked frequently during the heating season for creosote buildup and are cleaned when necessary.

3. The stove sits on a non-combustible or on a code-specified or listed floor protector.

4. Combustibles such as curtains, chairs, firewood, etc., are at least three feet away from the stove.

5. Only proper fuel is used in the stove.

6. A metal container with a tight-fitting lid is used for ash removal.

Recommendations:

- Do not use wood burning stoves and fireplaces unless they are properly installed and meet building codes.

- Follow the label instructions on the stove which recommends an inspection twice monthly. Have chimneys inspected and cleaned by a professional chimney sweep. Creosote is an unavoidable product of wood burning stoves. Creosote builds up in chimney flues and can cause a chimney fire. To cut down on creosote buildup, avoid smoldering fires.

- Use a code-specified or listed floor protector. It should extend 18 inches beyond the stove on all sides. This will reduce the possibility of the floor being ignited.

- Follow the instructions on the stove label for proper location of the stove from combustible walls.

- Never burn trash in a stove because this could over heat the stove. Gasoline and other flammable liquids should never be used to start wood stove fires. Gasoline will ignite and explode. Use coal only if designated as appropriate by the manufacturer.

Kerosene Heaters

You should be able to respond "yes" to the following safety statements.

1. Only 1-K kerosene is used and it is bought from a dealer who can certify that the product is 1-K kerosene.

2. The heater is placed out of the path of traffic areas such as doorways and hallways.

3. Kerosene is stored outdoors, and out of the reach of children in a tightly sealed, preferably blue plastic or metal container, labeled "kerosene."

4. No attempt is to be made to move the heater if flare-up (flames outside the heater cabinet) occurs. The fire department is called immediately.

5. The heater is used in well-ventilated rooms.

6. The heater is turned off while sleeping and is never left operating unattended.

7. The heater is placed at least three feet away from anything that might catch fire such as clothing, furniture, curtains, etc.

Recommendations:

- Check with your local fire marshal regarding local and state codes and regulations for using a kerosene heater.

- NEVER USE GASOLINE. Even small amounts of gasoline mixed with kerosene can increase the risk of fire.

- Use properly labeled containers. It reduces the likelihood of mistaking gasoline for kerosene.

- Place heater so it will not be knocked over or trap you in case of fire.

- Use 1-K kerosene because grades other than 1-K contain much more sulfur and will increase sulfur dioxide emissions, posing a possible health problem. If you buy kerosene from a gasoline station make sure you and/or the attendant are using the kerosene pump, not the gasoline pump.

- Never fill the heater while it is operating. Always refuel the heater outdoors to prevent spillage on floors and rugs, which could later result in fire ignition.

- Keep the room in which the heater operates ventilated (e.g. door open or the window ajar). This will prevent an indoor air pollution problem and minimize health problems. Kerosene heaters are not usually vented.

- Keep flammable liquids and fabrics away from an open flame.

- Never try to move the heater or try to smother the flames with a rug or a blanket if a flare up occurs. Activate the manual shut-off switch and call the fire department. Moving the heater may increase the height of the flames and cause leakage resulting in personal injury.

Gas-Fired Space Heaters

You should be able to respond "yes" to the following safety statements.

1. Only vented heaters are installed or used in sleeping quarters.

2. Vented heaters are properly vented to the outside.

3. The unvented gas-fired room heater has a warning label and instructions that are followed.

4. The unvented gas-fired room heater has a label stating it has a "pilot safety system" which turns off the gas if not enough fresh air is available.

5. The vented heater has a label stating that it is equipped with a vent safety shutoff system.

6. If the heater uses liquified petroleum (LP) gas, the container is located outside the house.

7. The manufacturer's instructions for lighting the pilot are followed.

8. Matches are lighted before turning on the gas if pilot lighting is required.

9. Flammable materials and liquids are kept away from gas heating appliances.

Recommendations:

- Follow the manufacturer's instructions regarding where and how to use gas space heaters. Unvented heaters should not be used in small enclosed areas, especially bedrooms because of the potential for carbon monoxide poisoning.

- Do not use a propane heater (LP) which has a gas cylinder stored in the body of the heater. Its use is prohibited in most states and localities in the United States.

- Follow the manufacturer's instructions for lighting the pilot. Gas vapors may accumulate and ignite explosively, burning your hand or face.

- Light matches, if needed for lighting, the pilot, before turning on the gas to prevent gas buildup.

- Do not operate a vented style heater unvented. It could allow combustion products, including carbon monoxide, to reach dangerous levels which will result in illness and death.

Portable Electric Heaters

The Commission estimates that half the deaths and one-third of the injuries resulting from electric heater fires occurred at night when family members are asleep and the heater unattended. The Commission is also concerned about the use of power or extension cords, which can be too small to supply the amount of current required by the typical portable electric heater.

You should be able to respond "yes" to the following safety statements.

1. The heater is operated at least three feet away from upholstered furniture, drapes, bedding and other combustible materials.

2. The extension cord (if used) is marked #14 or #12 American Wire Gauge (AWG).

3. The heater is used on the floor.

4. The heater is turned off when family members leave the house or are sleeping.

Recommendations:

• Operate heater away from combustible materials. Do not place heaters where towels or the like could fall on the appliance and trigger a fire.

• Avoid using extension cords unless absolutely necessary. If you must use an extension cord with your electric heater, make sure it is marked with a power rating at least as high as that of the heater itself. Keep the cord stretched out. Do not permit the cord to become buried under carpeting or rugs. Do not place anything on top of the cord.

• Never place heaters on cabinets, tables, furniture or the like. Never use heaters to dry wearing apparel or shoes.

Cooking Equipment

Cooking equipment is estimated to be associated with more than 100,000 fires annually, and almost 400 deaths, and 5,000 injuries. Gas cooking equipment accounts for about 30,000 fires, and electric cooking equipment for about 55,000 fires.

You should be able to respond "yes" to the following safety statements.

1. The storage area above the stove is free of flammable and combustible items.

2. Short or tight fitting sleeves, and tight fitting shirts, robes, gowns, etc., are worn while cooking.

3. Items that could attract children (e.g. cookies and candy) are not kept above the range and are kept out of the immediate area.

4. The stove is not left unattended when cooking especially when the burner is turned to a high setting.

Recommendations:

• Never place or store pot holders, plastic utensils, towels and other non-cooking equipment on or near the range because these items can be ignited.

• Roll up or fasten long loose sleeves with pins or elastic bands while cooking. Do not reach across a range while cooking. Long loose sleeves are more likely to catch on fire than are short sleeves. Long loose sleeves are also more apt to catch on pot handles, overturning pots and pans and cause scalds.

• Do not place candy or cookies over top of ranges. This will reduce the attraction kids may have for climbing on cooking equipment, thus reducing the possibility of their clothing catching fire.

• Keep constant vigilance on any cooking that is required above the "keep warm" setting.

Cigarette Lighters and Matches

Each year more than 200 deaths are associated with fires started by cigarette lighters. About two thirds of these result from children playing with lighters. Most of the victims are under five years old.

You should be able to answer "yes" to the safety statements below.

1. Cigarette lighters and matches are kept out of the reach of children.

2. Cigarette lighters are never used to entertain a child.

Recommendations:

- Keep lighters and matches out of sight and out of the reach of children. Children as young as two years old are capable of lighting cigarette lighters and matches.

- Never encourage or allow a child to play with a lighter or to think of it as a toy. Do not use it as a source of amusement for a child. Once their curiosity is aroused, children may seek out a lighter and try to light it.

- Always check to see that cigarettes are extinguished before emptying ashtrays. Stubs that are still burning can ignite trash.

Materials That Burn

Your home is filled with materials and products that will burn if ignited. Upholstered furniture, clothing, drapery fabrics, and liquids such as gasoline and volatile solvents are involved in many injury—causing fires each year. Most of these fires could be prevented.

Upholstered Furniture

You should be able to respond "yes" to the safety statements below.

1. Upholstered furniture fabrics made from vinyl, wool or thermoplastic fibers are generally selected for safety reasons.

2. I check thoroughly after parties for ashes or unextinguished cigarettes that may have fallen behind and between cushions and under furniture.

Recommendations:

- Look for furniture designed to reduce the likelihood of furniture fire from cigarettes. Much of the furniture manufactured today has significantly greater resistance to ignition by cigarettes than upholstered furniture manufactured 10 to 15 years ago. This is particularly true of furniture manufactured to comply with the requirements of the Upholstered Furniture Action Council's (UFAC) Voluntary Action Program. Such upholstered furniture may be identified by the gold colored tag on the furniture item. The legend on the front of the tag in red letters states: "Important Consumer Safety Information from UFAC."

- Always check the furniture where smokers have been sitting for improperly discarded smoking materials. Ashes and lighted cigarettes can fall unnoticed behind or between cushions or under furniture.

- Do not place or leave ashtrays on the arms of chairs where they can be knocked off.

- Look for fabrics made predominantly from thermoplastic fibers (nylon, polyester, acrylic, olefin) because they resist ignition by burning cigarettes better than cellulosic fabrics (rayon or cotton). In general, the higher the thermoplastic content, the greater the resistance to cigarette ignition.

Mattresses and Bedding

Smoldering fires in mattresses and bedding materials caused by cigarettes are a major cause of deaths in residential fires.

You should be able to respond "yes" to the following safety statements.

1. "No smoking in bed" is a rule that is practiced in my home.

2. Heaters, ash trays, smoking materials and other fire sources are located away from bedding.

Recommendations:

- DO NOT smoke in bed. Smoking in bed is a major cause of accidental fire deaths in homes.

- Locate heaters or other fire sources three feet from the bed to prevent the bed catching on fire.

- Consider replacing your old mattress with a new one if you are a smoker. Mattresses manufactured since 1973 are required to resist cigarette ignition.

Wearing Apparel

Most fibers used in clothing can burn, some more quickly than others. A significant number of clothing fires occur in the over 65 age group principally from nightwear (robes, pajamas, nightgowns). The severity of apparel burns is high. Hospital stays average over one month.

Small open flames, including matches, cigarette lighters, and candles are the major sources of clothing ignition. These are followed by ranges, open fires and space heaters. The most commonly worn garments that are associated with clothing ignition injuries are pajamas, nightgowns, robes, shirts/blouses, pants/slacks and dresses.

You should be able to respond "yes" to the following statements.

1. When purchasing wearing apparel I consider fiber content and fabric construction for safety purposes.

2. I purchase garments for my children that are intended for sleepwear since they are made to be flame resistant.

Recommendations:

*   Consider fabrics such as 100% polyester, nylon, wool and silk that are difficult to ignite and tend to self extinguish.

*   Consider the flammability of certain fabrics containing cotton, cotton/polyester blends, rayon, and acrylic. These are relatively easy to ignite and burn rapidly.

*   Look at fabric construction. It also affects ignitability. Tight weaves or knits and fabrics without a fuzzy or napped surface are less likely to ignite and burn rapidly than open knits or weaves, or fabrics with brushed or piled surfaces.

*   Consider purchasing garments that can be removed without having to pull them over the head. Clothes that are easily removed can help prevent serious burns. If a garment can be quickly stripped off when it catches fire, injury will be far less severe or avoided altogether.

*   Follow manufacturer's care and cleaning instructions on products labeled "flame resistant" to ensure that their flame resistant properties are maintained.

Flammable Liquids

One of the major causes of household fires is flammable liquids. These include gasoline, acetone, benzene, lacquer thinner, alcohol, turpentine, contact cements, paint thinner, kerosene, and charcoal lighter fluid. The most dangerous of all is gasoline.

You should be able to respond "yes" to the following safety statements.

1. Flammable liquids are stored in properly labeled, tightly closed non-glass containers.

2. These products are stored away from heaters, furnaces, water heaters, ranges, and other gas appliances.

3. Flammable liquids are stored out of reach of children.

Recommendation:

• Take extra precautions in storing and using flammable liquids, such as gasoline, paint thinners, etc. They produce invisible explosive vapors that can ignite by a small spark at considerable distances from the flammable substance. Store outside the house.

Early Warning and Escape

Even when you have complied with every item in this Home Fire Safety Checklist, you still need to have a plan for early warning and escape in case a fire does occur.

Many fire deaths and fire injuries are actually caused by smoke and gases. Victims inhale smoke and poisonous gases that rise ahead of the flames. Survival depends on being warned as early as possible and having an escape plan.

You should be able to respond "yes" to the following statements.

Smoke Detectors

1. At least one smoke detector is located on every floor of my home.

2. Smoke detectors are placed near bedrooms, either on the ceiling or 6-12 inches below the ceiling on the wall.

3. Smoke detectors are tested according to manufacturer's instructions on a regular basis (at least once a month) and are kept in working condition at all times.

4. Batteries are replaced according to manufacturer's instructions, at least annually.

5. Batteries are never disconnected.

173

6. The detector has a distinct warning signal that can be heard whether asleep or awake.

Recommendations:

- Purchase a smoke detector if you do not have one. Smoke detectors are inexpensive and are required by law in many localities. Check local codes and regulations before you buy your smoke detector because some codes require specific types of detectors. They provide an early warning which is critical because the longer the delay, the deadlier the consequences.

- Read the instructions that come with the detector for advice on the best place to install it. As a minimum detectors should be located near bedrooms and one on every floor.

- Follow the manufacturer's instructions for proper maintenance. Smoke detectors can save lives, but only if properly installed and maintained.

- Never disconnect a detector. Consider relocating the detector rather than disconnecting it if it is subject to nuisance alarms, e.g. from cooking.

- Replace the battery annually, or when a "chirping" sound is heard.

- Follow the manufacturer's instructions about cleaning your detector. Excessive dust, grease or other material in the detector may cause it to operate abnormally. Vacuum the grill work of your detector.

Escape Plan

Planning ahead, rehearsing, thinking, and acting clearly are keys to surviving a fire. How prepared are you?

You should be able to respond "yes" to the following statements.

1. The family has an escape plan and an alternate escape plan.

2. Escape routes and plans are rehearsed periodically.

3. The escape plan includes choosing a place safely outside the house where the family can meet to be sure everyone got out safely.

4. At least two exits from each part of the house are established.

5. The fire department number is posted on every telephone.

Recommendations:

- Establish advanced family planning for escape. It is an important partner with smoke detectors and it will prepare you for a fire emergency.

- Include small children as a part of the discussion and rehearsal. It is especially important to make sure they understand that they must escape; they can't hide from fire under a bed or in a closet.

Your life and that of your family can be saved by foresight, planning, discussing and rehearsal.

Chapter 17

Safer Cooking

Recipe for Safer Cooking

Follow these tips to protect you and your family when in the kitchen. Whether stirring up a quick dinner or creating a masterpiece four-course meal, here's a recipe for safer cooking you need to use daily.

To Prevent a Cooking Fire in Your Kitchen

- Keep an eye on your cooking and stay in the kitchen. Unattended cooking is the number one cause of cooking fires.

- Wear short or close-fitting sleeves. Loose clothing can catch fire.

- Watch children closely. When old enough, teach children to cook safely.

- Clean cooking surfaces to prevent food and grease build-up.

- Keep curtains, towels and pot holders away from hot surfaces, and store solvents and flammable cleaners away from heat sources. Never keep gasoline in the house.

- Turn pan handles inward to prevent food spills.

"Recipe for Safer Cooking," an undated fact sheet produced by the Consumer Product Safety Commission, available online at http://www.cpsc.gov/cpscpub/pubs/588.html; cited July 2001.

To Put Out a Cooking Fire in Your Kitchen

- Call the fire department immediately. In many cases, dialing 911 will give you Emergency Services.

- Slide a pan lid over flames to smother a grease or oil fire, then turn off the heat and leave the lid in place until the pan cools. Never carry the pan outside.

- Extinguish other food fires with baking soda. Never use water or flour on cooking fires.

- Keep the oven door shut and turn off the heat to smother an oven or broiler fire.

- Keep a fire extinguisher in the kitchen. Make sure you have the right type and training.

- Keep a working smoke detector in your home and test it monthly.

Aluminum Cookware Can Melt and Cause Severe Burns

The U.S. Consumer Product Safety Commission (CPSC) warns that placing aluminum cookware (or stainless cookware with an aluminum core) on high heat may cause it to melt. When aluminum cookware that is empty (or nearly empty) is placed on high heat, it can "boil dry." If a consumer picks up aluminum cookware that has "boiled dry," the molten aluminum can drip onto the consumer's arms, hands, legs, or feet. CPSC knows of several cases in which consumers were burned by dripping molten aluminum. Hot aluminum also can cause a fire.

CPSC urges consumers not to pre-heat aluminum cookware on "high" heat and not to leave aluminum cookware unattended on the stovetop burner. If an aluminum pan "boils dry" and melts, turn off the heat; do not pick up the pan until it cools.

High heat can melt aluminum cookware if it "boils dry." The dripping molten aluminum can cause severe burns.

Chapter 18

Safe Chimneys

Thousands of house fires each year are associated with metal factory-built chimneys connected to wood and coal burning stoves. The CSPC urgently warns consumers to be aware of the potential fire hazard associated with these chimneys.

If you have a stove or fireplace connected to a metal chimney, check for any damage that may have occurred in the past heating season. Look for signs of structural failure, such as deformation, cracks, or holes. If it is difficult to examine the chimney, a local chimney repairman, chimney "sweep", or dealer can help. Have any damage repaired NOW.

Most fires in metal factory-built chimneys occur because of improper installation, use or maintenance. The following are common causes:

- Improper chimney installation causing ignition of nearby wood framing.

- Structural damage to the chimney caused by burning creosote (a black tar-like substance which builds up inside the chimney).

- Chimney corrosion resulting in wood framing being exposed to excessive temperatures.

"Metal Chimneys: Safety Alert," an undated fact sheet produced by the Consumer Product Safety Commission, available online at http://www.cpsc.gov/cpscpub/pubs/5047.html; cited July 2001.

- Buckling and collapsing of the inner liner of the chimney. (This can result from too hot a fire, especially in high-efficiency stoves and in fireplace inserts, or from a creosote fire.)

Many serious fires also occur in masonry chimneys, usually from improper installation or when the tile inner liner and the surrounding brick or block structure crack and separate. Such cracks may be caused by the ignition of creosote. Smoke and heat can then escape and ignite material near the chimney.

Even when the heating appliance is properly installed, people with both metal and masonry chimney systems should frequently check the chimney for creosote deposits, soot build-up or physical damage. This involves only a simple visual examination, but it should be done as often as twice a month during heavy use. If you see heavy creosote build-up, suspect a problem, or have had a chimney fire, a qualified chimney repairman or chimney "sweep" should perform a complete safety inspection. They can arrange for any necessary repairs or creosote removal, which must be done before the heating appliance is used again.

Owners of these chimneys should:

- Be sure that the chimney and stove pipe were installed correctly in accordance with the manufacturers' recommendations and local building codes. If there is any doubt, a building inspector or fireman can determine whether the system is properly installed.

- Have the chimney checked routinely by a chimney "sweep" at least once a year, and more frequently if a stove is heavily used (for example, if it's used as a primary heat source for the home).

- Always operate your appliance within the manufacturers' recommended temperature limits. Too low a temperature increases creosote build-up and too high a temperature may lead to a fire. Chimney temperature monitors are available and should be used.

Chapter 19

Electric and Kerosene Space Heaters

What You Should Know about Space Heaters Used for Supplemental Room Heating

The purpose of this chapter is to provide safety information that should assist in the purchase operation, fueling, and maintenance of space heaters. A space heater is a self contained free standing air heating appliance intended for installation in the space being heated and not intended for duct connection. This document is not intended to be all inclusive, but it is intended to inform the reader about some of the safety aspects associated with using space heaters for supplemental room heating.

The U.S. Consumer Product Safety Commission estimates that more than 100 000 residential fires every year are associated with the use of room (space) heaters. Upwards of 600 persons die in these fires. In addition more than 100 persons are killed annually by non-fire related carbon monoxide poisoning from space heater operation. An estimated 20,000 persons receive hospital emergency room care for burn injuries associated with contacting hot surfaces of room heaters mostly in non-fire situations.

Text in this chapter was excerpted from the following undated fact sheets from the Consumer Product Safety Commission, "What You Should Know about Space Heaters," available online at http://www.cpsc/gov/cpscpub/pubs/463.html, "Electric Space Heaters," available online at http://www.cpsc/gov/cpscpub/pubs/098.html, "CPSC and KHA Stress Kerosene Heater Safety," available online at http://www.cpsc/gov/cpscpub/pubs/5052.html; cited July 2001.

Hazards

Consumers should be aware of the following hazards when buying and using gas, wood, kerosene. and electric space heaters.

1. Fires and burns caused by contact with or close proximity to the flame, heating element or hot surface area.

2. Fires and explosions caused by flammable fuels or defective wiring.

3. Indoor air pollution caused by improper venting or incomplete combustion.

4. Carbon monoxide poisoning caused by improper venting of fuel-burning equipment.

General Suggestions for All Space Heaters

CPSC offers the following general suggestions for selection safe use and maintenance of gas, wood, kerosene, and electric space heaters:

- Buy a space heater with a guard around the flame area or the heating coil. This will help keep children, pets, and clothing away from the heat source.

- When selecting a heater look for one that has been tested and labeled by a nationally-recognized testing laboratory. These heaters have been determined to meet specific safety standards and manufacturers are required to provide important use and care information to the consumer. You have less assurance that the safety features and operating instructions are adequate for a heater that has not been evaluated in such a manner.

- Read and follow the manufacturer s operating instructions. A good practice is to mad aloud the instructions and warning labels to all members of the household to be certain that everyone understands how the heater is to be operated safely. Keep the owner's manual in a convenient place to refer to when needed.

- Keep children and pets away from space heaters. Some heaters have very hot surfaces. Some heaters could operate dangerously if children are permitted to either adjust the controls or tip or jar the heater.

- Keep doors open to the rest of the house if you are using an unvented fuel-burning space heater. This helps to prevent pollutant build-up and promotes proper combustion Even vented heaters require ventilation for proper combustion.

- Never use a space heater overnight in the room where you are sleeping. Dangerous levels of carbon monoxide could accumulate from fuel-fired heaters, or uncontrolled burning could cause a fire.

- Never use or store flammable liquids (such as, gasoline) around a space heater. The flammable vapors can flow from one part of the room to another and be ignited by the open flame or by the electrical circuit of an electric heater.

- Be aware that mobile homes require specially designed heating equipment. Only electric or vented fuel-fired heaters should be used and a vented gas heater should be of the sealed combustion type (air for burning comes directly from the outside).

- Place heaters at least three feet away from objects such as bedding, furniture and drapes. Never use heaters to dry clothes or shoes. Do not place heaters where towels or other objects could fall on the heater and start a fire.

Specific Suggestions

Different types of space heaters present some different safety problems. You should be aware of important information and advice about these specific types of heaters.

- Have gas and kerosene space heaters inspected annually by qualified persons to ensure that they are property adjusted and clean. Keep the wick of the kerosene heater clean and property adjusted.

- Be certain that your heater is placed on a level surface.

- Keep the heater in a safe working condition. Replace missing guards and controls at once Never operate a defective heater. Have all necessary repairs done by qualified repair persons.

Kerosene Space Heaters

If you are using a kerosene heater, the U.S. Consumer Product Safety Commission and the National Kerosene Heater Association advise you to follow these suggestions in order to minimize the risk of fire and potential health effects from indoor air pollution.

- Use only water-clear 1 K grade kerosene. Never use gasoline. Gasoline is not the same as kerosene. Even small amounts of gasoline or other volatile fuels or solvents mixed with kerosene can substantially increase the risk of a fire or an explosion.

- Always store kerosene in a separate container intended for kerosene, not in a gasoline can or a can that has contained gasoline. This helps you avoid using contaminated fuel or the wrong fuel by mistake. Kerosene containers are usually blue; gasoline containers are usually red.

- When purchasing kerosene at the pump, make sure to use the kerosene pump, not the gasoline pump. Some service stations have separate islands for kerosene. Some oil companies have also established quality control programs to minimize the chances of gasoline contamination of kerosene.

- 1-K grade kerosene should be purchased from a dealer who can certify that what is being sold is 1-K. State operated and private sector certification programs that ensure the quality of kerosene are established in some states. Grades other than 1-K can lead to a release of more pollutants in your home, posing a possible health risk. Different grades of kerosene can look the same so it is important that the dealer certify that the product sold is 1-K grade kerosene.

- Never refuel the heater inside the home. Fill the tank outdoors, away from combustible materials, and only after the heater has been turned off and allowed to cool down. Do not refuel the heater when it is hot or is in operation. Do not fill the fuel tank above the "full" mark. The space above the "full" mark is to allow the fuel room to expand without causing leakage when the heater is operating.

- In case of flare-up or if uncontrolled flaming occurs, do not attempt to move or carry the heater. This can make the fire worse. If the heater is equipped with a manual shut-off switch, activate the switch to turn off the heater. If this does not extinguish the fire, leave the house immediately and call the fire department. As an added reminder and precaution, install at least one smoke detector near each sleeping area or on each level of the house.

- Reduce your exposure to indoor air pollutants by properly operating and maintaining your portable kerosene heater. Although portable kerosene heaters are very efficient in the burning of fuel to produce heat, low levels of certain pollutants such as carbon monoxide and nitrogen dioxide are produced. Exposure to low levels of these pollutants may be harmful, especially to individuals with chronic respiratory or circulatory health problems. To assure that you and family members are not exposed to significant levels of these pollutants, you should follow carefully the following rules of safe operation:

> Operate your heater in a room with a door open to the rest of the house.

> If you must operate your heater in a room with the door closed to the rest of the house, open an outside window approximately an inch to permit fresh air to effectively dilute the pollutants below a level of concern.

> Always operate your heater according to the manufacturer's instructions, making sure that the wick is set at the proper level as instructed by your manufacturer.

> Keep the wick in your heater clean and in good operating condition by following the cleaning and maintenance procedures recommended by the manufacturer.

> Keep an outside window opened approximately an inch to insure adequate fresh air infiltration. This is true regardless of whether you use a kerosene heater or some other conventional method of heating, if your home is relatively new and tight, or if it is older but has been winterized to reduce air infiltration from the outside.

CAUTION: Improper fuel may cause pollution and sooting of the burner. Use only water clear No. 1-K Kerosene.

DANGER: Risk of explosion. Never use gasoline in this heater.

CAUTION: Risk of indoor air pollution. Use this heater only in a well ventilated area. See operating instructions for details.

Portable Electric Space Heaters

The Statistics

The U.S. Consumer Product Safety Commission (CPSC) estimates that in 1994, electric space heaters were associated with 2,400 fires resulting 80 deaths, 240 injuries and $48.2 million in property loss.

The Problem

Even though electric space heaters don't have an open flame, the heating elements of some types of electric heaters are hot enough to ignite nearby combustibles like draperies, paper, clothing, furniture, and flammable liquids. It is, therefore, important to check surrounding objects periodically to see if they feel hot. Refer to the manufacturer's instructions to see how far the heater should be placed from combustible materials, and for how far the heater should be placed from the floor so that carpeting or flooring materials don't ignite.

Additionally, to prevent electrocutions, always keep portable electric heaters away from water, never use them in a bathroom or near a sink. (If you must use an appliance near water, always use a ground fault circuit interrupter).

Safety Tips

CPSC recommends the following when selecting an electric heater:

- Look for one that is listed with a nationally-recognized testing laboratory. These heaters have been tested to meet specific safety standards, and manufacturers are required to provide important use and care information to the consumer. On heaters that are not listed, consumers have less assurance that the safety features and operating instructions are adequate.

- Purchase a heater with a guard around the heating element. A wire grill or other protection is essential to keep fingers or fabrics from touching the hot element. Portable electric heaters that heat by circulating oil or water, however, usually have lower surface temperatures and may not need guards.

- Before using the heater, read and follow the instructions for its operation and maintenance.

- If you must use an extension cord, make sure it is a heavy duty cord marked with a #14 gauge or larger wire An incorrectly-sized cord may create a fire hazard. If the heater's plug has a grounding prong, use only a grounding (three-wire) extension cord.

- Never run the heater's cord (or any cord) under rugs or carpeting.

- Do not leave the heater operating unattended or operating while sleeping. Portable electric air heaters are designed for use only as temporary supplemental heating and only while attended.

- To prevent electrical shocks and electrocutions, always keep portable electric heaters away from water and never touch an electric heater if you are wet.

Safety Tips

- Do not use an electric heater as a dryer by placing clothing over it and never use it heater to thaw pipes.

- Keep the heater in safe working condition Replace missing guards and controls at once. Never operate a defective heater.

- Don't place the heater where children might play near it or where people might trip over or bump into it.

- Place the heater on a level surface for stability.

- Regardless of the type of heating system you have, install and maintain at least one smoke detector that is in good working condition on each floor of your home.

Wood Burning Heaters

- Existing building codes and manufacturer's instructions must be followed scrupulously during installation.

- Check chimney and stove pipes frequently during the heating season for creosote build-up and clean when necessary.

- Stoves must be placed on an approved floor protector or fire resistant floor.

- Do not burn trash or anything other than the proper fuel.

- Use a metal container for ash removal.

Gas Space Heaters

- All new unvented gas-fired space heaters should be equipped with an oxygen depletion sensor (ODS). An ODS detects a reduced level of oxygen in the area where the heater is operating and shuts off the heater before a hazardous level of carbon monoxide accumulates. These heaters also have labels that warn users about the hazards of carbon monoxide.

- Always have your gas heater and venting system professionally installed and inspected according to local codes.

- Vented gas-fired heaters can also cause carbon monoxide poisoning if they are not vented properly.

If your space heater is meant to be vented, be sure that the heater and flue are professionally installed according to local codes. Vent systems require regular maintenance and inspections. Many carbon monoxide poisoning deaths occur every year because this is not done. A voluntary standard requirement provides that a thermal shut-off device be installed on vented heaters manufactured after June 1, 1984. This device will interrupt heater operation if the appliance is not venting properly.

Be aware that older gas fired space heaters may not have the safety devices required by current voluntary standards such as an ODS or safety pilot valves that will turn off the gas to the heater if the pilot light should go out. If the pilot light or your heater should go out use the following safety tips:

- Light the match before you turn on the gas to the pilot. This avoids the risk of a flashback which could occur if you allow gas to accumulate before you are ready to light the pilot.

- IF YOU SMELL GAS, DO NOT ATTEMPT TO LIGHT THE APPLIANCE. Turn off all controls and open a window or door and leave the area. Then call a gas service person. Do not touch any electrical switches.

- Remember that LP-gas (propane), unlike natural gas supplied from the gas utility distribution pipes is heavier than air. If you believe a leak has occurred, go to a neighbor' phone to call your gas distributor or fire department. Do not operate any electrical switches or telephones in the building where the leak has occurred because a spark could cause an explosion.

Indoor Air Pollution from Space Heaters

The major pollutants from unvented kerosene and gas space heaters, woodstoves and fireplaces are carbon monoxide, nitrogen dioxide, and respirable particulates. Woodstoves, fireplace, and unvented kerosene heaters may also emit cancer-causing gases.

Other causes of combustion gases and particulates are chimneys and flues that are improperly installed or maintained. Down drafts in chimneys can bring pollutants back into the living space of homes.

Health Effects of Combustion Products

Carbon monoxide is a colorless odorless gas that interferes with the delivery of oxygen throughout the body. Carbon monoxide can cause headaches nausea dizziness weakness and confusion symptoms sometimes are contused with the flu. At high concentrations carbon monoxide can cause unconsciousness and death. Fetuses infants and people with anemia or with a history of heart disease may be especially sensitive to carbon monoxide exposures.

Nitrogen dioxide can irritate the skin and the mucous membranes in the eye nose, and throat. Depending upon the level and duration of exposure respiratory effects range from slight irritation to burning and pain in the chest and coughing and shortness of breath. In addition nitrogen dioxide may increase susceptibility to disease such as bronchitis. Children who are exposed to higher levels of nitrogen dioxide often show increased susceptibility to respiratory infections. Others who may be especially sensitive to nitrogen dioxide exposure include people with chronic respiratory disease including bronchitis, asthma, and emphysema.

Reducing Exposure to Combustion Products in Homes

Take special precautions when operating unvented space heater. Consider potential effects of indoor air pollution when deciding to use unvented kerosene or gas space heaters. Follow the manufacturer's directions especially about using the proper fuel and about providing fresh air while the heater is in use. This can be accomplished by keeping doors open to the rest of the house from the room where the heater is being used. In addition keep the heater properly adjusted.

Choose a space heater properly-sized for the room you wish to heat and make sure that it is installed correctly.

Keep flues and chimneys in good condition. Leaking chimneys and damaged flues can result in the release of harmful or even fatal concentrations of combustion gases, especially carbon monoxide.

General Home-Safety Information

Regardless of the method you use to heat your home, the Commission encourages you to:

- Equip your home with a least one smoke detector on each floor.

- Keep at least one dry-powder operative ABC-type fire extinguisher in the home at all times.

- Keep areas around heat sources free of papers and trash.

- Store paints, solvents, and flammable liquids away from all heat and ignition sources.

- Develop a fire-escape plan before a fire occurs. Be certain that all members of the household understand the plan and are able to carry out the plan in case of emergency.

- Be sure the plan includes a predetermined meeting place outside the house.

- If your clothing does catch fire don't run! Drop down immediately and roll to smother the flames. Teach your family how to do this.

Chapter 20

Gas Grill Safety

Introduction

Each year, thousands of people pull out their LP gas grills at the start of "barbecuing season." But before firing up the grill, there are several safety precautions to keep in mind. By following these guidelines, you'll help prevent possible gas explosions or fires.

LP gas is flammable. Many accidents occur after the grill has been unused over a period of time, or after a grill's gas container has been refilled and reattached.

Safety Checks Each Time You Use the Grill

- Check venturi tube for blockage by insects, spiders, or food drippings. Clear blockage, either with a pipe cleaner or with a wire. Push any blockages through the tube to the main part of the burner.

- Check grill's hoses for cracking, brittleness, holes, and leaks. Make sure there aren't sharp bends in the hose or tubing.

- Make sure hoses are as far away from the hot surface as possible. Make sure to keep hoses away from areas where grease could drip on them. If you can't move hoses, have a heat shield installed.

"Gas Grills Fact Sheet," an undated fact sheet produced by the Consumer Product Safety Commission, available online at http://www.cpsc.gov/cpscpub/ pubs/467.html; cited July 2001.

- Check connectors. If scratched or nicked, have them replaced; these conditions can cause leaks.

- Check for gas leaks whenever you reconnect the grill to the LP-gas container, or if you smell gas. To check for leaks, open the gas supply valve fully and apply a soapy solution (one part water, one part liquid detergent) with a brush at connection points. If bubbles appear, there is a leak. Turn off the gas and tighten the connection clockwise. (If it is the tank connection, tighten counterclockwise.) If this does not stop the leak, close the container valve and take the grill to your LP gas dealer or a qualified appliance repairperson.

- If a leak is detected, don't attempt to light the grill until the leak has been stopped. If you are using the grill, turn off the gas.

- Make sure there are no lighted cigarettes, matches, or open flames near a leaking grill.

- NEVER USE A GRILL INDOORS. And use the grill at least ten feet away from your house or any building. DO NOT USE THE GRILL in a garage, breezeway, carport, porch, or under a surface that will burn.

- Do not attempt to repair the container valve or appliance yourself. See your LP gas dealer or a qualified appliance repairperson.

- Always follow the instructions that accompany the grill.

LP Gas Container Tips

When Storing:

- Always keep containers upright.

- Never store a spare gas container under or near the grill.

- Never store or use flammable liquids, like gasoline, near the grill.

- Never use or store a gas container indoors.

When Transporting:

- Transport the container in a secure, upright position.

- Never keep a filled container in a hot car or car trunk.

- Heat will cause the gas pressure to increase which may open the relief valve and allow gas to escape.

When Refilling:

- Unless you have (the preferred) bar-coded container and are filling it at a facility that fills such containers, have the container refilled only by your LP gas dealer or by a qualified service station operator. DO NOT FILL THE CONTAINER YOURSELF.

When Connecting:

- Remove the container valve plug from the container valve.

- Thread the container connector securely into the container valve outlet (turn counter clock-wise).

- Tighten, but do not use excessive force.

- After connected, check for leaks.

When Disconnecting:

- Before disconnecting, turn off the gas burner and container valve.

- Disconnect the container (turn clockwise).

- Place the container valve plug securely into the container valve outlet.

Tips for Purchasing a Grill or Gas Container

- Buy a unit with a "quick connect" device at the container valve outlet.

- Buy a unit with an automatic thermal shut-off device.

- Buy a unit with a high pressure system shut-off regulator.

- Buy containers that bear the mark of a nationally-recognized testing laboratory.

Chapter 21

Portable Generator Safety Tips

Portable generators can be hazardous if used improperly. The hazards are: (1) carbon monoxide (CO) poisoning from the toxic engine exhaust and (2) electrocution from connecting the generator to the home electrical wiring system.

To avoid carbon monoxide (CO) poisoning:

- Never use a generator indoors or in attached garages.
- Only operate the generator outdoors in a well-ventilated, dry area, away from air intakes to the home, and protected from direct exposure to rain and snow, preferably under a canopy, open shed, or carport.

To avoid electrocution:

- Plug individual appliances into the generator using heavy duty, outdoor rated cords with a wire gauge adequate for the appliance load.
- Observe the generator manufacturer's instructions for safe operation.
- Do not plug the generator into a wall outlet.
- If connecting the generator into the house wiring is necessary, have a qualified electrician hook up the standby electrical system, or have the local utility install a linking device if available.

"Portable Generators: How to use them safely!" an undated fact sheet produced by the Consumer Product Safety Commission, available online at http://www.cpsc.gov/cpscpub/pubs/portgen.html; cited July 2001.

Never store gasoline in the home. Gasoline, kerosene and other flammable liquids should be stored outside of living areas in properly labeled, non-glass safety containers. They should also not be stored in a garage if a fuel-burning appliance is in the garage. The vapor from gasoline can travel invisibly along the ground and be ignited by pilot lights or arcs caused by activating electric switches.

If at all possible, avoid connecting the electrical output of the generator into the house wiring. Instead, connect individual appliances that have their own outdoor rated power cord directly to the receptacle outlet of the generator, or connect these cord-connected appliances to the generator's electrical outlet via a suitable, outdoor-rated extension cord having a sufficient wire gauge to handle the electrical load.

If connecting into the house wiring is necessary on a temporary basis to operate permanently wired equipment, such as a water pump, furnace blower/controls, room lighting, etc., there are important steps that require the utmost care to avoid electrocution. In some locations, the local utility company may offer to install a device at the electric meter socket to permit their customers to connect a portable generator to the household wiring during periods of power outages. If that service is not available or chosen, another method is to have a qualified electrician install a manual transfer switch.

A transfer switch permits transfer of the load from the household power source that is normally supplied by the electric utility over to the portable generator. The transfer switch should be certified by UL or other independent test lab for this application, and be mounted within an electrical box. Transfer switches and related accessories designed for connecting a standby system are available from electrical supply stores. These accessories equipment include:

1. cord sets with special locking and recessed connectors,
2. electrical boxes with controls for the branch circuits that will receive temporary power from the generator, and
3. feeder cable to connect the existing electrical panel to the transfer switch.

When properly installed, the transfer switch will isolate the circuits supplied by the generator from those normally supplied by the utility. This prevents inadvertently energizing circuits in both systems, and reduces the possibility of electrocution resulting from contact with conductors presumed to be de-energized.

Do not operate more appliances and equipment than the output rating of the generator.

Chapter 22

Tap Water Scalds

Each year, approximately 3,800 injuries and 34 deaths occur in the home due to scalding from excessively hot tap water. The majority of these accidents involve the elderly and children under the age of five. All users should lower their water heaters to 120 degrees Fahrenheit. In addition to preventing accidents, this decrease in temperature will conserve energy and save money.

Most adults will suffer third-degree burns if exposed to 150 degree water for two seconds. Burns will also occur with a six-second exposure to 140 degree water or with a thirty second exposure to 130 degree water. Even if the temperature is 120 degrees, a five minute exposure could result in third-degree burns.

Various procedures for lowering water temperature in the home exist, depending on the method of heating. Here are some suggestions:

Electric water heaters. Call your local electric company to adjust the thermostat. Some companies offer this service at no-charge. Hot water should not be used for at least two hours prior to setting. To make the adjustment yourself, start by shutting off current to the water heater, then turn off the circuit breaker to the heater or remove the fuse that serves the heater. Most electric water heaters have two thermostats, both of which must be set to a common temperature for proper operation. To

"Tap Water Scalds," an undated fact sheet produced by the Consumer Product Safety Commission, available online at http://www.cpsc.gov/cpscpub/pubs/5098.html; cited July 2001.

reach these thermostats you must remove the upper and lower access panels. Adjust the thermostat following the instructions provided with the appliance. Hold a candy or meat thermometer under the faucet to check water temperature.

Gas water heaters. Because thermostats differ, call your local gas company for instructions. Where precise temperatures are not given, hold a candy or meat thermometer under faucet for most accurate reading first thing in the morning or at least two hours after water use. If reading is too high, adjust thermostat on heater, according to manufacturers instructions, and check again with thermometer.

Furnace heater. If you do not have an electric, gas, or oil-fired water heater, you probably have an on-line hot water system. Contact your fuel supplier to have the temperature lowered. If you live in an apartment, contact the building manager to discuss possible options for lowering your tap water temperature. Reducing water temperature will not affect the heating capacity of the furnace.

A thermostat setting of 120 degrees Fahrenheit (49 degrees Celsius) may be necessary for residential water heaters to reduce or eliminate the risk of most tap water scald injuries. Consumers should consider lowering the thermostat to the lowest settings that will satisfy hot water needs for all clothing and dish washing machines.

Never take hot water temperature for granted. Always hand-test before using, especially when bathing children and infants. Leaving a child unsupervised in the bathroom, even if only for a second, could cause serious injuries. Your presence at all times is the best defense against accidents and scaldings to infants and young children.

Chapter 23

Clothes Dryers, Water Heaters, and Other Causes of House Fires

Overheated Clothes Dryers Can Cause Fires

The U.S. Consumer Product Safety Commission estimates that there are an estimated annual 15,500 fires, 10 deaths, and 310 injuries associated with clothes dryers. Some of these fires may occur when lint builds up in the filter or in the exhaust duct. Under certain conditions, when lint blocks the flow of air, excessive heat build-up may cause a fire in some dryers. To prevent fires:

- Clean the lint filter regularly and make sure the dryer is operating properly. Clean the filter after each load of clothes. While the dryer is operating, check the outside exhaust to make sure exhaust air is escaping normally, If it is not, look inside both ends of the duct and remove any lint. If there are signs that the dryer is hotter than normal, this may be a sign that the dryer's temperature control thermostat needs servicing.

Text in this chapter is excerpted from the following undated fact sheets produced by the Consumer Product Safety Commission, "Overheated Clothes Dryers Can Cause Fires," available at http://www.cpsc.gov/cpscpub/pubs/dryer.html, "CPSC and Gas-Fired Water Heaters," available at http://www.cpsc.gov/cpscpub/pubs/3007.html, "Child-Resistant Lighters Protect Young Children," available at http://www.cpsc.gov/cpscpub/pubs/5021.html, "Fire Hazard with Nightlights," available at http://www.cpsc.gov/cpscpub/pubs/5063.html, "Use Potpourri Pots Safely," available at http://www.cpsc.gov/cpscpub/pubs/5068.html; cited July 2001.

- Check the exhaust duct more often if you have a plastic, flexible duct. This type of duct is more apt to trap lint than ducting without ridges.

- Closely follow manufacturers' instructions for new installations. Most manufacturers that get their clothes dryers approved by Underwriters Laboratories specify the use of metal exhaust duct. If metal duct is not available at the retailer where the dryer was purchased, check other locations, such as hardware or builder supply stores. If you are having the dryer installed, insist upon metal duct unless the installer has verified that the manufacturer permits the use of plastic duct.

Gas-Fired Water Heaters

The Consumer Product Safety Commission has been working to reduce the risk of injuries and deaths from gas-fired water heaters.

The Commission was briefed on the issue by CPSC staff in June of 1994. The Commission let the industry know that it wanted to see a solution to this problem, and that it was considering development of a Federal regulation that would address the problem of flammable vapor ignition in gas-fired heaters.

Prior to 1994, the Commission staff had been seeking a permanent, technical solution to the hazard of flammable vapors. Commission staff believed that this problem required not only the education of consumers about the proper use and storage of flammable liquids, but also a redesign of water heaters.

Following the June 1994 Commission meeting, industry officials informed the Commission that they were working on a technical solution—a redesign of water heaters—that would eliminate the ignition of flammable vapors by water heaters. Industry also expressed a willingness to work closely in voluntary cooperation with CPSC on the issue.

Giving industry the opportunity to voluntarily develop the technology necessary to achieve a permanent solution has several advantages over regulation. The voluntary approach results in manufacturers investing their own resources in developing test methodologies—saving taxpayer dollars and making use of industry's knowledge and technical expertise about the product they manufacture.

In December, 1994, following the water heater manufacturers' offer to work with CPSC to eliminate the hazard, the Commission agreed to postpone the regulatory process. But, CPSC Chairman Ann

Brown expressly stated that industry must make real progress toward a technical solution and on developing a performance standard by which the safety of any new design could be measured.

As part of the CPSC's participation with industry in the efforts to reach a technical solution to this problem, CPSC staff has been closely monitoring the development of vapor-ignition resistant water heaters by the Water Heater Joint Research and Development Consortium. Three prototypes have already been tested and performed well in flammability tests.

The industry is funding the independent development of that performance test standard. The Gas Research Institute is developing a way to test gas-fired water heaters to ensure that they will not ignite flammable vapors. A technical advisory group consisting of representatives from the gas industry, manufacturers, industry trade associations and CPSC staff, oversees this project.

The Commission has also worked with industry to educate the public on the hazard of flammable vapors. The Commission endorsed a large public information campaign launched by the Gas Appliance Manufacturers Association in 1994 which included television commercials and materials designed to appeal to and inform children about the hazard. In addition, the Commission published its own information on the hazard in its home and fire safety brochures.

To reduce the hazard of flammable vapors, consumers should:

- Make sure gas-fired water heaters are installed according to code requirements;

- Where possible, elevate heaters 18 inches from the floor, whether installed in a basement or garage;

- Never use gasoline to clean equipment or tools;

- Use gasoline only as a motor fuel;

- Store gasoline only in tightly sealed red containers intended for gasoline; and

- Keep all flammable materials and liquids away from gas-fired water heaters.

Child-Resistant Lighters Protect Young Children

Children under 5 years old playing with lighters cause more than 5,000 residential fires a year, resulting in approximately 150 deaths and more than 1,000 injuries according to the U.S. Consumer Product

Safety Commission (CPSC). Approximately 30 million households own one or more working lighters. Lighters are frequently used for purposes other than lighting smoking materials and they are often left within a child's reach.

Although children as young as 2 years old are capable of operating lighters, the majority of the children who start fires by playing with lighters are ages 3 and 4. At these ages, children are curious about fire but don't understand the danger. Typically, when children start a fire, they will leave the room without telling anyone about the fire.

CPSC set a mandatory safety standard that requires disposable lighters and certain novelty lighters to be child-resistant. The standard covers more than 95 percent of the 600 million lighters purchased in the United States each year.

The standard became effective in summer 1994. Parents and caregivers are urged to:

- Purchase child-resistant lighters. Remember, these lighters are child resistant, not childproof.

- Keep lighters and matches out of the reach of children.

- Never use a lighter as a source of amusement for children. That may encourage children to think of lighters as a toy and try to light one on their own.

Fire Hazard with Nightlights

The U.S. Consumer Product Safety Commission (CPSC) warns that fires can start when flammable materials touch a nightlight. In an average year, CPSC receives about 10 reported incidents where nightlights were cited as being responsible for fires where flammable materials, such as bed spreads, pillows, and toilet paper were ignited. It appears that these nightlights were so close to a bed that falling pillows or blankets were able to touch the hot bulb of the nightlight and start a fire.

To reduce the chance of fire:

- Locate nightlights away from beds where the bulb might touch flammable materials.

- Look for nightlights that bear the mark of recognized testing laboratory.

- Consider using nightlights that have cooler, mini neon bulbs instead of four or seven watt bulbs.

Use Potpourri Pots Safely

During the past year the Consumer Product Safety Commission has received reports of approximately 130 incidents of flare-up of potpourri units. Usually the small candle, used to simmer the potpourri, has ignited accumulated soot, wax or candle debris. This caused flames to flare-up around the sides of the simmering potpourri unit. Also, the use of small candles contained in metal cups with the potpourri units can generate excess heat causing the unit to flare-up or ignite.

Potpourri units come in various designs. Two common characteristics are: (1) a base, in which a small warmer candle is placed and lit and, (2) a bowl or ladle, supported by the base, in which water and potpourri are placed and simmered to give off a pleasant scent.

Simmering potpourri units are sold nationwide. Holidays appear to generate the majority of sales. Consumers should be very cautious when using the simmering potpourri units and adhere to the following guidelines and instructions, which apply to all designs.

- Place unit in a clear and open area free from drafts or flammable materials.

- Never leave a burning potpourri unit (or any burning candle) unattended.

- If the unit should flare-up, smother the flames with a wet cloth.

- Do not throw water on the flame.

Chapter 24

Fire Hazards of Some Upholstered Furniture

Considering the purchase of upholstered furniture? Color, style, and fabric type are undoubtedly part of your considerations. Add one more factor safety. This can be taken into account without sacrificing other important requirements.

In 1983, an estimated 860 people lost their lives, approximately 2,900 people were injured, and ill million dollars in property loss resulted from fires started by a cigarette igniting upholstered furniture. Cigarette-ignited upholstered furniture fires kill more people every year than any other kind of fire. In a typical scenario, a burning cigarette is accidentally dropped on a furniture item—the family retires for the night—the burning cigarette ignites the fabric and the filling material underneath causing a fire that may not be discovered until too late.

Much of the furniture manufactured today has significantly greater resistance to ignition by cigarettes than upholstered furniture manufactured 10 to 15 years ago. This is particularly true of furniture manufactured to comply with the requirements of the Upholstered Furniture Action Council's (UFAC) Voluntary Action Program. Such upholstered furniture may be identified by the gold colored tag on the furniture item. The legend on the front of the tag in red letters states: "Important Consumer Safety Information from UFAC."

"Upholstered Furniture," an undated fact sheet produced by the Consumer Product Safety Commission, available online at http://www.cpsc.gov/cpscpub/pubs/5103.html; cited July 2001.

While today's furniture generally is more resistant to cigarette ignition, there are differences in ignition resistance. You can further improve your safety by careful selection of your new furniture:

- Fabrics made from vinyl, wool or thermoplastic fibers (nylon, polyester, olefin, acrylic) resist ignition by burning cigarettes better than fabrics made from other fiber types (cotton, rayon). In general, the higher the thermoplastic content, the greater the resistance to cigarette ignition. Studies indicate that as little as 35 percent thermoplastic fiber in a fabric can provide improved resistance to cigarette ignition.

- The resistance of fabrics made from cotton, rayon or linen to smouldering cigarettes depends on the weight of the fabric. The heavier the weight of the fabric, the more likely the fabric will burn.

- Upholstered furniture seat cushions are frequently made with box welts (raised edging around the upper and lower edges of the cushion). A special cord used in the box welt required by the UFAC Voluntary Action Program further improves cigarette ignition resistance. Furniture seat cushions made without UFAC box welts are less resistant to cigarette ignition.

Therefore, furniture made from thermoplastic fibers with seat cushions having UFAC special welt cord in the box welt provides increased protection against cigarette ignition.

In addition to upholstered furniture, your home contains many other items which will ignite and burn. As a back-up to the use of fire resistant materials, install smoke detectors on each level of your home and ensure that they are maintained in operating condition. These will provide an early warning if a fire does occur.

Chapter 25

Young Children and Teens Burned by Hair Curling Irons

In an average year children under 5 years of age suffer approximately 7,700 burn injuries which require hospital emergency room treatment when they touched hot curling irons. According to the U.S. Consumer Product Safety Commission (CPSC), burns to young children represented about 50 percent of all injuries with hair curling irons during these years. Teenagers and adults should never leave a hot curling iron where a young child can reach it.

Another hazard with hair curling irons is eye injury to the user. The CPSC estimates that there were 5,400 emergency room treated burns to the eye per year when users accidentally touched their eyes with the hot iron. Most victims were young women between 15 and 24 years old.

During the past few years, curling irons have been made to get hotter. These hotter curling irons may cause more severe injuries when young children touch them and when users inadvertently touch their eyes and face with the curling irons.

"Young Children and Teens Burned by Hair Curling Irons," an undated fact sheet produced by the Consumer Product Safety Commission; cited July 2001.

Chapter 26

Household Batteries Can Cause Chemical Burns

The U.S. Consumer Product Safety Commission (CPSC) estimates that approximately 3,700 people a year are treated in hospital emergency rooms for battery-related chemical burns. Approximately 20 percent of people treated in hospital emergency rooms for battery-related chemical burns are children under the age of 16.

Household batteries can overheat and rupture in several ways.

Re-Charging the Wrong Battery or Using the Wrong Charger

If you try to re-charge a battery not intended to be re-charged, the battery can overheat and rupture. If you have a rechargeable battery, be sure to use the proper battery charger intended for the size and type of battery you have. Do not use an automobile battery charger to recharge flashlight batteries because the batteries could rupture.

Mixing Batteries

If you use alkaline and carbon-zinc batteries together in the same appliance or if you mix old batteries with new freshly-charged ones in the same appliance, the batteries can overheat and rupture. Always

---

" Household Batteries Can Cause Chemical Burns," an undated fact sheet produced by the Consumer Product Safety Commission, available online at http://www.cpsc.gov/cpscpub/pubs/5088.html; cited July 2001.

use a complete set of new batteries of the same type when replacing batteries.

Putting Batteries in Backwards

If a battery is reversed (positive end where the negative end belongs and vice versa), it can overheat and rupture. This has happened when young children install batteries backwards. Warn children not to take out batteries or install them. Parents should install batteries in household appliances and children's toys.

Chapter 27

Ground Fault Circuit Interrupters (GFCIs)

The GFCI

A "GFCI" is a ground fault circuit interrupter. A ground fault circuit interrupter is an inexpensive electrical device that, if installed in household branch circuits, could prevent over two-thirds of the approximately 300 electrocutions still occurring each year in and around the home. Installation of the device could also prevent thousands of burn and electric shock injuries each year.

The GFCI is designed to protect people from severe or fatal electric shocks Because a GFCI detects ground faults, it can also prevent some electrical fires and reduce the severity of others by interrupting the flow of electric current.

The Problem

Have you ever experienced an electric shock? If you did, the shock probably happened because your hand or some other part of your body

Text in this chapter is from the following undated fact sheets produced by the Consumer Product Safety Commission, "GFCIs Fact Sheet," available at http://www.cpsc.gov/cpscpub/pubs/99.html, "Preventing Home Fires: Arc Fault Circuit Interrupters (AFCIs)," available at http://www.cpsc.gov/cpscpub/pubs/afci.html, "Use a Ground-Fault Circuit-Interrupter with Every Power Tool," available at http://www.cpsc.gov/cpscpub/pubs/5040.html, "Install Ground-Fault Circuit-Interrupter Protection for Pools, Spas and Hot Tubs," available at http://www.cpsc.gov/cpscpub/pubs/5039.html, and "Newer Hair Dryers Prevent Electrocutions," available at http://www.cpsc.gov/cpscpub/pubs/5037; all cited July 2001.

contacted a source of electrical current and your body provided a path for the electrical current to go to the ground, so that you received a shock.

An unintentional electric path between a source of current and a grounded surface is referred to as a "ground-fault." Ground faults occur when current is leaking somewhere, in effect, electricity is escaping to the ground. How it leaks is very important. If your body provides a path to the ground for this leakage, you could be injured, burned, severely shocked, or electrocuted.

Some examples of accidents that underscore this hazard include the following:

- Two children, ages five and six, were electrocuted in Texas when a plugged-in hair dryer fell into the tub in which they were bathing.

- A three-year-old Kansas girl was electrocuted when she touched a faulty countertop.

These two electrocutions occurred because the electrical current escaping from the appliance traveled through the victim to ground (in these cases, the grounded plumbing fixtures). Had a GFCI been installed, these deaths would probably have been prevented because a GFCI would have sensed the current flowing to ground and would have switched off the power before the electrocution occurred.

How the GFCI Works

In the home's wiring system, the GFCI constantly monitors electricity flowing in a circuit, to sense any loss of current. If the current flowing through the circuit differs by a small amount from that returning, the GFCI quickly switches off power to that circuit. The GFCI interrupts power faster than a blink of an eye to prevent a lethal dose of electricity. You may receive a painful shock, but you should not be electrocuted or receive a serious shock injury.

Here's how it may work in your house. Suppose a bare wire inside an appliance touches the metal case. The case is then charged with electricity. If you touch the appliance with one hand while the other hand is touching a grounded metal object, like a water faucet, you will receive a shock. If the appliance is plugged into an outlet protected by a GFCI, the power will be shut off before a fatal shock would occur.

Availability of GFCIs

Three common types of ground fault circuit interrupters are available for home use:

Receptacle Type

This type of GFCI is used in place of the standard duplex receptacle found throughout the house It fits into the standard outlet box and protects you against "ground faults" whenever an electrical product is plugged into the outlet Most receptacle-type GFCIs can be installed so that they also protect other electrical outlets further "down stream" in the branch circuit.

Circuit Breaker Type

In homes equipped with circuit breakers rather than fuses, a circuit breaker GFCI may be installed in a panel box to give protection to selected circuits The circuit breaker GFCI serves a dual purpose — not only will it shut off electricity in the event of a "ground-fault," but it will also trip when a short circuit or an overload occurs. Protection covers the wiring and each outlet, lighting fixture, heater, etc served by the branch circuit protected by the GFCI in the panel box.

Portable Type

Where permanent GFCIs are not practical, portable GFCIs may be used. One type contains the GFCI circuitry in a plastic enclosure with plug blades in the back and receptacle slots in the front. It can be plugged into a receptacle, then, the electrical product is plugged into the GFCI. Another type of portable GFCI is an extension cord combined with a GFCI. It adds flexibility in using receptacles that are not protected by GFCIs.

Where GFCIs Should Be Considered

In homes built to comply with the National Electrical Code (the Code), GFCI protection is required for most outdoor receptacles (since 1973), bathroom receptacle circuits (since 1975), garage wall outlets (since 1978), kitchen receptacles (since 1987), and all receptacles in crawl spaces and unfinished basements (since 1990).

Owners of homes that do not have GFCIs installed in all those critical areas specified in the latest version of the Code should consider having them installed. For broad protection, GFCI circuit breakers may be added in many panels of older homes to replace ordinary circuit breaker. For homes protected by fuses, you are limited to receptacle or portable-type GFCIs and these may be installed in areas of greatest exposure, such as the bathroom, kitchen, basement, garage, and outdoor circuits.

A GFCI should be used whenever operating electrically powered garden equipment (mower, hedge trimmer, edger, etc.). Consumers can obtain similar protection by using GFCIs with electric tools (drills, saws, sanders, etc.) for do-it-yourself work in and around the house.

Installing GFCIs

Circuit breaker and receptacle-type GFCIs may be installed in your home by a qualified electrician. Receptacle-type GFCIs may be installed by knowledgeable consumers familiar with electrical wiring practices who also follow the instructions accompanying the device. When in doubt about the proper procedure, contact a qualified electrician. Do not attempt to install it yourself.

The portable GFCI requires no special knowledge or equipment to install.

Testing the GFCIs

All GFCIs should be tested once a month to make sure they are working properly and are protecting you from fatal shock. GFCIs should be tested after installation to make sure they are working properly and protecting the circuit.

- To test the receptacle GFCI, first plug a nightlight or lamp into the outlet. The light should be on Then, press the "TEST" button on the GFCI. The GFCI's "RESET" button should pop out, and the light should go out.

- If the "RESET" button pops out but the light does not go out, the GFCI has been improperly wired. Contact an electrician to correct the wiring errors.

- If the "RESET" button does not pop out, the GFCI is defective and should be replaced.

- If the GFCI is functioning properly, and the lamp goes out, press the "RESET" button to restore power to the outlet.

Preventing Home Fires:
Arc Fault Circuit Interrupters (AFCIs)

Problems in home wiring, like arcing and sparking, are associated with more than 40,000 home fires each year. These fires claim over 350 lives and injure 1,400 victims annually.

A new electrical safety device for homes, called an arc fault circuit interrupter or AFCI, is expected to provide enhanced protection from fires resulting from these unsafe home wiring conditions.

Typical household fuses and circuit breakers do not respond to early arcing and sparking conditions in home wiring. By the time a fuse or circuit breaker opens a circuit to defuse these conditions, a fire may already have begun.

Several years ago, a CPSC study identified arc fault detection as a promising new technology. Since then, CPSC electrical engineers have tested the new AFCIs on the market and found these products to be effective.

Requiring AFCIs

AFCIs are already recognized for their effectiveness in preventing fires. The most recent edition of the National Electrical Code, the widely adopted model code for electrical wiring, will require AFCIs for bedroom circuits in new residential construction, effective January 2002.

Future editions of the code, which is updated every three years, could expand coverage.

AFCIs Versus GFCIs

AFCIs should not be confused with ground fault circuit interrupters or GFCIs. The popular GFCI devices are designed to provide protection from the serious consequences of electric shock.

While both AFCIs and GFCIs are important safety devices, they have different functions. AFCIs are intended to address fire hazards; GFCIs address shock hazards. Combination devices that include both AFCI and GFCI protection in one unit will become available soon.

AFCIs can be installed in any 15 or 20-ampere branch circuit in homes today and are currently available as circuit breakers with built-in AFCI features. In the near future, other types of devices with AFCI protection will be available.

215

Should You Install AFCIs?

You may want to consider adding AFCI protection for both new and existing homes. Older homes with ordinary circuit breakers especially may benefit from the added protection against the arcing faults that can occur in aging wiring systems.

For more information about AFCIs, contact an electrical supply store, an electrician, or the manufacturer of the circuit breakers already installed in your home. Sometimes these components can be replaced with AFCIs in the existing electrical panel box.

Be sure to have a qualified electrician install AFCIs; do not attempt this work yourself. The installation involves working within electrical panel boxes that are usually electrically live, even with the main circuit breakers turned off.

Use a Ground-Fault Circuit-Interrupter with Every Power Tool

The U S. Consumer Product Safety Commission (CPSC) recommends the use of a ground-fault circuit-interrupter (GFCI) with every power tool to protect against electrical shock hazards. Each year, CPSC learns of approximately 20 to 30 electrocution deaths associated with power drills, saws, sanders, hedge trimmers, and other electric power tools. Most of these deaths could be prevented by the use of a GFCI.

A GFCI constantly monitors current flowing in a circuit to sense any loss of current. If the current flowing through two circuit conductors differs by a very small amount, the GFCI instantly interrupts the current flow to prevent a lethal amount of electricity from reaching the consumer. The consumer may feet a painful shock but will not be electrocuted. Grounding may provide some protection for power equipment and double insulation of newer power tools presents lower risks of electrocution. However, GFCIs are the most effective means for protecting consumers against electrical shock hazards.

Since 1973, homes built according to the National Electrical Code have varying degrees of GFCI protection. GFCIs were first required in outdoor receptacle circuits In 1973, bathrooms in 1975, garage wall outlets in 1978, some kitchen receptacles since 1987, and all receptacle outlets in unfinished basements and crawl spaces since 1990.

Install Ground-Fault Circuit-Interrupter Protection for Pools, Spas and Hot Tubs

The U.S. Consumer Product Safety Commission (CPSC) recommends the installation of ground-fault circuit-interrupter (GFCI) protection for consumers against electrical shock hazards in pool underwater lighting circuits and in electric circuits of spas and hot tubs.

CPSC is aware of three recent electrical shock incidents involving the electric heater circuits of spas or hot tubs. Recently, a maintenance worker was electrocuted while repairing a pool light fixture.

The National Electrical Code provides for GFCI protection for cord-and-plug connected spas and hot tubs, and for lighting fixtures and receptacle outlets in the vicinity of pools, spas and hot tubs. However, the code does not require GFCI protection for all electrical equipment, particularly 240 volt equipment. Older pools, spas and hot tubs may not have adequate GFCI protection. In particular, pools older than 10-15 years may not have GFCI protection on underwater lighting circuits. Underwater swimming pool lighting fixtures and spa/hot tub heaters are a potential source of electrocution. Both 120 volt and 240 volt circuits should be protected by GFCIs.

Although grounding may provide some protection for pool, spa, and hot tub equipment, GFCIs are the most effective means for protecting consumers against electric shock hazards.

CPSC urges consumers to have an electrician install adequate GFCI protection for all spa and hot tub electrical equipment and for underwater swimming pool lighting fixtures.

Use a Ground-Fault Circuit-Interrupter with Electric Heaters in the Bathroom

The U.S. Consumer Product Safety Commission (CPSC) recommends the use of a ground-fault circuit-interrupter (GFCI) to protect against electrical shock hazards when electric heaters are used in bathrooms. CPSC knows of seven electrocution deaths since 1985 in which electric heaters fell into bathtubs and killed people. Electricity and water do not mix—consumers should keep electric heaters away from water. Most of these deaths could have been prevented by the use of a GFCI.

If you are considering the purchase of a heater and intend to use it in a bathroom, laundry area or similar indoor locations, look for models now specifically designed and certified by an independent testing laboratory for such uses. Even though such products are provided with built-in protection, never place your heater where it could easily fall into water.

Newer Hair Dryers Prevent Electrocutions

The U.S. Consumer Product Safety Commission (CPSC) recommends that consumers buy hair dryers that comply with the voluntary standard that gives added protection against electrocution.

To comply with the voluntary standard, hand-held hair dryers must protect against electrocution if they fall into water with the switch in either the "on" or "off" position.

Regardless of the improved protection, under no circumstances should consumers use a hair dryer where it could come in contact with water. Electricity and water are a potentially deadly combination, and in their presence children should always be supervised.

In the early 1980's an average of 18 electrocutions each year were caused by hand-held hair dryers falling or being pulled into water. That number has fallen to approximately 4 deaths per year since the voluntary standard to prevent electrocution went into effect. However, the CPSC estimates that there are millions of hair dryers still in use that do not provide any protection from electrocution in water. These older hair dryers continue to pose the risk of electrocution in bathrooms and other locations around water where permanent or portable ground-fault circuit-interrupters (GFCIs) are not used. Some hair dryers made before 1991 provide only partial protection from electrocution, in that they provide protection only when the switch is in the "off" position. These hair dryers may still be sold. CPSC encourages consumers to purchase the newer hair dryers that comply with the voluntary standards and thus provide the added measure of safety.

Chapter 28

Safe Use of Outlets, Extension Cords, and Other Electrical Equipment in the Home

Electrical Receptacle Outlets

Electrical receptacle outlets in walls and floors may present shock and electrical fire hazards to consumers. The U.S. Consumer Product Safety Commission estimates that 3,900 injuries associated with electrical receptacle outlets are treated in hospital emergency rooms each year. Approximately a third of these injuries occur when young children insert metal objects, such as hair pins and keys, into the outlet, resulting in electric shock or burn injuries to the hand or finger. CPSC also estimates that electric receptacles are involved in 5,300 fires annually which claim 40 lives and injured 110 consumers.

Older homes may have receptacles which are damaged or which, otherwise, may have deteriorated over the years. In one case of a damaged receptacle, a woman suffered severe burns to her hand as she was plugging in a floor lamp. Part of the plastic faceplate of the outlet had broken away, allowing the prongs of the plug to bridge from

The text in this chapter is from the following undated fact sheets produced by the Consumer Product Safety Commission, "Electrical Receptacle Outlets," available at http://www.cpsc.gov/cpscpub/pubs/5224.html, "Extension Cords Fact Sheet," available at http://www.cpsc.gov/cpscpub/pubs/16.html, "Household Extension Cords Can Cause Fires," available at http://www.cpsc.gov/cpscpub/pubs/5032.html, "New Electric Heat Tapes Help Prevent Fires," available at http://www.cpsc.gov/cpscpub/pubs/5045.html, "Metal Ladders and Electricity Don't Mix," available at http://www.cpsc.gov/cpscpub/pubs/5060.html; all cited July 2001.

the electrical contacts to the grounded strap, resulting in intense electrical arcing.

Outlets also deteriorate from repeated use, from plugging-in and unplugging appliances as is often done in kitchens and bathrooms. As a result, when plugs fit loosely into receptacles, especially the two-prong ungrounded type, they may slip partially or completely out of the receptacle with only slight movement of the attached cord. Receptacles in this condition may overheat and pose a serious fire hazard; if covered by a curtain or drape, the fire hazard is even greater.

Consumers should have a qualified person replace deteriorated and damaged receptacles and, at the same time, upgrade their home electrical system to present safety standards. The simplest and most effective method to protect against electrocution is through the installation of ground- fault circuit interrupters (GFCIs).

Another method of protection in the home is to install 3-wire receptacles which will accept either 2 or 3-prong plugs. This method, however, requires a grounding conductor, which may or may not be available in the outlet box. The least acceptable method is installing another 2-wire receptacle that requires the use of an adapter for accepting 3-wire plugs. Even thought the tab on the adapter may be properly connected to the cover-plate screw, the grounding path may not be adequate to protect against ground faults.

Outlets with poor internal contacts or loose wire terminals may become overheated and emit sparks. Even a receptacle with nothing plugged into it may run hot if it is passing current through to other outlets on the same circuit. To prevent damage to receptacles, appliances should be switched-off before unplugging from a receptacle.

- Have a qualified electrician replace damaged receptacles or those which feel hot, emit smoke or sparks, those with loose fitting plugs or those where plugged-in lamps flicker or fail to light.

- Do not unplug appliances by pulling on the cord at an angle. The brittle plastic face of the receptacle may crack and break away, leaving live parts of the receptacle exposed.

To protect young children, parents should consider some precautions:

- Insert plastic safety caps into unused outlets within reach of young children.

- Be sure that plugs are inserted completely into receptacles so that no part of the prongs are exposed.

Extension Cords

The Statistics

The U.S. Consumer Product Safety Commission (CPSO) estimates that each year, about 4,000 injuries associated with electric extension cords are treated in hospital emergency rooms. About half the injuries involve fractures, lacerations, contusions, or sprains from people tripping over extension cords. Thirteen percent of the injuries involve children under-five years of age; electrical burns to the mouth accounted for half the injuries to young children.

CPSC also estimates that about 3,300 residential fires originate in extension cords each year, killing 50 people and injuring about 270 others. The most frequent causes of such fires are short circuits, overloading, damage, and/or misuse of extension cords.

The Problem

Following injuries illustrate the major accident patterns associated with extension cords, namely children putting extension cords in their mouths, overloaded cords, worn or damaged cords, and tripping over cords:

- A 15-month-old girl put an extension cord in her mouth and suffered an electrical burn. She required surgery.

- Two young children were injured in a fire caused by an overloaded extension cord in their family's home. A lamp, TV set, and electric heater had been plugged into a single, light-duty extension cord.

- A 65-year old woman was treated for a fractured ankle after tripping over an extension cord.

The Standards

The National Electrical Code says that many cord-connected appliances should be equipped with polarized grounding type plugs. Polarized plugs have one blade slightly wider than the other and can only be inserted one way into the outlet. Polarization and grounding ensure that certain parts of appliances that could have a higher risk of electric shock when they become live are instead connected to the neutral, or grounded, side of the circuit. Such electrical products should only be used with polarized or grounding type extension cords.

Voluntary industry safety standards, including those of Underwriters Laboratories Inc. (UL), now require that general use extension cords have safety closures, warning labels, rating information about the electrical current, and other added features for the protection of children and other consumers.

In addition, UL-listed extension cords now must be constructed with #16 gauge or larger wire, or be equipped with integral fuses. The #16 gauge wire is rated to carry 13 amperes (up to 1560 watts), as compared to the formerly-used #18 gauge cords that were rated for 10 amperes (up to 1200 watts).

Safety Suggestions

The following are recommendations for the purchase and safe use of extension cords:

- Use extension cords only when necessary and only on a temporary basis.

- Use polarized extension cords with polarized appliances.

- Make sure cords do not dangle from the counter or table tops where they can be pulled down or tripped over.

- Replace cracked or worn extension cords with new #16 gauge cords that have the listing, of a nationally-recognized testing laboratory, safety closures, and other safety features.

- With cords lacking safety closures, cover any unused outlets with electrical tape or with plastic caps to prevent the chance of a child making contact with the live circuit.

- Insert plugs fully so that no part of the prongs are exposed when the extension cord is in use.

- When disconnecting cords, pull the plug rather than the cord itself.

- Teach children not to play with plugs and outlets.

- Use only three-wire extension cords for appliances with three-prong plugs. Never remove the third (round or U-shaped) prong, which is a safety feature designed to reduce the risk of shock and electrocution.

- In locations where furniture or beds may be pushed against an extension cord where the cord joins the plug, use a special "angle extension cord," which is specifically designed for use in these instances.

- Check the plug and the body of the extension cord while the cord is in use. Noticeable warming of these plastic parts is expected when cords are being used at their maximum rating, however, if the cord feels hot or if there is a softening of the plastic, this is a warning that the plug wires or connections are failing and that the extension cord should be discarded and replaced.

- Never use an extension cord while it is coiled or looped. Never cover any part of an extension cord with newspapers, clothing, rugs, or any objects while the cord is in use. Never place an extension cord where it is likely to be damaged by heavy furniture or foot traffic.

- Don't use staples or nails to attach extension cords to a baseboard or to another surface. This could damage the cord and present a shock or fire hazard.

- Don't overload extension cords by plugging in appliances that draw a total of more watts than the rating of the cord.

- Use special, heavy duty extension cords for high wattage appliances such as air conditioners, portable electric heaters, and freezers.

- When using outdoor tools and appliances, use only extension cords labeled for outdoor use.

Household Extension Cords Can Cause Fires

Overheating of the entire cord is usually caused by overloading (connecting appliances that need too many watts for the wire size of the cord). Many older extension cords made with small (No. 18 gauge) wire that can overheat at 15 or 20 amps are in use.

Consumers should feel the temperature of the cords when they are in use. If they are hot to the touch, disconnect the appliances).

If there is any sign of overheating, replace the extension cords with new ones having No. 16 or heaver gauge wire (the lower the gauge number, the heavier the wire and the more electrical current the cord can safely carry).

The difference between the cord sizes is not obvious, but the new No. 16 cords usually have 16 / 2 or 16 / 3 stamped on the cord and will have the wire size printed on the package.

Check new cords to make sure they are listed by a recognized national testing laboratory.

Electric Heat Tape

Electric heat tapes are used to keep water pipes from freezing. Heat tapes are usually installed in attics or underneath porches and homes, especially mobile homes. CPSC estimates there are about 2,000 fires, 10 deaths, and 100 injuries each year involving heat tapes. The use of certified heat tapes can help to reduce the frequency of these fires.

To help prevent fires, replace uncertified heat tapes more than three years old. Uncertified heat tapes should be replaced with new heat tapes certified to meet recognized voluntary standards. The following organizations are certifying heat tapes to meet recognized voluntary standards:

- Underwriters Laboratories (UL)
- The Canadian Standards Association (CSA)
- Factory Mutual Research Corporation (FMRC)

The following are safety tips for purchasing, installing, and maintaining electric heat tapes:

- Replace uncertified heat tapes more than 3 years old with new heat tapes certified to meet recognized voluntary standards. All new heat tapes will have a 3-prong plug.

- Always plug the 3-prong plug into a 3-prong outlet to make sure the heat tape is grounded.

- Use a ground-fault circuit-interrupter (GFCI) wherever heat tapes are plugged in.

- Do not wrap heat tape over itself unless specifically permitted in the manufacturer's instructions.

- Apply heat tapes directly on the pipe to be protected, never on top of the insulation covering the pipe.

- Do not cover the heat tape with insulation unless advised by the manufacturer. Use nonflammable insulation such as fiber glass.

- Do not use foam or vinyl insulation that could catch fire from a failing heat tape.

- Keep the end-cap sealed and off the ground to prevent water from getting in. Moisture can lead to a fire.

- Do not use heat tapes designed for water pipes on gutters, driveways, or fuel lines.

- If heat tape has a thermostat, check instructions to see if the thermostat should be placed against the pipe and covered with insulation or if it should be left hanging and uncovered.

- Inspect heat tapes each year and replace them if you notice signs of deterioration. Look for discolored surfaces (especially at the plug), charring, cuts or breaks in the insulation, or bare wires.

- Check installation instructions when you change types or brands of heat tape because different heat tapes have different installation requirements.

Metal Ladders and Electricity Don't Mix

Consumers can be electrocuted when they use metal ladders near overhead wires. Consumers often use metal ladders near overhead wires to clean gutters, paint structures, trim trees, and repair roofs and chimneys.

Electrocutions often occur when:

- Metal ladders are moved and accidentally touch an overhead electrical wire near the house or street. Metal ladders conduct electricity, which can kill anyone touching the ladder.

- Metal ladders shift position. Wind, uneven ground or reaching to the side while on the ladder can cause the ladder or person to contact an overhead wire.

- Metal ladders are used while handling an improperly grounded power tool or contacting an electrical source, such as a light socket.

Metal stepladders and extension ladders meeting Underwriters Laboratories and American National Standards Institute voluntary standards have labels warning about this hazard. The labels typically state with words and graphic:

"Danger! Metal conducts electricity! Keep ladder away from power lines and live electrical wires."

Despite these and other warnings, electrocutions still occur each year. To avoid this hazard, CPSC advises you to use a ladder that does not conduct electricity, such as fiberglass or wood, when working near overhead wires.

If you must use a metal ladder, follow these precautions:

1. Carefully check the location of all overhead wires before using a ladder, especially where the lines connect to the house. Any power line (including the line running from the street to your house) can permit electricity to flow into a piece of metal or 3 other object, such as a wet tree branch, that touches it.

    Power lines and phone lines often appear similar. Assume all overhead wires carry electricity. Some overhead lines are coated to extend the life of the line. The coating is not intended to protect against electrocution.

2. Lower the ladder when carrying or moving it, to avoid touching an overhead wire. Since long ladders can be unwieldy, have someone help carry and set up the ladder.

3. Never work on a windy day a gust of wind can cause the ladder to shift and touch an overhead wire.

4. Never place a ladder where it could slide into an overhead line. Make sure the distance to the nearest overhead line is at least twice the length of the ladder.

5. Place the ladder's feet on solid, level ground before climbing it. When the ground is not level or is soft, put a flat piece of wood under one or both feet of the ladder to provide a solid, level base. If possible, tie off the ladder to prevent it from moving.

6. If the ladder should start to fall into an overhead line, let it go. Never try to move it. Do not leave the ladder unattended Have someone call the power company and ask them to cut off electricity to the line, before you move the ladder. If someone is holding the ladder when it contacts the overhead line, never try to pull them away with your hands. Use something that does not conduct electricity, such as a long piece of dry wood or rope, to push or pull them loose.

Chapter 29

Smoke Detectors

Test All Smoke Detectors and Annually Replace Batteries

Tragedies can be prevented simply by testing your smoke detector once a month and by annually replacing smoke detector batteries. Owner neglect of testing and battery replacement has been a major cause of smoke detector failure in fires.

Every year in the United States, approximately 5,000 people are killed by residential fires. Most fire victims die from inhalation of smoke and toxic gases, not as a result of burns. Most deaths and injuries occur in fires that happen at night while the victims are asleep.

Properly installed and maintained, the home smoke detector is considered one of the best and least expensive means of providing an early warning when a fire begins, before the concentration of smoke reaches a dangerous level or before the fire becomes too intense. There is no doubt about it—smoke detectors save lives, prevent injuries, and minimize property damage by enabling residents to detect fires early in their development. The risk of dying from fires in homes without smoke detectors is twice as high as in homes that have functioning detectors.

Both wired-in and battery-powered smoke detectors should be tested at least once a month or in accordance with the detector manufacturer's recommendation (if more frequent) to make sure they

The text in this chapter is from the following fact sheets produced by the Consumer Product Safety Commission, "Test All Smoke Detectors and Annually Replace Batteries," available at http://www.cpsc.gov/cpscpub/pubs/5077.html, and "Smoke Detectors Can Save Your Life," available at http://www.cpsc.gov/cpscpub/pubs/557.html; both cited July 2001.

are operating properly. If the smoke detector is battery operated, test it and replace the batteries according to the manufacturer's instructions. Fresh batteries should last approximately one year.

Follow manufacturer's directions for testing the detector.

If your battery-powered detector begins to emit its low-power warning, such as a chirping sound, replace the battery immediately with a fresh one. Better yet, consider making routine replacement of batteries a seasonal task, such as when resetting clocks in the fall or spring, or in conjunction with a major event, such as New Year's Day or a birthday. This practice will ensure that your smoke detectors will continue to provide protection for you without your having to purchase a battery when a smoke detector begins to produce its periodic "low battery warning" chirping.

If "nuisance" alarms occur during cooking, or from a smoking fireplace, etc., do not disable your smoke detector. Either fan away the smoke, relocate the detector, or purchase one with a delay switch.

At least one smoke detector should be properly placed on every floor of the home. The most important location is near the bedrooms to provide early warning to all sleeping occupants. A smoke detector should be placed in any bedroom occupied by a smoker.

Rehearse an escape plan, so that when the smoke detector sounds, family members will react appropriately.

Don't wait for a fire in your home to test your smoke detector ... Do it now: test it, replace its batteries, and sleep with peace of mind.

Make sure detectors are placed either on the ceiling or 6-12 inches below the ceiling on the wall. Locate smoke detectors away from air vents or registers; high air flow or "dead" spots are to be avoided.

Smoke Detectors Can Save Your Life

- Smoke detectors warn you in time to escape from a fire
- The best place for your smoke detectors are outside the bedrooms and at each level in the home
- Test them monthly and replace the battery once a year or when they make a "chirping" sound

Know How to Escape

- always help those who need help
- plan your escape route and practice leaving your home
- decide one place outside where family members should meet.

Part Four

Water Hazards

Chapter 30

Prevent Child Drownings in the Home

Frequently Asked Questions

How large is the problem of unintentional drowning in the United States?

- In 1998, 4,406 people drowned, including 1,003 children younger than 15 years old.[1]

- In 1992, the U.S. Coast Guard received reports of 6,000 crashes involving recreational boats that resulted in 3,700 injuries and 816 deaths.[2]

Which groups of people are more likely to drown?

Children: Drowning is the second leading cause of injury-related death for children (aged 1 through 14 years), accounting for 940 deaths in 1998.[1]

The text is this chapter is from the following undated fact sheets produced by the Consumer Product Safety Commission, "Prevent Child Drownings in the Home," available at http://www.cpsc.gov/cpscpub/pubs/5013.html, "How to Plan for the Unexpected: Preventing Child Drownings," available at http://www.cpsc.gov/cpscpub/pubs/359.html, and "Infants and Toddlers Can Drown in 5-Gallon Buckets," available at http://www.cpsc.gov/cpscpub/pubs/5006.html; all cited July 2001; "Drowning Prevention," an undated factsheet produced by the Centers for Disease Control and Prevention (CDC); cited August 2001.

Males: In 1998, males comprised 81% of people who drowned in the United States.[1]

Blacks: In 1998, the overall age-adjusted drowning rate for blacks was 1.6 times higher than for whites. Black children ages 5 through 19 years drowned at 2.5 times the rate of whites.[1] Black children ages 1 through 4 years had a lower drowning rate than white children, largely because drownings in that age group typically occur in residential swimming pools, which are not as accessible to minority children in the United States.[1,3,4]

Where do childhood drownings occur most often?

Most children drown in swimming pools. According to the U.S. Consumer Product Safety Commission (CPSC), emergency departments reported that among children younger than 5 years old, about

Table 30.1. States with the Highest Rates of Unintentional Drowning per 100,000 population* (1998)[1]

State	Number of people drowned	Rate per 100,000 persons (1996)
Alaska	47	7.41
Mississippi	95	3.47
Louisiana	129	3.03
Idaho	34	2.90
Florida	396	2.64
Alabama	112	2.60
Arkansas	59	2.53
Hawaii	33	2.53
South Carolina	92	2.49
Oregon	76	2.38
United States	**4,406**	**1.65**

*Ranking based on age-adjusted rate.
Source: NCHS 2000 Vital Statistics System

320 fatal drownings in 1991 and nearly 2,300 non-fatal near-drownings in 1993 occurred in residential swimming pools. Between 60-90% of drownings among children aged 0-4 years occur in residential pools; more than half of these occur at the child's own home. Compared with in-ground pools without four-sided fencing, 60% fewer drownings occur in in-ground pools with four-sided isolation fencing.[5]

How often is alcohol use involved in drownings?

Alcohol use is involved in about 25-50% of adolescent and adult deaths associated with water recreation. It is a major contributing factor in up to 50% of drownings among adolescent boys.[6,7]

What can government agencies do to prevent drownings?

- Mandate and enforce legal limits for blood alcohol levels during water recreation activities.

- Provide public service announcements about the danger of combining alcohol with water recreation.

- Eliminate advertisements that encourage alcohol use during boating.

- Restrict the sale of alcohol at water recreation facilities.

How can people guard against drowning?

You can greatly reduce the chances of you or your children becoming drowning or near-drowning victims by following a few simple safety tips:

- Whenever young children are swimming, playing, or bathing in water, make sure an adult is constantly watching them. By definition this means that the supervising adult should not read, play cards, talk on the phone, mow the lawn, or do any other distracting activity while watching children.

- Never swim alone or in unsupervised places. Teach children to always swim with a buddy.

- Keep small children away from buckets containing liquid: 5-gallon industrial containers are a particular danger. Be sure to empty buckets when household chores are done.

- Never drink alcohol during or just before swimming, boating, or water skiing. Never drink alcohol while supervising children. Teach teenagers about the danger of drinking alcohol and swimming, boating, or water skiing.

- To prevent choking, never chew gum or eat while swimming, diving, or playing in water.

- Learn to swim. Enroll yourself and/or your children aged 4 and older in swimming classes. Swimming classes are not recommended for children under age 4.

- Learn CPR (cardio-pulmonary resuscitation). This is particularly important for pool owners and individuals who regularly participate in water recreation.

- Do NOT use air-filled swimming aids (such as "water wings") in place of life jackets or life preservers with children. These can give parents and children a false sense of security and increase the risk of drowning.

- Check the water depth before entering. The American Red Cross recommends 9 feet as a minimum depth for diving or jumping.

Young children can drown in as little as two inches of water. Caregivers must be aware of the hidden drowning hazard associated with many products found in and around the home.

Available data show that accidental drowning is the third leading cause of death for children under 5 years of age. Many of these deaths are associated with common household products. For example:

- About 100 children under age 5 have drowned each year in bathtubs. Some of these bathtub drownings occurred when children were in bath seats or rings.

- 5-gallon buckets, often used for household chores, have been associated with more than 275 drownings since 1984.

- Over 20 young children, most around one year of age, have drowned in toilets since 1990—usually when they fell in head first.

- Childhood drownings have also happened in other containers that may contain liquids, including diaper pails, picnic coolers, wash tubs and basins.

The following safety tips can help prevent childhood drownings in and around the home.

- ALWAYS provide supervision when children are around any type of containers containing liquids.

- NEVER leave young children alone or with young siblings in a bathtub even if you are using a bath seat or ring. Children can drown in just a few minutes.

- Keep young children out of the bathroom unless you are watching them closely.

- Be sure all containers that may contain liquids are emptied immediately after use. Do not leave empty containers in yards or around the house where they may accumulate water and attract young children. day they are issued.

How to Plan for the Unexpected

In some of the nation's sunbelt, drowning has been the leading cause of accidental death in the home of children under 5 years old. The information below can help parents and caregivers provide young children with the protection they deserve.

Each year, nationwide, more than 300 children under 5 years old drown in residential swimming pools, usually a pool owned by their family. In addition, more than 2,000 children in that age group are treated in hospital emergency rooms for submersion injures.

Medical costs for submersion victims during the initial hospitalization alone can be quite high. Costs can range from an estimated $2,000 for a victim who recovers fully to $80,000 for a victim with severe brain damage. Some severely brain damaged victims have initial hospital stays in excess of 120 days and expenses in excess of $150,000.

Many communities have enacted safety regulations governing residential swimming pools—inground and aboveground. It's up to parents to comply with these regulations. Apart from these laws, parents who own pools, can take their own precautions to reduce the chances of their youngsters accessing the family pool or spa without adult supervision.

Facts and Figures

Following are just a few facts uncovered by the U.S. Consumer Product Safety Commission (CPSC) in a comprehensive study of drowning and submersion incidents involving children under 5 years old in Arizona, California, and Florida.

- Seventy-five percent of the submersion victims studied by CPSC were between 1 and 3 years old; 65 percent of this group were boys. Toddlers, in particular, often do something unexpected because their capabilities change daily.

- At the time of the incidents, most victims were being supervised by one or both parents. Forty-six percent of the victims were last seen in the house; 23 percent were last seen in the yard or on the porch or patio; and 31 percent were in or around the pool before the accident. In all, 69 percent of the children were not expected to be at or in the pool, yet they were found in the water.

- Submersion incidents involving children usually happen in familiar surroundings. Sixty-five percent of the incidents happened in a pool owned by the child's family and 33 percent of the incidents happened in a pool owned by friends or relatives.

- Pool submersions involving children happen quickly. A child can drown in the time it takes to answer a phone. Seventy-seven percent of the victims had been missing from sight for 5 minutes or less.

- Survival depends on rescuing the child quickly and restarting the breathing process, even while the child is still in the water. Seconds count in preventing death or brain damage.

- Child drowning is a silent death. There's no splashing to alert anyone that the child is in trouble.

Barriers

The following barrier recommendations are the result of identifying key parameters that typically contribute to child drowning in backyard pools. These recommendations are the minimum steps you can take to make your home a safe place for your child.

Barriers are not childproof, but they provide layers of protection for a child who strays from supervision. Barriers give parents additional time to locate a child before the unexpected becomes a reality.

Barriers include a fence or wall, door alarms for the house, and a power safety cover over the pool. Barriers also may be used to protect children from accessing hot tubs and spas. Use the following recommendations as a guide:

Fences and Gates

- Install a fence or other barrier, such as a wall, completely around the pool. If the house is part of the barrier, the doors leading from the house to the pool should be protected with an alarm or the pool should have a power safety cover. Alarm and cover details follow.

- The fence or other barrier should be at least 4 feet high. It should have no foot or handholds that could help a young child to climb it.

- Vertical fence slats should be less than 4 inches apart to prevent a child from squeezing through.

- Use this as a guide when the release mechanism is located less than 54 inches from the bottom of the gate.

- If horizontal members are equal to or more than 45 inches apart, vertical spacing shall not exceed 4 inches.

- If the fence is chain link, then no part of the diamond-shaped opening should be larger than 1-3/4 inches.

- Fence gates should be self-closing and self-latching. The gate should be well maintained to close and latch easily. The latch should be out of a child's reach.

- When the release mechanism of the self-latching device is less than 54 inches from the bottom of the gate, the release mechanism for the gate should be at least 3 inches below the top of the gate on the side facing the pool. Placing the release mechanism at this height prevents a young child from reaching over the top of a gate and releasing the latch. Also, the gate and barrier should have no opening greater than 1/2 inch within 18 inches of the latch release mechanism. This prevents a young child from reaching through the gate and releasing the latch.

There are a wide variety of fencing construction materials available to compliment your house and pool surroundings. Your local fence company or pool enclosure company can provide you with information and assist you in making a selection.

The weak link in the strongest and highest fence is a gate that fails to close and latch completely. For a gate to close completely every time, it must be in proper working order.

Door Alarms

- If the house forms one side of the barrier, then doors leading from the house to the pool should be protected with alarms that produce an audible sound when a door is unexpectedly opened.

- Install an alarm that can be temporarily turned off by an adult for a single opening of the door by using a keypad or switch that is out of a child's reach.

Battery and electrically powered alarms are available. The key pad switch can be used by adults who wish to pass through the door without setting off the alarm. It should be placed high on all doors leading from the house to the pool. Affordable and easily installed alarms are available. An alarm signal immediately tells a parent that a door has been opened.

Power Safety Covers

Power safety covers over the pool may be used as an alternative to door alarms. A power safety cover should meet the requirements of the ASTM pool cover standard which addresses labeling requirements and performance. ASTM requires that a cover withstand the weight of two adults and a child to allow a rescue should an individual fall onto the cover. The standard also requires quick removal of water from the cover. A young child can drown in just inches of water.

A power safety cover is a motor powered barrier that can be placed over the water area. Motor-driven covers easily open and close over the pool. When the power safety cover is properly in place over the pool, it provides a high level of safety for children under 5 years old by inhibiting their access to the water.

Above-Ground Pools

- Steps and ladders leading from the ground to the pool should be secured and locked, or removed when the pool is not in use.

Rules For Pools

- Instruct babysitters about potential pool hazards to young children and about the use of protective devices, such as door alarms and latches. Emphasize the need for constant supervision.

- Never leave a child unsupervised near a pool. During social gatherings at or near a pool, appoint a "designated watcher" to protect young children from pool accidents. Adults may take turns being the "watcher." When adults become preoccupied, children are at risk.

- If a child is missing, check the pool first. Seconds count in preventing death or disability. Go to the edge of the pool and scan the entire pool, bottom and surface, as well as the pool area.

- Do not allow a young child in the pool without an adult.

- Do not consider young children to be drownproof because they have had swimming lessons. Children must be watched closely while swimming.

- Do not use flotation devices as a substitute for supervision.

- Learn CPR (cardiopulmonary resuscitation). Babysitters and other caretakers, such as grandparents and older siblings, should also know CPR.

- Keep rescue equipment by the pool. Be sure a telephone is poolside with emergency numbers posted nearby.

- Remove toys from in and around the pool when it is not in use. Toys can attract young children to the pool.

- Never prop open the gate to a pool barrier.

Infants and Toddlers Can Drown in 5-Gallon Buckets

Large buckets and young children can be a deadly combination. The U.S. Consumer Product Safety Commission (CPSC) has received reports of over 275 young children who have drowned in buckets since 1984. Over 30 other children have been hospitalized. Almost all of the containers were 5-gallon buckets containing liquids. Most were used for mopping floors or other household chores. Many were less than half full.

Of all buckets, the 5-gallon size presents the greatest hazard to young children because of its tall, straight sides and weight, even with just a small amount of liquid. At 14-inches high, a 5-gallon bucket is about half the height of a young child. That, combined with the stability, makes it nearly impossible for top-heavy infants and toddlers to free themselves when they fall into the bucket head first. A child can drown in a small amount of water.

Children are naturally curious and easily attracted to water. At the crawling and pulling up stages while learning to walk, they can quickly get into trouble. CPSC believes that bucket drownings happen when children are left momentarily unattended, crawl to a bucket, pull themselves up, and lean forward to reach for an object or play in the water.

Parents and caregivers who are using 5-gallon buckets for household chores are warned not to leave a bucket containing even a small amount of liquid unattended where a young child may gain access to it. A child can drown in the time it takes to answer a telephone.

Resources

CDC-Healthy Swimming
Reducing the spread of recreational water illnesses
Internet; http://www.cdc.gov/healthyswimming

SafeUSA
Internet: http://www.cdc.gov/safeusa

US Consumer Product Safety Commission Clearinghouse
For information about pool-related drownings and injuries.
Internet: http://www.cpsc.gov

The United States Lifesaving Association (USLA)
USLA works to reduce the incidence of death and injury in the aquatic environment through public education, national lifeguard standards, training programs, promotion of high levels of lifeguard readiness, and other means.
Internet: http://www.usla.org

References

1. National Center for Health Statistics (NCHS). *National Mortality Data, 1998*. Hyattsville (MD): NCHS 2000.

2. *US Coast Guard Boating Statistics, 1992*. Washington, DC: US Department of Transportation (COMDTPUB P16754.8).

3. Branche, C.M., What is happening with drowning rates in the United States? In: JR Fletemeyer and SJ Freas (eds). *Drowning: New perspectives on intervention and prevention*. Boca Raton, Florida: CRC Press LLC, 1999.

4. Branche-Dorsey, C.M., Russell, J.C., Greenspan, A.I., Chorba, T.C. Unintentional injuries: the problems and some preventive strategies. In: IL Livingston (ed). *Handbook of Black American Health: The mosaic of conditions, issues, policies and prospects*. Westport, CT: Greenwood Publishing Group, 1994.

5. US Consumer Product Safety Commission Clearinghouse, Washington DC, (301) 504-0424.

6. National Safety Council, 1993. *Accident Facts, 1993 Ed.* Itasca, Illinois: Author.

7. Howland, J., Hingson, R.. Alcohol as a risk factor for drowning: a review of the literature (1950-1985). *Accident Analysis and Prevention* 1988;20:19-25.

Chapter 31

Safety Barrier Guidelines for Home Pools

Swimming pools should always be happy places. Unfortunately, each year thousands of American families confront swimming pool tragedies—drownings and near-drownings of young children. These tragedies are preventable.

The swimming pool barrier guidelines are not a CPSC standard and are not mandatory requirements. Therefore, the Commission does not endorse these guidelines as the sole method to minimize pool drownings of young children. The Commission believes, however, that the safety features recommended in this chapter will help make pools safer.

Some localities have incorporated the guidelines in this chapter into their building codes. Check with your local authorities to see whether these guidelines are included in your area's building code or in other regulations.

Why the Swimming Pool Guidelines Were Developed

Each year, hundreds of young children die and thousands come close to death due to submersion in residential swimming pools. CPSC has estimated that each year about 300 children under 5 years old drown in residential swimming pools. The Commission estimates hospital emergency room treatment is required for approximately another 2,300 children under 5 years of age who were submerged in residential pools.

"Safety Barrier Guidelines for Home Pools," an undated fact sheet produced by the Consumer Product Safety Commission; cited July 2001.

In the late 1980s, CPSC did an extensive study of swimming pool accidents, both fatal drownings and near-fatal submersions, in California, Arizona and Florida, states in which home swimming pools are very popular and in use during much of the year. The findings from that study led Commission staff to develop the guidelines in this chapter.

- In California, Arizona and Florida, drowning was the leading cause of accidental death in and around the home for children under the age of 5 years.

- 75 percent of the children involved in swimming pool submersion or drowning accidents were between 1 and 3 years old.

- Boys between 1 and 3 years old were the most likely victims of fatal drownings and near-fatal submersions in residential swimming pools.

- Most of the victims were being supervised by one or both parents when the swimming pool accident occurred.

- Nearly half of the child victims were last seen in the house before the pool accident occurred. In addition, 23 percent of the accident victims were last seen on the porch or patio, or in the yard. This means that fully 69 percent of the children who became victims in swimming pool accidents were not expected to be in or at the pool, but were found drowned or submerged in the water.

- 65 percent of the accidents occurred in a pool owned by the victim's immediate family, and 33 percent of the accidents occurred in pools owned by relatives or friends.

- Fewer than 2 percent of the pool accidents were a result of children trespassing on property where they didn't live or belong.

- 77 percent of the swimming pool accident victims had been missing for five minutes or less when they were found in the pool drowned or submerged.

The speed with which swimming pool drownings and submersions can occur is a special concern: by the time a child's absence is noted, the child may have drowned. Anyone who has cared for a toddler knows how fast young children can move. Toddlers are inquisitive and impulsive and lack a realistic sense of danger. These behaviors, coupled with a child's ability to move quickly and unpredictably, make swimming pools particularly hazardous for households with young children.

Swimming pool drownings of young children have another particularly insidious feature: these are silent deaths. It is unlikely that splashing or screaming will occur to alert a parent or caregiver that a child is in trouble.

CPSC staff have reviewed a great deal of data on drownings and child behavior, as well as information on pool and pool barrier construction. The staff concluded that the best way to reduce child drownings in residential pools was for pool owners to construct and maintain barriers that would prevent young children from gaining access to pools. However, there are no substitutes for diligent supervision.

The Swimming Pool Barrier Guidelines

The definition of pool includes spas and hot tubs; the swimming pool barrier guidelines therefore apply to these structures as well as to conventional swimming pools.

A successful pool barrier prevents a child from getting OVER, UNDER, or THROUGH and keeps the child from gaining access to the pool except when supervising adults are present.

How to Prevent a Child from Getting OVER a Pool Barrier

A young child can get over a pool barrier if the barrier is too low or if the barrier has handholds or footholds for a child to use when climbing.

The guidelines recommend that the top of a pool barrier be at least 48 inches above grade, measured on the side of the barrier which faces away from the swimming pool.

Guidelines recommend eliminating handholds and footholds and minimizing the size of openings in a barrier's construction.

For a Solid Barrier:

No indentations or protrusions should be present, other than normal construction tolerances and masonry joints.

For a Barrier (Fence) Made Up of Horizontal and Vertical Members:

If the distance between the tops of the horizontal members is less than 45 inches, the horizontal members should be on the swimming pool side of the fence. The spacing of the vertical members should not exceed 1 3/4 inches. This size is based on the foot width of a young child and is intended to reduce the potential for a child to gain a foothold. If there are any decorative cutouts in the fence, the space within the cutouts should not exceed 1 3/4 inches.

If the distance between the tops of the horizontal members is more than 45 inches, the horizontal members can be on the side of the fence facing away from the pool. The spacing between vertical members should not exceed 4 inches. This size is based on the head breadth and chest depth of a young child and is intended to prevent a child from passing through an opening. Again, if there are any decorative cutouts in the fence, the space within the cutouts should not exceed 1 3/4 inches.

For a Chain Link Fence:

The mesh size should not exceed 1 1/4 inches square unless slats, fastened at the top or bottom of the fence, are used to reduce mesh openings to no more than 1 3/4 inches.

For a Fence Made Up of Diagonal Members (Latticework):

The maximum opening in the lattice should not exceed 1 3/4 inches.

For Aboveground Pools:

Aboveground pools should have barriers. The pool structure itself serves as a barrier or a barrier is mounted on top of the pool structure.

Then, there are two possible ways to prevent young children from climbing up into an aboveground pool. The steps or ladder can be designed to be secured, locked or removed to prevent access, or the steps or ladder can be surrounded by a barrier such as those described above.

How to Prevent a Child From Getting UNDER a Pool Barrier

For any pool barrier, the maximum clearance at the bottom of the barrier should not exceed 4 inches above grade, when the measurement is done on the side of the barrier facing away from the pool.

Aboveground Pool with Barrier on Top of Pool:

If an aboveground pool has a barrier on the top of the pool, the maximum vertical clearance between the top of the pool and the bottom of the barrier should not exceed 4 inches.

How to Prevent a Child from Getting THROUGH a Pool Barrier

Preventing a child from getting through a pool barrier can be done by restricting the sizes of openings in a barrier and by using self-closing and self-latching gates.

To prevent a young child from getting through a fence or other barrier, all openings should be small enough so that a 4 inch diameter sphere can not pass through. This size is based on the head breadth and chest depth of a young child.

Gates:

There are two kinds of gates which might be found on a residential property. Both can play a part in the design of a swimming pool barrier.

Pedestrian Gate: These are the gates people walk through. Swimming pool barriers should be equipped with a gate or gates which restrict access to the pool. A locking device should be included in the gate design. Gates should open out from the pool and should be self-closing and self-latching. If a gate is properly designed, even if the gate is not completely latched, a young child pushing on the gate in order to enter the pool area will at least close the gate and may actually engage the latch.

When the release mechanism of the self-latching device is less than 54 inches from the bottom of the gate, the release mechanism for the gate should be at least 3 inches below the top of the gate on the side facing the pool. Placing the release mechanism at this height prevents a young child from reaching over the top of a gate and releasing the latch.

Also, the gate and barrier should have no opening greater than 1/2 inch within 18 inches of the latch release mechanism. This prevents a young child from reaching through the gate and releasing the latch.

All Other Gates (Vehicle Entrances, Etc.): Other gates should be equipped with self-latching devices. The self-latching devices should be installed as described for pedestrian gates.

When the House Wall Forms Part of the Pool Barrier:

In many homes, doors open directly onto the pool area or onto a patio which leads to the pool.

In such cases, the wall of the house is an important part of the pool barrier, and passage through any doors in the house wall should be controlled by security measures. The importance of controlling a young child's movement from house to pool is demonstrated by the statistics obtained during CPSC's study of pool incidents in California, Arizona and Florida: almost half (46 percent) of the children who became victims of pool accidents were last seen in the house just before they were found in the pool.

All doors which give access to a swimming pool should be equipped with an audible alarm which sounds when the door and/or screen are opened. The alarm should sound for 30 seconds or more immediately after the door is opened. The alarm should be loud: at least 85 dBA (decibels) when measured 10 feet away from the alarm mechanism. The alarm sound should be distinct from other sounds in the house, such as the telephone, doorbell and smoke alarm. The alarm should have an automatic reset feature.

Because adults will want to pass through house doors in the pool barrier without setting off the alarm, the alarm should have a switch that allows adults to temporarily deactivate the alarm for up to 15 seconds. The deactivation switch could be a touchpad (keypad) or a manual switch, and should be located at least 54 inches above the threshold of the door covered by the alarm. This height was selected based on the reaching ability of young children.

Power safety covers can be installed on pools to serve as security barriers. Power safety covers should conform to the specifications in ASTM F 1346-91. This standard specifies safety performance requirements for pool covers to protect young children from drowning.

Self-closing doors with self-latching devices could also be used to safeguard doors which give ready access to a swimming pool.

Indoor Pools:

When a pool is located completely within a house, the walls that surround the pool should be equipped to serve as pool safety barriers. Measures recommended above where a house wall serves as part of a safety barrier also apply for all the walls surrounding an indoor pool.

Barriers for Residential Swimming Pool, Spas, and Hot Tubs

The preceding explanations of the US. Consumer Product Safety Commission's pool barrier guidelines were provided in order to make it easier for pool owners, purchasers, builders, technicians and others to understand and apply the guidelines themselves.

Application

The guidelines presented in this chapter are intended to provide a means of protection against potential drownings and near-drownings to children under 5 years of age by restricting access to residential swimming pools, spas, and hot tubs.

Definitions

Aboveground/onground pool: See definition of swimming pool.

Barrier: A fence, a wall, a building wall or a combination thereof which completely surrounds the swimming pool and obstructs access to the swimming pool.

Hot tub: See definition of swimming pool.

Inground pool: See definition of swimming pool.

Residential: That which is situated on the premises of a detached one- or two-family dwelling or a one-family townhouse not more than three stories in height.

Spa, nonportable: See definition of swimming pool.

Spa, portable: A non-permanent structure intended for recreational bathing, in which all controls, water-heating, and water-circulating equipment are an integral part of the product and which is cord-connected (not permanently electrically wired).

Swimming pool: Any structure intended for swimming or recreational bathing that contains water over 24 inches deep. This includes inground, aboveground, and onground swimming pools, hot tubs, and spas.

Swimming pool, indoor: A swimming pool which is totally contained within a structure and surrounded on all four sides by walls of said structure.

Swimming pool, outdoor: Any swimming pool which is not an indoor pool.

Guidelines

Section I. Outdoor Swimming Pool

An outdoor swimming pool, including an inground, aboveground, or onground pool, hot tub, or spa, should be provided with a barrier which complies with the following:

1. The top of the barrier should be at least 48 inches above grade measured on the side of the barrier which faces away from the swimming pool. The maximum vertical clearance between grade and the bottom of the barrier should be 4 inches measured on the side of the barrier which faces away from the swimming pool. Where the top of the pool structure is above grade, such as an aboveground pool, the barrier may be at ground level, such as the pool structure, or mounted on top of the pool structure. Where the barrier is mounted on top of the pool structure, the maximum vertical clearance between the top of the pool structure and the bottom of the barrier should be 4 inches.

2. Openings in the barrier should not allow passage of a 4-inch diameter sphere.

3. Solid barriers, which do not have openings, such as a masonry or stone wall, should not contain indentations or protrusions except for normal construction tolerances and tooled masonry joints.

4. Where the barrier is composed of horizontal and vertical members and the distance between the tops of the horizontal members is less than 45 inches, the horizontal members should be located on the swimming pool side of the fence. Spacing between vertical members should not exceed 1 3/4 inches in width. Where there are decorative cutouts, spacing within the cutouts should not exceed 1 3/4 inches in width.

5. Where the barrier is composed of horizontal and vertical members and the distance between the tops of the horizontal members is 45 inches or more, spacing between vertical members should not exceed 4 inches. Where there are decorative cutouts, spacing within the cutouts should not exceed 1 3/4 inches in width.

6. Maximum mesh size for chain link fences should not exceed 1 1/4 inch square unless the fence is provided with slats fastened at the top or the bottom which reduce the openings to no more than 1 3/4 inches.

7. Where the barrier is composed of diagonal members, such as a lattice fence, the maximum opening formed by the diagonal members should be no more than 1 3/4 inches.

8. Access gates to the pool should comply with Section I, Paragraphs 1 through 7, and should be equipped to accommodate a locking device. Pedestrian access gates should open outward, away from the pool, and should be self-closing and have a self-latching device. Gates other than pedestrian access gates should have a self-latching device. Where the release mechanism of the self-latching device is located less than 54 inches from the bottom of the gate, (a) the release mechanism should be located on the pool side of the gate at least 3 inches below the top of the gate and (b) the gate and barrier should have no opening greater than 1/2 inch within 18 inches of the release mechanism.

9. Where a wall of a dwelling serves as part of the barrier, one of the following should apply:

    (a). All doors with direct access to the pool through that wall should be equipped with an alarm which produces an audible warning when the door and its screen, if present, are opened. The alarm should sound continuously for a minimum of 30 seconds, immediately after the door is opened. The alarm should have a minimum sound pressure rating of 85 dBA at 10 feet and the sound of the alarm should be distinctive from other household sounds, such as smoke alarms, telephones, and door bells. The alarm should automatically reset under all conditions. The alarm should be equipped with manual means, such as touchpads or switches, to temporarily deactivate the alarm for a single opening of the door from either direction. Such deactivation should last for no more than 15 seconds. The deactivation touchpads or switches should be located at least 54 inches above the threshold of the door.

(b). The pool should be equipped with a power safety cover which complies with ASTM F1346-91 listed below.

(c). Other means of protection, such as self-closing doors with self-latching devices, are acceptable so long as the degree of protection afforded is not less than the protection afforded by (a) or (b) described above.

10. Where an aboveground pool structure is used as a barrier or where the barrier is mounted on top of the pool structure, and the means of access is a ladder or steps, then (a) the ladder to the pool or steps should be capable of being secured, locked or removed to prevent access, or (b) the ladder or steps should be surrounded by a barrier which meets Section I, Paragraphs 1 through 9. When the ladder or steps are secured, locked, or removed, any opening created should not allow the passage of a 4-inch diameter sphere.

Section II. Indoor Swimming Pool.

All walls surrounding an indoor swimming pool should comply with Section I, Paragraph 9.

Section III. Barrier Locations.

Barriers should be located so as to prohibit permanent structures, equipment or similar objects from being used to climb the barriers.

Exemptions

A portable spa with a safety cover which complies with ASTM F1346-91 mentioned in the following paragraph, should be exempt from the guidelines presented in this document. But, swimming pools, hot tubs, and non-portable spas with safety covers should not be exempt from the provisions of this document.

ASTM F1346-91. Standard Performance Specification for Safety Covers and Labeling Requirements for All Covers for Swimming Pools, Spas and Hot Tubs.

Chapter 32

Safe Spas, Pools, and Hot Tubs

Backyard Pool: Always Supervise Children

According to the U.S. Consumer Product Safety Commission, an estimated 260 children under five years of age drown each year in residential swimming pools and spas. The Commission estimates that another 3,000 children under age five are treated in hospital emergency rooms following submersion accidents each year. Some of these submersion accidents result in permanent brain damage.

Nationally, drowning is the fourth leading cause of death to children under five. In some states such as California, Florida and Arizona, drowning is the leading cause of accidental death to children under five.

CPSC offers the following tips for pool owners:

- Never leave a child unsupervised near a pool.

- Instruct babysitters about potential hazards to young children in and around swimming pools and the need for constant supervision.

The text in this chapter is from the following undated fact sheets produced by the Consumer Product Safety Commission, "Backyard Pools," available at http://www.cpsc.gov/cpscpub/pubs/5097.html, "Children Drown, and More are Injured from Hair Entrapment in Drain Covers," available at http://www.cpsc.gov/cpscpub/pubs/5067.html, and "Spas, Hot Tubs, and Whirlpools," available at http://www.cpsc.gov/cpscpub/pubs/5112.html; all cited July 2001.

- Completely fence the pool. Install self-closing and self-latching gates. Position latches out of reach of young children. Keep all doors and windows leading to the pool area secure to prevent small children from getting to the pool. Effective barriers and locks are necessary preventive measures, but there is no substitute for supervision.

- Do not consider young children "drown proof" because they have had swimming lessons; young children should always be watched carefully while swimming.

- Do not use flotation devices as a substitute for supervision.

- Never use a pool with its pool cover partially in place, since children may become entrapped under it. Remove the cover completely.

- Place tables and chairs well away from the pool fence to prevent children from climbing into the pool area.

- Keep toys away from the pool area because a young child playing with the toys could accidentally fall in the water.

- Remove steps to above ground pools when not in use.

- Have a telephone at poolside to avoid having to leave children unattended in or near the pool to answer a telephone elsewhere. Keep emergency numbers at the poolside telephone.

- Learn CPR (cardiopulmonary resuscitation).

- Keep rescue equipment by the pool.

Parents And Guardians: Only you can prevent a drowning. Watch your child closely at all times. Make sure doors leading to the pool area are closed and locked. Young children can quickly slip away and into the pool.

Improper Diving Practices

Diving injuries can result in quadriplegia, paralysis below the neck, to divers who hit the bottom or side of a swimming pool, according to CPSC. Divers should observe the following precautions:

- Never dive into above-ground pools. They are too shallow.

- Don't dive from the side of an in-ground pool. Enter the water feet first.

- Dive only from the end of the diving board and not from the sides.

- Dive with your hands in front of you and always steer up immediately upon entering the water to avoid hitting the bottom or sides of the pool.

- Don't dive if you have been using alcohol or drugs because your reaction time may be too slow.

- Improper use of pool slides presents the same danger as improper diving techniques. Never slide down head first-slide down feet first only.

Hair Entrapment in Drain Covers for Spas, Hot Tubs, and Whirlpool Bathtubs

Incidents, including deaths, have occurred in which people's hair was sucked into the suction fitting drain of a spa, hot tub, or whirlpool bathtub, causing the victims' heads to be held under water. The suction from drain outlets is strong enough to cause entrapment of hair or body parts, and drowning. Most accidents with drain outlets involve people with hair that is shoulder-length or longer.

Hair entrapment occurs when a bather's hair becomes entangled in a suction fitting drain cover as the water and hair are drawn powerfully through the drain. In several incidents, children were playing a "hold your breath the longest" game, leaning forward in the water and permitting their long hair to be sucked into the drain.

Here are some safety precautions to help prevent hair entrapment in your spa, hot tub, or whirlpool bathtub:

- There is a voluntary standard for drain covers (ASME/ANSI A112.19.8M-1987) that should help reduce hair entrapment. Ask your dealer about drain covers that meet this voluntary standard.

- Keep long hair away from the suction fitting drain cover. Wear a bathing cap or pin hair up if you have long hair.

- Never allow a child to play in a way that could permit the child's hair to come near the drain cover. Always supervise children around a spa, hot tub, whirlpool bathtub, wading pool, or swimming pool.

- If drain cover is missing or broken, shut down the spa until drain cover is replaced.

Spas, Hot Tubs, and Whirlpools

The U.S. Consumer Product Safety Commission (CPSC) helped develop standards to prevent hair entanglement and body part entrapment in spas, hot tubs, and whirlpools. These standards should help prevent deaths and injuries. Consumers should fix their old spas, hot tubs, and whirlpools with new, safer drain covers. CPSC warns about these hazards:

Drownings

The main hazard from hot tubs and spas is the same as that from pools—drowning. Since 1980, CPSC has reports of more than 700 deaths in spas and hot tubs. About one-third of those were drownings to children under age five. Consumers should keep a locked safety cover on the spa whenever it is not in use and keep children away unless there is constant adult supervision.

Hair Entanglement

CPSC helped develop a voluntary standard for drain covers that helps reduce the risk of hair entrapment. Consumers should be sure they have new drain covers that meet this standard. If you are not sure, call a pool or spa professional to check the spa. Never allow a child to play in a way that could permit the child's hair to come near the drain cover. If a drain cover is missing or broken, shut down the spa until the cover is replaced.

Body Part Entrapment

CPSC knows of 18 incidents since 1980 in which parts of the body have been entrapped by the strong suction of the drain of pools, wading pools, spas, and hot tubs. Of these, 10 resulted in disembowelment and 5 other people died. CPSC helped develop a standard requiring dome-shaped drain outlets and two outlets for each pump. This reduces the powerful suction if one drain is blocked. Consumers with older spas should have new drain covers installed and may want to consider getting a spa with two drains.

Hot Tub Temperatures

CPSC knows of several deaths from extremely hot water (approximately 110 degrees Fahrenheit) in a spa. High temperatures can cause drowsiness which may lead to unconsciousness, resulting in drowning. In addition, raised body temperature can lead to heat stroke and death. In 1987, CPSC helped develop requirements for temperature controls to make sure that spa water temperatures never exceed 104 degrees Fahrenheit. Pregnant women and young children should not use a spa before consulting with a physician.

CPSC Recommends These Safety Precautions when Using a Hot Tub, Spa, or Whirlpool

1. Always use a locked safety cover when the spa is not in use and keep young children away from spas or hot tubs unless there is constant adult supervision.

2. Make sure the spa has the dual drains and drain covers required by current safety standards.

3. Regularly have a professional check your spa or hot tub and make sure it is in good, safe working condition, and that drain covers are in place and not cracked or missing. Check the drain covers yourself throughout the year.

4. Know where the cut-off switch for your pump is so you can turn it off in an emergency.

5. Be aware that consuming alcohol while using a spa could lead to drowning.

6. Keep the temperature of the water in the spa at 104 degrees Fahrenheit or below.

Chapter 33

Safety Tips for Flood Victims

The U.S. Consumer Product Safety Commission (CPSC) recommends several safety tips to the victims of floods. This chapter illustrates some dangerous practices which consumers may be tempted to engage in during efforts to rebuild or while staying in temporary housing, tents, or partially damaged homes. This information is provided in an effort to prevent injuries and deaths from consumer products as flood survivors make new beginnings.

For more disaster-related information or help with emergency preparedness, visit the Federal Emergency Management Agency (FEMA).

Electricity and Water Don't Mix

Do not use electrical appliances that have been wet. Water can damage the motors in electrical appliances, such as furnaces, freezers, refrigerators, washing machines, and dryers.

If electrical appliances have been under water, have them dried out and reconditioned by a qualified service repairman. Do not turn on damaged electrical appliances because the electrical parts can become grounded and pose an electric shock hazard or overheat and cause a fire. Before flipping a switch or plugging in an appliance, have an electrician check the house wiring and appliance to make sure it is safe to use.

"Safety Tips for Flood Victims," an undated fact sheet produced by the Consumer Product Safety Commission, available online at http://www.cpsc.gov/cpscpub/pubs/fema/flood.html; cited July 2001.

Use a ground fault circuit interrupter (GFCI) to help prevent electrocutions and electrical shock injuries. Portable GFCIs require no tools to install and are available at prices ranging from $12 to $30.

To Prevent a Gas Explosion and Fire, Have Gas Appliances (Natural Gas And LP Gas) Inspected and Cleaned after Flooding

If gas appliances have been under water, have them inspected and cleaned and their gas controls replaced. The gas company or a qualified appliance repair person or plumber should do this work. Water can damage gas controls so that safety features are blocked, even if the gas controls appear to operate properly. If you suspect a gas leak, don't light a match, use any electrical appliance, turn lights on or off, or use the phone. These may produce sparks. Sniff for gas leaks, starting at the water heater. If you smell gas or hear gas escaping, turn off the main valve, open windows, leave the area immediately, and call the gas company or a qualified appliance repair person or plumber for repairs. Never store flammable materials near any gas appliance or equipment.

Check to Make Sure Your Smoke Detector Is Functioning

Smoke detectors can save your life in a fire. Check the battery frequently to make sure it is operating. Fire extinguishers also are a good idea.

Gasoline Is Made to Explode!

Never use gasoline around ignition sources such as cigarettes, matches, lighters, water heaters, or electric sparks. Gasoline vapors can travel and be ignited by pilot light or other ignition sources. Make sure that gasoline powered generators are away from easily combustible materials.

Chain Saws Can Cause Serious Injuries

Chain saws can be hazardous, especially if they "kick back." To help reduce this hazard, make sure that your chain saw in equipped with the low-kickback chain. Look for other safety features on chain saws, including hand guard, safety tip, chain brake, vibration reduction system, spark arrestor on gasoline models, trigger or throttle lock-out, chain catcher, and bumper spikes. Always wear shoes, gloves, and protective glasses. On new saws, look for certification to the ANSI B-175.1 standard.

When Cleaning Up from a Flood, Store Medicines and Chemicals Away from Young Children

Poisonings can happen when young children swallow medicines and household chemicals.

Keep household chemicals and medicines locked up away from children. Use the child resistant closures that come on most medicines and chemicals.

Burning Charcoal Gives Off Carbon Monoxide. Carbon Monoxide Has No Odor and Can Kill You

Never burn charcoal inside homes, tents, campers, vans, cars, trucks, garages, or mobile homes.

WARNING! Submerged Gas Control Valves, Circuit Breakers, and Fuses Pose Explosion and Fire Hazard!

Replace all gas control valves, circuit breakers, and fuses that have been under water. Gas control valves on furnaces, water heaters, and other gas appliances that have been under water are unfit for continued use. If they are used, they could cause a fire or an explosion. Silt and corrosion from flood water can damage internal components of control valves and prevent proper operation. Gas can leak and result in an explosion or fire. Replace ALL gas control valves that have been under water.

Electric Circuit Breakers and Fuses Can Malfunction When Water and Silt Get Inside.

Discard ALL circuit breakers and fuses that have been submerged.

Part Five

Choking, Strangulation, and Suffocation Hazards

Chapter 34

Choking Hazards

Preventing Choking among Infants and Young Children

Many infants and children die each year from choking. These deaths can be prevented if parents and care givers watch their children more closely and keep dangerous toys, foods, and household items out of their reach.

Tips for Preventing Choking

If you are the parent or care giver of an infant or child under 4 years old, follow these tips from the American Academy of Pediatrics, the American Red Cross, and the Centers for Disease Control and Prevention (CDC) to reduce the chances of choking.

At Mealtime

- Insist that your children eat at the table, or at least sitting down. Watch young children while they eat. Encourage them to eat slowly and chew their food well.

The text in this chapter is from the following undated fact sheets produced by the Consumer Product Safety Commission, "Dangers with Infant Rattles," available at http://www.cpsc.gov/cpscpub/pubs/5070.html, "Choking on Small Balls Can Be Fatal to Young Children," available at http://www.cpsc.gov/cpscpub/pubs/5075.html, and "Infants Can Choke on Plastic Decals," available at http://www.cpsc.gov/cpscpub/pubs/5083.html; all cited July 2001; and "Preventing Choking among Infants and Young Children," produced by Centers for Disease Control and Prevention (CDC), 2001.

- Cut up foods that are firm and round and can get stuck in your child's airway, such as:

    hotdogs-always cut hotdogs length-wise and then into small pieces

    grapes-cut them into quarters

    raw vegetables-cut them into small strips or pieces that are not round

- Other foods that can pose a choking hazard include:

    hard or sticky candy, like whole peppermints or caramels

    nuts and seeds (don't give peanuts to children under age 7)

    popcorn

    spoonfuls of peanut butter

During Playtime

- Follow the age recommendations on toy packages. Any toy that is small enough to fit through a 11/4-inch circle or is smaller than 21/4 inches long is unsafe for children under 4 years old.

- Don't allow young children to play with toys designed for older children. Teach older children to put their toys away as soon as they finish playing so young siblings can't get them.

- Frequently check under furniture and between cushions for dangerous items young children could find, including:

    coins

    marbles

    watch batteries (the ones that look like buttons)

    pen or marker caps

    cars with small rubber wheels that come off

    small balls or foam balls that can be compressed to a size small enough to fit in a child's mouth

- Never let your child play with or chew on uninflated or broken latex balloons. Many young children have died from swallowing or inhaling them.

- Don't let your small child play on bean bag chairs made with small foam pellets. If the bag opens or rips, the child could inhale these tiny pieces.

If you're a parent, grandparent, or other care giver, learn how to help a choking child and how to perform CPR in case of an emergency.

Who Is Affected?

More than 2,800 people die each year from choking; many of them are children. According to one study, nearly two-thirds of the children who choked to death during a 20-year period were 3 years old or younger.

The majority of choking deaths are caused by toys and household items. One study found that nearly 70 percent of choking deaths among children age 3 and under were caused by toys and other products made for children. According to CDC, balloons account for 7 to 10 deaths a year. And the U.S. Consumer Product Safety Commission has received reports of five deaths from bean bag chairs, resulting from children choking on the small foam pellets inside.

The most common cause of nonfatal choking incidents is food. In one study, nearly 70 percent of choking cases presented in the emergency department were caused by foods such as hotdogs, nuts, and vegetable and fruit pieces.

Dangers with Infant Rattles

The U.S. Consumer Product Safety Commission (CPSC) is concerned about several rattles recently sold as novelty items or decorations for cakes, gifts, floral arrangements, etc., which do not meet the safety requirements the Commission has established for rattles. These novelty rattles are small enough to enter an infant's mouth and become lodged in the back of the throat. To prevent choking accidents, CPSC urges consumers to discard these hazardous rattles.

In 1978, after receiving reports of several choking deaths involving children's rattles, CPSC established safety requirements which all rattles must meet. The regulations require that rattles be large enough so that they cannot enter an infant's mouth and become lodged in the back of the throat, and be constructed so they will not separate into small pieces which can be swallowed or inhaled.

While all rattles intended for children must meet these regulations, the CPSC has become aware of some non-complying rattles which have been sold recently as party favors or as decorations on gifts, floral arrangements, cakes, etc. These rattles could be removed and given to infants, although they do not meet the safety requirements the CPSC has established. Distributors have been advised that these rattles are banned; they have stopped selling the rattles and have begun recalling them from retailers. CPSC is concerned, however, about the possibility of children choking on rattles that may still be in consumers' hands.

Check all rattles carefully before giving them to a child. An infant's mouth is extremely pliable and can stretch to hold larger shapes than one might expect. To test rattles for minimum permissible size, CPSC uses a device which has an oval opening that measures approximately 1-3/8 inches (35mm) by 2 inches (50mm), and is 1-3/16 inches (30mm) deep. Any portion of a rattle, such as its handle, which passes through this opening is small enough to enter an infant's mouth and become lodged in the back of the throat. To reduce the chance of a choking accident, parents should choose rattles which are at least as large, and preferably larger, than these dimensions.

Choking on Small Balls Can be Fatal to Young Children

During a recent one-year period, CPSC received reports of 7 deaths of children involving small balls. The youngest child was 10 months old. Due to the small size of the balls they can easily become lodged in the airway of young children.

Caregivers are warned that young or handicapped children can choke on these small balls and that they should not be available to them. Care should also be taken to assure that older children don't play with small balls around younger siblings.

Since these small balls are found in many types of retail establishments, in vending machines, and some games intended for older children, caregivers should be aware of the choking hazard and keep all such small balls away from children who may have a tendency to put them into their mouths.

The packages and vending machines containing small balls, with a diameter of 1.75 inches, must be labeled with the following cautionary statement:

WARNING: CHOKING HAZARD—This toy is a small ball. Not for children under 3 yrs.

Infants Can Choke on Plastic Decals from Baby Walkers and Other Products

The U.S. Consumer Product Safety Commission (CPSC) knows of incidents in which young children peeled off and choked on plastic labels and decals from baby walkers. The CPSC also has reports of young children choking on plastic labels and decals from other products. Fortunately none of these incidents resulted in deaths but the potential exists for a tragedy to occur.

Parents and other child care providers are strongly urged to pull off and throw away all plastic labels and decals from baby walkers and other juvenile products to prevent choking. However, do not remove permanent paper warning labels. Parents also should throw away loose plastic labels and decals from other products to which the children may have access.

Chapter 35

Strangulation Hazards of Toys

Strangulation with Crib Toys

Crib gyms, exercisers, kickers, and similar toys are attractive additions to a child's environment, but they are DANGEROUS as well. The risk of strangulation begins when children are just starting to push up on hands and knees, usually about 5 months old. These children can pull themselves up to a hanging crib toy and become entangled or fall forward over it; but they cannot disentangle themselves, support their own weight, or lift themselves off the toy. The results can be injury or death.

Completely remove such toys from the crib or playpen. Do not merely untie one end and allow the toy to dangle because strangulation is still a possibility.

Remove all crib toys which are strung across crib or playpen area when your child is beginning to push up on hands and knees or is 5 months of age, whichever comes earliest.

Strings and Straps on Toys Can Strangle Young Children

Strings and straps on toys, such as toy guitar straps, can strangle a young child if they become twisted around the neck. CPSC knows

The text in this chapter is from the following undated fact sheets produced by the Consumer Product Safety Commission, "CPSC Warns of Strangulation with Crib Toys," available at http://www.cpsc.gov/cpscpub/pubs/5024.html, and "Strings and Straps on Toys Can Strangle Young Children," available at http://www.cpsc.gov/cpscpub/pubs/5100.html; both cited July 2001.

of several incidents where a toy strap twisted around a child's neck. The children were primarily under the age of three.

Strangulation deaths have resulted from necklaces, cords, or ribbons being wrapped around a child's neck.

Parents should never give young children toys with cords, strings, or straps that fit around the neck. Only a few pounds of force on the neck's blood vessels can cause strangulation. Most young children cannot untwist a cord or strap.

To prevent strangulation, parents should cut off the cords, strings, and straps on toy guitars or other toys given to young children. Give toys with straps only to older children.

Chapter 36

Strangulation Dangers in the Home

Wall Decorations with Ribbons and Streamers Can Be Hazardous

Children can strangle if they become entangled in ribbons or streamers hanging from wall decorations near the crib or within reach of children. CPSC knows of incidents involving young children who became entangled in the ribbons of a wall decoration. The padded fabric wall decoration was hung near the crib where the child could reach the ribbons and streamers on the decoration.

Parents should keep wall decorations with ribbons or streamers away from cribs and well out of reach where children play to prevent entanglement and strangulation.

Window Covering Cords

The U.S. Consumer Product Safety Commission (CPSC) and the Window Covering Safety Council are joining with major manufacturers, importers, and retailers across the United States to warn parents and caregivers that young children can become entangled and strangle in pull cords- for window coverings. CPSC is aware of at least

The text in this chapter if from the following undated fact sheets produced by the Consumer Product Safety Commission, "Children Can Strangle When They Become Entangled in Wall Decorations," available at http://www.cpsc.gov/cpscpub/pubs/5105.html, and "Children Can Strangle in Window Covering Cords," available at http://www.cpsc.gov/cpscpub/pubs/5114; both cited July 2001.

194 deaths since 1981. With the continuing number of strangulation deaths, CPSC is reissuing this warning which was first issued in 1985.

Window covering cords are one of the products most frequently associated with strangulation of children under five. The younger victims, usually between 10 to 15 months of age, typically are in cribs which have been placed near window covering pull cords.

Although a few older children, usually from two to four years old, find cords hanging near the floor, most of these victims become entangled in cords while climbing on furniture to look out the window. Entanglement and strangulation can occur when a child is alone in a room for only a short time. The CPSC and the Window Covering Safety Council urge parents to eliminate the loop in two-corded horizontal blinds, and pleated and cellular shades by using any of the following technical fixes:

Horizontal Blinds

Cut the cord above the tassel, remove the equalizer buckle, and add a separate tassel at the end of each cord, or cut the cord above the tassel, remove the equalizer buckle, and add a breakaway tassel which will separate if a child becomes entangled in the loop.

Pleated or Cellular Shades

Leave the cord stop near the headrail in place. Cut the cord above the tassel and add a separate tassel at the end of each cord. Warning: When shades are raised, a loop will appear above the cord stop. Keep cord out of the reach of children.

Vertical Blinds, Continuous Loop Systems, and Drapery Cords

Install a cord tie-down device. Permanently attach and use the tie-down to floor, wall, or window jamb.

Keep all window covering cords out of the reach of children. Unless the cords can be completely removed from a child's reach, including when a child climbs on furniture, CPSC recommends against knotting or tying the cords together which creates a new loop for a child to become entangled.

CPSC also recommends that when you install window coverings, adjust the cords to their shortest length possible. When you order new custom window coverings, specify that you want a short cord.

Chapter 37

Suffocation Hazards

Suffocating with Plastic Bags

The U.S. Consumer Product Safety Commission (CPSC) has received an average of about 25 reports a year describing deaths to children who suffocated due to plastic bags. Almost 90 percent of them were under one year of age. Recent reports often describe bags originally used for dry cleaning or storage. Some may have been used to protect bedding and furniture, and others just were not carefully discarded.

Most dry cleaning bags and some other plastic bags bear a voluntary label such as:

"Warning: To avoid danger of suffocation, keep this plastic bag away from babies and children. Do not use this bag in cribs, beds, carriages or playpens. The plastic bag could block nose and mouth and prevent breathing. This bag is not a toy."

Text in this chapter is from the following undated fact sheets produced by the Consumer Product Safety Commission, "Children Still Suffocating with Plastic Bags," available at http://www.cpsc.gov/cpscpub/pubs/5064.html, "Suffocation Danger Associated with Children's Balloons," available at http://www.cpsc.gov/cpscpub/pubs/5087.html, "Dangers with Toy Chest Lids," available at http://www.cpsc.gov/cpscpub/pubs/5099.html, "Suffocation and Death of Children in Old Refrigerators," available at http://www.cpsc.gov/cpscpub/pubs/5072.html, and "Soft Bedding May Be Hazardous to Babies," available at http://www.cpsc.gov/cpscpub/pubs/5049.html; all cited July 2001.

The CPSC has reports of children suffocating with plastic bags in cases like these:

- Child pulled plastic dry-cleaning bag over face while lying on adult bed.

- Plastic garbage bag (filled with clothes) fell over victim's face and mouth while victim was on adult bed.

- Child crawled into plastic garbage bag.

- Child rolled off mattress onto plastic bag filled with clothes.

- Child slept on mattress covered by plastic bag.

Never put children to sleep on or near plastic bags.

Suffocation Danger Associated with Children's Balloons

Of all children's products, balloons are the leading cause of suffocation death, according to CPSC injury data. Since 1973, more than 110 children have died as a result of suffocation involving uninflated balloons or pieces of balloons. Most of the victims were under six years of age, but the CPSC does know of several older children who have suffocated on balloons.

Accidents involving balloons tend to occur in two ways. Some children have sucked uninflated balloons into their mouths, often while attempting to inflate them. This can occur when a child who is blowing up the balloon inhales or takes a breath to prepare for the next blow, and draws the balloon back into the mouth and throat. Some deaths may have resulted when children swallowed uninflated balloons they were sucking or chewing on. The CPSC knows of one case in which a child was chewing on an uninflated balloon when she fell from a swing. The child hit the ground and, in a reflex action, inhaled sharply. She suffocated on the balloon.

The second kind of accident involves balloon pieces. Children have drawn pieces of broken balloons that they were playing with into their throats. If a balloon breaks and is not discarded, for example, some children may continue to play with it, chewing on pieces of the balloon or attempting to stretch it across their mouths and suck or blow bubbles in it. These balloon pieces are easily sucked into the throat and lungs. Balloons mold to the throat and lungs and can completely block breathing.

Because of the danger of suffocation, the CPSC recommends that parents and guardians do not allow children under the age of eight to play with uninflated balloons without supervision. The CPSC does not believe that a completely inflated balloon presents a hazard to young children. If the balloon breaks, however, CPSC recommends that parents immediately collect the pieces of the broken balloon and dispose of them out of the reach of young children.

Dangers with Toy Chest Lids

The U.S. Consumer Product Safety Commission (CPSC) knows of 45 children who died when lids of containers used for toy storage fell on their heads or necks. There have been at least three incidents of permanent brain damage. Many deaths involved products specifically manufactured as toy boxes or chests, although children have died in other containers used for toy storage, such as trunks, footlockers, decorator cubes, and blanket chests. Fatal suffocation incidents have also happened when children climbed into storage containers such as cedar chests to play or hide and became trapped.

Typically, accidents occurred when children used the chest to pull themselves up, causing the lid to fall from the upright, open position, and when young children attempted to open the lids themselves. Children were reaching over and into the chest when the lid dropped and either fell on their heads or trapped them at the neck between the lid and the edge of the toy chest.

Parents and guardians of young children should avoid any toy chest or other container which has a hinged lid that can fall freely.

Open chests or bins which have no lids; chests with lightweight, removable lids; or chests with sliding doors or panels will not present the risk of a falling lid. If they do choose a new toy chest with a vertically opening lid, parents should look for a chest which uses a lid support that will hold the lid open in any position in which it is placed. Parents should check the support provided to make sure that it does, in fact, prevent the lid from falling.

If you already own a chest or trunk that has a freely falling, hinged lid, the lid should be completely removed to avert possible tragedy. Alternatively, parents may wish to install a lid support which will hold the lid open in any position. Once a support is installed, it is important to check it frequently to make certain that it is working properly. Some supports may need to be adjusted or tightened periodically so that they continue to hold the lid open.

Suffocation and Death of Children in Old Refrigerators

The U.S. Consumer Product Safety Commission (CPSC) urges that all unused old-style refrigerators around the home be rendered "childproof" or, if on public property, appropriate authorities be called to safely dispose of the products. CPSC continues to receive reports about the tragic deaths of young children who are suffocated because of entrapment in old refrigerators.

The Refrigerator Safety Act was enacted August 2, 1956. The Act's regulations which became effective October 30, 1958 require a mechanism (usually a magnetic latch) which enables the door to be opened from the inside in the event of accidental entrapment. This type of latch, therefore, makes the hazardous refrigerators manufactured before that date easy to identify. The serious entrapment hazard occurs when children, during play, climb inside the old abandoned or carelessly stored refrigerators to hide. Many of these refrigerators are still in use, and when they are carelessly discarded or stored where they are accessible to children, they become a danger.

Double deaths are not uncommon because children naturally enjoy playing together, and old refrigerators provide an interesting place to play. However, when the door slams shut, it is dark and the normally innocent and familiar refrigerator becomes a death trap. Suffocation then ensues because the tight fitting gasket, which is on the inside of the door to seal in the cold, cuts off the child's air. This along with the insulated construction of a refrigerator also prevents the children's screams for help from being heard.

There are several ways to "childproof" these old discarded refrigerators. The surest method is to take off the door completely and in most cases this is a simple process using a screwdriver. If the door will not come off, chain and padlock the door permanently and tightly closed. A third alternative is to remove or disable the latch completely so the door will no longer lock when closed. A wooden block screwed to the door to keep it from closing is also a possibility. Another helpful deterrent is to leave the shelves in the refrigerator to discourage children from getting inside. It is unlawful in many local jurisdictions to discard old refrigerators without first removing the door.

Old electric refrigerators are not the only killer of children. Self-locking ice refrigerators can also present a suffocation hazard to small children because they cannot be opened from the inside.

Soft Bedding May Be Hazardous to Babies

To prevent infant deaths due to soft bedding, the U.S. Consumer Product Safety Commission, the American Academy of Pediatrics, and the National Institute of Child Health and Human Development are revising their recommendations on safe bedding practices when putting infants down to sleep. Here are the revised recommendations to follow for infants under 12 months:

A Safe Sleeping Environment for Your Baby: Safe Bedding Practices For Infants

- Place baby on his/her back on a firm tight-fitting mattress in a crib that meets current safety standards.

- Remove pillows, quilts, comforters, sheepskins, stuffed toys, and other soft products from the crib.

- Consider using a sleeper or other sleep clothing as an alternative to blankets, with no other covering.

- If using a blanket, put baby with feet at the foot of the crib. Tuck a thin blanket around the crib mattress, reaching only as far as the baby's chest.

- Make sure your baby's head remains uncovered during sleep.

- Do not place baby on a waterbed, sofa, soft mattress, pillow, or other soft surface to sleep.

Placing babies to sleep on their backs instead of their stomachs has been associated with a dramatic decrease in deaths from Sudden Infant Death Syndrome (SIDS). Babies have been found dead on their stomachs with their faces, noses, and mouths covered by soft bedding, such as pillows, quilts, comforters and sheepskins. However, some babies have been found dead with their heads covered by soft bedding even while sleeping on their backs.

Part Six

Other Household Hazards

Chapter 38

Cordless Telephones and Hearing Loss Hazards

The U.S. Consumer Product Safety Commission (CPSC) and the Electronic Industries Association (EIA), recently issued a joint consumer alert urging owners of "cordless" or portable telephones to exercise caution when using the product. Cordless telephones offer the user the convenience of placing or receiving calls in their home or in the immediate vicinity outside their home. The CPSC and EIA, however, caution users always to place the phone in the talk position before moving the telephone to their ear. Otherwise, they may be exposed to a loud and possibly painful ring.

Since December 1982, the CPSC has received over 20 consumer complaints about the loud sound which is made when the telephone rings or when someone near the base station of these telephones presses the intercom or page button while the handset is close to the user's ear.

Several of these complaints, including some from physicians, claim that some loss of hearing has resulted from the loudness of the ring.

Currently most cordless telephones are designed so that the ring or page signal comes through the earphone of the unit. From the information provided in the complaints it is clear that the users were not expecting their telephone to ring and had placed it against or near their ear without placing the phone in the talk position. In at least one case the user was preparing to place a call when the phone rang

"Alert on Cordless Telephones," an undated fact sheet produced by the Consumer Product Safety Commission, available online at http://www.cpsc.gov/cpscpub/pubs/5023.html; cited July 2001.

unexpectedly. Some users have encountered unexpected ringing of the cordless telephone while they were first learning to use it or while the telephone was being used by someone otherwise unfamiliar with its operation.

People who now have one of these telephones in their home or office should be sure that everyone using the product is thoroughly familiar with its proper operation. Carefully read any user manual or instructions provided with the telephone at the time of purchase. Also, provide assistance to children or visitors in the home or office who may use the cordless telephone.

A number of manufacturers and distributors of cordless telephones who are members of EIA have been attaching labels to their products alerting the user about the loud ring. These labels and accompanying information in the telephone's user manuals or instructions direct users to place the phone in the talk position before moving the handset to the ear.

Chapter 39

Preventing Window Falls

Every year, thousands of young children are killed or injured in falls from windows. To help prevent these tragedies, take the following actions—especially for windows in bedrooms.

- Safeguard your windows with window guards or window stops.

  Install window guards to prevent children from falling out of windows. (For windows on the 6th floor and below, install window guards that adults and older children can open easily in case of fire.)

  Install window stops so that windows open no more than 4 inches.

- Never depend on screens to keep children from falling out of windows.

- Whenever possible, open windows from the top—not the bottom.

- Keep furniture away from windows, to discourage children from climbing near windows.

"Preventing Window Falls," an undated fact sheet produced by the Consumer Product Safety Commission, available online at http://www.cpsc.gov/cpscpub/pubs/5124.html; cited July 2001.

Chapter 40

Child Accidents in Recliner Chairs

The Consumer Product Safety Commission (CPSC) is concerned about possible accidental death or injury to young children using or playing on recliner chairs. Since January 1980, the CPSC has received reports of 8 deaths and several serious brain injuries to children involving recliner chairs.

Information available to the CPSC about the accidents shows the victims:

- were between the ages of 12 months and 5 years;

- were usually unsupervised at the time of the accident;

- were apparently climbing or playing on the leg rest of the chair while the chair was in a reclined position;

- were trapped when their heads entered the opening between the chair seat and the leg rest as their own body weight forced the leg rest down.

After receiving this information from CPSC, the recliner chair industry established voluntary guidelines that called for improvements in new recliner chairs. These guidelines specify:

"Child Accidents in Recliner Chairs," an undated fact sheet produced by the Consumer Product Safety Commission, available online at http://www.cpsc.gov/cpscpub/pubs/5071.html; cited July 2001.

1. that a device(s) will be installed that will reduce the opening created between the leg rest and seat cushion when the chair is in the reclined position

2. that the following caution be attached to all recliner chairs

   "**CAUTION:** DO NOT ALLOW CHILDREN TO PLAY ON THIS MECHANIZED FURNITURE OR OPERATE THE MECHANISM. LEG REST FOLDS DOWN ON CLOSING SO THAT A CHILD COULD POSSIBLY BE INJURED. ALWAYS LEAVE IN AN UPRIGHT AND CLOSED POSITION. KEEP HANDS AND FEET CLEAR OF MECHANISM. ONLY THE OCCUPANT SHOULD OPERATE IT."

Consumers who have the older design of recliner chairs in their homes are urged to use appropriate precautions in preventing young children from playing on these chairs. Consumers who are shopping for new recliner chairs should look for chairs that meet the voluntary industry guidelines.

Chapter 41

Mobile Folding Tables Can Be Hazardous

Children cannot safely move mobile folding tables commonly found in school cafeterias and meeting rooms. The tall heavy tables can tip-over and seriously injure or kill a child.

Several deaths and injuries to children in schools when these tables tipped over while being moved in their folded positions, have been reported. The tables are about 6 feet tall and may weigh up to 350 pounds. Some of the tables have benches or seats attached. The tables are on wheels so they can be moved and then unfolded when in the desired location. Most of the accidents happened during after-school or non-school sponsored activities. The tables overturned when the wheel or bottom edge of the table apparently hit a child's foot or when the child attempted to ride on the table while it was being moved. Typically, two children were moving the table, one child pulling and the other pushing. The child pulling was the one injured or killed.

To avoid injuries and deaths from the tip-over of folded tables, school administrators and those supervising after school or non-school activities, such as scouting organization meetings, and social and church group meetings, should follow these safety rules:

- Do not allow children to move the folded tables. Only adults should move them.

"Children Should Not Move or Play with Mobile Folding Tables," an un-dated fact sheet produced by the Consumer Product Safety Commission, available online at http://www.cpsc.gov/cpscpub/pubs/5062.html; cited July 2001.

- Do not allow the children to play with the folded tables.

- Keep children away from the tables while they are being moved. Once the tables start to fall, it is difficult to stop them.

The Consumer Product Safety Commission is reviewing the safety of folding tables. Some manufacturers of mobile folding tables have provided, or will soon provide, warning labels to be affixed to the tables. In the meantime, if folding tables do not have warning labels, we suggest that each table be prominently labeled with the above safety rules.

Part Seven

Indoor Air Quality

Chapter 42

A Guide to Indoor Air Quality

Indoor Air Quality Concerns

All of us face a variety of risks to our health as we go about our day-to-day lives. Driving in cars, flying in planes, engaging in recreational activities, and being exposed to environmental pollutants all pose varying degrees of risk. Some risks are simply unavoidable. Some we choose to accept because to do otherwise would restrict our ability to lead our lives the way we want. And some are risks we might decide to avoid if we had the opportunity to make informed choices. Indoor air pollution is one risk that you can do something about.

In the last several years, a growing body of scientific evidence has indicated that the air within homes and other buildings can be more seriously polluted than the outdoor air in even the largest and most industrialized cities. Other research indicates that people spend approximately 90 percent of their time indoors. Thus, for many people, the risks to health may be greater due to exposure to air pollution indoors than outdoors.

In addition, people who may be exposed to indoor air pollutants for the longest periods of time are often those most susceptible to the effects of indoor air pollution. Such groups include the young, the elderly, and the chronically ill, especially those suffering from respiratory or cardiovascular disease.

"A Guide to Indoor Air Quality," an undated fact sheet produced by the Consumer Product Safety Commission, available online at http://www.cpsc.gov/cpscpub/pubs/450.html; cited July 2001.

While pollutant levels from individual sources may not pose a significant health risk by themselves, most homes have more than one source that contributes to indoor air pollution. There can be a serious risk from the cumulative effects of these sources. Fortunately, there are steps that most people can take both to reduce the risk from existing sources and to prevent new problems from occurring.

Because so many people spend a lot of time in offices with mechanical heating, cooling, and ventilation systems, there is also a short section on the causes of poor air quality in offices and what you can do if you suspect that your office may have a problem.

Indoor Air Quality in Your Home

What Causes Indoor Air Problems?

Indoor pollution sources that release gases or particles into the air are the primary cause of indoor air quality problems in homes. Inadequate ventilation can increase indoor pollutant levels by not bringing in enough outdoor air to dilute emissions from indoor sources and by not carrying indoor air pollutants out of the home. High temperature and humidity levels can also increase concentrations of some pollutants.

Pollutant Sources

There are many sources of indoor air pollution in any home. These include combustion sources such as oil, gas, kerosene, coal, wood, and tobacco products; building materials and furnishings as diverse as deteriorated, asbestos-containing insulation, wet or damp carpet, and cabinetry or furniture made of certain pressed wood products; products for household cleaning and maintenance, personal care, or hobbies; central heating and cooling systems and humidification devices; and outdoor sources such as radon, pesticides, and outdoor air pollution.

The relative importance of any single source depends on how much of a given pollutant it emits and how hazardous those emissions are. In some cases, factors such as how old the source is and whether it is properly maintained are significant. For example, an improperly adjusted gas stove can emit significantly more carbon monoxide than one that is properly adjusted.

Some sources, such as building materials, furnishings, and household products like air fresheners, release pollutants more or less continuously. Other sources, related to activities carried out in the home, release pollutants intermittently. These include smoking, the use of unvented or malfunctioning stoves, furnaces, or space heaters, the use of solvents in cleaning and hobby activities, the use of paint strippers in redecorating activities, and the use of cleaning products and pesticides in housekeeping. High pollutant concentrations can remain in the air for long periods after some of these activities.

Amount of Ventilation

If too little outdoor air enters a home, pollutants can accumulate to levels that can pose health and comfort problems. Unless they are built with special mechanical means of ventilation, homes that are designed and constructed to minimize the amount of outdoor air that can "leak" into and out of the home may have higher pollutant levels than other homes. However, because some weather conditions can drastically reduce the amount of outdoor air that enters a home, pollutants can build up even in homes that are normally considered "leaky."

How Does Outdoor Air Enter a House?

Outdoor air enters and leaves a house by: infiltration, natural ventilation, and mechanical ventilation. In a process known as infiltration, outdoor air flows into the house through openings, joints, and cracks in walls, floors, and ceilings, and around windows and doors. In natural ventilation, air moves through opened windows and doors. Air movement associated with infiltration and natural ventilation is caused by air temperature differences between indoors and outdoors and by wind. Finally, there are a number of mechanical ventilation devices, from outdoor-vented fans that intermittently remove air from a single room, such as bathrooms and kitchen, to air handling systems that use fans and duct work to continuously remove indoor air and distribute filtered and conditioned outdoor air to strategic points throughout the house. The rate at which outdoor air replaces indoor air is described as the air exchange rate. When there is little infiltration, natural ventilation, or mechanical ventilation, the air exchange rate is low and pollutant levels can increase.

What If You Live in an Apartment?

Apartments can have the same indoor air problems as single-family homes because many of the pollution sources, such as the interior building materials, furnishings, and household products, are similar.

Indoor air problems similar to those in offices are caused by such sources as contaminated ventilation systems, improperly placed outdoor air intakes, or maintenance activities.

Solutions to air quality problems in apartments, as in homes and offices, involve such actions as: eliminating or controlling the sources of pollution, increasing ventilation, and installing air cleaning devices. Often a resident can take the appropriate action to improve the indoor air quality by removing a source, altering an activity, unblocking an air supply vent, or opening a window to temporarily increase the ventilation; in other cases, however, only the building owner or manager is in a position to remedy the problem. You can encourage building management to follow guidance in EPA and NIOSH's *Building Air Quality: A Guide for Building Owners and Facility Managers*.

Improving the Air Quality in Your Home

Indoor Air and Your Health

Health effects from indoor air pollutants may be experienced soon after exposure or, possibly, years later.

Immediate effects may show up after a single exposure or repeated exposures. These include irritation of the eyes, nose, and throat, headaches, dizziness, and fatigue. Such immediate effects are usually short-term and treatable. Sometimes the treatment is simply eliminating the person's exposure to the source of the pollution, if it can be identified. Symptoms of some diseases, including asthma, hypersensitivity pneumonitis, and humidifier fever, may also show up soon after exposure to some indoor air pollutants.

The likelihood of immediate reactions to indoor air pollutants depends on several factors. Age and preexisting medical conditions are two important influences. In other cases, whether a person reacts to a pollutant depends on individual sensitivity, which varies tremendously from person to person. Some people can become sensitized to biological pollutants after repeated exposures, and it appears that some people can become sensitized to chemical pollutants as well.

Certain immediate effects are similar to those from colds or other viral diseases, so it is often difficult to determine if the symptoms are a result of exposure to indoor air pollution. For this reason, it is important to pay attention to the time and place the symptoms occur. If the symptoms fade or go away when a person is away from the home and return when the person returns, an effort should be made to identify indoor air sources that may be possible causes. Some effects may be made worse by an inadequate supply of outdoor air or from the heating, cooling, or humidity conditions prevalent in the home.

Other health effects may show up either years after exposure has occurred or only after long or repeated periods of exposure. These effects, which include some respiratory diseases, heart disease, and cancer, can be severely debilitating or fatal. It is prudent to try to improve the indoor air quality in your home even if symptoms are not noticeable.

While pollutants commonly found in indoor air are responsible for many harmful effects, there is considerable uncertainty about what concentrations or periods of exposure are necessary to produce specific health problems. People also react very differently to exposure to indoor air pollutants. Further research is needed to better understand which health effects occur after exposure to the average pollutant concentrations found in homes and which occur from the higher concentrations that occur for short periods of time.

Identifying Air Quality Problems

Some health effects can be useful indicators of an indoor air quality problem, especially if they appear after a person moves to a new residence, remodels or refurnishes a home, or treats a home with pesticides. If you think that you have symptoms that may be related to your home environment, discuss them with your doctor or your local health department to see if they could be caused by indoor air pollution. You may also want to consult a board-certified allergist or an occupational medicine specialist for answers to your questions.

Another way to judge whether your home has or could develop indoor air problems is to identify potential sources of indoor air pollution. Although the presence of such sources does not necessarily mean that you have an indoor air quality problem, being aware of the type and number of potential sources is an important step toward assessing the air quality in your home.

A third way to decide whether your home may have poor indoor air quality is to look at your lifestyle and activities. Human activities can be significant sources of indoor air pollution. Finally, look for signs of problems with the ventilation in your home. Signs that can indicate your home may not have enough ventilation include moisture condensation on windows or walls, smelly or stuffy air, dirty central heating and air cooling equipment, and areas where books, shoes, or other items become moldy. To detect odors in your home, step outside

297

for a few minutes, and then upon reentering your home, note whether odors are noticeable.

Measuring Pollutant Levels

The federal government recommends that you measure the level of radon in your home. Without measurements there is no way to tell whether radon is present because it is a colorless, odorless, radioactive gas. Inexpensive devices are available for measuring radon. EPA provides guidance as to risks associated with different levels of exposure and when the public should consider corrective action. There are specific mitigation techniques that have proven effective in reducing levels of radon in the home.

For pollutants other than radon, measurements are most appropriate when there are either health symptoms or signs of poor ventilation and specific sources or pollutants have been identified as possible causes of indoor air quality problems. Testing for many pollutants can be expensive.

Before monitoring your home for pollutants besides radon, consult your state or local health department or professionals who have experience in solving indoor air quality problems in nonindustrial buildings.

Weatherizing Your Home

The federal government recommends that homes be weatherized in order to reduce the amount of energy needed for heating and cooling. While weatherization is underway, however, steps should also be taken to minimize pollution from sources inside the home.

In addition, residents should be alert to the emergence of signs of inadequate ventilation, such as stuffy air, moisture condensation on cold surfaces, or mold and mildew growth. Additional weatherization measures should not be undertaken until these problems have been corrected.

Weatherization generally does not cause indoor air problems by adding new pollutants to the air. (There are a few exceptions, such as caulking, that can sometimes emit pollutants.) However, measures such as installing storm windows, weather stripping, caulking, and blown-in wall insulation can reduce the amount of outdoor air infiltrating into a home. Consequently, after weatherization, concentrations of indoor air pollutants from sources inside the home can increase.

Three Basic Strategies

Source Control

Usually the most effective way to improve indoor air quality is to eliminate individual sources of pollution or to reduce their emissions. Some sources, like those that contain asbestos, can be sealed or enclosed; others, like gas stoves, can be adjusted to decrease the amount of emissions. In many cases, source control is also a more cost-efficient approach to protecting indoor air quality than increasing ventilation because increasing ventilation can increase energy costs. Specific sources of indoor air pollution in your home are listed later in this section.

Ventilation Improvements

Another approach to lowering the concentrations of indoor air pollutants in your home is to increase the amount of outdoor air coming indoors. Most home heating and cooling systems, including forced air heating systems, do not mechanically bring fresh air into the house. Opening windows and doors, operating window or attic fans, when the weather permits, or running a window air conditioner with the vent control open increases the outdoor ventilation rate. Local bathroom or kitchen fans that exhaust outdoors remove contaminants directly from the room where the fan is located and also increase the outdoor air ventilation rate.

It is particularly important to take as many of these steps as possible while you are involved in short-term activities that can generate high levels of pollutants—for example, painting, paint stripping, heating with kerosene heaters, cooking, or engaging in maintenance and hobby activities such as welding, soldering, or sanding. You might also choose to do some of these activities outdoors, if you can and if weather permits.

Advanced designs of new homes are starting to feature mechanical systems that bring outdoor air into the home. Some of these designs include energy-efficient heat recovery ventilators (also known as air-to-air heat exchangers).

Air Cleaners

There are many types and sizes of air cleaners on the market, ranging from relatively inexpensive table-top models to sophisticated and expensive whole-house systems. Some air cleaners are highly effective at particle removal, while others, including most table-top models, are much less so. Air cleaners are generally not designed to remove gaseous pollutants.

The effectiveness of an air cleaner depends on how well it collects pollutants from indoor air (expressed as a percentage efficiency rate) and how much air it draws through the cleaning or filtering element (expressed in cubic feet per minute). A very efficient collector with a low air-circulation rate will not be effective, nor will a cleaner with a high air-circulation rate but a less efficient collector. The long-term performance of any air cleaner depends on maintaining it according to the manufacturer's directions.

Another important factor in determining the effectiveness of an air cleaner is the strength of the pollutant source. Table-top air cleaners, in particular, may not remove satisfactory amounts of pollutants from strong nearby sources. People with a sensitivity to particular sources may find that air cleaners are helpful only in conjunction with concerted efforts to remove the source.

Over the past few years, there has been some publicity suggesting that houseplants have been shown to reduce levels of some chemicals in laboratory experiments. There is currently no evidence, however, that a reasonable number of houseplants remove significant quantities of pollutants in homes and offices. Indoor houseplants should not be over-watered because overly damp soil may promote the growth of microorganisms which can affect allergic individuals.

At present, EPA does not recommend using air cleaners to reduce levels of radon and its decay products. The effectiveness of these devices is uncertain because they only partially remove the radon decay products and do not diminish the amount of radon entering the home. EPA plans to do additional research on whether air cleaners are, or could become, a reliable means of reducing the health risk from radon. EPA's booklet, *Residential Air-Cleaning Devices*, provides further information on air-cleaning devices to reduce indoor air pollutants.

For most indoor air quality problems in the home, source control is the most effective solution. This section takes a source-by-source look at the most common indoor air pollutants, their potential health effects, and ways to reduce levels in the home.

A Look at Source-Specific Controls

Radon (Rn)

The most common source of indoor radon is uranium in the soil or rock on which homes are built. As uranium naturally breaks down, it releases radon gas which is a colorless, odorless, radioactive gas. Radon gas enters homes through dirt floors, cracks in concrete walls and floors, floor drains, and sumps. When radon becomes trapped in buildings and concentrations build up indoors, exposure to radon becomes a concern.

Any home may have a radon problem. This means new and old homes, well-sealed and drafty homes, and homes with or without basements.

Sometimes radon enters the home through well water. In a small number of homes, the building materials can give off radon, too. However, building materials rarely cause radon problems by themselves.

Health Effects of Radon

The predominant health effect associated with exposure to elevated levels of radon is lung cancer. Research suggests that swallowing water with high radon levels may pose risks, too, although these are believed to be much lower than those from breathing air containing radon. Major health organizations (like the Centers for Disease Control and Prevention (CDC), the American Lung Association (ALA), and the American Medical Association (AMA) agree with estimates that radon causes thousands of preventable lung cancer deaths each year. EPA estimates that radon causes about 14,000 deaths per year in the United States—however, this number could range from 7,000 to 30,000 deaths per year. If you smoke and your home has high radon levels, your risk of lung cancer is especially high.

Reducing Exposure to Radon in Homes

Measure levels of radon in your home.

You can't see radon, but it's not hard to find out if you have a radon problem in your home. Testing is easy and should only take a little of your time.

There are many kinds of inexpensive, do-it-yourself radon test kits you can get through the mail and in hardware stores and other retail outlets. Make sure you buy a test kit that has passed EPA's testing program or is state-certified. These kits will usually display the phrase "Meets EPA Requirements." If you prefer, or if you are buying or selling a home, you can hire a trained contractor to do the testing for you. EPA's voluntary National Radon Proficiency Program (RPP) evaluated testing (measurement) contractors. A contractor who had met EPA's requirements carried an EPA-generated RPP identification card. EPA provides a list of companies and individual contractors available online at http://www.cpsc.gov/cpscpub/pubs/450.html which is also available to state radon offices. You should call your state radon office to obtain a list of qualified contractors in your area.

Refer to the EPA guidelines on how to test and interpret your test results.

You can learn more about radon through EPA's publications, *A Citizen's Guide to Radon: The Guide to Protecting Yourself and Your Family From Radon* and *Home Buyer's and Seller's Guide to Radon*, which are also available from your state radon office.

Learn about radon reduction methods.

Ways to reduce radon in your home are discussed in EPA's *Consumer's Guide to Radon Reduction*. You can get a copy from your state radon office. There are simple solutions to radon problems in homes. Thousands of homeowners have already fixed radon problems. Lowering high radon levels requires technical knowledge and special skills. You should use a contractor who is trained to fix radon problems.

A trained radon reduction contractor can study the problem in your home and help you pick the correct treatment method. Check with your state radon office for names of qualified or state-certified radon-reduction contractors in your area.

Stop smoking and discourage smoking in your home.

Scientific evidence indicates that smoking combined with radon is an especially serious health risk. Stop smoking and lower your radon level to reduce lung cancer risk.

Treat radon-contaminated well water.

While radon in water is not a problem in homes served by most public water supplies, it has been found in well water. If you've tested the air in your home and found a radon problem, and you have a well, contact a lab certified to measure radiation in water to have your water tested. Radon problems in water can be readily fixed.

Environmental Tobacco Smoke (ETS)

Environmental tobacco smoke (ETS) is the mixture of smoke that comes from the burning end of a cigarette, pipe, or cigar, and smoke exhaled by the smoker. It is a complex mixture of over 4,000 compounds, more than 40 of which are known to cause cancer in humans or animals and many of which are strong irritants. ETS is often referred to as "secondhand smoke" and exposure to ETS is often called "passive smoking."

Health Effects of Environmental Tobacco Smoke

In 1992, EPA completed a major assessment of the respiratory health risks of ETS concludes that exposure to ETS is responsible for approximately 3,000 lung cancer deaths each year in nonsmoking adults and impairs the respiratory health of hundreds of thousands of children.

Infants and young children whose parents smoke in their presence are at increased risk of lower respiratory tract infections (pneumonia and bronchitis) and are more likely to have symptoms of respiratory irritation like cough, excess phlegm, and wheeze. EPA estimates that passive smoking annually causes between 150,000 and 300,000 lower respiratory tract infections in infants and children under 18 months of age, resulting in between 7,500 and 15,000 hospitalizations each year. These children may also have a build-up of fluid in the middle ear, which can lead to ear infections. Older children who have been exposed to secondhand smoke may have slightly reduced lung function.

Asthmatic children are especially at risk. EPA estimates that exposure to secondhand smoke increases the number of episodes and severity of symptoms in hundreds of thousands of asthmatic children, and may cause thousands of nonasthmatic children to develop the disease each year. EPA estimates that between 200,000 and 1,000,000 asthmatic children have their condition made worse by exposure to secondhand smoke each year. Exposure to secondhand smoke causes eye, nose, and throat irritation. It may affect the cardiovascular system and some studies have linked exposure to secondhand smoke with the onset of chest pain.

Reducing Exposure to Environmental Tobacco Smoke

Don't smoke at home or permit others to do so. Ask smokers to smoke outdoors.

The 1986 Surgeon General's report concluded that physical separation of smokers and nonsmokers in a common air space, such as different rooms within the same house, may reduce—but will not eliminate—non-smokers' exposure to environmental tobacco smoke.

If smoking indoors cannot be avoided, increase ventilation in the area where smoking takes place.

Open windows or use exhaust fans. Ventilation, a common method of reducing exposure to indoor air pollutants, also will reduce but not eliminate exposure to environmental tobacco smoke. Because smoking produces such large amounts of pollutants, natural or mechanical ventilation techniques do not remove them from the air in your home as quickly as they build up. In addition, the large increases in ventilation it takes to significantly reduce exposure to environmental tobacco smoke can also increase energy costs substantially. Consequently, the most effective way to reduce exposure to environmental tobacco smoke in the home is to eliminate smoking there.

Do not smoke if children are present, particularly infants and toddlers.

Children are particularly susceptible to the effects of passive smoking. Do not allow babysitters or others who work in your home to smoke indoors. Discourage others from smoking around children. Find out about the smoking policies of the day care center providers, schools, and other care givers for your children. The policy should protect children from exposure to ETS.

Biological Contaminants

Biological contaminants include bacteria, molds, mildew, viruses, animal dander and cat saliva, house dust mites, cockroaches, and pollen. There are many sources of these pollutants. Pollens originate from plants; viruses are transmitted by people and animals; bacteria are carried by people, animals, and soil and plant debris; and household pets are sources of saliva and animal dander. The protein in urine from rats and mice is a potent allergen. When it dries, it can become airborne. Contaminated central air handling systems can become breeding grounds for mold, mildew, and other sources of biological contaminants and can then distribute these contaminants through the home.

By controlling the relative humidity level in a home, the growth of some sources of biologicals can be minimized. A relative humidity of 30-50 percent is generally recommended for homes. Standing water, water-damaged materials, or wet surfaces also serve as a breeding ground for molds, mildews, bacteria, and insects. House dust mites, the source of one of the most powerful biological allergens, grow in damp, warm environments.

Health Effects from Biological Contaminants

Some biological contaminants trigger allergic reactions, including hypersensitivity pneumonitis, allergic rhinitis, and some types of asthma. Infectious illnesses, such as influenza, measles, and chicken pox are transmitted through the air. Molds and mildews release disease-causing toxins. Symptoms of health problems caused by biological pollutants include sneezing, watery eyes, coughing, shortness of breath, dizziness, lethargy, fever, and digestive problems.

Allergic reactions occur only after repeated exposure to a specific biological allergen. However, that reaction may occur immediately upon re-exposure or after multiple exposures over time. As a result, people who have noticed only mild allergic reactions, or no reactions at all, may suddenly find themselves very sensitive to particular allergens.

Some diseases, like humidifier fever, are associated with exposure to toxins from microorganisms that can grow in large building ventilation systems. However, these diseases can also be traced to microorganisms that grow in home heating and cooling systems and humidifiers. Children, elderly people, and people with breathing problems, allergies, and lung diseases are particularly susceptible to disease-causing biological agents in the indoor air.

Reducing Exposure to Biological Contaminants

Install and use exhaust fans that are vented to the outdoors in kitchens and bathrooms and vent clothes dryers outdoors.

These actions can eliminate much of the moisture that builds up from everyday activities. There are exhaust fans on the market that produce little noise, an important consideration for some people. Another benefit to using kitchen and bathroom exhaust fans is that they can reduce levels of organic pollutants that vaporize from hot water used in showers and dishwashers.

Ventilate the attic and crawl spaces to prevent moisture build-up.

Keeping humidity levels in these areas below 50 percent can prevent water condensation on building materials.

If using cool mist or ultrasonic humidifiers, clean appliances according to manufacturer's instructions and refill with fresh water daily.

Because these humidifiers can become breeding grounds for biological contaminants, they have the potential for causing diseases such as hypersensitivity pneumonitis and humidifier fever. Evaporation trays in air conditioners, dehumidifiers, and refrigerators should also be cleaned frequently.

Thoroughly clean and dry water-damaged carpets and building materials (within 24 hours if possible) or consider removal and replacement.

Water-damaged carpets and building materials can harbor mold and bacteria. It is very difficult to completely rid such materials of biological contaminants.

Keep the house clean. House dust mites, pollens, animal dander, and other allergy-causing agents can be reduced, although not eliminated, through regular cleaning.

People who are allergic to these pollutants should use allergen-proof mattress encasements, wash bedding in hot (130 degrees Fahrenheit) water, and avoid room furnishings that accumulate dust, especially if they cannot be washed in hot water. Allergic individuals should also leave the house while it is being vacuumed because vacuuming can actually increase airborne levels of mite allergens and other biological contaminants. Using central vacuum systems that are vented to the outdoors or vacuums with high efficiency filters may also be of help.

Take steps to minimize biological pollutants in basements.

Clean and disinfect the basement floor drain regularly. Do not finish a basement below ground level unless all water leaks are patched and outdoor ventilation and adequate heat to prevent condensation are provided. Operate a dehumidifier in the basement if needed to keep relative humidity levels between 30-50 percent.

Stoves, Heaters, Fireplaces, and Chimneys

In addition to environmental tobacco smoke, other sources of combustion products are unvented kerosene and gas space heaters, woodstoves, fireplaces, and gas stoves. The major pollutants released are carbon monoxide, nitrogen dioxide, and particles. Unvented kerosene heaters may also generate acid aerosols.

Combustion gases and particles also come from chimneys and flues that are improperly installed or maintained and cracked furnace heat exchangers. Pollutants from fireplaces and woodstoves with no dedicated outdoor air supply can be "back-drafted" from the chimney into the living space, particularly in weatherized homes.

Health Effects of Combustion Products

Carbon monoxide (CO) is a colorless, odorless gas that interferes with the delivery of oxygen throughout the body. At high concentrations it can cause unconsciousness and death. Lower concentrations can cause a range of symptoms from headaches, dizziness, weakness, nausea, confusion, and disorientation, to fatigue in healthy people and episodes of increased chest pain in people with chronic heart disease. The symptoms of carbon monoxide poisoning are sometimes confused with the flu or food poisoning. Fetuses, infants, elderly people, and people with anemia or with a history of heart or respiratory disease can be especially sensitive to carbon monoxide exposures.

Nitrogen dioxide (NO2) is a colorless, odorless gas that irritates the mucous membranes in the eye, nose, and throat and causes shortness of breath after exposure to high concentrations. There is evidence that high concentrations or continued exposure to low levels of nitrogen dioxide increases the risk of respiratory infection; there is also evidence from animal studies that repeated exposures to elevated nitrogen dioxide levels may lead, or contribute, to the development of lung disease such as emphysema. People at particular risk from exposure to nitrogen dioxide include children and individuals with asthma and other respiratory diseases.

Particles, released when fuels are incompletely burned, can lodge in the lungs and irritate or damage lung tissue. A number of pollutants, including radon and benzo(a)pyrene, both of which can cause cancer, attach to small particles that are inhaled and then carried deep into the lung.

Reducing Exposure to Combustion Products in Homes

Take special precautions when operating fuel-burning unvented space heaters.

Consider potential effects of indoor air pollution if you use an unvented kerosene or gas space heater. Follow the manufacturer's directions, especially instructions on the proper fuel and keeping the heater properly adjusted. A persistent yellow-tipped flame is generally an indicator of maladjustment and increased pollutant emissions. While a space heater is in use, open a door from the room where the heater is located to the rest of the house and open a window slightly.

Install and use exhaust fans over gas cooking stoves and ranges and keep the burners properly adjusted.

Using a stove hood with a fan vented to the outdoors greatly reduces exposure to pollutants during cooking. Improper adjustment, often indicated by a persistent yellow-tipped flame, causes increased pollutant emissions. Ask your gas company to adjust the burner so that the flame tip is blue. If you purchase a new gas stove or range, consider buying one with pilotless ignition because it does not have a pilot light that burns continuously. Never use a gas stove to heat your home. Always make certain the flue in your gas fireplace is open when the fireplace is in use.

Keep woodstove emissions to a minimum. Choose properly sized new stoves that are certified as meeting EPA emission standards.

Make certain that doors in old woodstoves are tight-fitting. Use aged or cured (dried) wood only and follow the manufacturer's directions for starting, stoking, and putting out the fire in woodstoves. Chemicals are used to pressure-treat wood; such wood should never be burned indoors. (Because some old gaskets in woodstove doors contain asbestos, when replacing gaskets refer to the instructions in the CPSC, ALA, and EPA booklet, *Asbestos in Your Home*, to avoid creating an asbestos problem. New gaskets are made of fiberglass.)

Have central air handling systems, including furnaces, flues, and chimneys, inspected annually and promptly repair cracks or damaged parts.

Blocked, leaking, or damaged chimneys or flues release harmful combustion gases and particles and even fatal concentrations of carbon monoxide. Strictly follow all service and maintenance procedures recommended by the manufacturer, including those that tell you how frequently to change the filter. If manufacturer's instructions are not readily available, change filters once every month or two during periods of use. Proper maintenance is important even for new furnaces because they can also corrode and leak combustion gases, including carbon monoxide.

Household Products

Organic chemicals are widely used as ingredients in household products. Paints, varnishes, and wax all contain organic solvents, as do many cleaning, disinfecting, cosmetic, degreasing, and hobby products. Fuels are made up of organic chemicals. All of these products can release organic compounds while you are using them, and, to some degree, when they are stored.

EPA's Total Exposure Assessment Methodology (TEAM) studies found levels of about a dozen common organic pollutants to be 2 to 5 times higher inside homes than outside, regardless of whether the homes were located in rural or highly industrial areas. Additional TEAM studies indicate that while people are using products containing organic chemicals, they can expose themselves and others to very high pollutant levels, and elevated concentrations can persist in the air long after the activity is completed.

Health Effects of Household Chemicals

The ability of organic chemicals to cause health effects varies greatly, from those that are highly toxic, to those with no known health effect. As with other pollutants, the extent and nature of the health effect will depend on many factors including level of exposure and length of time exposed. Eye and respiratory tract irritation, headaches, dizziness, visual disorders, and memory impairment are among the immediate symptoms that some people have experienced soon after exposure to some organics. At present, not much is known about what health effects occur from the levels of organics usually found in homes. Many organic compounds are known to cause cancer in animals; some are suspected of causing, or are known to cause, cancer in humans.

Reducing Exposure to Household Chemicals

Follow label instructions carefully.

Potentially hazardous products often have warnings aimed at reducing exposure of the user. For example, if a label says to use the product in a well-ventilated area, go outdoors or in areas equipped with an exhaust fan to use it. Otherwise, open up windows to provide the maximum amount of outdoor air possible.

Throw away partially full containers of old or unneeded chemicals safely.

Because gases can leak even from closed containers, this single step could help lower concentrations of organic chemicals in your home. (Be sure that materials you decide to keep are stored not only in a well-ventilated area but are also safely out of reach of children.) Do not simply toss these unwanted products in the garbage can. Find out if your local government or any organization in your community sponsors special days for the collection of toxic household wastes. If such days are available, use them to dispose of the unwanted containers safely. If no such collection days are available, think about organizing one.

Buy limited quantities.

If you use products only occasionally or seasonally, such as paints, paint strippers, and kerosene for space heaters or gasoline for lawn mowers, buy only as much as you will use right away.

Keep exposure to emissions from products containing methylene chloride to a minimum.

Consumer products that contain methylene chloride include paint strippers, adhesive removers, and aerosol spray paints. Methylene chloride is known to cause cancer in animals. Also, methylene chloride is converted to carbon monoxide in the body and can cause symptoms associated with exposure to carbon monoxide. Carefully read the labels containing health hazard information and cautions on the proper use of these products. Use products that contain methylene chloride outdoors when possible; use indoors only if the area is well ventilated.

Keep exposure to benzene to a minimum.

Benzene is a known human carcinogen. The main indoor sources of this chemical are environmental tobacco smoke, stored fuels and paint supplies, and automobile emissions in attached garages. Actions that will reduce benzene exposure include eliminating smoking within the home, providing for maximum ventilation during painting, and discarding paint supplies and special fuels that will not be used immediately.

Keep exposure to perchloroethylene emissions from newly dry-cleaned materials to a minimum.

Perchloroethylene is the chemical most widely used in dry cleaning. In laboratory studies, it has been shown to cause cancer in animals. Recent studies indicate that people breathe low levels of this chemical both in homes where dry-cleaned goods are stored and as they wear dry-cleaned clothing. Dry cleaners recapture the perchloroethylene during the dry-cleaning process so they can save money by re-using it, and they remove more of the chemical during the pressing and finishing processes. Some dry cleaners, however, do not remove as much perchloroethylene as possible all of the time. Taking steps to minimize your exposure to this chemical is prudent. If dry-cleaned goods have a strong chemical odor when you pick them up, do not accept them until they have been properly dried. If goods with a chemical odor are returned to you on subsequent visits, try a different dry cleaner.

Formaldehyde

Formaldehyde is an important chemical used widely by industry to manufacture building materials and numerous household products. It is also a by-product of combustion and certain other natural processes. Thus, it may be present in substantial concentrations both indoors and outdoors.

Sources of formaldehyde in the home include building materials, smoking, household products, and the use of unvented, fuel-burning appliances, like gas stoves or kerosene space heaters. Formaldehyde, by itself or in combination with other chemicals, serves a number of purposes in manufactured products. For example, it is used to add permanent-press qualities to clothing and draperies, as a component of glues and adhesives, and as a preservative in some paints and coating products.

In homes, the most significant sources of formaldehyde are likely to be pressed wood products made using adhesives that contain urea-formaldehyde (UF) resins. Pressed wood products made for indoor use include: particleboard (used as subflooring and shelving and in cabinetry and furniture); hardwood plywood paneling (used for decorative wall covering and used in cabinets and furniture); and medium density fiberboard (used for drawer fronts, cabinets, and furniture tops). Medium density fiberboard contains a higher resin-to-wood ratio than any other UF pressed wood product and is generally recognized as being the highest formaldehyde-emitting pressed wood product.

Other pressed wood products, such as softwood plywood and flake or oriented strandboard, are produced for exterior construction use and contain the dark, or red/black-colored phenolformaldehyde (PF) resin. Although formaldehyde is present in both types of resins, pressed woods that contain PF resin generally emit formaldehyde at considerably lower rates than those containing UF resin.

Since 1985, the Department of Housing and Urban Development (HUD) has permitted only the use of plywood and particleboard that conform to specified formaldehyde emission limits in the construction of prefabricated and mobile homes. In the past, some of these homes had elevated levels of formaldehyde because of the large amount of high-emitting pressed wood products used in their construction and because of their relatively small interior space.

The rate at which products like pressed wood or textiles release formaldehyde can change. Formaldehyde emissions will generally decrease as products age. When the products are new, high indoor temperatures or humidity can cause increased release of formaldehyde from these products.

During the 1970s, many homeowners had urea-formaldehyde foam insulation (UFFI) installed in the wall cavities of their homes as an energy conservation measure. However, many of these homes were found to have relatively high indoor concentrations of formaldehyde soon after the UFFI installation. Few homes are now being insulated with this product. Studies show that formaldehyde emissions from UFFI decline with time; therefore, homes in which UFFI was installed many years ago are unlikely to have high levels of formaldehyde now.

Health Effects of Formaldehyde

Formaldehyde, a colorless, pungent-smelling gas, can cause watery eyes, burning sensations in the eyes and throat, nausea, and difficulty in breathing in some humans exposed at elevated levels (above 0.1 parts per million). High concentrations may trigger attacks in people with asthma. There is evidence that some people can develop a sensitivity to formaldehyde. It has also been shown to cause cancer in animals and may cause cancer in humans.

Reducing Exposure to Formaldehyde in Homes

Ask about the formaldehyde content of pressed wood products, including building materials, cabinetry, and furniture before you purchase them.

If you experience adverse reactions to formaldehyde, you may want to avoid the use of pressed wood products and other formaldehyde-emitting goods. Even if you do not experience such reactions, you may wish to reduce your exposure as much as possible by purchasing exterior-grade products, which emit less formaldehyde.

Some studies suggest that coating pressed wood products with polyurethane may reduce formaldehyde emissions for some period of time. To be effective, any such coating must cover all surfaces and edges and remain intact. Increase the ventilation and carefully follow the manufacturer instructions while applying these coatings. (If you are sensitive to formaldehyde, check the label contents before purchasing coating products to avoid buying products that contain formaldehyde, as they will emit the chemical for a short time after application.) Maintain moderate temperature and humidity levels and provide adequate ventilation. The rate at which formaldehyde is released is accelerated by heat and may also depend somewhat on the humidity level. Therefore, the use of dehumidifiers and air conditioning to control humidity and to maintain a moderate temperature can help reduce formaldehyde emissions. (Drain and clean dehumidifier collection trays frequently so that they do not become a breeding ground for microorganisms.) Increasing the rate of ventilation in your home will also help in reducing formaldehyde levels.

Pesticides

According to a recent survey, 75 percent of U.S. households used at least one pesticide product indoors during the past year. Products used most often are insecticides and disinfectants. Another study suggests that 80 percent of most people's exposure to pesticides occurs indoors and that measurable levels of up to a dozen pesticides have been found in the air inside homes. The amount of pesticides found in homes appears to be greater than can be explained by recent pesticide use in those households; other possible sources include contaminated soil or dust that floats or is tracked in from outside, stored pesticide containers, and household surfaces that collect and then release the pesticides. Pesticides used in and around the home include products to control insects (insecticides), termites (termiticides), rodents (rodenticides), fungi (fungicides), and microbes (disinfectants). They are sold as sprays, liquids, sticks, powders, crystals, balls, and foggers.

In 1990, the American Association of Poison Control Centers reported that some 79,000 children were involved in common household pesticide poisonings or exposures. In households with children under five years old, almost one-half stored at least one pesticide product within reach of children.

EPA registers pesticides for use and requires manufacturers to put information on the label about when and how to use the pesticide. It is important to remember that the "-cide" in pesticides means "to kill." These products can be dangerous if not used properly.

In addition to the active ingredient, pesticides are also made up of ingredients that are used to carry the active agent. These carrier agents are called "inerts" in pesticides because they are not toxic to the targeted pest; nevertheless, some inerts are capable of causing health problems.

Health Effects from Pesticides

Both the active and inert ingredients in pesticides can be organic compounds; therefore, both could add to the levels of airborne organics inside homes. Both types of ingredients can cause the effects discussed in this chapter under "Household Products," however, as with other household products, there is insufficient understanding at present about what pesticide concentrations are necessary to produce these effects.

Exposure to high levels of cyclodiene pesticides, commonly associated with misapplication, has produced various symptoms, including headaches, dizziness, muscle twitching, weakness, tingling sensations, and nausea. In addition, EPA is concerned that cyclodienes might cause long-term damage to the liver and the central nervous system, as well as an increased risk of cancer.

There is no further sale or commercial use permitted for the following cyclodiene or related pesticides: chlordane, aldrin, dieldrin, and heptachlor. The only exception is the use of heptachlor by utility companies to control fire ants in underground cable boxes.

Reducing Exposure to Pesticides in Homes

Read the label and follow the directions. It is illegal to use any pesticide in any manner inconsistent with the directions on its label.

Unless you have had special training and are certified, never use a pesticide that is restricted to use by state-certified pest control operators. Such pesticides are simply too dangerous for application by a noncertified person. Use only the pesticides approved for use by the general public and then only in recommended amounts; increasing the amount does not offer more protection against pests and can be harmful to you and your plants and pets.

Ventilate the area well after pesticide use.

Mix or dilute pesticides outdoors or in a well-ventilated area and only in the amounts that will be immediately needed. If possible, take plants and pets outside when applying pesticides to them.

Use nonchemical methods of pest control when possible.

Since pesticides can be found far from the site of their original application, it is prudent to reduce the use of chemical pesticides outdoors as well as indoors. Depending on the site and pest to be controlled, one or more of the following steps can be effective: use of biological pesticides, such as *Bacillus thuringiensis*, for the control of gypsy moths; selection of disease-resistant plants; and frequent washing of indoor plants and pets. Termite damage can be reduced or prevented by making certain that wooden building materials do not come into direct contact with the soil and by storing firewood away from the home. By appropriately fertilizing, watering, and aerating lawns, the need for chemical pesticide treatments of lawns can be dramatically reduced.

If you decide to use a pest control company, choose one carefully.

Ask for an inspection of your home and get a written control program for evaluation before you sign a contract. The control program should list specific names of pests to be controlled and chemicals to be used; it should also reflect any of your safety concerns. Insist on a proven record of competence and customer satisfaction.

Dispose of unwanted pesticides safely.

If you have unused or partially used pesticide containers you want to get rid of, dispose of them according to the directions on the label or on special household hazardous waste collection days. If there are no such collection days in your community, work with others to organize them.

Keep exposure to moth repellents to a minimum.

One pesticide often found in the home is paradichlorobenzene, a commonly used active ingredient in moth repellents. This chemical is known to cause cancer in animals, but substantial scientific uncertainty exists over the effects, if any, of long-term human exposure to paradichlorobenzene. EPA requires that products containing paradichlorobenzene bear warnings such as "avoid breathing vapors" to warn users of potential short-term toxic effects. Where possible, paradichlorobenzene, and items to be protected against moths, should be placed in trunks or other containers that can be stored in areas that are separately ventilated from the home, such as attics and detached garages. Paradichlorobenzene is also the key active ingredient in many air fresheners (in fact, some labels for moth repellents recommend that these same products be used as air fresheners or deodorants). Proper ventilation and basic household cleanliness will go a long way toward preventing unpleasant odors.

Asbestos

Asbestos is a mineral fiber that has been used commonly in a variety of building construction materials for insulation and as a fire-retardant. EPA and CPSC have banned several asbestos products. Manufacturers have also voluntarily limited uses of asbestos. Today, asbestos is most commonly found in older homes, in pipe and furnace insulation materials, asbestos shingles, millboard, textured paints and other coating materials, and floor tiles.

Elevated concentrations of airborne asbestos can occur after asbestos-containing materials are disturbed by cutting, sanding or other remodeling activities. Improper attempts to remove these materials can release asbestos fibers into the air in homes, increasing asbestos levels and endangering people living in those homes.

Health Effects of Asbestos

The most dangerous asbestos fibers are too small to be visible. After they are inhaled, they can remain and accumulate in the lungs. Asbestos can cause lung cancer, mesothelioma (a cancer of the chest and abdominal linings), and asbestosis (irreversible lung scarring that can be fatal). Symptoms of these diseases do not show up until many years after exposure began. Most people with asbestos-related diseases were exposed to elevated concentrations on the job; some developed disease from exposure to clothing and equipment brought home from job sites.

Reducing Exposure to Asbestos in Homes

If you think your home may have asbestos, don't panic!

Usually it is best to leave asbestos material that is in good condition alone. Generally, material in good condition will not release asbestos fiber. There is no danger unless fibers are released and inhaled into the lungs.

Do not cut, rip, or sand asbestos-containing materials.

Leave undamaged materials alone and, to the extent possible, prevent them from being damaged, disturbed, or touched. Periodically inspect for damage or deterioration. Discard damaged or worn asbestos gloves, stove-top pads, or ironing board covers. Check with local health, environmental, or other appropriate officials to find out about proper handling and disposal procedures.

If asbestos material is more than slightly damaged, or if you are going to make changes in your home that might disturb it, repair or removal by a professional is needed. Before you have your house remodeled, find out whether asbestos materials are present.

When you need to remove or clean up asbestos, use a professionally trained contractor.

Select a contractor only after careful discussion of the problems in your home and the steps the contractor will take to clean up or remove them. Consider the option of sealing off the materials instead of removing them.

Lead

Lead has long been recognized as a harmful environmental pollutant. In late 1991, the Secretary of the Department of Health and Human Services called lead the "number one environmental threat to the health of children in the United States." There are many ways in which humans are exposed to lead: through air, drinking water, food, contaminated soil, deteriorating paint, and dust. Airborne lead enters the body when an individual breathes or swallows lead particles or dust once it has settled. Before it was known how harmful lead could be, it was used in paint, gasoline, water pipes, and many other products.

Old lead-based paint is the most significant source of lead exposure in the U.S. today. Harmful exposures to lead can be created when lead-based paint is improperly removed from surfaces by dry scraping, sanding, or open-flame burning. High concentrations of airborne lead particles in homes can also result from lead dust from outdoor sources, including contaminated soil tracked inside, and use of lead in certain indoor activities such as soldering and stained-glass making.

Health Effects of Exposure to Lead

Lead affects practically all systems within the body. At high levels it can cause convulsions, coma, and even death. Lower levels of lead can adversely affect the brain, central nervous system, blood cells, and kidneys.

The effects of lead exposure on fetuses and young children can be severe. They include delays in physical and mental development, lower IQ levels, shortened attention spans, and increased behavioral problems. Fetuses, infants, and children are more vulnerable to lead exposure than adults since lead is more easily absorbed into growing bodies, and the tissues of small children are more sensitive to the damaging effects of lead. Children may have higher exposures since they are more likely to get lead dust on their hands and then put their fingers or other lead-contaminated objects into their mouths.

Get your child tested for lead exposure. To find out where to do this, call your doctor or local health clinic.

Ways to Reduce Exposure to Lead

Keep areas where children play as dust-free and clean as possible.

Mop floors and wipe window ledges and chewable surfaces such as cribs with a solution of powdered automatic dishwasher detergent in warm water. (Dishwasher detergents are recommended because of their high content of phosphate.) Most multi-purpose cleaners will not remove lead in ordinary dust. Wash toys and stuffed animals regularly. Make sure that children wash their hands before meals, nap time, and bedtime.

Reduce the risk from lead-based paint.

Most homes built before 1960 contain heavily leaded paint. Some homes built as recently as 1978 may also contain lead paint. This paint could be on window frames, walls, the outside of homes, or other surfaces. Do not burn painted wood since it may contain lead.

Leave lead-based paint undisturbed if it is in good condition — do not sand or burn off paint that may contain lead.

Lead paint in good condition is usually not a problem except in places where painted surfaces rub against each other and create dust (for example, opening a window).

Do not remove lead paint yourself.

Individuals have been poisoned by scraping or sanding lead paint because these activities generate large amounts of lead dust. Consult your state health or housing department for suggestions on which private laboratories or public agencies may be able to help test your home for lead in paint. Home test kits cannot detect small amounts of lead under some conditions. Hire a person with special training for correcting lead paint problems to remove lead-based paint. Occupants, especially children and pregnant women, should leave the building until all work is finished and clean-up is done.

Do not bring lead dust into the home.

If you work in construction, demolition, painting, with batteries, in a radiator repair shop or lead factory, or your hobby involves lead, you may unknowingly bring lead into your home on your hands or clothes. You may also be tracking in lead from soil around your home. Soil very close to homes may be contaminated from lead paint on the outside of the building. Soil by roads and highways may be contaminated from years of exhaust fumes from cars and trucks that used leaded gas. Use doormats to wipe your feet before entering the home. If you work with lead in your job or a hobby, change your clothes before you go home and wash these clothes separately. Encourage your children to play in sand and grassy areas instead of dirt, which sticks to fingers and toys. Try to keep your children from eating dirt, and make sure they wash their hands when they come inside.

Find out about lead in drinking water.

Most well and city water does not usually contain lead. Water usually picks up lead inside the home from household plumbing that is made with lead materials. The only way to know if there is lead in drinking water is to have it tested. Contact the local health department or the water supplier to find out how to get the water tested. Send for the EPA pamphlet, "Lead and Your Drinking Water," for more information about what you can do if you have lead in your drinking water.

Eat right.

A child who gets enough iron and calcium will absorb less lead. Foods rich in iron include eggs, red meats, and beans. Dairy products are high in calcium. Do not store food or liquid in lead crystal glassware or imported or old pottery. If you reuse old plastic bags to store or carry food, keep the printing on the outside of the bag.

What about Carpet?

In recent years, a number of consumers have associated a variety of symptoms with the installation of new carpet. Scientists have not been able to determine whether the chemicals emitted by new carpets are responsible. If you are installing new carpet, you may wish to take the following steps:

- Talk to your carpet retailer. Ask for information on emissions from carpet.

- Ask the retailer to unroll and air out the carpet in a well-ventilated area before installation.

- Ask for low-emitting adhesives if adhesives are needed.

- Consider leaving the premises during and immediately after carpet installation. You may wish to schedule the installation when most family members or office workers are out.

- Be sure the retailer requires the installer to follow the Carpet and Rug Institute's installation guidelines.

- Open doors and windows. Increasing the amount of fresh air in the home will reduce exposure to most chemicals released from carpet. During and after installation, use window fans, room air conditioners, or other mechanical ventilation equipment you may have installed in your house, to exhaust fumes to the outdoors. Keep them running for 48 to 72 hours after the new carpet is installed.

- Contact your carpet retailer if objectionable odors persist.

- Follow the manufacturer's instructions for proper carpet maintenance.

When Building a New Home

Building a new home provides the opportunity for preventing indoor air problems. However, it can result in exposure to higher levels of indoor air contaminants if careful attention is not given to potential pollution sources and the air exchange rate.

Express your concerns about indoor air quality to your architect or builder and enlist his or her cooperation in taking measures to provide good indoor air quality. Talk both about purchasing building materials and furnishings that are low-emitting and about providing an adequate amount of ventilation.

The American Society of Heating, Refrigerating, and Air-Conditioning Engineers (ASHRAE) recommends a ventilation rate of 0.35 ach (air changes per hour) for new homes, and some new homes are built to even tighter specifications. Particular care should be given in such homes to preventing the build-up of indoor air pollutants to high levels.

Here are a few important actions that can make a difference:

- Use radon-resistant construction techniques.

  Obtain a copy of the EPA booklet, *Model Standards and Techniques for Control of Radon in New Residential Buildings*, from your state radon office or health agency, your state homebuilders' association, or your EPA regional office.

- Choose building materials and furnishings that will keep indoor air pollution to a minimum.

  There are many actions a homeowner can take to select products that will prevent indoor air problems from occurring—a couple of them are mentioned here. First, use exterior-grade pressed wood products made with phenol-formaldehyde resin in floors, cabinetry, and wall surfaces. Or, as an alternative, consider using solid wood products. Secondly, if you plan to install wall-to-wall carpet on concrete in contact with the ground, especially concrete in basements, make sure that an effective moisture barrier is installed prior to installing the carpet. Do not permanently adhere carpet to concrete with adhesives so that the carpet can be removed if it becomes wet.

- Provide proper drainage and seal foundations in new construction.

  Air that enters the home through the foundation can contain more moisture than is generated from all occupant activities.

- Become familiar with mechanical ventilation systems and consider installing one.

  Advanced designs of new homes are starting to feature mechanical systems that bring outdoor air into the home. Some of these designs include energy-efficient heat recovery ventilators (also known as air-to-air heat exchangers).

- Ensure that combustion appliances, including furnaces, fireplaces, woodstoves, and heaters, are properly vented and receive enough supply air.

Combustion gases, including carbon monoxide, and particles can be back-drafted from the chimney or flue into the living space if the combustion appliance is not properly vented or does not receive enough supply air. Back-drafting can be a particular problem in weatherized or tightly constructed homes. Installing a dedicated outdoor air supply for the combustion appliance can help prevent backdrafting.

Do You Suspect Your Office Has an Indoor Air Problem?

Indoor air quality problems are not limited to homes. In fact, many office buildings have significant air pollution sources. Some of these buildings may be inadequately ventilated. For example, mechanical ventilation systems may not be designed or operated to provide adequate amounts of outdoor air. Finally, people generally have less control over the indoor environment in their offices than they do in their homes. As a result, there has been an increase in the incidence of reported health problems.

Health Effects

A number of well-identified illnesses, such as Legionnaires' disease, asthma, hypersensitivity pneumonitis, and humidifier fever, have been directly traced to specific building problems. These are called building-related illnesses. Most of these diseases can be treated, nevertheless, some pose serious risks.

Sometimes, however, building occupants experience symptoms that do not fit the pattern of any particular illness and are difficult to trace to any specific source. This phenomenon has been labeled sick building syndrome. People may complain of one or more of the following symptoms: dry or burning mucous membranes in the nose, eyes, and throat; sneezing; stuffy or runny nose; fatigue or lethargy; headache; dizziness; nausea; irritability and forgetfulness. Poor lighting, noise, vibration, thermal discomfort, and psychological stress may also cause, or contribute to, these symptoms.

There is no single manner in which these health problems appear. In some cases, problems begin as workers enter their offices and diminish as workers leave; other times, symptoms continue until the illness is treated. Sometimes there are outbreaks of illness among many workers in a single building; in other cases, health symptoms show up only in individual workers.

In the opinion of some World Health Organization experts, up to 30 percent of new or remodeled commercial buildings may have unusually high rates of health and comfort complaints from occupants that may potentially be related to indoor air quality.

What Causes Problems?

Three major reasons for poor indoor air quality in office buildings are the presence of indoor air pollution sources; poorly designed, maintained, or operated ventilation systems; and uses of the building that were unanticipated or poorly planned for when the building was designed or renovated.

Sources of Office Air Pollution

As with homes, the most important factor influencing indoor air quality is the presence of pollutant sources. Commonly found office pollutants and their sources include environmental tobacco smoke; asbestos from insulating and fire-retardant building supplies; formaldehyde from pressed wood products; other organics from building materials, carpet, and other office furnishings, cleaning materials and activities, restroom air fresheners, paints, adhesives, copying machines, and photography and print shops; biological contaminants from dirty ventilation systems or water-damaged walls, ceilings, and carpets; and pesticides from pest management practices.

Ventilation Systems

Mechanical ventilation systems in large buildings are designed and operated not only to heat and cool the air, but also to draw in and circulate outdoor air. If they are poorly designed, operated, or maintained, however, ventilation systems can contribute to indoor air problems in several ways.

For example, problems arise when, in an effort to save energy, ventilation systems are not used to bring in adequate amounts of outdoor air. Inadequate ventilation also occurs if the air supply and return vents within each room are blocked or placed in such a way that outdoor air does not actually reach the breathing zone of building occupants. Improperly located outdoor air intake vents can also bring in air contaminated with automobile and truck exhaust, boiler emissions, fumes from dumpsters, or air vented from restrooms. Finally, ventilation systems can be a source of in door pollution themselves by spreading biological contaminants that have multiplied in cooling towers, humidifiers, dehumidifiers, air conditioners, or the inside surfaces of ventilation duct work.

Use of the Building

Indoor air pollutants can be circulated from portions of the building used for specialized purposes, such as restaurants, print shops, and dry-cleaning stores, into offices in the same building. Carbon monoxide and other components of automobile exhaust can be drawn from underground parking garages through stairwells and elevator shafts into office spaces.

In addition, buildings originally designed for one purpose may end up being converted to use as office space. If not properly modified during building renovations, the room partitions and ventilation system can contribute to indoor air quality problems by restricting air recirculation or by providing an inadequate supply of outdoor air.

What to Do If You Suspect a Problem

If you or others at your office are experiencing health or comfort problems that you suspect may be caused by indoor air pollution, you can do the following:

- Talk with other workers, your supervisor, and union representatives to see if the problems are being experienced by others and urge that a record of reported health complaints be kept by management, if one has not already been established.

- Talk with your own physician and report your problems to the company physician, nurse, or health and safety officer.

- Call your state or local health department or air pollution control agency to talk over the symptoms and possible causes.

- Encourage building management to obtain a copy of *Building Air Quality: A Guide for Building Owners and Facility Managers* from the EPA. Building Air Quality (BAQ) is simply written, yet provides comprehensive information for identifying, correcting, and preventing indoor air quality problems. BAQ also provides supporting information such as when and how to select outside technical assistance, how to communicate with others regarding indoor air issues, and where to find additional sources of information.

Chapter 43

Carbon Monoxide

Questions and Answers

What is carbon monoxide (CO) and how is it produced in the home?

Carbon monoxide (CO) is a colorless, odorless, poisonous gas. It is produced by the incomplete burning of solid, liquid, and gaseous fuels. Appliances fueled with natural gas, liquified petroleum (LP gas), oil, kerosene, coal, or wood may produce CO. Burning charcoal produces CO. Running cars produce CO.

How many people are unintentionally poisoned by CO?

Every year, over 200 people in the United States die from CO produced by fuel-burning appliances (furnaces, ranges, water heaters, room heaters). Others die from CO produced while burning charcoal inside a home, garage, vehicle or tent. Still others die from CO produced

The text in this chapter is from the following undated fact sheets produced by the Consumer Product Safety Commission, "Carbon Monoxide Questions and Answers," available at http://www.cpsc/gov/cpscpub/pubs/466.html, "Carbon Monoxide Detectors Can Save Lives," available at http://www.cpsc/gov/cpscpub/pubs/5010.html, and "Burning Charcoal in Homes, Vehicles, and Tents Causes 25 Deaths from Carbon Monoxide Each Year," available at http://www.cpsc/gov/cpscpub/pubs/5012.html, "What You Should Know About Combustion Appliances," available at http://www.cpsc.gov/cpscpub/pubs/452.html; all cited July 2001.

by cars left running in attached garages. Several thousand people go to hospital emergency rooms for treatment for CO poisoning.

What are the symptoms of CO poisoning?

The initial symptoms of CO poisoning are similar to the flu (but without the fever). They include:

- Headache

- Fatigue

- Shortness of breath

- Nausea

- Dizziness

Many people with CO poisoning mistake their symptoms for the flu or are misdiagnosed by physicians, which sometimes results in tragic deaths.

What should you do to prevent CO poisoning?

- Make sure appliances are installed according to manufacturer's instructions and local building codes. Most appliances should be installed by professionals. Have the heating system (including chimneys and vents) inspected and serviced annually. The inspector should also check chimneys and flues for blockages, corrosion, partial and complete disconnections, and loose connections.

- Install a CO detector/alarm that meets the requirements of the current UL standard 2034 or the requirements of the IAS 6-96 standard. A carbon monoxide detector/alarm can provide added protection, but is no substitute for proper use and upkeep of appliances that can produce CO. Install a CO detector/alarm in the hallway near every separate sleeping area of the home. Make sure the detector cannot be covered up by furniture or draperies.

- Never burn charcoal inside a home, garage, vehicle, or tent.

- Never use portable fuel-burning camping equipment inside a home, garage, vehicle, or tent.

328

- Never leave a car running in an attached garage, even with the garage door open.

- Never service fuel-burning appliances without proper knowledge, skills, and tools. Always refer to the owner's manual when performing minor adjustments or servicing fuel-burning appliances.

- Never use gas appliances such as ranges, ovens, or clothes dryers for heating your home.

- Never operate unvented fuel-burning appliances in any room with closed doors or windows or in any room where people are sleeping.

- Do not use gasoline-powered tools and engines indoors. If use is unavoidable, ensure that adequate ventilation is available and whenever possible place engine unit to exhaust outdoors.

What CO level is dangerous to your health?

The health effects of CO depend on the level of CO and length of exposure, as well as each individual's health condition. The concentration of CO is measured in parts per million (ppm). Health effects from exposure to CO levels of approximately 1 to 70 ppm are uncertain, but most people will not experience any symptoms. Some heart patients might experience an increase in chest pain. As CO levels increase and remain above 70 ppm, symptoms may become more noticeable (headache, fatigue, nausea). As CO levels increase above 150 to 200 ppm, disorientation, unconsciousness, and death are possible.

What should you do if you are experiencing symptoms of CO poisoning?

If you think you are experiencing any of the symptoms of CO poisoning, get fresh air immediately. Open windows and doors for more ventilation, turn off any combustion appliances, and leave the house. Call your fire department and report your symptoms. You could lose consciousness and die if you do nothing. It is also important to contact a doctor immediately for a proper diagnosis. Tell your doctor that you suspect CO poisoning is causing your problems. Prompt medical attention is important if you are experiencing any symptoms of CO poisoning when you are operating fuel-burning appliances. Before turning your fuel-burning appliances back on, make sure a qualified serviceperson checks them for malfunction.

What has changed in CO detectors/alarms recently?

CO detectors/alarms always have been and still are designed to alarm before potentially life-threatening levels of CO are reached. The UL standard 2034 (1998 revision) has stricter requirements that the detector/alarm must meet before it can sound. As a result, the possibility of nuisance alarms is decreased.

What should you do when the CO detector/alarm sounds?

Never ignore an alarming CO detector/alarm. If the detector/alarm sounds: Operate the reset button. Call your emergency services (fire department or 911). Immediately move to fresh air—outdoors or by an open door/window.

How should a consumer test a CO detector/alarm to make sure it is working?

Consumers should follow the manufacturer's instructions. Using a test button, some detectors/alarms test whether the circuitry as well as the sensor, which senses CO is working, while the test button on other detectors only tests whether the circuitry is working. For those units, which test the circuitry only, some manufacturers sell separate test kits to help the consumer test the CO sensor inside the alarm.

What is the role of the U.S. Consumer Product Safety Commission (CPSC) in preventing CO poisoning?

CPSC worked closely with Underwriters Laboratories (UL) to help develop the safety standard (UL 2034) for CO detectors/alarms. CPSC helps promote carbon monoxide safety awareness to raise awareness of CO hazards and the need for regular maintenance of fuel-burning appliances. CPSC recommends that every home have a CO detector/alarm that meets the requirements of the most recent UL standard 2034 or the IAS 6-96 standard in the hallway near every separate sleeping area. CPSC also works with industry to develop voluntary and mandatory standards for fuel-burning appliances.

Do some cities require that CO detectors/alarms be installed?

On September 15, 1993, Chicago, Illinois became one of the first cities in the nation to adopt an ordinance requiring, effective October 1,

1994, the installation of CO detectors/alarms in all new single-family homes and in existing single-family residences that have new oil or gas furnaces. Several other cities also require CO detectors/alarms in apartment buildings and single-family dwellings.

Should CO detectors/alarms be used in motor homes and other recreational vehicles?

CO detectors/alarms are available for boats and recreational vehicles and should be used. The Recreation Vehicle Industry Association requires CO detectors/alarms in motor homes and in towable recreational vehicles that have a generator or are prepped for a generator.

Carbon Monoxide Detectors Can Save Lives

The U.S. Consumer Product Safety Commission (CPSC) recommends that consumers purchase and install carbon monoxide detectors with labels showing they meet the requirements of the new Underwriters Laboratories, Inc. (UL) voluntary standard (UL 2034). The UL standard, published in April 1992, requires detectors to sound an alarm when exposure to carbon monoxide reaches potentially hazardous levels over a period of time. Detectors that meet the requirements of UL 2034 provide a greater safety margin than previously manufactured detectors.

About 200 people die each year from carbon monoxide poisoning associated with home fuel-burning heating equipment. Carbon monoxide is a colorless, odorless gas that is produced when any fuel is incompletely burned. Symptoms of carbon monoxide poisoning are similar to flu-like illnesses and include dizziness, fatigue, headaches, nausea, and irregular breathing. Carbon monoxide can leak from faulty furnaces or fuel-fired heaters or can be trapped inside by a blocked chimney or flue. Burning charcoal inside the house or running an automobile engine in an attached garage also will produce carbon monoxide in the home.

The first line of defense against carbon monoxide is to make sure that all fuel-burning appliances operate properly. Consumers should have their home heating systems (including chimneys and flues) inspected each year for proper operations and leakage. Inspectors should check all heating appliances and their electrical and mechanical components, thermostat controls and automatic safety devices.

Properly working carbon monoxide detectors can provide an early warning to consumers before the deadly gas builds up to a dangerous level. Exposure to a low concentration over several hours can be as dangerous as exposure to high carbon monoxide levels for a few minutes—the new detectors will detect both conditions. Most of the devices cost under $100. Each home should have at least one carbon monoxide detector in the area outside individual bedrooms. CPSC believes that carbon monoxide detectors are as important to home safety as smoke detectors are.

Burning Charcoal in Homes, Vehicles, and Tents is Hazardous

The U.S. Consumer Product Safety Commission (CPSC) warns consumers—including hunters and campers—never to burn charcoal inside homes, vehicles, or tents. Burning charcoal produces carbon monoxide. Carbon monoxide has no odor, cannot be seen, and can kill you. Consumers may not realize that burning charcoal produces carbon monoxide and that it will build up to a dangerous level. Opening a window or using a fan will not assure that carbon monoxide will be reduced to safe levels.

Each year, approximately 25 people die and hundreds more suffer from carbon monoxide poisoning when they burn charcoal in enclosed areas such as their homes, in campers or vans, or in tents. Some of the victims die from carbon monoxide poisoning after they burn charcoal in a bedroom or living room for heat or cooking. Some are campers who burn charcoal inside a tent or camper to keep warm. Others are hunters who burn charcoal inside their trucks, cars, or vans. Those who do not die can suffer headaches, drowsiness, dizziness, weakness, nausea, vomiting, confusion, disorientation, or collapse.

Never use charcoal to cook or provide heat inside enclosed areas such as tents, campers, vans, cars, trucks, homes, garages, or mobile homes because the carbon monoxide can kill you.

What You Should Know about Combustion Appliances and Indoor Air Pollution

Hazards may be associated with almost all types of appliances. Combustion appliances are those which burn fuels for warmth, cooking, or decorative purposes. Typical fuels are gas, both natural and liquefied petroleum (LP); kerosene; oil; coal; and wood. Examples of the appliances are space heaters, ranges, ovens, stoves, furnaces, fireplaces, water heaters, and clothes dryers. These appliances are usually safe. However, under certain conditions, these appliances can produce combustion pollutants that can damage your health, or even kill you.

Possible health effects range from headaches, dizziness, sleepiness, and watery eyes to breathing difficulties or even death. Similar effects may also occur because of common medical problems or other indoor air pollutants.

What Are Combustion Pollutants?

Combustion pollutants are gases or particles that come from burning materials. The combustion pollutants discussed in this chapter come from burning fuels in appliances. The common fuels burned in these appliances are natural or LP gas, fuel oil, kerosene, wood, or coal.

The types and amounts of pollutants produced depend upon the type of appliance, how well the appliance is installed, maintained, and vented, and the kind of fuel it uses. Some of the common pollutants produced from burning these fuels are carbon monoxide, nitrogen dioxide, particles, and sulfur dioxide. Particles can have hazardous chemicals attached to them. Other pollutants that can be produced by some appliances are unburned hydrocarbons and aldehydes.

Combustion always produces water vapor. Water vapor is not usually considered a pollutant, but it can act as one. It can result in high humidity and wet surfaces. These conditions encourage the growth of biological pollutants such as house dust mites, molds, and bacteria.

Where Do Combustion Pollutants Come from?

Combustion pollutants found indoors include: outdoor air, tobacco smoke, exhaust from car and lawn mower internal combustion engines, and some hobby activities such as welding, woodburning, and soldering. Combustion pollutants can also come from vented or unvented combustion appliances. These appliances include space heaters, gas ranges and ovens, furnaces, gas water heaters, gas clothes dryers, wood or coal-burning stoves, and fireplaces. As a group these are called "combustion appliances."

What Are Vented and Unvented Appliances?

Vented appliances are appliances designed to be used with a duct, chimney, pipe, or other device that carry the combustion pollutants

Table 43.1. Combustion Appliances and Potential Problems

Appliances	Fuel	Typical Potential Problems
Central Furnaces; Room Heaters; Fireplaces	Natural or Liquefied Petroleum Gas	Cracked heat exchanger; Not enough air to burn fuel properly; Defective/blocked flue; Maladjusted burner
Central Furnaces	Oil	Cracked heat exchanger; Not enough air to burn fuel properly; Defective/blocked flue; Maladjusted burner
Central Heaters; Room Heaters	Wood	Cracked heat exchanger; Not enough air to burn fuel properly; Defective/blocked flue; Green or treated wood
Central Furnaces; Stoves	Coal	Cracked heat exchanger; Not enough air to burn fuel properly; Defective grate
Room Heaters; Central Heaters	Kerosene	Improper adjustment; Wrong fuel (not-K-1); Wrong wick or wick height; Not enough air to burn fuel properly
Water Heaters	Natural or Liquefied Petroleum Gas	Not enough air to burn fuel properly; Defective/blocked flue; Maladjusted burner
Ranges; Ovens	Natural or Liquefied Petroleum Gas	Not enough air to burn fuel properly; Maladjusted burner; Misuse as a room heater
Stoves; Fireplaces	Wood; Coal	Not enough air to burn fuel properly; Defective/blocked flue; Green or treated wood; Cracked heat exchanger or firebox

outside the home. These appliances can release large amounts of pollutants directly into your home, if a vent is not properly installed, or is blocked or leaking.

Unvented appliances do not vent to the outside, so they release combustion pollutants directly into the home.

Can I Use Charcoal Grills or Charcoal Hibachis Indoors?

No. Never use these appliances inside homes, trailers, truck-caps, or tents. Carbon monoxide from burning and smoldering charcoal can kill you if you use it indoors for cooking or heating.

There are about 25 deaths each year from the use of charcoal grills and hibachis indoors.

NEVER burn charcoal inside homes, trailers, tents, or other enclosures. The carbon monoxide can kill you.

What Are the Health Effects of Combustion Pollutants?

The health effects of combustion pollutants range from headaches and breathing difficulties to death. The health effects may show up immediately after exposure or occur after being exposed to the pollutants for a long time. The effects depend upon the type and amount of pollutants and the length of time of exposure to them. They also depend upon several factors related to the exposed person. These include the age and any existing health problems. There are still some questions about the level of pollutants or the period of exposure needed to produce specific health effects. Further studies to better define the release of pollutants from combustion appliances and their health effects are needed.

Carbon Monoxide

Each year, according to CPSC, there are more than 200 carbon monoxide deaths related to the use of all types of combustion appliances in the home. Exposure to carbon monoxide reduces the blood's ability to carry oxygen. Often a person or an entire family may not recognize that carbon monoxide is poisoning them. The chemical is odorless and some of the symptoms are similar to common illnesses. This is particularly dangerous because carbon monoxide's deadly effects will not be recognized until it is too late to take action against them.

Carbon monoxide exposures especially affect unborn babies, infants, and people with anemia or a history of heart disease. Breathing low levels of the chemical can cause fatigue and increase chest pain in people with chronic heart disease. Breathing higher levels of carbon monoxide causes symptoms such as headaches, dizziness, and weakness in healthy people. Carbon monoxide also causes sleepiness, nausea, vomiting, confusion, and disorientation. At very high levels it causes loss of consciousness and death.

Nitrogen Dioxide

Breathing high levels of nitrogen dioxide causes irritation of the respiratory tract and causes shortness of breath. Compared to healthy people, children, and individuals with respiratory illnesses such as asthma, may be more susceptible to the effects of nitrogen dioxide.

Some studies have shown that children may have more colds and flu when exposed to low levels of nitrogen dioxide. When people with asthma inhale low levels of nitrogen dioxide while exercising, their lung airways can narrow and react more to inhaled materials.

Particles

Particles suspended in the air can cause eye, nose, throat, and lung irritation. They can increase respiratory symptoms, especially in people with chronic lung disease or heart problems. Certain chemicals attached to particles may cause lung cancer, if they are inhaled. The risk of lung cancer increases with the amount and length of exposure. The health effects from inhaling particles depend upon many factors, including the size of the particle and its chemical make-up.

Sulfur Dioxide

Sulfur dioxide at low levels of exposure can cause eye, nose, and respiratory tract irritation. At high exposure levels, it causes the lung airways to narrow. This causes wheezing, chest tightness, or breathing problems. People with asthma are particularly susceptible to the effects of sulfur dioxide. They may have symptoms at levels that are much lower than the rest of the population.

Other Pollutants

Combustion may release other pollutants. They include unburned hydrocarbons and aldehydes. Little is known about the levels of these pollutants in indoor air and the resulting health effects.

What Do I Do If I Suspect That Combustion Pollutants Are Affecting My Health?

If you suspect you are being subjected to carbon monoxide poisoning get fresh air immediately. Open windows and doors for more ventilation, turn off any combustion appliances, and leave the house. You could lose consciousness and die from carbon monoxide poisoning if you do nothing. It is also important to contact a doctor IMMEDIATELY for a proper diagnosis.

Remember to tell your doctor that you suspect carbon monoxide poisoning is causing your problems. Prompt medical attention is important.

Remember that some symptoms from combustion pollutants — headaches, dizziness, sleepiness, coughing, and watery eyes — may also occur because of common medical problems.

These medical problems include colds, the flu, or allergies. Similar symptoms may also occur because of other indoor air pollutants. Contact your doctor for a proper diagnosis.

To help your doctor make the correct diagnosis, try to have answers to the following questions:

- Do your symptoms occur only in the home? Do they disappear or decrease when you leave home, and reappear when you return?

- Is anyone else in your household complaining of similar symptoms, such as headaches, dizziness, or sleepiness? Are they complaining of nausea, watery eyes, coughing, or nose and throat irritation?

- Do you always have symptoms?

- Are your symptoms getting worse?

- Do you often catch colds or get the flu?

- Are you using any combustion appliances in your home?

- Has anyone inspected your appliances lately? Are you certain they are working properly?

Your doctor may take a blood sample to measure the level of carbon monoxide in your blood if he or she suspects carbon monoxide poisoning. This sample will help determine whether carbon monoxide is affecting your health.

Contact qualified appliance service people to have your appliances inspected and adjusted if needed. You should be able to find a qualified person by asking your appliance distributor or your fuel supplier. In some areas, the local fuel company may be able to inspect and adjust the appliance.

How Can I Reduce My Exposure to Combustion Pollutants?

Proper selection, installation, inspection and maintenance of your appliances are extremely important in reducing your exposure to these pollutants. Providing good ventilation in your home and correctly using your appliance can also reduce your exposure to these pollutants.

Additionally, there are several different residential carbon monoxide detectors for sale. The CPSC is encouraging the development of detectors that will provide maximum protection. These detectors would warn consumers of harmful carbon monoxide levels in the home. They may soon be widely available to reduce deaths from carbon monoxide poisoning.

Appliance Selection

- Choose vented appliances whenever possible.

- Only buy combustion appliances that have been tested and certified to meet current safety standards. Examples of certifying organizations are Underwriters Laboratories (UL) and the American Gas Association (AGA) Laboratories. Look for a label that clearly shows the certification.

- All currently manufactured vented gas heaters are required by industry safety standards to have a safety shut-off device. This device helps protect you from carbon monoxide poisoning by shutting off an improperly vented heater.

- Check your local and state building codes and fire ordinances to see if you can use an unvented space heater, if you consider purchasing one. They are not allowed to be used in some communities, dwellings, or certain rooms in the house.

- If you must replace an unvented gas space heater with another, make it a new one. Heaters made after 1982 have a pilot light safety system called an oxygen depletion sensor (ODS). This system shuts off the heater when there is not enough fresh air, before the heater begins producing large amounts of carbon

338

monoxide. Look for the label that tells you that the appliance has this safety system. Older heaters will not have this protection system.

- Consider buying gas appliances that have electronic ignitions rather than pilot lights. These appliances are usually more energy efficient and eliminate the continuous low-level pollutants from pilot lights.

- Buy appliances that are the correct size for the area you want to heat. Using the wrong size heater may produce more pollutants in your home and is not an efficient use of energy.

- Talk to your dealer to determine the type and size of appliance you will need. You may wish to write to the appliance manufacturer or association for more information on the appliance.

- All new woodstoves are EPA-certified to limit the amounts of pollutants released into the outdoor air. For more information on selecting, installing, operating, and maintaining wood-burning stoves. Before buying a woodstove check your local laws about the installation and use of woodstoves.

Proper Installation

You should have your appliances professionally installed. Professionals should follow the installation directions and applicable building codes. Improperly installed appliances can release dangerous pollutants in your home and may create a fire hazard. Be sure that the installer checks for backdrafting on all vented appliances. A qualified installer knows how to do this.

Ventilation

- To reduce indoor air pollution, a good supply of fresh outdoor air is needed. The movement of air into and out of your home is very important. Normally, air comes through cracks around doors and windows. This air helps reduce the level of pollutants indoors. This supply of fresh air is also important to help carry pollutants up the chimney, stovepipe, or flue to the outside.

- Keep doors open to the rest of the house from the room where you are using an unvented gas space heater or kerosene heater, and crack open a window. This allows enough air for proper combustion and reduces the level of pollutants, especially carbon monoxide.

- Use a hood fan, if you are using a range. They reduce the level of pollutants you breath, if they exhaust to the outside. Make sure that enough air is coming into the house when you use an exhaust fan. If needed, slightly open a door or window, especially if other appliances are in use. For proper operation of most combustion appliances and their venting system, the air pressure in the house should be greater than that outside. If not, the vented appliances could release combustion pollutants into the house rather than outdoors. If you suspect that you have this problem you may need the help of a qualified person to solve it.

- Make sure that your vented appliance has the vent connected and that nothing is blocking it. Make sure there are no holes or cracks in the vent. Do not vent gas clothes dryers or water heaters into the house for heating. This is unsafe.

- Open the stove's damper when adding wood. This allows more air into the stove. More air helps the wood burn properly and prevents pollutants from being drawn back into the house instead of going up the chimney. Visible smoke or a constant smoky odor inside the home when using a woodburning stove is a sign that the stove is not working properly. Soot on furniture in the rooms where you are using the stove also tells this. Smoke and soot are signs that the stove is releasing pollutants into the indoor air.

Correct Use

- Read and follow the instructions for all appliances so you understand how they work. Keep the owner's manual in a convenient place to refer to when needed. Also, read and follow the warning labels because they tell you important safety information that you need to know. Reading and following the instructions and warning labels could save your life.

- Always use the correct fuel for the appliance.

- Only use water-clear ASTM 1-K kerosene for kerosene heaters. The use of kerosene other than 1-K could lead to a release of more pollutants in your home. Never use gasoline in a kerosene heater because it can cause a fire or an explosion. Using even small amounts of gasoline could cause a fire.

- Use seasoned hardwoods (elm, maple, oak) instead of softwoods (cedar, fir, pine) in woodburning stoves and fireplaces. Hardwoods are better because they burn hotter and form less creosote, an oily, black tar that sticks to chimneys and stove pipes. Do not use green or wet woods as the primary wood because they make more creosote and smoke. Never burn painted scrap wood or wood treated with preservatives, because they could release highly toxic pollutants, such as arsenic or lead. Plastics, charcoal, and colored paper such as comics, also produce pollutants. Never burn anything that the stove or fireplace manufacturer does not recommend.

- Never use a range, oven, or dryer to heat your home. When you misuse gas appliances in this way, they can produce fatal amounts of carbon monoxide. They can produce high levels of nitrogen dioxide, too.

- Never use an unvented combustion heater overnight or in a room where you are sleeping. Carbon monoxide from combustion heaters can reach dangerous levels.

- Never ignore a safety device when it shuts off an appliance. It means that something is wrong. Read your appliance instructions to find out what you should do or have a professional check out the problem.

- Never ignore the smell of fuel. This usually indicates that the appliance is not operating properly or is leaking fuel. Leaking fuel will not always be detectible by smell. If you suspect that you have a fuel leak have it fixed as soon as possible. In most cases you should shut off the appliance, extinguish any other flames or pilot lights, shut off other appliances in the area, open windows and doors, call for help, and leave the area.

Inspection and Maintenance

- Have your combustion appliance regularly inspected and maintained to reduce your exposure to pollutants. Appliances that are not working properly can release harmful and even fatal amounts of pollutants, especially carbon monoxide.

- Have chimneys and vents inspected when installing or changing vented heating appliances. Some modifications may be required. For example, if a change was made in your heating system from oil to natural gas, the flue gas produced by the gas system could be hot enough to melt accumulated oil combustion debris in the chimney or vent. This debris could block the vent forcing pollutants into the house. It is important to clean your chimney and vents especially when changing heating systems.

The best advice is to follow for maintenance is the recommendations of the manufacturer. The same combustion appliance may have different inspection and maintenance requirements, depending upon where you live.

In general, check the flame in the furnace combustion chamber at the beginning of the heating season. Natural gas furnaces should have a blue flame with perhaps only a slight yellow tip. Call your appliance service representative to adjust the burner if there is a lot of yellow in the flame, or call your local utility company for this service. LP units should have a flame with a bright blue center that may have a light yellow tip. Pilot lights on gas water heaters and gas cooking appliances should also have a blue flame. Have a trained service representative adjust the pilot light if it is yellow or orange.

Before each heating season, have flues and chimneys inspected and cleaned before each heating season for leakage and for blockage by creosote or debris. Creosote buildup or leakage could cause black stains on the outside of the chimney or flue. These stains can mean that pollutants are leaking into the house.

Table 43.2 shows how and when to take care of your appliance.

Table 43.2. Inspection and Maintenance Schedules

Appliance	*Inspection/Frequency*	*Maintenance/Frequency*
Gas Hot Air Heating System	Air Filters: Clean/change filter monthly as needed; look at flues for rust and soot yearly	Qualified person check/clean chimney, clean/adjust burners, check heat exchanger and operation yearly (at start of heating season)
Gas/Oil, Water/Steam Heating Systems and Water Heaters	Look at flues for rust and soot yearly	Qualified person check/clean chimney, clean combustion chamber, adjust burners, check operation yearly (at start of heating season)
Kerosene Space Heaters	Look to see that mantle is properly seated daily when in use; Look to see that fuel tank is free of water and other contaminants daily or before refueling	Check and replace wick yearly (at start of heating season); Clean Combustion chamber yearly (at start of heating season); Drain fuel tank yearly (at end of heating season)
Wood/Coal Stoves	Look at flues for rust and soot yearly	Qualified person check/clean chimney, check seams and gaskets, check operation yearly (at start of heating season)

Chapter 44

Asbestos

Asbestos in the Home

This chapter will help you understand asbestos: what it is, its health effects, where it is in your home, and what to do about it.

Even if asbestos is in your home, this is usually NOT a serious problem. The mere presence of asbestos in a home or a building is not hazardous. The danger is that asbestos materials may become damaged over time. Damaged asbestos may release asbestos fibers and become a health hazard.

The best thing to do with asbestos material in good condition is to leave it alone! Disturbing it may create a health hazard where none existed before.

Where Asbestos Hazards May Be Found in the Home

1. Some roofing and siding shingles are made of asbestos cement.

2. Houses built between 1930 and 1950 may have asbestos as insulation.

Text in this chapter is from the following undated fact sheets produced by the Consumer Product Safety Commission, "Asbestos in the Home," available at http://www.cpsc.gov/cpscpub/pubs/453.html, and "CPSC Warns about Asbestos in Consumer Products," available at http://www.cpsc.gpv/cpscpub/pubs/5080.html; both cited July 2001.

3. Asbestos may be present in textured paint and in patching compounds used on wall and ceiling joints. Their use was banned in 1977.

4. Artificial ashes and embers sold for use in gas-fired fireplaces may contain asbestos.

5. Older products such as stove-top pads may have some asbestos compounds.

6. Walls and floors around woodburning stoves may be protected with asbestos paper, millboard, or cement sheets.

7. Asbestos is found in some vinyl floor tiles and the backing on vinyl sheet flooring and adhesives.

8. Hot water and steam pipes in older houses may be coated with an asbestos material or covered with an asbestos blanket or tape.

9. Oil and coal furnaces and door gaskets may have asbestos insulation.

What Is Asbestos?

Asbestos is a mineral fiber. It can be positively identified only with a special type of microscope. There are several types of asbestos fibers. In the past, asbestos was added to a variety of products to strengthen them and to provide heat insulation and fire resistance.

How Can Asbestos Affect My Health?

From studies of people who were exposed to asbestos in factories and shipyards, we know that breathing high levels of asbestos fibers can lead to an increased risk of:

*   lung cancer:

    mesothelioma, a cancer of the lining of the chest and the abdominal cavity; and

    asbestosis, in which the lungs become scarred with fibrous tissue.

The risk of lung cancer and mesothelioma increases with the number of fibers inhaled. The risk of lung cancer from inhaling asbestos fibers is also greater if you smoke. People who get asbestosis have usually been exposed to high levels of asbestos for a long time. The symptoms of these diseases do not usually appear until about 20 to 30 years after the first exposure to asbestos.

Most people exposed to small amounts of asbestos, as we all are in our daily lives, do not develop these health problems. However, if disturbed, asbestos material may release asbestos fibers, which can be inhaled into the lungs. The fibers can remain there for a long time, increasing the risk of disease. Asbestos material that would crumble easily if handled, or that has been sawed, scraped, or sanded into a powder, is more likely to create a health hazard.

Where Can I Find Asbestos and When Can It Be a Problem?

Most products made today do not contain asbestos. Those few products made which still contain asbestos that could be inhaled are required to be labeled as such. However, until the 1970s, many types of building products and insulation materials used in homes contained asbestos.

Common products that might have contained asbestos in the past, and conditions which may release fibers, include:

- STEAM PIPES, BOILERS, and FURNACE DUCTS insulated with an asbestos blanket or asbestos paper tape. These materials may release asbestos fibers if damaged, repaired, or removed improperly.

- RESILIENT FLOOR TILES (vinyl asbestos, asphalt, and rubber), the backing on VINYL SHEET FLOORING, and ADHESIVES used for installing floor tile. Sanding tiles can release fibers. So may scraping or sanding the backing of sheet flooring during removal.

- CEMENT SHEET, MILLBOARD, and PAPER used as insulation around furnaces and woodburning stoves. Repairing or removing appliances may release asbestos fibers. So may cutting, tearing, sanding, drilling, or sawing insulation.

- DOOR GASKETS in furnaces, wood stoves, and coal stoves. Worn seals can release asbestos fibers during use.

- SOUNDPROOFING OR DECORATIVE MATERIAL sprayed on walls and ceilings. Loose, crumbly, or water-damaged material may release fibers. So will sanding, drilling, or scraping the material.

347

- PATCHING AND JOINT COMPOUNDS for walls and ceilings, and TEXTURED PAINTS. Sanding, scraping, or drilling these surfaces may release asbestos.

- ASBESTOS CEMENT ROOFING, SHINGLES, and SIDING. These products are not likely to release asbestos fibers unless sawed, dilled, or cut.

- ARTIFICIAL ASHES AND EMBERS sold for use in gas-fired fireplaces. Also, other older household products such as FIRE-PROOF GLOVES, STOVE-TOP PADS, IRONING BOARD COVERS, and certain HAIRDRYERS.

- AUTOMOBILE BRAKE PADS AND LININGS, CLUTCH FACINGS, and GASKETS.

What Should Be Done about Asbestos in the Home?

If you think asbestos may be in your home, don't panic! Usually the best thing is to leave asbestos material that is in good condition alone.

Generally, material in good condition will not release asbestos fibers. THERE IS NO DANGER unless fibers are released and inhaled into the lungs.

Check material regularly if you suspect it may contain asbestos. Don't touch it, but look for signs of wear or damage such as tears, abrasions, or water damage. Damaged material may release asbestos fibers. This is particularly true if you often disturb it by hitting, rubbing, or handling it, or if it is exposed to extreme vibration or air flow.

Sometimes, the best way to deal with slightly damaged material is to limit access to the area and not touch or disturb it. Discard damaged or worn asbestos gloves, stove-top pads, or ironing board covers. Check with local health, environmental, or other appropriate officials to find out proper handling and disposal procedures.

If asbestos material is more than slightly damaged, or if you are going to make changes in your home that might disturb it, repair or removal by a professional is needed. Before you have your house remodeled, find out whether asbestos materials are present.

How to Identify Materials That Contain Asbestos

You can't tell whether a material contains asbestos simply by looking at it, unless it is labeled. If in doubt, treat the material as if it contains asbestos or have it sampled and analyzed by a qualified professional. A professional should take samples for analysis, since a professional knows what to look for, and because there may be an increased health risk if fibers are released. In fact, if done incorrectly, sampling can be more hazardous than leaving the material alone. Taking samples yourself is not recommended. If you nevertheless choose to take the samples yourself, take care not to release asbestos fibers into the air or onto yourself. Material that is in good condition and will not be disturbed (by remodeling, for example) should be left alone. Only material that is damaged or will be disturbed should be sampled. Anyone who samples asbestos-containing materials should have as much information as possible on the handling of asbestos before sampling, and at a minimum, should observe the following procedures:

- Make sure no one else is in the room when sampling is done.

- Wear disposable gloves or wash hands after sampling.

- Shut down any heating or cooling systems to minimize the spread of any released fibers.

- Do not disturb the material any more than is needed to take a small sample.

- Place a plastic sheet on the floor below the area to be sampled.

- Wet the material using a fine mist of water containing a few drops of detergent before taking the sample. The water/detergent mist will reduce the release of asbestos fibers.

- Carefully cut a piece from the entire depth of the material using, for example, a small knife, corer, or other sharp object. Place the small piece into a clean container (for example, a 35 mm film canister, small glass or plastic vial, or high quality resealable plastic bag).

- Tightly seal the container after the sample is in it.

- Carefully dispose of the plastic sheet. Use a damp paper towel to clean up any material on the outside of the container or around the area sampled. Dispose of asbestos materials according to state and local procedures.

- Label the container with an identification number and clearly state when and where the sample was taken.

- Patch the sampled area with the smallest possible piece of duct tape to prevent fiber release.

- Send the sample to an EPA-approved laboratory for analysis. The National Institute for Standards and Technology (NIST) has a list of these laboratories.

How to Manage an Asbestos Problem

If the asbestos material is in good shape and will not be disturbed, do nothing! If it is a problem, there are two types of corrections: repair and removal.

Repair usually involves either sealing or covering asbestos material.

Sealing (encapsulation) involves treating the material with a sealant that either binds the asbestos fibers together or coats the material so fibers are not released. Pipe, furnace, and boiler insulation can sometimes be repaired this way. This should be done only by a professional trained to handle asbestos safely.

Covering (enclosure) involves placing something over or around the material that contains asbestos to prevent release of fibers. Exposed insulated piping may be covered with a protective wrap or jacket.

With any type of repair, the asbestos remains in place. Repair is usually cheaper than removal, but it may make later removal of asbestos, if necessary, more difficult and costly. Repairs can either be major or minor.

Asbestos Do's and Don'ts for the Homeowner

- Do keep activities to a minimum in any areas having damaged material that may contain asbestos.

- Do take every precaution to avoid damaging asbestos material.

- Do have removal and major repair done by people trained and qualified in handling asbestos. It is highly recommended that sampling and minor repair also be done by asbestos professionals.

- Don't dust, sweep, or vacuum debris that may contain asbestos.

- Don't saw, sand, scrape, or drill holes in asbestos materials.

- Don't use abrasive pads or brushes on power strippers to strip wax from asbestos flooring.

- Never use a power stripper on a dry floor.

350

- Don't sand or try to level asbestos flooring or its backing. When asbestos flooring needs replacing, install new floorcovering over it, if possible.

- Don't track material that could contain asbestos through the house. If you cannot avoid walking through the area, have it cleaned with a wet mop. If the material is from a damaged area, or if a large area must be cleaned, call an asbestos professional.

Major repairs must be done only by a professional trained in methods for safely handling asbestos.

Minor repairs should also be done by professionals since there is always a risk of exposure to fibers when asbestos is disturbed.

Doing minor repairs yourself is not recommended since improper handling of asbestos materials can create a hazard where none existed. If you nevertheless choose to do minor repairs, you should have as much information as possible on the handling of asbestos before doing anything. Contact your state or local health department or regional EPA office for information about asbestos training programs in your area. Your local school district may also have information about asbestos professionals and training programs for school buildings. Even if you have completed a training program, do not try anything more than minor repairs. Before undertaking minor repairs, carefully examine the area around the damage to make sure it is stable. As a general matter, any damaged area which is bigger than the size of your hand is not a minor repair.

Before undertaking minor repairs, be sure to follow all the precautions described earlier for sampling asbestos material. Always wet the asbestos material using a fine mist of water containing a few drops of detergent. Commercial products designed to fill holes and seal damaged areas are available. Small areas of material such as pipe insulation can be covered by wrapping a special fabric, such as rewettable glass cloth, around it. These products are available from stores (listed in the telephone directory under "Safety Equipment and Clothing") which specialize in asbestos materials and safety items.

Removal is usually the most expensive method and, unless required by state or local regulations, should be the last option considered in most situations. This is because removal poses the greatest risk of fiber release. However, removal may be required when remodeling or making major changes to your home that will disturb asbestos material. Also, removal may be called for if asbestos material is damaged extensively and cannot be otherwise repaired. Removal is complex and must be done only by a contractor with special training. Improper removal may actually increase the health risks to you and your family.

Asbestos Professionals: Who Are They and What Can They Do?

Asbestos professionals are trained in handling asbestos material. The type of professional will depend on the type of product and what needs to be done to correct the problem. You may hire a general asbestos contractor or, in some cases, a professional trained to handle specific products containing asbestos.

Asbestos professionals can conduct home inspections, take samples of suspected material, assess its condition, and advise about what corrections are needed and who is qualified to make these corrections. Once again, material in good condition need not be sampled unless it is likely to be disturbed. Professional correction or abatement contractors repair or remove asbestos materials.

Some firms offer combinations of testing, assessment, and correction. A professional hired to assess the need for corrective action should not be connected with an asbestos-correction firm. It is better to use two different firms so there is no conflict of interest. Services vary from one area to another around the country.

The federal government has training courses for asbestos professionals around the country. Some state and local governments also have or require training or certification courses. Ask asbestos professionals to document their completion of federal or state-approved training. Each person performing work in your home should provide proof of training and licensing in asbestos work, such as completion of EPA-approved training. State and local health departments or EPA regional offices may have listings of licensed professionals in your area.

If you have a problem that requires the services of asbestos professionals, check their credentials carefully. Hire professionals who are trained, experienced, reputable, and accredited—especially if accreditation is required by state or local laws. Before hiring a professional, ask for references from previous clients. Find out if they were satisfied. Ask whether the professional has handled similar situations. Get cost estimates from several professionals, as the charges for these services can vary.

Though private homes are usually not covered by the asbestos regulations that apply to schools and public buildings, professionals should still use procedures described during federal or state-approved training. Homeowners should be alert to the chance of misleading claims by asbestos consultants and contractors. There have been reports of firms incorrectly claiming that asbestos materials in homes must be replaced. In other cases, firms have encouraged unnecessary removals or performed them improperly. Unnecessary removals are a waste of money. Improper removals may actually increase the health risks to you and your family. To guard against this, know what services are available and what procedures and precautions are needed to do the job properly.

In addition to general asbestos contractors, you may select a roofing, flooring, or plumbing contractor trained to handle asbestos when it is necessary to remove and replace roofing, flooring, siding, or asbestos-cement pipe that is part of a water system. Normally, roofing and flooring contractors are exempt from state and local licensing requirements because they do not perform any other asbestos-correction work.

Asbestos-containing automobile brake pads and linings, clutch facings, and gaskets should be repaired and replaced only by a professional using special protective equipment. Many of these products are now available without asbestos.

If You Hire a Professional Asbestos Inspector

- Make sure that the inspection will include a complete visual examination and the careful collection and lab analysis of samples. If asbestos is present, the inspector should provide a written evaluation describing its location and extent of damage, and give recommendations for correction or prevention.

- Make sure an inspecting firm makes frequent site visits if it is hired to assure that a contractor follows proper procedures and requirements. The inspector may recommend and perform checks after the correction to assure the area has been properly cleaned.

If You Hire a Corrective-Action Contractor

- Check with your local air pollution control board, the local agency responsible for worker safety, and the Better Business Bureau. Ask if the firm has had any safety violations. Find out if there are legal actions filed against it.

- Insist that the contractor use the proper equipment to do the job. The workers must wear approved respirators, gloves, and other protective clothing.

- Before work begins, get a written contract specifying the work plan, cleanup, and the applicable federal, state, and local regulations which the contractor must follow (such as notification requirements and asbestos disposal procedures). Contact your state and local health departments, EPA's regional office, and the Occupational Safety and Health Administration's regional office to find out what the regulations are. Be sure the contractor follows local asbestos removal and disposal laws. At the end of the job, get written assurance from the contractor that all procedures have been followed.

- Assure that the contractor avoids spreading or tracking asbestos dust into other areas of your home. They should seal the work area from the rest of the house using plastic sheeting and duct tape, and also turn off the heating and air conditioning system. For some repairs, such as pipe insulation removal, plastic glove bags may be adequate. They must be sealed with tape and properly disposed of when the job is complete.

- Make sure the work site is clearly marked as a hazard area. Do not allow household members and pets into the area until work is completed.

- Insist that the contractor apply a wetting agent to the asbestos material with a hand sprayer that creates a fine mist before removal. Wet fibers do not float in the air as easily as dry fibers and will be easier to clean up.

- Make sure the contractor does not break removed material into small pieces. This could release asbestos fibers into the air. Pipe insulation was usually installed in preformed blocks and should be removed in complete pieces.

- Upon completion, assure that the contractor cleans the area well with wet mops, wet rags, sponges, or HEPA (high efficiency particulate air) vacuum cleaners. A regular vacuum cleaner must never be used. Wetting helps reduce the chance of spreading asbestos fibers in the air. All asbestos materials and disposable equipment and clothing used in the job must be placed in sealed, leakproof, and labeled plastic bags. The work site should be visually free of dust and debris. Air monitoring (to make sure there is no increase of asbestos fibers in the air) may be necessary to assure that the contractor's job is done properly. This should be done by someone not connected with the contractor.

Caution!

Do not dust, sweep, or vacuum debris that may contain asbestos. These steps will disturb tiny asbestos fibers and may release them into the air. Remove dust by wet mopping or with a special HEPA vacuum cleaner used by trained asbestos contractors.

Asbestos in Consumer Products

The Consumer Product Safety Commission warns consumers about the hazard of exposure to consumer products containing asbestos. These products include:

- Asbestos paper and millboard
- Asbestos-cement sheet
- Dry-mix asbestos furnace or boiler cement
- Asbestos wood/coal stove door gaskets
- Asbestos laboratory gloves and pads
- Asbestos stove mats and iron rests
- Central hot-air furnace duct connectors containing asbestos
- Bulk asbestos fibers

Some of these products still are for sale or may be in consumers' homes. Handling these products may release asbestos fibers; breathing asbestos fibers is known to cause cancer. The risk of asbestos-related cancer may be substantially higher among smokers at the levels of asbestos encountered in homes. If these products must be handled:

- Wear a respirator approved for use with asbestos.
- Do not dry sweep; use wet procedures for clean-up. Dispose of any residue or unused material along with the clean-up materials in a manner that will not release airborne fibers.
- Do not use power operated or other tools to cut or drill because this can create respirable dust levels.
- Keep these products out of the reach of children.

The extent of current asbestos product labeling is limited. Except for products which are sold unwrapped, such as millboard; and asbestos-cement sheet, all products are labeled with the name of the manufacturer or distributor. Only asbestos paper and furnace cement are labeled as containing asbestos. Non-asbestos substitutes for all asbestos products are widely available to the public for household uses.

CPSC requires that the labeling requirements of the Federal Hazardous Substances Act apply to asbestos products. Asbestos products not labeled according to these provisions will be considered misbranded, and thus will be subject to enforcement action by the Commission.

Chapter 45

Formaldehyde

What Is Formaldehyde?

Formaldehyde is an important industrial chemical used to make other chemicals, building materials, and household products. It is one of the large family of chemical compounds called volatile organic compounds or "VOCs." The term volatile means that the compounds vaporize, that is, become a gas, at normal room temperatures. Formaldehyde serves many purposes in products. It is used as a part of:

- the glue or adhesive in pressed wood products (particleboard, hardwood plywood, and medium density fiberboard [MDF]);

- preservatives in some paints, coatings, and cosmetics;

- the coating that provides permanent press quality to fabrics and draperies;

- the finish used to coat paper products; and

- certain insulation materials (urea-formaldehyde foam and fiberglass insulation).

Formaldehyde is released into the air by burning wood, kerosene or natural gas, by automobiles, and by cigarettes. Formaldehyde can

"An Update on Formaldehyde," an undated fact sheet produced by the Consumer Product Safety Commission, available online at http://www.cpsc.gov/cpscpub/pubs/725.html; cited July 2001.

off-gas from materials made with it. It is also a naturally occurring substance.

This chapter tells you where you may come in contact with formaldehyde, how it may affect your health, and how you might reduce your exposure to it.

Why Should You Be Concerned?

Formaldehyde is a colorless, strong-smelling gas. When present in the air at levels above 0.1 ppm (parts in a million parts of air), it can cause watery eyes, burning sensations in the eyes, nose and throat, nausea, coughing, chest tightness, wheezing, skin rashes, and allergic reactions. It also has been observed to cause cancer in scientific studies using laboratory animals and may cause cancer in humans. Typical exposures to humans are much lower; thus any risk of causing cancer is believed to be small at the level at which humans are exposed.

Formaldehyde can affect people differently. Some people are very sensitive to formaldehyde while others may not have any noticeable reaction to the same level.

Persons have developed allergic reactions (allergic skin disease and hives) to formaldehyde through skin contact with solutions of formaldehyde or durable-press clothing containing formaldehyde. Others have developed asthmatic reactions and skin rashes from exposure to formaldehyde.

Formaldehyde is just one of several gases present indoors that may cause illnesses. Many of these gases, as well as colds and flu, cause similar symptoms.

What Levels of Formaldehyde Are Normal?

Formaldehyde is normally present at low levels, usually less than 0.03 ppm, in both outdoor and indoor air. The outdoor air in rural areas has lower concentrations while urban areas have higher concentrations. Residences or offices that contain products that release formaldehyde to the air can have formaldehyde levels of greater than 0.03 ppm. Products that may add formaldehyde to the air include particleboard used as flooring underlayment, shelving, furniture and cabinets; MDF in cabinets and furniture; hardwood plywood wall panels, and urea-formaldehyde foam used as insulation. As formaldehyde levels increase, illness or discomfort is more likely to occur and may be more serious.

Efforts have been made by both the government and industry to reduce exposure to formaldehyde. CPSC voted to ban urea-formaldehyde foam insulation in 1982. That ban was over-turned in the courts, but this action greatly reduced the residential use of the insulation product.

CPSC, the Department of Housing and Urban Development (HUD) and other federal agencies have historically worked with the pressed wood industry to further reduce the release of the chemical from their products. A 1985 HUD regulation covering the use of pressed wood products in manufactured housing was designed to ensure that indoor levels are below 0.4 ppm. However, it would be unrealistic to expect to completely remove formaldehyde from the air. Some persons who are extremely sensitive to formaldehyde may need to reduce or stop using these products.

What Affects Formaldehyde Levels?

Formaldehyde levels in the indoor air depend mainly on what is releasing the formaldehyde (the source), the temperature, the humidity, and the air exchange rate (the amount of outdoor air entering or leaving the indoor area). Increasing the flow of outdoor air to the inside decreases the formaldehyde levels. Decreasing this flow of outdoor air by sealing the residence or office increases the formaldehyde level in the indoor air.

As the temperature rises, more formaldehyde is emitted from the product. The reverse is also true; less formaldehyde is emitted at lower temperature. Humidity also affects the release of formaldehyde from the product. As humidity rises more formaldehyde is released.

The formaldehyde levels in a residence change with the season and from day-to-day and day-to-night. Levels may be high on a hot and humid day and low on a cool, dry day. Understanding these factors is important when you consider measuring the levels of formaldehyde.

Some sources—such as pressed wood products containing urea-formaldehyde glues, urea-formaldehyde foam insulation, durable-press fabrics, and draperies—release more formaldehyde when new. As they age, the formaldehyde release decreases.

What are the Major Sources?

Urea-formaldehyde foam insulation: During the 1970s, many homeowners installed this insulation to save energy. Many of these homes had high levels of formaldehyde soon afterwards. Sale of urea-formaldehyde foam insulation has largely stopped. Formaldehyde released from this product decreases rapidly after the first few months and reaches background levels in a few years. Therefore, urea-formaldehyde foam insulation installed 5 to 10 years ago is unlikely to still release formaldehyde.

Durable-press fabrics, draperies and coated paper products: In the early 1960s, there were several reports of allergic reactions to form-aldehyde from durable-press fabrics and coated paper products. Such reports have declined in recent years as industry has taken steps to reduce formaldehyde levels. Draperies made of formaldehyde-treated durable press fabrics may add slightly to indoor formaldehyde levels.

Cosmetics, paints, coatings, and some wet-strength paper products: The amount of formaldehyde present in these products is small and is of slight concern. However, persons sensitive to formaldehyde may have allergic reactions.

Pressed wood products: Pressed wood products, especially those containing urea-formaldehyde glues, are a source of formaldehyde. These products include particleboard used as flooring underlayment, shelves, cabinets, and furniture; hardwood plywood wall panels; and medium density fiberboard used in drawers, cabinets and furniture. When the surfaces and edges of these products are unlaminated or uncoated they have the potential to release more formaldehyde. Manu-facturers have reduced formaldehyde emissions from pressed wood products by 80-90% from the levels of the early 1980s.

Combustion sources: Burning materials such as wood, kerosene, cigarettes and natural gas, and operating internal combustion engines (e.g. automobiles), produce small quantities of formaldehyde. Com-bustion sources add small amounts of formaldehyde to indoor air.

Products such as carpets or gypsum board do not contain signifi-cant amounts of formaldehyde when new. They may trap formalde-hyde emitted from other sources and later release the formaldehyde into the indoor air when the temperature and humidity change.

Do You Have Formaldehyde-Related Symptoms?

There are several formaldehyde-related symptoms, such as watery eyes, runny nose, burning sensation in the eyes, nose, and throat, headaches and fatigue. These symptoms may also occur because of the common cold, the flu or other pollutants that may be present in the indoor air. If these symptoms lessen when you are away from home or office but reappear upon your return, they may be caused by indoor pollutants, including formaldehyde. Examine your environment. Have you recently moved into a new or different home or office? Have you recently remodeled or installed new cabinets or furniture? Symptoms may be due to formaldehyde exposure. You should contact your physician and/or state or local health department for help. Your physician can help to determine if the cause of your symptoms is formaldehyde or other pollutants.

Should You Measure Formaldehyde?

Only trained professionals should measure formaldehyde because they know how to interpret the results. If you become ill, and the illness persists following the purchase of furniture or remodeling with pressed wood products, you might not need to measure formaldehyde. Since these are possible sources, you can take action. You may become ill after painting, sealing, making repairs, and/or applying pest control treatment in your home or office. In such cases, indoor air pollutants other than formaldehyde may be the cause. If the source is not obvious, you should consult a physician to determine whether or not your symptoms might relate to indoor air quality problems. If your physician believes that you may be sensitive to formaldehyde, you may want to make some measurements. As discussed earlier, many factors can affect the level of formaldehyde on a given day in an office or residence. This is why a professional is best suited to make an accurate measurement of the levels.

Do-it-yourself formaldehyde measuring devices are available, however these devices can only provide a "ball park" estimate for the formaldehyde level in the area. If you use such a device, carefully follow the instructions.

How Do You Reduce Formaldehyde Exposure?

Every day you probably use many products that contain formaldehyde. You may not be able to avoid coming in contact with some formaldehyde in your normal daily routine. If you are sensitive to formaldehyde, you will need to avoid many everyday items to reduce symptoms. For most people, a low-level exposure to formaldehyde (up to 0.1 ppm) does not produce symptoms. People who suspect they are sensitive to formaldehyde should work closely with a knowledgeable physician to make sure that it is formaldehyde causing their symptoms.

You can avoid exposure to higher levels by:

- Purchasing pressed wood products such as particleboard, MDF, or hardwood plywood for construction or remodeling of homes, or for do-it-yourself projects, that are labeled or stamped to be in conformance with American National Standards Institute (ANSI) criteria. Particleboard should be in conformance with ANSI A208.1-1993. For particleboard flooring, look for ANSI grades "PBU", "D2", or "D3" actually stamped on the panel. MDF should be in conformance with ANSI A208.2-1994; and hardwood plywood with ANSI/HPVA HP-1-1994. These standards all specify lower formaldehyde emission levels.

- Purchasing furniture or cabinets that contain a high percentage of panel surface and edges that are laminated or coated. Unlaminated or uncoated (raw) panels of pressed wood products will generally emit more formaldehyde than those that are laminated or coated.

- Using alternative products such as wood panel products not made with urea-formaldehyde glues, lumber or metal.

- Avoiding the use of foamed-in-place insulation containing formaldehyde, especially urea-formaldehyde foam insulation.

- Washing durable-press fabrics before use.

How Do You Reduce Existing Formaldehyde Levels?

The choice of methods to reduce formaldehyde is unique to your situation. People who can help you select appropriate methods are your state or local health department, physician, or professional expert in indoor air problems. Here are some of the methods to reduce indoor levels of formaldehyde.

1. Bring large amounts of fresh air into the home. Increase ventilation by opening doors and windows and installing an exhaust fan(s).

2. Seal the surfaces of the formaldehyde-containing products that are not already laminated or coated. You may use a vapor barrier such as some paints, varnishes, or a layer of vinyl or polyurethane-like materials. Be sure to seal completely, with a material that does not itself contain formaldehyde. Many paints

and coatings will emit other VOCs when curing, so be sure to ventilate the area well during and after treatment.

3. Remove from your home the product that is releasing formaldehyde in the indoor air. When other materials in the area such as carpets, gypsum boards, etc., have absorbed formaldehyde, these products may also start releasing it into the air. Overall levels of formaldehyde can be lower if you increase the ventilation over an extended period.

One method NOT recommended by CPSC is a chemical treatment with strong ammonia (28-29% ammonia in water) which results in a temporary decrease in formaldehyde levels. We strongly discourage such treatment since ammonia in this strength is extremely dangerous to handle.

Ammonia may damage the brass fittings of a natural gas system, adding a fire and explosion danger.

For more information about biological pollutants, combustion pollutants, asbestos, and indoor air quality in your home, write to:

U.S. Consumer Product Safety Commission
Washington, DC 20207
Tel: CPSC's toll-free hotline: 800-638-2772
Internet: http://www.cpsc.gov

American Lung Association
1740 Broadway
New York, NY 10019-4374
Tel: 212-315-8700
Internet: http://www.lungusa.org
E-mail: info@lungusa.org

Local and State Health Departments

Chapter 46

Methylene Chloride Risks

Use of Proper Ventilation While Using Methylene Chloride

When working with paint strippers and adhesive removers containing methylene chloride, use the products outdoors or ventilate the work area. Methylene chloride has been shown to cause cancer in certain laboratory animals. To properly ventilate the work area, open all windows and doors and use a fan to exhaust the air outside. Since 1987, when warning labels were required for household products containing methylene chloride, there has been a 55 percent reduction in the estimated number of cancers to be caused annually in the U.S. from these products. However, CPSC is still concerned about the potential risk to consumers who inhale high levels of fumes when using paint strippers and adhesive removers.

The CPSC staff is studying various substitutes for methylene chloride to evaluate the flammability and chronic hazards of those formulations. In addition, the Commission staff is studying current warning labels and consumer education materials and may propose

Text in this chapter is from the following undated fact sheets produced by the Consumer Product Safety Commission, "Ventilation to Reduce Methylene Chloride Cancer Risk," available at http://www.cpsc.gov/cpscpub/pubs/5059.html, "What You Should Know about Using Paint Strippers," available at http://www.cpsc.gov/cpscpub/pubs/423.html, and "Do Not Use Indoors Any Water Sealers Intended for Outdoor Use," available at http://www.cpsc.gov/cpscpub/pubs/5107.html; all cited July 2001.

revisions to them in the future, emphasizing the importance of ventilation when working with methylene chloride products.

If Not Properly Used, Paint Strippers Are Hazardous to Your Health and Safety.

Paint strippers contain chemicals that loosen paint from surfaces. These chemicals can harm you if not used properly. Some paint stripping chemicals can irritate the skin and eyes, or cause headaches, drowsiness, nausea, dizziness, or loss of coordination. Some may cause cancer, reproductive problems, or damage of the liver, kidney, or brain. Others catch fire easily. Proper handling and use of paint strippers will reduce your exposure to these chemicals and lessen your health risk.

General Safety Precautions

Paint strippers contain different chemicals, and the potential hazards are different for various products. Each product has specific safety precautions. However, there are some general safety steps to keep in mind when using any paint stripper. If you use paint strippers frequently, it is particularly important that you follow these steps:

1. Always read and follow all the instructions and safety precautions on the label. Do not assume you already know how to use the product. The hazards may be different from one product to another, and the ingredients in individual products often change over time. The label tells you what actions you should take to reduce hazards and the first aid measures to use.

2. Wear chemical-resistant gloves appropriate to the type of stripper being used. Common kitchen latex gloves do not provide enough protection.

3. Avoid getting the paint stripper on your skin or in your eyes. Wear protective clothing and goggles appropriate for the project and type of stripper.

4. Use paint strippers outdoors if possible. If you must use them indoors, cross-ventilate by opening all doors and windows. Make sure there is fresh air movement throughout the room.

Ventilate the area before, during, and after applying and stripping. Never use any paint stripper in a poorly ventilated area. If work must be done indoors under low ventilation conditions, consider having the work done professionally instead of attempting it yourself.

5. If you must work indoors, always work so the stripper fumes are blowing away from you and to the outside. A fan can be used to improve cross-ventilation and to ensure fresh air movement. A fan is particularly important for nonflammable products that evaporate quickly, such as methylene chloride. Electrical sparks from fans may increase the chance of flammable paint strippers fumes to catch fire.

6. Do not use flammable paint strippers near any source of sparks, flame, or high heat. Do not work near gas stoves, kerosene heaters, gas or electric water heaters, gas or electric clothes dryers, gas or electric furnaces, gas or electric space heaters, sanders, buffers, or other electric hand tools. Open flames, cigarettes, matches, lighters, pilot lights, or electric sparks can cause the chemicals in the paint strippers to suddenly catch fire.

7. Only strip paint with chemicals that are marketed as paint strippers. Never use gasoline, lighter fluid, or kerosene to strip paint.

8. Dispose of paint strippers according to the instructions on the label. If you have any questions, ask your local environmental sanitation department about proper disposal.

Types of Paint Strippers

Solvent-Based Strippers

Most paint strippers are solvent-based. Solvents dissolve the bond between wood and paint. Solvents also can dissolve other materials, including the latex or rubber of common household or dish washing gloves. Some solvents will irritate or burn the skin. Some solvents may cause serious health effects even if contact does not immediately cause pain. In addition, many solvents evaporate quickly and you can easily inhale them. Inhalation of these solvents can produce health effects immediately or years after exposure.

367

It is especially important to use paint strippers containing solvents that evaporate quickly either outdoors or in an indoor area with strong fresh air movement. Some paint strippers contain solvents that do not evaporate quickly. When using these strippers indoors, be sure to open windows and doors to provide fresh air movement in and out of the work site. You should always follow the manufacturer's instructions and safety precautions. Use the amount of stripper recommended by the manufacturer to avoid buildup of harmful fumes.

The different types of solvent-based paint strippers and their potential hazards and safety precautions are:

Methylene chloride (also called dichloromethane, or DCM)

Methylene chloride is the most commonly used chemical in paint strippers. Methylene chloride products come in two varieties. One type is nonflammable, while the other type is flammable. The flammable paint strippers have less methylene chloride but have other flammable chemicals, including acetone, toluene, or methanol.

Methylene chloride causes cancer in laboratory animals. The U.S. Environmental Protection Agency (EPA) and the U.S. Consumer Product Safety Commission (CPSC) consider the chemical to be a potential cause of cancer in humans. Methylene chloride evaporates quickly, and you can inhale it easily. Breathing high levels of methylene chloride over short periods can irritate the eyes, skin, nose, and lungs. It can also cause dizziness, headache, and lack of coordination. Your body changes some inhaled methylene chloride to carbon monoxide. Carbon monoxide lowers the blood's ability to carry oxygen. This can cause problems for people with heart, lung, or blood diseases who use methylene chloride paint strippers indoors without fresh air cross-ventilation.

High exposures to methylene chloride for long periods can also cause liver and kidney damage.

- It is very important to reduce your exposure to methylene chloride vapors.

- It is very important to have a lot of fresh air when using methylene chloride products.

- Use methylene chloride paint strippers outdoors if possible. If you must use them indoors, open all doors and windows to ensure that the fresh air is moving in and out of the room.

- For indoor use of nonflammable methylene chloride strippers, also use a fan to keep fresh air moving throughout the work area. Electrical sparks from fans may increase the chance of flammable paint strippers fumes to catch fire.

- The safest place to use flammable methylene chloride strippers is outdoors away from any source of sparks, flame, or high heat.

Acetone, Toluene, and Methanol

These chemicals are commonly used together. All three chemicals evaporate quickly and are very flammable. Breathing high levels of these chemicals can cause a variety of effects, including drowsiness, dizziness, and headache. Breathing high levels of toluene may harm unborn children. Breathing very high levels for a long period may cause brain damage. Toluene and methanol are poisonous if swallowed.

- To avoid fire and health problems, it is very important to use products containing these chemicals only in areas with plenty of fresh air.

- Do not work near an open flame, pilot lights, or electrical sparks when using flammable paint strippers. Do not use strippers near gas stoves, kerosene heaters, gas or electric water heaters, gas or electric clothes dryers, gas or electric furnaces, gas or electric space heaters, sanders, buffers, or other electric hand tools.

N-Methylpyrrolidone (NMP)

Excessive contact with NMP may cause skin swelling, blistering, and burns. These skin reactions may not appear until some time after exposure. N-methylpyrrolidone can readily get into the body through the skin and may cause health problems. NMP may cause reproductive problems and harm to unborn children.

- It is very important to wear chemical-resistant gloves and avoid skin contact when using this solvent.

- Wash hands immediately after use, even when wearing gloves.

- Gloves should fit properly and be chemical-resistant. Common kitchen latex gloves do not provide enough protection.

- Avoid using this product for extended periods in an enclosed area without open doors or windows to the outside for cross-ventilation.

Dibasic Esters (DBE), Including Dimethyl Adipate Ester, Dimethyl Succinate Ester, and Dimethyl Glutarate Ester

Much less is known about the possible health effects of these chemicals than about most of the other paint stripping chemicals. Some people using DBE products without fresh air have reported temporary blurred vision. Repeatedly breathing DBE damages the cells lining the nose of laboratory animals. Some strippers include a mixture of DBE products and NMP.

- Avoid using this product for extended periods in an enclosed area without open doors or windows to the outside for cross-ventilation.

- Use appropriate protective clothing and provide fresh air to the work site when using these products.

Caustic-Based Strippers (Not Flammable)

Caustic Alkalis

Caustic alkalis react with the paint coating and loosen it from the surface. One of the chemicals in this type of stripper is sodium hydroxide (lye). Some people do not use caustic alkalis because caustic products can darken wood and raise the grain. Caustics can cause severe burns to skin and eyes even on short contact. Therefore, be very careful to keep caustic chemicals away from skin and eyes and wear protective clothing. If contact occurs, wash off immediately with cold water. Caustics are also highly toxic if swallowed.

- It is very important to avoid skin and eye contact when using caustic alkalis.

- Use gloves that fit properly and are appropriate for caustic alkalis.

- Wear appropriate protective clothing and goggles when using caustic alkalis.

Other Types of Paint Strippers

Some paint strippers have a citrus smell or make "environmentally friendly" claims. However, these paint strippers may be hazardous despite the smell and environmental claims.

- It is important to use appropriate protective clothing and fresh air for cross-ventilation when using these products.

Water Sealers

The U.S. Consumer Product Safety Commission has reports of 19 incidents in which consumers suffered health problems after being exposed to water sealers. In some cases, consumers reported they had to leave their homes because of fumes. Two people died after exposure to water sealers.

Some of the symptoms reported by consumers after exposure to water sealers were headaches, nausea, dizziness, and breathing difficulties. The chemicals identified in these incidents included petroleum distillates, mineral spirits, xylene, toluene, and naphtha. Many of these water sealers have labels warning not to use them inside. Use solvent-based water sealers outside unless labels give specific directions on how to use them safely indoors. If a water sealer is labeled for indoor use but does not have instructions for ventilation, open all windows and doors and use a fan to exhaust the air outside during application and drying. Be sure the air moves throughout the area in which the product is used. Observe all flammability warnings on the product label.

Chapter 47

Biological Pollutants in Your Home

This chapter will help you understand:

1. What Indoor Biological Pollution Is
2. Whether Your Home or Lifestyle Promotes Its Development
3. How to Control Its Growth and Buildup

Outdoor air pollution in cities is a major health problem. Much effort and money continues to be spent cleaning up pollution in the outdoor air. But air pollution can be a problem where you least expect it, in the place you may have thought was safest—your home. Many ordinary activities such as cooking, heating, cooling, cleaning, and redecorating can cause the release and spread of indoor pollutants at home. Studies have shown that the air in our homes can be even more polluted than outdoor air.

Many Americans spend up to 90 percent of their time indoors, often at home. Therefore, breathing clean indoor air can have an important impact on health. People who are inside a great deal may be at greater risk of developing health problems, or having problems made worse by indoor air pollutants. These people include infants, young children the elderly and those with chronic illnesses.

Text in this chapter is from the following undated fact sheets produced by the Consumer Product Safety Commission, "Biological Pollutants in Your Home," available at http://www.cpsc.gov/cpscpub/pubs/425.html, and "Care of Room Humidifiers," available at http://www.cpsc.gov/cpscpub/pubs/5046; both cited July 2001.

What Are Biological Pollutants?

Biological pollutants are or were living organisms. They promote poor indoor air quality and may be a major cause of days lost from work or school, and of doctor and hospital visits. Some can even damage surfaces inside and outside your house. Biological pollutants can travel through the air and are often invisible.

Some common indoor biological pollutants are:

- Animal Dander (minute scales from hair, feathers, or skin)

- Dust Mite and Cockroach parts

- Infectious agents (bacteria or viruses)

- Pollen

Some of these substances are in every home. It is impossible to get rid of them all. Even a spotless home may permit the growth of biological pollutants. Two conditions are essential to support biological growth nutrients and moisture. These conditions can be found in many locations, such as bathrooms, damp or flooded basements, wet appliances (such as humidifiers or air conditioners), and even some carpets and furniture.

Modern materials and construction techniques may reduce the amount of outside air brought into buildings which may result in high moisture levels inside. Using humidifiers, unvented heaters, and air conditioners in our homes has increased the chances of moisture forming on interior surfaces. This encourages the growth of certain biological pollutants.

The Scope of the Problem

Most information about sources and health effects of biological pollutants is based on studies of large office buildings and two surveys of homes in northern U.S. and Canada. These surveys show that 30% to 50% of all structures have damp conditions which may encourage the growth and buildup of biological pollutants. This percentage is likely to be higher in warm, moist climates.

Some diseases or illnesses have been linked with biological pollutants in the indoor environment. However, many of them also have causes unrelated to the indoor environment. Therefore, we do nut know how many health problems relate only to poor indoor air.

Health Effects of Biological Pollutants

All of us are exposed to biological pollutants. However, the effects on our health depend upon the type and amount of biological pollution and the individual person. Some people do not experience health reactions from certain biological pollutants, while others may experience one or more of the following reactions:

- Allergic
- Infectious
- Toxic

Except for the spread of infections indoors, allergic reactions may be the most common health problem with indoor air quality in homes. They are often connected with animal dander (mostly from cats and dogs), with house dust mites (microscopic animals living in household dust), and with pollen. Allergic reactions can range from mildly uncomfortable to life-threatening, as in a severe asthma attack. Some common signs and symptoms are:

- Watery eyes
- Runny nose and sneezing
- Nasal congestion
- Itching
- Coughing
- Wheezing and difficulty breathing
- Headache
- Fatigue

Health experts are especially concerned about people with asthma These people have very sensitive airways that can react to various irritants, making breathing difficult. The number of people who have asthma has greatly increased in recent years. The number of people with asthma has gone up by 59 percent since 1970, to a total of 9.6 million people. Asthma in children under 15 years of age has increased 41 percent in the same period, to a total of 2.6 million children. The number of deaths from asthma is up by 68 percent since 1979, to a total of almost 4,400 deaths per year.

Talking to Your Doctor

Are you concerned about the effects on your health that may be related to biological pollutants in your home? Before you discuss your concerns with your doctor, you should know the answers to the following questions. This information can help the doctor determine whether your health problems may be related to biological pollution.

- Does anyone in the family have frequent headaches, fevers, itchy watery eyes, a stuffy nose, dry throat, or a cough? Does anyone complain of feeling tired or dizzy all the time? Is anyone wheezing or having difficulties breathing on a regular basis?

- Did these symptoms appear after you moved to a new or different home?

- Do the symptoms disappear when you go to school or the office or go away on a trip, and return when you come back?

- Have you recently remodeled your home or done any energy conservation work, such as installing insulation, storm windows, or weather stripping? Did your symptoms occur during or after these activities?

- Does your home feel humid? Can you see moisture on the windows or on other surfaces, such as walls and ceilings?

- What is the usual temperature in your home? Is it very hot or cold?

- Have you recently had water damage?

- Is your basement wet or damp?

- Is there any obvious mold or mildew?

- Does any part of your home have a musty or moldy odor?

- Is the air stale?

- Do you have pets?

- Do your house plants show signs of mold?

- Do you have air conditioners or humidifiers that have not been properly cleaned?

- Does your home have cockroaches or rodents?

Infectious diseases caused by bacteria and viruses, such as flu, measles, chicken pox, and tuberculosis, may be spread indoors. Most infectious diseases pass from person to person through physical contact. Crowded conditions with poor air circulation can promote this spread. Some bacteria and viruses thrive in buildings and circulate through indoor ventilation systems. For example, the bacterium causing Legionnaire's disease, a serious and sometimes lethal infection, and Pontiac Fever, a flu-like illness, have circulated in some large buildings.

Toxic reactions are the least studied and understood health problem caused by some biological air pollutants in the home. Toxins can damage a variety of organs and tissues in the body, including the liver, the central nervous system, the digestive tract, and the immune system.

Coping with the Problem

Checking Your Home

There is no simple and cheap way to sample the air in your home to determine the level of all biological pollutants. Experts suggest that sampling for biological pollutants is not a useful problem-solving tool. Even if you had your home tested, it is almost impossible to know which biological pollutant(s) cause various symptoms or health problems. The amount of most biological substances required to cause disease is unknown and varies from one person to the next.

Does this make the problem sound hopeless? On the contrary, you can take several simple, practical actions to help remove sources of biological pollutants, to help get rid of pollutants, and to prevent their return.

Self-Inspection: A Walk through Your Home

Begin by touring your household. Follow your nose, and use your eyes. Two major factors help create conditions for biological pollutants to grow nutrients and constant moisture with poor air circulation.

- Dust and construction materials, such as wood, wallboard, and insulation, contain nutrients that allow biological pollutants to grow. Firewood also is a source of moisture, fungi, and bugs.

- Appliances such as humidifiers, kerosene and gas heaters, and gas stoves add moisture to the air.

377

- A musty odor, moisture on hard surfaces, or even water stains, may be caused by:

    Air-conditioning units

    Basements, attics, and crawlspaces

    Bathrooms

    Carpets

    Heating and air-conditioning ducts

    Humidifiers and dehumidifiers

    Refrigerator drip pans

What You Can Do about Biological Pollutants

Before you give away the family pet or move, there are less drastic steps that can be taken to reduce potential problems. Properly cleaning and maintaining your home can help reduce the problem and may avoid interrupting your normal routine. People who have health problems such as asthma, or are allergic, may need to do this and more. Discuss this with your doctor.

Moisture Control

Water in your home can come from many sources. Water can enter your home by leaking or by seeping through basement floors. Showers or even cooking can add moisture to the air in your home. The amount of moisture that the air in your home can hold depends on the temperature of the air. As the temperature goes down, the air is able to hold less moisture. This is why, in cold weather, moisture condenses on cold surfaces (for example, drops of water form on the inside of a window). This moisture can encourage biological pollutants to grow.

There are many ways to control moisture in your home:

- Fix leaks and seepage. If water is entering the house from the outside, your options range from simple landscaping to extensive excavation and waterproofing. (The ground should slope away from the house). Water in the basement can result from the lack of gutters or a water flow toward the house. Water leaks in pipes or around tubs and sinks can provide a place for biological pollutants to grow.

- Put a plastic cover over dirt crawlspaces to prevent moisture from coming in from the ground. Be sure crawlspaces are well-ventilated.

- Use exhaust fans in bathrooms and kitchens to remove moisture to the outside (not into the attic) Vent your clothes dryer to the outside.

- Turn off certain appliances (such as humidifiers or kerosene heaters) if you notice moisture on windows and other surfaces.

- Use dehumidifiers and air conditioners, especially in hot, humid climates, to reduce moisture in the air, but be sure that the appliances themselves don't become sources of biological pollutants.

- Raise the temperature of cold surfaces where moisture condenses. Use insulation or storm windows. (A storm window installed on the inside works better than one installed on the outside.) Open doors between rooms (especially doors to closets which may be colder than the rooms) to increase circulation. Circulation carries heat to the cold surfaces. Increase air circulation by using fans and by moving furniture from wall corners to promote air and heat circulation. Be sure that your house has a source of fresh air and can expel excessive moisture from the home.

- Pay special attention to carpet on concrete floors. Carpet can absorb moisture and serve as a place for biological pollutants to grow. Use area rugs which can be taken up and washed often In certain climates, if carpet is to be installed over a concrete floor, it maybe necessary to use a vapor barrier (plastic sheeting) over the concrete and cover that with sub-flooring (insulation covered with plywood) to prevent a moisture problem.

- Moisture problems and their solutions differ from one climate to another. The Northeast is cold and wet, the Southwest is hot and dry, the South is hot and wet, and the Western Mountain states are cold and dry. All of these regions can have moisture problems. For example, evaporative coolers used in the Southwest can encourage the growth of biological pollutants. In other hot regions, the use of air conditioners which cool the air too quickly may prevent the air conditioners from running long enough to remove excess moisture from the air. The types of construction and weatherization for the different climates can lead to different problems and solutions.

Where Biological Pollutants May Be Found in the Home

1. Dirty air conditioners

2. Dirty humidifiers and/or dehumidifiers

3. Bathroom without vents or windows

4. Kitchen without vents or windows

5. Dirty refrigerator drip pans

6. Laundry room with unvented dryer

7. Unventilated attic

8. Carpet on damp basement floor

9. Bedding

10. Closet on outside wall

11. Dirty heating/air conditioning system

12. Dogs or cats

13. Water damage (around windows, the roof or the basement)

Maintain and Clean All Appliances That Come in Contact with Water

Have major appliances, such as furnaces, heat pumps and central air conditioners, inspected and cleaned regularly by a professional, especially before seasonal use. Change filters on heating and cooling systems according to manufacturer's directions. (In general, change filters monthly during use.) When first turning on the heating or air conditioning at the start of the season, consider leaving your home until it airs out.

Have window or wall air-conditioning units cleaned and serviced regularly by a professional, especially before the cooling season. Air conditioners can help reduce the entry of allergy-causing pollen. But they may also become a source of biological pollutants if not properly maintained. Clean the coils and rinse the drain pans according to manufacturer's instructions, so water can-not collect in pools.

Have furnace-attached humidifiers cleaned and serviced regularly by a professional, especially before the heating season.

Follow manufacturer's instructions when using any type of humidifier Experts differ on the benefits of using humidifiers. If you do use a portable humidifier (approximately 1 to 2 gallon tanks), be sure to empty its tank every day and refill with distilled or demineralized water, or even fresh tap water if the other types of water are unavailable. For larger portable humidifiers, change the water as recommended by the manufacturer. Unplug the appliance before cleaning. Every third day, clean all surfaces coming in contact with water with a 3% solution of hydrogen peroxide, using a brush to loosen deposits Some manufacturers recommend using diluted household bleach for cleaning and maintenance, generally in a solution of one-half cup bleach to one gallon water. When any household chemical, rinse well to remove all traces of chemical before refilling humidifier.

Empty dehumidifiers daily and clean often. If possible, have the appliance drip directly into a drain. Follow manufacturer's instructions for cleaning and maintenance. Always disconnect the appliance before cleaning.

Clean refrigerator drip pans regularly according to manufacturer's instructions. If refrigerator and freezer doors don't seal properly, moisture may build up and mold can grow. Remove any mold on door gaskets and replace faulty gaskets.

Clean moist surfaces, such as showers and kitchen counters.

Remove mold from walls, ceilings, floors, and paneling. Do not simply cover mold with paint, stain, varnish, or a moisture-proof sealer, as it may resurface.

Replace moldy shower curtains, or remove them and scrub well with a household cleaner and rinse before rehanging them.

Dust Control

Controlling dust is very important for people who are allergic to animal dander and mites. You cannot see mites, but you can either remove their favorite breeding grounds or keep these areas dry and clean. Dust mites can thrive in sofas, stuffed chairs, carpets, and bedding. Open shelves, fabric wallpaper, knickknacks, and Venetian blinds are also sources of dust mites. Dust mites live deep in the carpet and are not removed by vacuuming. Many doctors suggest that their mite-allergic patients use washable area rugs rather than wall-to-wall carpet.

Always wash bedding in hot water (at least 130 degrees F) to kill dust mites. Cold water won't do the job. Launder bedding at least every 7 to 10 days.

Use synthetic or foam rubber mattress pads and pillows, and plastic mattress covers if you are allergic Do not use fuzzy wool blankets, feather or wool-stuffed comforters, and feather pillows.

Clean rooms and closets well, dust and vacuum often to remove surface dust. Vacuuming and other cleaning may not remove all animal dander, dust mite material, and other biological pollutants. Some particles are so small they can pass through vacuum bags and remain in the air If you are allergic to dust, wear a mask when vacuuming or dusting. People who are highly allergy-prone should not perform these tasks. They may even need to leave the house when someone else is cleaning.

Before You Move

Protect yourself by inspecting your potential new home. If you identify problems, have the landlord or seller correct them before you move in, or even consider moving elsewhere.

- Have professionals check the heating and cooling system, including humidifiers and vents. Have duct lining and insulation checked for growth.

- Check for exhaust fans in bathrooms and kitchens If there are no vents, do the kitchen and bathrooms have at least one window a piece? Does the cook top have a hood vented outside? Does the clothes dryer vent outside? Are all vents to the outside of the building, not in attics or crawlspaces?

- Look for obvious mold growth throughout the house, including attics, basements, and crawlspaces and around the foundation. See if there are many plants close to the house, particularly if they are damp and rotting. They are a potential source of biological pollutants. Downspouts from roof gutters should route water away from the building.

- Look for stains on the walls, floor or carpet (including any carpet over concrete floors) as evidence of previous flooding or moisture problems. Is there moisture on windows and surfaces? Are there signs of leaks or seepage in the basement?

- Look for rotted building materials which may suggest moisture or water damage.

- If you or anyone else in the family has a pet allergy, ask if any pets have lived in the home.

- Examine the design of the building. Remember that in cold climates, overhanging areas, rooms over unheated garages, and closets on outside walls may be prone to problems with biological pollutants.

- Look for signs of cockroaches.

Warning!

Carefully read instructions for use and any cautionary labeling on cleaning products before beginning cleaning procedures.

- Do not mix any chemical products. Especially, never mix cleaners containing bleach with any product (such as ammonia) which does not have instructions for such mixing. When chemicals are combined, a dangerous gas can sometimes be formed.

- Household chemicals may cause burning or irritation to skin and eyes.

- Household chemicals may be harmful if swallowed, or inhaled.

- Avoid contact with skin, eyes, mucous membranes and clothing.

- Avoid breathing vapor. Open all windows and doors and use an exhaust fan that sends the air outside.

- Keep household chemicals out of reach of children.

- Rinse treated surface areas well to remove all traces of chemicals.

Correcting Water Damage

What if damage is already done? Follow these guidelines for correcting water damage:

- Throw out mattresses, wicker furniture, straw baskets and the like that have been water damaged or contain mold. These cannot be recovered.

- Discard any water-damaged furnishings such as carpets, drapes, stuffed toys, upholstered furniture and ceiling tales, unless they can be recovered by steam cleaning or hot water washing and thorough drying.

- Remove and replace wet insulation to prevent conditions where biological pollutants can grow.

383

Care of Room Humidifiers

Dirty Humidifiers May Cause Health Problems

Bacteria and fungi often grow in the tanks of portable and console room humidifiers and can be released in the mist. Breathing dirty mist may cause lung problems ranging from flu-like symptoms to serious infection. This information is of special concern to allergy or asthma sufferers whose symptoms may be increased.

Film or scum appearing on the water surface, on the sides or bottom of the tank, or on exposed motor parts may indicate that the humidifier tank contains bacteria or fungi. A crusty deposit or scale may also form within the tank or on parts in the water. This scale is composed of minerals that have settled out of the water creating a surface on which bacteria or fungi may grow.

Minerals can also be released in the mist and settle as fine white dust. This white dust may contain particles that are small enough to enter the lungs. The health effects from inhaling this humidifier dust are not clear, any impact on human health will depend upon the types and amounts of minerals found in the water used.

To reduce the possibility of health hazards from dirty room humidifiers, take the following precautions:

- Do not allow film and scale to develop in your humidifier. If possible, change the water in your room humidifier daily. Empty the tank before you fill it. If the tank is not removable, clean it often according to manufacturer's instructions.

- Use distilled or demineralized water in your room humidifier to reduce the buildup of scale and the release of dust. Do not use tap water because it contains more minerals. Use demineralization cartridges or filters if supplied or recommended for use with your humidifier.

- Drain and clean the tank of your room humidifier before you store it. Clean it after summer storage. Remove dust on the outside of your unit.

- Clean your room humidifier well and often during the heating season. Be sure to unplug the humidifier before cleaning. Follow the manufacturer's suggested cleaning methods. If chlorine bleach or other cleaning product or disinfectant is used, make sure to rinse the tank well to avoid breathing harmful chemicals.

Use a brush or other scrubber to clean the tank. Be careful not to damage the motor or to scratch the inner surface. Clean or replace sponge filters or belts when needed.

- Maintain the relative humidity in your home between 30% and 50% if possible. Humidity levels above 60% may allow moisture to build up indoors and condense on surfaces, where bacteria and fungi can settle and grow. You can measure humidity with an instrument called a hygrometer, available at your local hardware store.

Part Eight

Nurseries, Toys, Playgrounds, and Other Equipment

Chapter 48

Crib Safety

Your Used Crib Could Be Deadly

An unsafe used crib could be very dangerous for your baby. Each year, about 50 babies suffocate or strangle when they become trapped between broken crib parts or in cribs with older, unsafe designs.

A safe crib is the best place to put your baby to sleep. Look for a crib with a certification seal showing that it meets national safety standards.

If your crib does not meet these guidelines, destroy it and replace it with a safe crib. A safe crib has:

- No missing, loose, broken, or improperly installed screws, brackets, or other hardware on the crib or the mattress support.

- No more than 2 3/8 inches between crib slats so a baby's body cannot fit through the slats.

Text in this chapter is from the following undated fact sheets produced by the Consumer Product Safety Commission, "Your Used Crib Could Be Deadly," available at http://www.cpsc.gov/cpscpub/pubs/5020.html, "Crib Safety Tips," available at http://www.cpsc.gov/cpscpub/pubs/cribs.html, "Some Crib Cornerposts May be Dangerous," available at http://www.cpsc.gov/cpscpub/pubs/5027.html, "CPSC Warns Parents about Infant Strangulations Caused by Failure of Crib Hardware," available at http://www.cpsc.gov/cpscpub/pubs/5025.html, "CPSC Warns Against Placing Babies in Adult Beds," available at http://www.cpsc.gov/cpscpub/pubs/5091.html, and "SIDS Awareness Survey,"; all cited July 2001.

- A firm, snug-fitting mattress so a baby cannot get trapped between the mattress and the side of the crib.

- No corner posts over 1/16 of an inch above the end panels (unless they are over 16 inches high for a canopy) so a baby cannot catch clothing and strangle.

- No cutout areas on the headboard or foot board so a baby's head cannot get trapped.

- A mattress support that does not easily pull apart from the corner posts so a baby cannot get trapped between mattress and crib.

- No cracked or peeling paint to prevent lead poisoning.

- No splinters or rough edges.

Crib Safety Tips

Use Your Crib Safely

For infants under 12 months of age, follow these practices to prevent suffocation and keep your baby safe:

- Place baby on his/her back in a crib with a firm, tight-fitting mattress.

- Do not put pillows, quilts, comforters, sheepskins, pillow-like bumper pads or pillow-like stuffed toys in the crib.

- Consider using a sleeper instead of a blanket.

- If you do use a blanket, place baby with feet to foot of the crib. Tuck a thin blanket around the crib mattress, covering baby only as high as his/her chest.

- Use only a fitted bottom sheet specifically made for crib use.

Check Your Crib for Safety

There should be:

- A firm, tight-fitting mattress so a baby cannot get trapped between the mattress and the crib.

- No missing, loose, broken or improperly installed screws, brackets or other hardware on the crib or mattress support.

- No more than 2 3/8 inches (about the width of a soda can) between crib slats so a baby's body cannot fit through the slats; no missing or cracked slats.

- No corner posts over 1/16th inch high so a baby's clothing cannot catch.

- No cutouts in the headboard or foot board so a baby's head cannot get trapped.

For mesh-sided cribs or play yards, look for:

- Mesh less than 1/4 inch in size, smaller than the tiny buttons on a baby's clothing.

- Mesh with no tears, holes or loose threads that could entangle a baby.

- Mesh securely attached to top rail and floor plate.

- Top rail cover with no tears or holes.

- If staples are used, they are not missing, loose or exposed.

Some Crib Cornerposts May Be Dangerous

The U.S. Consumer Product Safety Commission warns of a strangulation hazard that may exist with some cribs that have projections on the corner-posts. Decorative knobs or cornerposts, which extend above the crib end or side, have caught clothing, necklaces and pacifier cords as the child moves about in the corner areas of the crib. These knobs or posts have been implicated in two cases of brain damage and 48 deaths due to strangulation. The CPSC urges that parents never tie pacifiers around a child's neck.

The Juvenile Products Manufacturers Association (JPMA), after being alerted to this hazard by the CPSC, developed a voluntary standard that restricts the height of crib cornerpost extensions to 1/16 inch unless the posts are high and the tops are out of reach of a child, such as where the posts are supports for a canopy. Most crib manufacturers have already ceased to produce cribs with post extensions. However, there may be thousands of such cribs still in consumers' homes, at garage sales, or in second-hand furniture stores.

If you already own a crib with cornerpost extensions more than 1/16 inch in height, you should remove the extensions and discard them. Some may be removed merely by unscrewing, while others may have to be sawed off and sanded smooth. If you are purchasing a new or used crib, look for one that has cornerpost extensions less than 1/16 inch above the top edge of the end or side.

Failure of Crib Hardware May Cause Strangulation

The U.S. Consumer Product Safety Commission (CPSC) is concerned about possible accidental death or injury to young children in cribs that are in need of repair. The CPSC has investigated or received reports of numerous incidents in which cribs have come apart. Many of these resulted in death.

For example, a 5-month-old infant died when he became lodged between the mattress and the side rail of his crib. A support hanger on the mattress frame had come off the hook attached to the crib end panel or corner post creating a space in which the infant's head became entrapped. In another accident, a 6-month-old baby became entrapped and choked to death when screws securing the side rail pulled loose from the corner post of the crib creating a space between the rail and the mattress.

In yet another accident, a missing bolt caused a side rail to separate from the mattress and a 6-month-old baby became entrapped in a space between the mattress and side rail and suffocated. Similar reports of fatal accidents are repeated many times in Commission files and many more non-fatal incidents are on record in which an entrapped child was rescued.

Accidents such as these may occur when hardware intended to hold parts of the crib together has worked loose, come apart, or broken. Hardware can become worn or over-stressed as a result of children's playing; repeated disassembling and reassembling of cribs, such as during household moves; when new babies are born in the family; and when cribs are sold or given to another family.

Hardware also can work loose as a result of moving or cleaning the crib. On some cribs, the design is such that the mattress support hanger may easily come out of the supporting hook, allowing the mattress to drop at one corner. This can happen when changing the sheets, raising or lowering the drop side, or simply when the baby moves in the crib. The CPSC also knows of cases in which wood screws have pulled out of the wood, machine screws and nuts have worked loose, and hooks which support the mattress have broken or bent.

A project has been initiated to work with crib manufacturers to examine the need for product standards for crib hardware and to determine the extent to which such standards would prevent injuries and deaths. If you have a crib, you are urged to inspect it frequently for hardware which has disengaged or needs to be repaired or replaced. The Commission also suggests:

- When buying a new crib, physically examine it for stability. Look for adequate strength in the frame and headboard, a secure fitting mattress support structure, and a label certifying that the crib complies with the Commission's standards for cribs.

- If you buy a used crib, make sure all the hardware is present and in good condition. Make sure that when the crib is assembled, all the pieces of the crib are securely attached and the mattress fits snugly. Also, check the wood joints to be sure they are not coming apart. Check to see that the slats are no more than 2-3/8 inch apart—the distance required by law for all new cribs.

- On cribs in which the mattress support hanger easily disengages from the hooks on corner posts, secure the mattress support hanger firmly to the hook on the post.

Placing Babies in Adult Beds May Cause Suffocation

Parents and caregivers should be aware of the dangers of placing babies to sleep in adult beds. According to a CPSC study, placing babies to sleep in adult beds puts them at risk of suffocation or strangulation and is a danger of which many parents and caregivers are unaware. The study revealed an average 64 deaths per year to babies under the age of 2 years placed to sleep in adult beds, including waterbeds and daybeds.

A review of incident data from January 1990 to December 1997 linked adult beds to at least 515 baby deaths. Analysis of the deaths revealed four major hazard patterns:

- Suffocation associated with the co-sleeping of adult and baby.

- Suffocation where an infant becomes entrapped or wedged between the mattress and another object.

- Suffocation due to airway obstruction when the baby is face down on a waterbed mattress.

- Strangulation in rails or openings on beds that allow a baby's body to pass through while entrapping the head.

CPSC's study is the first to quantify the number of fatalities resulting from the practice of co-sleeping with babies. Of the 515 deaths, 121 were reported to be due to a parent, caregiver or sibling rolling on top of or against the baby while sleeping. More that three-quarters of these deaths occurred to infants younger than three months.

One of the most tragic aspects of these deaths is that they are largely preventable. In many cases, the adult placing the baby on the adult bed was unaware of or underestimated the danger posed. The practice of co-sleeping can result in the adult rolling on top of or next to the baby smothering him or her. Mothers who breast-feed should be alerted to this hazard and should be encouraged to return the baby to the crib after breast-feeding.

The other 394 deaths resulted from suffocation or strangulation caused by entrapment of the child's head in various structures of the bed. Entrapments occurred between the mattress and the wall, bed frame, headboard, footboard, bed railings or adjacent furniture.

"Don't sleep with your baby or put the baby down to sleep in an adult bed," said CPSC Chairman Ann Brown. "The only safe place for babies is in a crib that meets current safety standards and has a firm, tight-fitting mattress. Place babies to sleep on their backs and remove all soft bedding and pillow like items from the crib."

SIDS Awareness Survey

The survey polled almost 500 parents with children under the age of three years about their practices for placing their babies to sleep (before they were old enough to roll over). It also polled parents' attitudes about a safe sleeping environment to reduce the risk of Sudden Infant Death Syndrome (SIDS).

Key Findings

Sleep Position

- Only 31% of African-American parents surveyed put their babies to sleep on their backs as recommended to reduce the risk of SIDS.

- African-American parents are more likely to believe incorrectly that putting babies to sleep on their stomachs is the best way to reduce the risk of SIDS.

- 43% of all parents say they put their babies to sleep on their backs.

Soft Bedding in Crib

- In general, parents are not following recommendations to avoid soft bedding such as quilts, comforters and pillows in the crib with a baby under 12 months. 67% of all parents put these items in the crib with their baby and 85% of African-American parents put these items in the crib.

How Parent Learned about Sleep Position

- 39% of African-American parents say they learned about sleep position from their baby's grandparents while 22% said they learned it from a pediatrician or nurse practitioner. That compares to 12% of Caucasians who say they learned about sleep position from their baby's grandparent, while 45% say they learned about it from a pediatrician or nurse practitioner.

- African-American parents are more likely than Caucasian parents to place their babies to sleep on their stomachs because that's the way their families have always done it.

Table 48.1. Primary sleep position for children under 3 (see note on page 398).

Parent places baby on his/her back	43% all
	47% Caucasian
	31% African-American
	39% Hispanic
Parent places baby on his/her side	36% all
	36% Caucasian
	38% African-American
	43% Hispanic
Parent places baby on his/her stomach	15% all
	14% Caucasian
	20% African-American
	12% Hispanic

Table 48.2. Items placed in crib with baby (see note on page 398).

Comforters and quilts	67% all
	63% Caucasian
	85% African-American
	76% Hispanic
Pillows	22% all
	18% Caucasian
	36% African-American
	25% Hispanic
No soft bedding in crib	28% all
	32% Caucasian
	13% African-American
	16% Hispanic

Table 48.3. How did parent get information about sleep position? (See note on page 398.)

From pediatrician or Nurse practitioner	40% all
	45% Caucasian
	22% African-American
	35% Hispanic
From baby's grandparents	18% all
	12% Caucasian
	39% African-American
	20% Hispanic
Other family, friends	13% all
	12% Caucasian
	17% African-American
	16% Hispanic

Table 48.4. Reasons for not placing baby to sleep on back (see note on page 398).

Fear baby will choke on vomit	52% all 47% Caucasian 71% African-American 72% Hispanic
Family tradition	22% all 18% Caucasian 40% African-American 32% Hispanic
Fear baby will develop flat spot	15% all 13% Caucasian 21% African-American 17% Hispanic

Table 48.5. Safest sleep position to reduce risk of SIDS (see note on page 398).

Baby on its back	44% all 49% Caucasian 27% African-American 29% Hispanic
Baby on its side	34% all 31% Caucasian 41% African-American 39% Hispanic
Baby on its stomach	5% all 4% Caucasian 12% African-American 3% Hispanic

Note to Tables 48.1–5.

The survey was conducted by Caravan(r) Opinion Research Corporation International. Telephone interviews were conducted among a national probability sample of 5,078 adults comprising 2,542 men and 2,536 women 18 years of age and older, living in private households in the continental United States. Interviewing for the survey was conducted among 460 parents of children under the age of three during the period of March 23-April 16, 2000. All participants were contacted via random digit dialing to ensure a representative sample of parents nationwide. The margin of error for this sample is ± 5 percent.

Chapter 49

Bunk Bed Safety

Bunk beds are frequently used as a child's first regular bed after he/she outgrows a crib—either at about age 2 or 35 inches (890 mm) in height. Some bunk beds also are used separately as twin beds for older children and even adults.

Each year, thousands of children under age 15 receive hospital emergency room treatment for injuries associated with bunk beds. Most of these injuries are fairly minor and occur when children fall from the beds. Horseplay frequently contributes to these accidents. There are other less obvious yet potentially very serious hazards associated with bunk bed structures that have entrapped children and resulted in suffocation or strangulation deaths.

Guardrail Spacing

On some beds, the space between the guardrail and mattress or the bed frame and mattress is large enough to allow a young child to slip through. Deaths have occurred when children became suspended by the head in these spaces and strangled.

Text in this chapter is from the following undated fact sheets produced by the Consumer Product Safety Commission, "Bunk Bed Fact Sheet," available at http://www.cpsc.gov/cpscpub/pubs/071.html, "CPSC Warns That Tubular Metal Bunk Beds May Collapse," available at http://www.cpsc.gov/cpscpub/pubs/5034.html, and "CPSC Warns Consumers of Bunk Bed Entrapment Hazard and Mattress Support Collapse," available at http://www.cpsc.gov/cpscpub/pubs/5007.html; all cited July 2001.

Guardrails which are attached to the bed by hooks and remain in place by their own weight can dislodge, allowing a child to become entrapped under the guardrail or fall.

Attach additional boards to the bunk bed to close up any gap more than 31/2 inches (89 mm) between the lower edge of the guardrails and the upper edge of the bed frame to prevent possible entrapment and strangulation.

Use of the Bed without Rails on Both Sides

Most bunk beds are used with one side located against a wall and are sold with only one guardrail for the upper bunk to prevent falls from the side away from the wall. Deaths have occurred when very young children ratted off the bed and became entrapped between the wall and the side of the bed not having a guardrail. This hazard is not unique to bunk beds. Regular beds can present the same hazard.

Dislodgement of Mattress Foundation

The mattress foundation and some bunk beds merely rests on small ledges attached to the bed frame. They can dislodge, particularly if a child, underneath the bunk, pushes or kicks upwards on the mattress. Suffocation deaths have occurred when mattress foundations fell on children playing on the floor or occupying the lower bunk. Fasten additional cross ties underneath the mattress foundation of both beds.

Wrong Size Mattress

Bunk bed structures and mattresses come in two lengths—regular and extra long. Extra long is 5 inches (127 mm) longer than regular. Therefore, if a regular length mattress is purchased for an extra long bed, there can be a 5-inch (127 mm) opening between the mattress and headboard or footboard. Strangulation deaths have occurred when children fell through openings created between the mattress and headboard or footboard when a regular length mattress was used in an extra long bed frame.

Safety Tips for Selecting, Using, and Maintaining Bunk Beds

Selection

Choose bunk beds that have:

- Guardrails on all sides which are screwed, bolted or otherwise firmly attached to the bed structure.

- Spacing between bed frame and bottom of guard rails that is no greater than 3-1/2 inches (89 mm).

- Guardrails that extend at least 5 inches (127 mm) above the mattress surface to prevent a child from rolling off.

- Cross ties under the mattress foundation which can be securely attached.

- A ladder that is secured to the bed frame and will not slip when a child climbs on it.

- A feature which permits the beds to be separated to form two single beds if you have children too young to sleep safety on the upper bunk.

- Choose a mattress that correctly fits your bed, whether regular or extra long.

Use

- Always use two side guardrails on the upper bunk. Keep guardrails securely in place at all times no matter what the age of the child. Children move about during sleep and may roll out of bed.

- Do not permit children under 6 years of age to sleep in the upper bunk.

- Be sure crossties are under the mattress foundation of each bed and that they are secured in place even if bunks are used as twin beds.

- Emphasize to children to use the ladder and not chairs or other pieces of furniture to climb into or out of the top bunk.

- Teach children that rough play is unsafe around and on beds and other furniture.

- Consider using a night light so that children will be able to see the ladder if they get up during the night.

Maintenance or Safety Repair

- If spacing between guard rails and bed frames is more than 3 1/2 inches (89 mm), nail or screw another rail to close the space to prevent head entrapment.

- Keep guardrails in good repair and securely in place.

- Replace loose or missing ladder rungs immediately.

- Repair or replace loose or missing hardware, including cross ties immediately.

Tubular Metal Bunk Beds May Collapse

The U. S. Consumer Product Safety Commission (CPSC) advises owners of children's tubular metal bunk beds to inspect the beds for metal or weld cracks which may lead to collapse and serious injury. The bunk beds may have been welded poorly or have inadequate material thickness around the mattress support fins, which connect to the side rails.

The CPSC is aware of numerous incidents in which the bunk beds collapsed during use. Many of the incidents occurred on the currently popular twin-size on top/full-size on bottom bunk beds. Injuries reported include broken bones, lacerations, bruises, and sprains.

These bunk beds are often imported from Malaysia, Taiwan, and Mexico. They are distributed in the United States by a large number of importers and retailers and sold to consumers nationwide.

The beds are constructed of tubular metal and are usually painted with high gloss red, white, blue, or black paint. They have been sold for approximately $150 to $250 each. The beds frequently have no identifying markings or manufacturer labels.

In 1994, CPSC announced the repair-recall of imported metal bunk beds because of the risk of collapse during use. If consumers have a tubular metal bunk bed, they should:

- Inspect all eight mattress support corners for cracks in the paint or metal. If cracks are found, stop using it immediately. Do not wait for the bed to break.

- Whether or not cracks are present, call the retailer where the bed was bought to see if it is under recall. Get the telephone number of the importer and call for repair instructions. Consumers will receive a repair kit consisting of reinforcement brackets. In cases where the bed has cracks in the corner supports, consumers should receive a new bed.

To help avoid bunk bed collapse, CPSC urges consumers to inspect all eight mattress support fin tabs and pockets for breaks or cracks in the metal and welds. The fin tabs are inserted into pockets located near each of the bed's eight corners. Stop using damaged beds as bunks and contact the importer for repair or replacement.

Bunk Bed Entrapment Hazard and Mattress Support Collapse

Deaths to children under age six that involved head entrapment under bunk bed guard rails have been reported. To reduce the risk of your child slipping feet first into the space between the lower edge of a guardrail and the top surface of the mattress, CPSC advises:

- Never allow children under 6 years-old on the upper bunk.

- Close the space between the lower edge of the guardrail and upper edge of the bed frame to 3-1/2 inches or less.

In addition, CPSC received reports that children, primarily age one and under, died when they became entrapped between the bed and the wall. A guardrail placed next to the wall, on the lower bunk as well as the upper bunk, will help reduce this risk of entrapment.

CPSC is also aware of young children who died when their bunk bed mattress and mattress foundation collapsed while they were playing on or under the beds. Mattresses and/or foundations resting only on ledges need fastened cross wires, or other means of support to help prevent dislodgement, even when beds are used as twin beds.

Chapter 50

Walkers, Strollers, and Other Devices

Baby Walkers

New walkers are available that have features that will reduce the stair fall injuries associated with traditional baby walkers.

More children are injured with baby walkers than with any other nursery product. CPSC estimates that, in 1997, walkers were involved in 14,300 hospital emergency-room-treated injuries to children younger than 15 months. Walkers also have been involved in 34 deaths since 1973.

Most children sustained injuries when their walker fell down stairs.

To make walkers safer, CPSC worked with the industry to develop a new standard. Each walker meeting the new standard and certified by the Juvenile Products Manufacturers Association (JPMA) must meet one of two requirements:

1. It must be too wide to fit through a standard doorway, or

Text in this chapter is from the following undated fact sheets produced by the Consumer Product Safety Commission, "New, Safer Baby Walkers," available at http://www.cpsc.gov/cpscpub/pubs/5086.html, "Infants Can Die When Their Heads Become Trapped in Strollers," available at http://www.cpsc.gov/cpscpub/pubs/5096, "Safety Tips for Infant Carrier Seats," available at http://www.cpsc.gov/cpscpub/pubs/5048.html, "Infants Can Suffocate in Mesh Drop-Sided Playpens," available at http://www.cpsc.gov/cpscpub/pubs/5058.html, and "Old Accordion Style Baby Gates Are Dangerous," available at http://www.cpsc.gov/cpscpub/pubs/5085; all cited July 2001.

2. It must have features, such as a gripping mechanism, to stop the walker at the edge of a step.

If you choose to use baby walkers, replace your old walkers with a new generation baby walker, which meets the requirements of the standard. Consumers should look for the "Meets New Safety Standard" label.

If you want a wheeled walker, buy one that has new safety features to help prevent falls down stairs. Another alternative is the stationary activity center, which does not have wheels. Whichever new product you choose, you should follow these safety tips when using a baby walker or an activity center:

- Close the door or gate at the top of the stairs.

- Keep children within view.

- Keep children away from hot surfaces and containers.

- Beware of dangling appliance cords.

- Keep children away from toilets, swimming pools and other sources of water.

CPSC said that without the new standard, baby walker-related injuries would increase to as many as 32,000 injuries in 2002. With CPSC's intervention in getting the new standard in place, the number of baby walker-related injuries is estimated to decrease to less than 10,000 per year by 2002.

Stroller Hazards

Babies can die if they are left unattended to sleep in strollers. They may slip feet first, through a leg opening, and become entrapped by the head between the seat and the hand rest bar. In a recent one-year period, an estimated 14,400 children under age 5 were treated in hospital emergency rooms for injuries associated with strollers. Most of the injuries resulted from falls, and almost 90 percent of the fall injuries were to the head. On average, about two children die each year from stroller-related incidents. Many of these deaths happen when children are left unattended to sleep in strollers reclined to the "carriage" position. They may slip feet first through a leg opening and become entrapped by the head between the seat and restraint bar. To avoid incidents of entrapment in stroller leg openings, CPSC advises infant caretakers to:

1.   Never leave a child unattended in a stroller. This is especially important if the stroller seat's backrest is in the flat "carriage" position.

2.   Be aware that infants only a few weeks old can creep or move when asleep. The youngest victim was an infant just seven weeks old.

NEVER leave a child unattended in a stroller because the child may slip into a leg opening, become entrapped by the head, and die.

Infant Carrier Seats

Parents should keep a close watch when a child is in an infant carrier seat because the seat can fall or turn over and the child can be injured or killed. CPSC knows of at least 5 deaths a year involving various types of carriers used to hold infants. In addition, there were over 13,000 estimated injuries in a recent one-year period. (This does not include incidents involving motor vehicles.) The deaths happened when infants became entangled in restraining straps, when carrier seats toppled over on soft surfaces such as beds, or when unrestrained children fell from the carrier seat to the floor. In almost all of the cases, infants were left unattended in the infant carrier seat. Active infants can move or tip carrier seats by their movements or by pushing off on other objects with their feet.

To prevent injuries and deaths with infant carrier seats, parents should:

* Choose a carrier with a wide, sturdy base for stability.

* Stay within arm's reach of the baby when the carrier seat is on tables or counters. Infant seats can move when the baby moves or bounces. Never place a carrier seat on soft, plush surfaces that will make it unstable.

* Always use the safety belts.

* Do not use infant carriers as a substitute for infant car seats.

Infants Can Suffocate in Mesh Drop-Sided Playpens

Do not leave the drop side of mesh-sided playpens down while children are in them. Playpens used with sides down can present a suffocation hazard to infants. When the drop side is down, the mesh net material forms a loose pocket leaving a gap between the edge of the playpen floor and the mesh side. Infants can easily fall or roll into this pocket. Once an infant's head is entrapped in this pocket, the infant can suffocate.

In recent years, CPSC has investigated an average of about three deaths annually of infants who suffocated between the floor or mattress and mesh side of the playpen.

The CPSC and members of the Juvenile Products Manufacturers Association (JPMA) developed a warning label that appears on the saddle cover of the top rail around mesh-sided playpens which reads:

*"**WARNING!** NEVER LEAVE an infant in playpen with SIDES DOWN. Infant may roll into space between mattress and loose mesh side, causing suffocation."*

This warning label has been placed on mesh-sided playpens with drop sides produced since 1985. A similar warning has appeared on mesh-sided portable cribs with drop sides produced since 1980.

The drop sides of mesh-sided playpens and portable cribs should always be up and locked securely in position whenever a child is in the playpen or crib.

Old Accordion Style Baby Gates Are Dangerous

An entrapment and strangulation hazard exists with accordion-style baby gates manufactured prior to February 1985. These gates have V-shaped openings along the top edge and diamond-shaped openings in the sides that are large enough to entrap a child's head. CPSC knows of 9 deaths and at least 25 "near-misses" because of the entrapment hazard of these gates. Most of the deaths occurred when children's heads became entrapped in the V-shaped openings.

In contrast, other styles of baby gates—such as a straight top edge and rigid mesh screen, or openings too small for a child's head to enter—do not present the entrapment/strangulation hazard.

CPSC worked with the Juvenile Products Manufacturers Association (JPMA) to develop an ASTM (formerly the American Society for Testing and Materials) voluntary standard to address the entrapment/strangulation hazard. The standard restricts the width of V-shaped openings in the top edge of a gate to no more than 1.5 inches and limits the diamond-shaped openings to a size that prevents entry of the head of a 6 month old child. Gates that meet the requirements in the ASTM voluntary standard are safer than the old accordion-style gates. CPSC has no reports of deaths or near misses due to head entrapment in these newer gates.

Caregivers who have the old gates with large V- or diamond-shaped openings should discontinue their use.

Of course, in order to prevent falls when using any type of baby gates, care should be taken to be sure they're securely latched and that children do not attempt to climb on them.

Chapter 51

Toy Safety

When Buying Toys

Protecting children from unsafe toys is the responsibility of everyone. Careful toy selection and proper supervision of children at play is still—and always will be—the best way to protect children from toy-related injuries.

- Choose toys with care. Keep in mind the child's age, interests and skill level.

- Look for quality design and construction in all toys for all ages.

- Make sure that all directions or instructions are clear—to you, and, when appropriate, to the child. Plastic wrappings on toys should be discarded at once before they become deadly playthings.

- Be a label reader. Look for and heed age recommendations, such as *"Not recommended for children under three"*. Look for other safety labels including: *"Flame retardant / Flame resistant"* on fabric products and *"Washable / hygienic materials"* on stuffed toys and dolls.

Text in this chapter is from the following undated fact sheets produced by the Consumer Product Safety Commission, "Think Toy Safety," available at http://www.cpsc.gov/cpscpub/pubs/281.html, "Toy safety Shopping Tips," available at http://www.cpsc.gov/cpscpub/pubs/grand/toy/toysafe.html, "The Dangers of Electric Toys," available at http://www.cpsc.gov/cpscpub/pubs/287.html, and "Law Requires Review and Labeling of Art Materials," available at http://www.cpsc.gov/cpscpub/pubs/5016.html; all cited July 2001.

When Maintaining Toys

Check all toys periodically for breakage and potential hazards. A damaged or dangerous toy should be thrown away or repaired immediately.

Edges on wooden toys that might have become sharp or surfaces covered with splinters should be sanded smooth. When repainting toys and toy boxes, avoid using leftover paint, unless purchased recently, since older paints may contain more lead than new paint, which is regulated by CPSC. Examine all outdoor toys regularly for rust or weak parts that could become hazardous.

When Storing Toys

Teach children to put their toys safely away on shelves or in a toy chest after playing to prevent trips and falls.

Toy boxes, too, should be checked for safety. Use a toy chest that has a lid that will stay open in any position to which it is raised, and will not fall unexpectedly on a child. For extra safety, be sure there are ventilation holes for fresh air. Watch for sharp edges that could cut and hinges that could pinch or squeeze. See that toys used outdoors are stored after play—rain or dew can rust or damage a variety of toys and toy parts creating hazards.

Sharp Edges

New toys intended for children under eight years of age should, by regulation, be free of sharp glass and metal edges.

With use, however, older toys may break, exposing cutting edges.

Small Parts

Older toys can break to reveal parts small enough to be swallowed or to become lodged in a child's windpipe, ears or nose. The law bans small parts in new toys intended for children under three. This includes removable small eyes and noses on stuffed toys and dolls, and small, removable squeakers on squeeze toys.

Loud Noises

Toy caps and some noisemaking guns and other toys can produce sounds at noise levels that can damage hearing. The law requires the following label on boxes of caps producing noise above a certain level: *"WARNING—Do not fire closer than one foot to the ear. Do not use indoors."* Caps producing noise that can injure a child's hearing are banned.

Cords and Strings

Toys with long strings or cords may be dangerous for infants and very young children. The cords may become wrapped around an infant's neck, causing strangulation. Never hang toys with long strings, cords, loops, or ribbons in cribs or playpens where children can become entangled.

Remove crib gyms for the crib when the child can pull up on hands and knees; some children have strangled when they fell across crib gyms stretched across the crib.

Sharp Points

Toys which have been broken may have dangerous points or prongs. Stuffed toys may have wires inside the toy which could cut or stab if exposed. A CPSC regulation prohibits sharp points in new toys and other articles intended for use by children under eight years of age.

Propelled Objects

Projectiles—guided missiles and similar flying toys—can be turned into weapons and can injure eyes in particular. Children should never be permitted to play with adult lawn darts or other hobby or sporting equipment that have sharp points. Arrows or darts used by children should have soft cork tips, rubber suction cups or other protective tips intended to prevent injury. Check to be sure the tips are secure. Avoid those dart guns or other toys which might be capable of firing articles not intended for use in the toy, such as pencils or nails.

The Dangers of Electric Toys

Electric toys and other electrically operated products intended for use by children can be extremely hazardous if improperly used, used without supervision, or not properly designed and/or constructed. The possible dangers are many: electric shock, burns, especially if the product has a heating element; and a wide variety of mechanical hazards common to toys in general, such as sharp edges and points and dangerous moving parts.

In 1973, the U.S. Consumer Product Safety Commission (CPSC) issued safety regulations under the Federal Hazardous Substances Act for electrically operated toys intended to be operated from 110-125 volt branch circuits. These safety regulations specify, manufacturing, construction and performance requirements intended to reduce the risk of injury from these products. In addition, the regulations call for mandatory cautionary labels on both the articles and their shelf packages. Also issued were complementary toy regulations for sharp points, edges, and small parts. In addition, there are applicable industry toy voluntary standards.

While these standards and mandatory regulations have reduced the risk of injury from electric toys and other electric products for children, adults must still be selective in purchasing toys, supervise their use at home, inspect them periodically, and repair, replace, or discard deteriorating toys.

Selecting a Toy

Do not buy an electrical toy, or any toy, for a child too young to use it safely. Always check the age recommendation on the shelf package. Remember that this is a minimum age recommendation. If a toy is labeled *"Not Recommended for Children under 8 Years of Age,"* this does not mean that every child who is 8 years old is mature enough to operate it. The buyer must still take into account an individual child's capabilities.

Use of a Toy

Read the instructions accompanying the product carefully and then read them with any child who will be using the product and follow the manufacturers recommendations. Be sure that the child knows how to use the items safely, understands all the instructions and warning labels, and is aware of the hazards of misusing the toy. The instructions should be kept with the toy or in a safe place where they can be found easily.

Supervision

Supervise the use of any electrical product. Just how much supervision is necessary is again a matter of judgment. Consider both the maturity of the child and the nature of the toy.

Be sure that the plug of an electrical product fits snugly into wall outlets or (if they must be used) extension cord receptacles. To prevent electrical shock, no prongs should be exposed. Teach children always to disconnect an electrical appliance after use by grasping the plug, not by pulling on the cord.

Keep infants and toddlers out of the area in which an electrical toy is being used.

Storage

All electrical toys should be put away immediately after use in a dry storage area out of the reach of younger children.

Maintenance and Disposal

Deterioration of electrically operated toys can present many hazards. Therefore, check on their condition periodically. Be alert for broken parts, frayed cords, and damage to enclosures of wiring and other protected components.

Only an adult or responsible older child should replace a light bulb on an electrical toy, as it is extremely important that the replacement bulb be of the proper wattage and that the plug is disconnected when the change is made.

Any product that has been so severely damaged that adequate repairs cannot be made should be discarded immediately.

Regulations

The CPSCs regulations address the major electrical, mechanical and thermal hazards of electric toys and other electrically operated children's articles. All electric toys must meet these provisions to be sold in the U.S. Some of the most important provisions are listed below.

Electrical

All live electrical components must be securely enclosed. These enclosures must be designed so that they cannot be opened even with common household tools, such as a screwdriver or pliers. This does not apply, however, to the housings of replaceable light bulbs.

Switches, motors, transformers, and the like must be securely mounted to prevent any non-functional movement and possible damage.

Heating elements must be supported and prevented from making contacts that might produce shock hazards.

Products designed for use with water must have electrical components in a sealed chamber completely separate from the water reservoir (as in toy steam engines).

Products requiring cleaning with a wet cloth must be designed to prevent seepage of water into areas with electrified parts, to prevent corrosion and electrical shock.

Electrical plugs must have a finger/thumb grasping area and must have a safety shield to protect small fingers from accidentally contacting energized prongs while the toy is being plugged into a wall outlet.

Mechanical

Enclosures must be strong and rigid enough to preserve the safety and integrity of the electrical components, even when the toy is subjected to foreseeable abuse.

The toy's potentially hazardous moving parts must be enclosed or guarded to minimize the chance of contact.

For pressurized enclosures such as steam chambers, there must be an automatic pressure-relief valve that will discharge in the safest possible direction.

Thermal

Products must not exceed maximum surface temperature requirements. These temperatures are determined on the basis of accessibility of a particular surface, its function, and the material from which it is made. A surface to which a child cannot gain access, for instance. is allowed to reach a higher temperature than a knob or a carrying handle.

Containers for holding molten compounds and hot liquids must be designed and constructed to minimize spills. No container should melt or become deformed when heated.

Toys must comply with the CPSC's toy safety requirements, which incorporate rigorous "use and abuse" test procedures for toys intended for various age groups.

Labeling

The labeling requirements specify that certain precautionary information shall be listed on labels on children's electrical products. The labeling is designed to help buyers choose the right toy for the right age and to warn the user of potential hazards.

The package of every such product must carry a cautionary message and a minimum age recommendation. No item with a heating element may be recommended for children under 8 years of age. There are some hobby items, such as woodburning kits, that reach very high temperatures and that been exempted from certain maximum surface temperature regulations. These items cannot be recommended for, and should be kept out of reach of children under 12 years of age.

Certain areas of the product itself must also be labeled:

- accessible surfaces that exceed certain specified temperatures must carry a warning of the danger

- toys with replaceable electric lights must carry a warning of the maximum safe wattage for a replacement bulb and a notice to disconnect the plug before changing the bulb

- products with nonreplaceable lights will be so marked; and—products not designed to be immersed in water must carry a notice to that effect

Instructions

All cautionary statements that appear on the toy or its package must also appear in the instructions that accompany it. These instructions must cover all aspects of safe use and maintenance and must advise parents of the necessity for examining the product periodically to be sure it is in safe working order.

These requirements help assure that electrically operated products for children will be as safe as can reasonably be expected.

Reminder

When electric toys or other electrical products are in use, the CPSC recommends plugging them into GFCI-protected circuits. A GFCI (Ground Fault Circuit Interrupter) will prevent many electrocutions.

All Toys Are Not for All Children

Keep toys designed for older children out of the hands of little ones. Follow labels that give age recommendations—some toys are recommended for older children because they may be hazardous in the hands of a younger child. Teach older children to help keep their toys away from younger brothers and sisters.

Even balloons, when uninflated or broken, can choke or suffocate if young children try to swallow them. More children have suffocated on uninflated balloons and pieces of broken balloons than on any other type of toy.

Infant Toys

Infant toys, such as rattles, squeeze toys, and teethers, should be large enough so that they cannot enter and become lodged in an infant's throat.

Our Responsibility

Under the Federal Hazardous Substances Act and the Consumer Product Safety Act, the Commission has set safety regulations for certain toys and other children's articles. Manufacturers must design and manufacture their products to meet these regulations so that hazardous products are not sold.

U.S. Consumer Product Safety Commission Child Safety Protection Act Fact Sheet

November 1995

- Effective January 1, 1995 products that are manufactured in or imported into the United States on or after that date must comply with the Child Safety Protection Act (CSPA).

- Any ball with a diameter of 1.75 inches (44.4mm) or less that is intended for use by children younger than 3 years of age is banned.

- Any ball with a diameter of 1.75 inches (44.4mm) or less that is intended for use by children 3 years or older must be labeled:

  "WARNING: CHOKING HAZARD — This toy is a small ball. Not for children under 3 yrs."

- Any toy or game intended for children 3 years or older but less than 8 years that contains a small ball shall bear the following cautionary label:

  "WARNING: CHOKING HAZARD — Toy contains a small ball. Not for children under 3 yrs."

- Toys and games with small parts intended for use by children at least 3 years old but under 6 years must be labeled as follows:

  "WARNING: CHOKING HAZARD — Small parts. Not for children under 3 yrs."

- Any latex balloon, or toy or game that contains a latex balloon, shall be labeled as follows:

  "WARNING: CHOKING HAZARD — Children under eight yrs. Can choke or suffocate on uninflated or broken balloons. Adult supervision required. Keep uninflated balloons from children. Discard broken balloons at once."

- Any marble intended for children 3 years or older shall be labeled:

  "WARNING: CHOKING HAZARD — This toy is a marble. Not for children under 3 yrs."

- Any toys and games intended for children at least 3 years old but less than 8 years which contain a marble shall be labeled:

  "WARNING: CHOKING HAZARD — Toy contains a marble. Not for children under 3 yrs.

Toy Safety Shopping Tips

Children Under 3 Years Old

Children under 3 tend to put everything in their mouths. Avoid buying toys intended for older children which may have small parts that pose a choking danger.

Never let children of any age play with uninflated or broken balloons because of the choking danger.

Avoid marbles, balls, and games with balls, that have a diameter of 1.75 inches or less. These products also pose a choking hazard to young children.

Children at this age pull, prod and twist toys. Look for toys that are well-made with tightly secured eyes, noses and other parts.

Avoid toys that have sharp edges and points.

Children Ages 3 through 5

Avoid toys that are constructed with thin, brittle plastic that might easily break into small pieces or leave jagged edges.

Look for household art materials, including crayons and paint sets, marked with the designation "ASTM D-4236." This means the product has been reviewed by a toxicologist and, if necessary, labeled with cautionary information.

Teach older children to keep their toys away from their younger brothers and sisters.

Children Ages 6 through 12

For all children, adults should check toys periodically for breakage and potential hazards. Damaged or dangerous toys should be repaired or thrown away.

If buying a toy gun, be sure the barrel, or the entire gun, is brightly colored so that it's not mistaken for a real gun.

If you buy a bicycle for any age child, buy a helmet too, and make sure the child wears it. Teach all children to put toys away when they're finished playing so they don't trip over them or fall on them.

Read the Label

The U.S. Consumer Product Safety Commission requires toy manufacturers to meet stringent safety standards and to label certain toys that could be a hazard for younger children. Look for labels that give age recommendations and use that information as a guide. Labels on toys that state *"not recommended for children under three ... contains small parts,"* are labeled that way because they may pose a choking hazard to children under three. Toys should be developmentally appropriate to suit the skills, abilities and interests of the child.

Shopping for toys during the holidays can be exciting and fun, but it can also be frustrating. There can be thousands of toys to choose from in one store, and it's important to choose the right toy for the right age child. Toys that are meant for older children can be dangerous for younger children.

Last year, an estimated 140,700 children were treated in U.S. hospital emergency rooms after toy-related incidents and 13 children died.

Law Requires Review and Labeling of Art Materials Including Children's Art and Drawing Products

On November 18, 1988, the President signed into law the Labeling of Hazardous Art Materials Act (Public Law 100-695).This law requires that all art materials be reviewed to determine the potential for causing a chronic hazard and that appropriate warning labels be put on those art materials found to pose a chronic hazard. The term "art material" includes "any substance marketed or represented by the producer or repackager as suitable for use in any phase of the creation of any work of visual or graphic art of any medium." (15 U.S.C. 1277(b)(1). The law applies to many children's toy products such as crayons, chalk, paint sets, modeling clay, coloring books, pencils, and any other products used by children to produce a work of visual or graphic art.

The "Labeling of Hazardous Art Materials Act" (LHAMA) amended the Federal Hazardous Substances Act (FHSA) by adding Section 23 and designating the ASTM Standard Practice for Labeling Art Materials for Chronic Health Hazards (ASTM D-4236-88) as a regulation under Section 3(b) of the FHSA. The requirements of the LHAMA became effective on November 18,1990.These requirements apply to art materials that are intended for use in the household or by children, which are initially introduced into interstate commerce on and after November 18, 1990.

The Commission believes that under the broad statutory definition of "art material" three general categories can be seen:

1. Those products which actually become a component of the work of visual or graphic art, such as paint, canvas, inks, crayons, chalk, solder, brazing rods, flux, paper, clay, stone, thread, cloth, and photographic film.

2. Those products which are closely and intimately associated with the creation of the final work of art, such as brush cleaners, solvents, ceramic kilns, brushes, silk screens, molds or mold making material, and photo developing chemicals.

3. Those tools, implements, and furniture that are used in the process of the creation of a work of art, but do not become part of the work of art. Examples are drafting tables and chairs, easels, picture frames, canvas stretchers, potter's wheels, hammers, chisels, and air pumps for air brushes.

The CPSC does not believe that Congress intended products in the third category to be considered "art materials." Therefore, as an enforcement policy, the CPSC is not requiring that products falling in this third category comply with the standard for art materials. However, manufacturers still have the responsibility under the FHSA to assure that these products comply with any FHSA labeling or other requirements due to chronic toxicity or other hazards.

Parents and others buying art materials, school supplies and toys such as crayons, paint sets, or modeling clay should be alert and purchase only those products which are accompanied by the statement "Conforms to ASTM D-4236."

The LHAMA does not change the fact that products which are hazardous are banned for distribution to young children, whether the hazard is based on chronic toxicity, acute toxicity, flammability, or other hazard identified by the FHSA. There is an exception for art materials if they meet all three of the exemption criteria of Section 2(q) of the FHSA in that they:

1. require the inclusion of the hazardous substances for their functional purpose

2. bear labeling giving adequate directions and warnings for safe use

3. are intended for use by children who have attained sufficient maturity, and may reasonably be expected, to read and heed such directions and warnings.

Chapter 52

Safe Playground Equipment

Questions and Answers

How large is the problem of playground-related injuries?

- Each year in the United States, 200,000 preschool and elementary school children visit emergency departments for care of injuries sustained on playground equipment (about 1 injury every 2½ minutes).[1]

- About 35% of all playground-related injuries are severe (e.g., fractures, internal injuries, concussions, dislocations, amputations, crushes).[1]

- Public playgrounds account for about 70% of injuries related to playground equipment.[1]

Text in this chapter is from the following undated fact sheets produced by the Consumer Product Safety Commission, "Playground Surfacing Material," available at http://www.cpsc.gov/cpscpub/pubs/3005.html, "Never Put Children's Climbing Gyms on Hard Surfaces," available at http://www.cpsc.gov/cpscpub/pubs/5119.html, "Strangulation Hazard with Playground Cargo Nets," available at http://www.cpsc.gov/cpscpub/pubs/5065.html, "Prevent Burns on Hot Metal Playground Equipment," available at http://www.cpsc.gov/cpscpub/pubs/5036.html, and "Soft Contained Play Equipment Safety Checklist," available at http://www.cpsc.gov/cpscpub/pubs/328.html; all cited July 2001; and "Playground Injuries," an undated fact sheet produced by the Centers for Disease Control and Prevention (CDC); cited August 2001.

- In schools, most injuries to students between the ages of 5 and 14 years occur on playgrounds.[2]

Which playground equipment causes the most injury?

- Most injuries occur when children fall off swings, monkey bars, climbers, or slides.[1]

- Falls off of playground equipment to the ground account for more than 60% of all playground-related injuries.[1,3]

How many injuries require hospitalization?

- Slightly less than 3% of all playground injuries require hospitalization.[1]

How many children die each year because of playground-related injuries?

- Each year, nearly 20 children die from playground-related injuries. More than half of these deaths result from strangulation and about one-third result from falls.[2]

What costs are associated with playground-related injury?

- In 1995, the costs were $1.2 billion for children younger than 15 years old.[2]

What is CDC doing to prevent playground-related injuries?

The National Center for Injury Prevention and Control, CDC, funds the National Program for Playground Safety (NPPS), which works to prevent playground-related injuries and the attendant suffering and costs. This program is based at the University of Northern Iowa in Cedar Falls, Iowa.

What are the goals of NPPS?

- To implement a national plan for the prevention of playground-related injuries.

- To maintain a clearinghouse of materials on playground safety and make those materials available to anyone who requests them.

- To provide an information hotline on preventing playground-related injury.

- To hold training programs for teachers and playground safety inspectors.

- To research the impact attenuation characteristics of playground surfaces under a variety of conditions.

What material is available from NPPS?

Brochures

- *Inspection Guide for Parents*
- *A Blueprint for Increasing Playground Safety*
- *Supervision Means . . .*
- *All Children Should Play on Age-Appropriate Equipment*
- *Falls to Surface Should Be Cushioned*
- *Equipment Should Be Safe*
- *Planning a Play Area for Children*
- *The National Action Plan for Playground Safety*
- *Funding Tips for Playgrounds*
- *SAFE Playground Resources*

Videos

- *ABC's of Supervision (training for elementary school supervisors)*
- *America's Playgrounds—Make Them Safe (NPPS overview)*
- *Sammy's Playground (for grades K-3)*
- *SAFE Playgrounds—General Description of SAFE Playgrounds*

Other Materials

- Summary Report for NPPS
- SAFE Playground Workbook
- SAFE Playground Handbook

Playground Surfacing Materials

The surface under and around playground equipment can be a major factor in determining the injury—causing potential of a fall. It is self evident that a fall onto a shock absorbing surface is less likely to cause a serious injury than a fall onto a hard surface. Because head impact injuries from a fall have the potential for being life threatening,

425

the more shock absorbing a surface can be made, the more is the likelihood that the severity of the injury will be reduced. However, it should be recognized that all injuries due to falls cannot be prevented no matter what playground surfacing material is used.

Acceptability of Various Surfacing Materials

Hard surfacing materials, such as asphalt or concrete, are unsuitable for use under and around playground equipment of any height unless they are required as a base for a shock absorbing unitary material such as a rubber mat. Earth surfaces such as soils and hard packed dirt are also not recommended because their shock absorbing properties can vary considerably depending on climatic conditions such as moisture and temperature. Similarly, grass and turf are not recommended because their effectiveness in absorbing shock during a fall can be reduced considerably due to wear and environmental conditions.

Acceptable playground surfacing materials are available in two basic types, *Unitary* or *Loose-Fill*.

Unitary Materials

Unitary Materials are generally rubber mats or a combination of rubberlike materials held in place by a binder that may be poured in place at the playground site and cures to form a unitary shock absorbing surface. Unitary materials are available from a number of different manufacturers many of whom have a range of materials with differing shock absorbing properties. Persons wishing to install a unitary material as a playground surface should request test data from the manufacturer that should identify the "Critical Height" of the desired material. In addition, site requirements should be obtained from the manufacturer because, as stated above, some unitary materials require installation over a hard surface while for others this is not required.

Loose-Fill Materials

Loose-fill materials can also have acceptable shock absorbing properties when installed at a sufficient depth. These materials include, but are not confined to, sand, gravel, and shredded wood products. Loose-fill materials should not be installed over hard surfaces such as asphalt or concrete.

Because loose-fill materials are generally sold for purposes other than playground surfacing, many vendors are unlikely to be able to provide information on their shock absorbing performance. For that reason, CPSC staff has conducted tests to determine the relative shock absorbing properties of some loose-fill materials commonly used as surfaces under and around playground equipment.

The tests were conducted in accordance with the procedure in the voluntary standard for playground surfacing systems, ASTM F1292.

The "Critical Heights" of loose-fill materials may be used as a guide in selecting the type and depth of materials that will provide the necessary safety for equipment of various heights.

The depth of any loose-fill material could be reduced during use resulting in different shock-absorbing properties. For this reason, a margin of safety should be considered in selecting a type and depth of material for a specific use.

Other Characteristics of Surfacing Materials

Selection of a surfacing material for a specific location may be governed by the environmental conditions at that location.

Organic Loose Material

Examples of organic loose materials would be wood chips, bark mulch, etc.

Fall Absorbing Characteristics

Cushioning effect depends on air trapped within and between individual particles, and presupposes an adequate depth of material.

Installation / Maintenance

Organic loose material should not be installed over existing hard surfaces (e.g., asphalt, concrete). Requires a method of containment (e.g., retaining barrier, excavated pit). Requires good drainage underneath material. Requires periodic renewal or replacement and continuous maintenance (e.g., leveling, grading, sifting, raking) to maintain appropriate depth and remove foreign matter.

Advantages

Low initial cost. Ease of installation. Good drainage. Less abrasive than sand. Less attractive to cats and dogs (compared to sand). Attractive appearance. Readily available.

Disadvantages

The following conditions may reduce cushioning potential:

1. Environmental conditions; rainy weather, high humidity, freezing temperatures.

2. With normal use over time, combines with dirt and other foreign materials.

3. Over time, decomposes, is pulverized, and compacts.

4. Depth may be reduced by displacement due to children's activities or by material being blown by wind. Can be blown or thrown into children's eyes. Subject to microbial growth when wet. Conceals animal excrement and trash (e.g., broken glass, nails, pencils, and other sharp objects that can cause cut and puncture wounds. Spreads easily outside of containment area. Can be flammable. Subject to theft by neighborhood residents for use as mulch.

Inorganic Loose Material

Examples of inorganic loose materials are sand and gravel.

Installation / Maintenance

Should not be installed over existing hard surfaces (e.g., asphalt, rock). Method of containment needed (e.g., retaining barrier, excavated pit). Good drainage required underneath material. Requires periodic renewal or replacement and continuous maintenance (e.g., leveling, grading, sifting, raking) to maintain appropriate depth and remove foreign matter. Compacted sand should periodically be turned over, loosened, and cleaned. Gravel may require periodic break up and removal of hard pan.

Advantages

Low initial cost. Ease of installation. Does not pulverize. Not ideal for microbial growth. Nonflammable. Materials are readily available. Not susceptible to vandalism except by contamination. Gravel is less attractive to animals than sand.

Disadvantages

The following conditions reduce cushioning potential:

1. Environmental conditions: rainy weather, high humidity, freezing temperatures.

2. With normal use, combines with dirt and other foreign materials.

3. Depth may be reduced due to displacement by children's activities and sand may be blown by wind. May be swallowed. Conceals animal excrement and trash (e.g., broken glass, nails, pencils, and other sharp objects that can cause cut and puncture wounds).

Sand: Spreads easily outside of containment area. Small particles bind together and become less cushioning when wet; when thoroughly wet, sand reacts as a rigid material. May be tracked out of play area on shoes; abrasive to floor surfaces when tracked indoors; abrasive to plastic materials. Adheres to clothing. Susceptible to fouling by animals.

Gravel: Difficult to walk on. If displaced onto nearby hard surface pathways, could present a fall hazard. Hard pan may form under heavily traveled areas.

Unitary Synthetic Materials

Examples of unitary synthetic materials are rubber or rubber over foam mats or tiles, poured in place urethane and rubber compositions.

Fall Absorbing Characteristics

Manufacturer should be contacted for information on Critical Height of materials when tested according to ASTM F1292.

Installation / Maintenance

Some unitary materials can be laid directly on hard surfaces such as asphalt or concrete. Others may require expert under-surface preparation and installation by the manufacturer or a local contractor. Materials generally require no additional means of containment. Once installed, the materials require minimal maintenance.

Advantages

Low maintenance. Easy to clean. Consistent shock absorbency. Material not displaced by children during play activities. Generally low life cycle costs. Good footing (depends on surface texture). Harbor few foreign objects. Generally no retaining edges needed. Is accessible to the handicapped.

Disadvantages

Initial cost relatively high. Under surfacing may be critical for thinner materials. Often must be used on almost level uniform surfaces. May be flammable. Subject to vandalism (e.g., ignited, defaced, cut). Full rubber tiles may curl up and cause tripping. Some designs susceptible to frost damage.

Description of Loose Fill Surfacing Materials

Wood Mulch: Random sized wood chips, twigs, and leaves collected from a wood chipper being fed tree limbs, branches, and brush.

Double Shredded Bark Mulch: Similar to shredded mulch commonly used by homeowners to mulch shrubs and flower beds.

Uniform Wood Chips: Relatively uniform sized shredded wood fibers from recognized hardwoods. Sample contained no bark or leaves.

Fine Sand: Particles of white sand purchased in bags marked "play sand."

Plastic Climbing Gyms on Hard Surfaces, Indoors or Outdoors, May Be Hazardous

The U.S. Consumer Product Safety Commission (CPSC) is warning parents and daycare providers that children's plastic climbing equipment should not be used indoors on wood or cement floors, even if covered with carpet, such as indoor/out-door, shag or other types of carpet. Carpet does not provide adequate protection to prevent injuries.

CPSC has reports of two children killed and hundreds injured at home and at day-care centers when they fell from climbing equipment placed indoors on cement, wood or carpeted floors.

Parents and child care-givers should put all climbing equipment outdoors on surfaces such as sand or mulch to prevent children's head injuries. Manufacturers of plastic climbing equipment are labeling their products with warnings to NEVER put the equipment on concrete, asphalt, wood, or other hard surfaces and that carpet may NOT prevent injury.

Strangulation Hazard with Playground Cargo Nets

The U.S. Consumer Product Safety Commission (CPSC) advises parents to check outdoor play equipment with cargo nets before allowing children to climb them. Nets having openings with a perimeter length (sum of the length of the four sides) of between 17 and 28 inches could allow head entrapment resulting in strangulation.

CPSC knows of incidents at fast food restaurants where a child's head was entrapped and an adult had to cut the net to release the child. Although no serious injuries occurred, the potential for strangulation exists. CPSC staff are working with firms to correct any cargo nets which may be potentially hazardous.

Parents should check for playground cargo nets that could allow head entrapment and strangulations. Net openings should either be too small to permit entry of a child's body or large enough to permit free passage of a child's head.

Prevent Burns on Hot Metal Playground Equipment

Parents should check for hot surfaces on metal playground equipment before allowing young children to play on it. Solid steel decks, slides, or steps in direct sunlight may reach temperatures high enough to cause serious contact burn injuries in a matter of seconds.

CPSC knows of incidents in which children suffered second and third degree burns to their hands, legs, and buttocks when they sat on metal stairs, decks, or slides. Young children are most at risk because, unlike older children who react quickly by pulling away their hands or by getting off a hot surface, very young children may remain in place when they contact a hot surface.

Soft Contained Play Equipment Safety Checklist

The following checks will help parents and children use Soft Contained Play Equipment safely.

Equipment Check

Check the safety netting for tears or frays.

- Torn netting could allow a child to climb onto the outer portions of the equipment and fall onto a hard surface.

Check cargo webbing and rope equipment for tears or frays.

- Torn rope equipment or loose sewing connections in the cargo webbing may be an entrapment or tripping hazard.

Check floor surfacing for tears.

- Floor surfacing should not be torn, in order to prevent trips or ankle sprains.

- If mats are used outside of the Soft Contained Play Equipment, they should be placed tightly together and should not be torn, in order to prevent trips or ankle sprains.

Check the equipment for general cleanliness.

- Dirty equipment is an indication that the owner/operator may not have kept up with the routine maintenance and repair.

- Walkways should be clear of trash and clutter to prevent tripping.

Safe Use Check

Obey the posted safety guidelines of the Soft Contained Play Equipment.

- Guidelines should explain proper equipment use.

Follow use and size recommendations.

- Smaller children are at a disadvantage in a collision with a larger child.

- If your child meets the size restriction for the toddler section. do not bring him/her into the older children's section.

- Keep older, larger children from playing in the toddler section.

Remove clothing strings, necklaces, earrings and all loose items in pockets before the child enters the Soft Contained Play Equipment.

- Loose hanging strings and jewelry can get caught in play equipment.

- Items inside pockets can fall into the ball pools.

Do not allow children to play or linger in front of slide exits or to climb up slides.

- A child playing in front of a slide exit or climbing up a slide could be struck, by a child coming down the slide.

- Children like to bury themselves under the balls in a ball pool. If a slide exits into the ball pool, a child playing in the balls in front of the exit may be struck.

Do not allow children to play or linger at the base of climbing equipment in a ball pool.

- Children jump off equipment such as the mountain climb into the ball pool. A child playing at the base of the equipment could be struck.

Accessibility to the Disabled

The Americans with Disabilities Act of 1990 (ADA) prohibits discrimination on the basis of disability in employment, public services, transportation, public accommodations—including many services operated by private entities—and telecommunications. Title III of the legislation includes within the definition of public accommodation: "a park, zoo, amusement park, or other place of recreation"; a school, including nursery schools; a day care center; and a gymnasium, health spa, or "other places of exercise or recreation." Specific Federal requirements for accessibility to playgrounds by the disabled are expected to be published.

The Department of Parks and Recreation in the State of California has advised that after January 1, 1991, regulations requiring that all types of play activity in new and redone play areas must be accessible to the disabled. Other states may similarly issue accessibility requirements. Playground designers, installers and operators are reminded that they should determine what Federal and State requirements for accessibility are in effect. These requirements could necessitate changes to existing playgrounds as well as when new playgrounds are planned or existing playgrounds refurbished.

Resources

SafeUSA

Internet: http://www.cdc.gov/safeusa
Toll Free: 888-252-7751

National Program for Playground Safety
Tel: 800-554-PLAY
Internet: http://www.uni.edu/playground

Consumer Product Safety Commission
Tel: 800-638-2772
Internet: http://www.cpsc.gov

References

1. Consumer Product Safety Commission (CPSC). National Electronic Injury Surveillance System 1990-94. Washington (DC): CPSC.

2. Office of Technology Assessment. *Risks to students in school.* Washington (DC): U.S. Government Printing Office, 1995.

3. U.S. Consumer Product Safety Commission (CPSC). *Handbook for public playground safety.* Washington, DC: author, 1997. Publication No. 325, available at: www.cpsc.gov/cpscpub/pubs/playbk97.pdf.

Chapter 53

Trampoline Safety

The U. S. Consumer Product Safety Commission (CPSC) wants you and your family to be safe when using trampolines. The CPSC estimates that in 1998 there were 95,000 hospital emergency room-treated injuries associated with trampolines. About 75 percent of the victims are under 15 years of age, and 10 percent are under 5 years of age. Since 1990, CPSC has received reports of 6 deaths involving trampolines. The hazards that result in injuries and deaths are:

- Colliding with another person on the trampoline.

- Landing improperly while jumping or doing stunts on the trampoline.

- Falling or jumping off the trampoline.

- Falling on the trampoline springs or frame.

- Almost all of the trampolines associated with injuries were at private homes, usually in backyards. Most of the injuries occurred on full-size trampolines.

Here are the steps you can take to help prevent serious trampoline injuries, especially sprains, fractures, scrapes, bruises, and cuts.

"Trampoline Safety Alert," an undated fact sheet produced by the Consumer Product Safety Commission, available online at http://www.cpsc.gov/cpscpub/pubs/085.html; cited July 2001.

- Allow only one person on the trampoline at a time.

- Do not attempt or allow somersaults.

- Do not allow trampoline to be used without shock-absorbing pads that completely cover the springs, hooks, and the frame.

- Place the trampoline away from structures and other play areas. Use shock-absorbent material on the ground around the perimeter.

- Do not use a ladder with the trampoline because it provides unsupervised access by small children. No child under 6 years of age should use a regular-size trampoline. Secure the trampoline to prevent unauthorized and unattended use.

- Always supervise children who use a trampoline.

Chapter 54

Guidelines for Moveable Soccer Goal Safety

Movable soccer goals can fall over and kill children who climb on them or hang from the crossbar. The U.S. Consumer Product Safety Commission (CPSC) has reports of at least 24 deaths since 1979 resulting from soccer goals falling over. In addition, an estimated 120 injuries involving falling goals are treated each year in U.S. hospital emergency rooms.

Almost all of the goals involved in these tipovers appeared to be "homemade" by high school shop classes, custodial members, or local welders, not professionally manufactured. These "homemade" goals are often very heavy and unstable.

Since 1990, the CPSC has worked with the Coalition to Promote Soccer Goal Safety to address risks presented by these soccer goals and to make movable soccer goals more stable. The Commission and the Coalition strongly recommend that soccer coaches, school officials, and soccer field maintenance personnel prevent goals falling over by anchoring goals to the ground. They should chain goals to a fence or permanent structure when not in use and warn students not to climb on goals.

Follow these safety suggestions/guidelines:

The text in this chapter is from the following undated fact sheets produced by the Consumer Product Safety Commission, "Movable Soccer Goals Can Fall Over On Children," available at http://www.cpsc.gov/cpscpub/pubs/5118.html, and "Guidelines for Movable Soccer Goal Safety," available at http://www.cpsc.gov/cpscpub/pubs/326.html; both cited July 2001.

- Securely anchor or counter-weight movable goals at all times.

- Never climb on the net or goal framework.

- Remove nets when goals are not in use.

- Anchor or chain goals to nearby fence posts, dugouts, or any other similar sturdy fixture when not in use.

- Check all connecting hardware before every use. Replace damaged or missing fasteners immediately.

- Ensure safety labels are clearly visible.

- Fully disassemble goals for seasonal storage.

- Always use extreme caution when moving goals.

- Always instruct players on the safe handling of and potential dangers associated with movable soccer goals.

- Use movable soccer goals only on level (flat) fields.

Soccer Goal Injuries and Deaths

According to the 1994 National Soccer Participation Survey (Soccer Industry Council of America), over 16 million persons in the United States play soccer at least once a year. Seventy-four percent (over 12 million) of these persons are under the age of 18. Soccer ranks fourth in participation for those under 18, following basketball, volleyball, and softball and well ahead of baseball, which has an annual participation of 9.7 million.

There are approximately 225,000 to 500,000 soccer goals in the United States. Many of these soccer goals are unsafe because they are unstable and are either unanchored or not properly anchored or counter-balanced. These movable soccer goals pose an unnecessary risk of tipover to children who climb on goals (or nets) or hang from the crossbar.

The majority of movable soccer goals are constructed of metal, typically weighing 150-500 pounds. The serious injuries and deaths are a result of blunt force trauma to the head, neck, chest, and limbs of the victims. In most cases this occurred when the goal tipped or was accidentally tipped onto the victim. In one case an 8-year-old child was fatally injured when the movable soccer goal he was climbing tipped over and struck him on the head. In another case, a 20-year-old male died from a massive head trauma when he pulled a goal down on himself while attempting to do chin-ups. In a third case, while attempting to tighten a net to its goal post, the victim's father lifted the back base of the goal causing it to tip over striking his 3-year-old child on the head, causing a fatal injury.

High winds can also cause movable soccer goals to fall over. For example, a 9-year-old was fatally injured when a goal was tipped over by a gust of wind. In another incident, a 19-year-old goalie suffered stress fractures to both legs when the soccer goal was blown on top of her.

Rules of Soccer

From the Federation of Internationale De Football Associations (FIFA) Laws of the Game, Guide for Referees, July 1993.

- "Goal-posts and cross-bars must be made of wood, metal, or other approved material as decided from time to time by the International Football Association Board. They may be square, rectangular, round. half round, or elliptical in shape."

- "Goal-posts and cross-bars made of other materials and in other shapes are not permitted. The goal-posts must be white in color."

- "The width and depth of the cross-bar shall not exceed 5 inches(12 cm)."

From the National Federation of State High School Associations' (NFSHSA) 1994-95 National Federation Edition-Soccer Rules Book.

- "They shall consist of 2 upright (posts) 4 inches but not more than 5 inches (0.10m by 0.12m)...the tops of the posts shall be joined by a 4 inches but not more than 5 inches (0.10m by 0.12m) horizontal crossbar..."

From the National Collegiate Athletic Associations (NCAA) Rules for Soccer.

- "...and shall consist of two wooden or metal posts, ...the width or diameter of the goal-posts and crossbar shall not be less than 4 inches (10.16 cm) nor more than 5 inches (12.7 cm)."

Design/Construction Guidelines

While a movable soccer goal appears to be a simple structure, a correctly designed goal is carefully constructed with counterbalancing measures incorporated into the product. The common dimensions of a full-size goal are approximately 7.3 m (24 ft.) in width by 2.4 m (8 ft.) in height and 1.8 m (6 ft.) in depth. The stability of a soccer goal depends on several factors. One effective design alternative uses a counterbalancing strategy by lengthening the overall depth of the goal to effectively place more weight further from the goal's front posts (more weight at the back of the goal). A second design selects lightweight materials for the goal's front posts and crossbar and provides much heavier materials for the rear ground bar and frame members. This tends to counterbalance the forces working to tip the goal forward. Another design uses a heavy rear framework and folds flat when not in use, making the goal much less likely to tip over. Finally, after these various designs are considered, it is imperative that ALL movable soccer goals be anchored firmly in place at all times.

Anchoring/Securing/Counterweighting Guidelines

A properly anchored/counterweighted movable soccer goal is much less likely to tip over. Remember to secure the goal to the ground (preferably at the rear of the goal), making sure the anchors are flush with the ground and clearly visible. It is IMPERATIVE that ALL movable soccer goals are always anchored properly. There are several different ways to secure your soccer goal. The number and type of anchors to be used will depend on a number of factors, such as soil type, soil moisture content, and total goal weight.

Anchor Types

Auger Style

This style anchor is "helical" shaped and is screwed into the ground. A flange is positioned over the ground shoes (bar) and rear ground shoe (bar) to secure them to the ground. A minimum of two auger-style anchors (one on each side of the goal) are recommended. More may be required, depending on the manufacturer's specifications, the weight of the goal, and soil conditions.

Semipermanent

This anchor type is usually comprised of two or more functional components. The main support requires a permanently secured base that is buried underground. One type (3.2a) of semipermanent anchor connects the underground base to the soccer goal by means of 2 tethers. Another design (3.2b) utilizes a buried anchor tube with a threaded opening at ground level. The goal is positioned over the buried tube and the bolt is passed through the goal ground shoes (bar) and rear ground shoe (bar) and screwed into the threaded hole of the buried tube.

Peg or Stake Style (Varying Lengths)

Typically two to four pegs or stakes are used per goal (more for heavier goals). The normal length of a peg or stake is approximately 10 inches (250mm). Care should be taken when installing pegs or stakes. Pegs or stakes should be driven into the ground with a sledgehammer as far as possible and at an angle if possible, through available holes in the ground shoes (bar) and rear ground shoe (bar) to secure them to the ground. If the peg or stake is not flush with the ground, it should be clearly visible to persons playing near the soccer goal. Stakes with larger diameters or textured surfaces have greater holding capacity.

J-Hook Shaped Stake Style

This style is used when holes are not pre-drilled into the ground shoes (bars) or rear ground shoe (bar) of the goal. Similar to the peg or stake style, this anchor is hammered, at an angle if possible, directly into the earth. The curved (top) portion of this anchor fits over the goal member to secure it to the ground. Typically, two to four stakes of this type are recommended (per goal), depending on stake structure, manufacturers specifications, weight of goal, and soil conditions. Stakes with larger diameters or textured surfaces have greater holding capacity.

Sandbags / Counterweights

Sandbags or other counterweights could be an effective alternative on hard surfaces, such as artificial turf, where the surface can not be penetrated by a conventional anchor (i.e., an indoor practice facility). The number of bags or weights needed will vary and must be adequate for the size and total weight of the goal being supported.

Net Pegs

These tapered, metal stakes should be used to secure only the NET to the ground. Net pegs should NOT be used to anchor the movable soccer goal.

Guidelines for Goal Storage or Securing When Goal is Not in Use

The majority of the incidents investigated by CPSC did not occur during a soccer match. Most of the incidents occurred when the goals were unattended. Therefore, it is imperative that all goals are stored properly when not being used. When goals are not being used always:

- Remove the net

- Take appropriate steps to secure goals such as:

    Place the goal frames face to face and secure them at each goalpost with a lock and chain

    Lock and chain to a suitable fixed structure such as a permanent fence

    Lock unused goals in a secure storage room after each use

    If applicable, fully disassemble the goals for seasonal storage, or

    If applicable, fold the face of the goal down and lock it to its base.

Conclusions/Safety Tips

- Securely anchor or counterweight movable soccer goals at ALL times.

- Anchor or chain one goal to another, to itself in a folded down position, or to nearby fence posts, dugouts, or any other similar sturdy fixture when not in use. If this is not practical, store movable soccer goals in a place where children cannot have access to them.

- Remove nets when goals are not in use.

- Check for structural integrity and proper connecting hardware before every use. Replace damaged or missing parts or fasteners immediately.

- NEVER allow anyone to climb on the net or goal framework.

- Ensure safety/warning labels are clearly visible (placed under the crossbar and on the sides of the down-posts at eye level).

- Fully disassemble goals for seasonal storage.

- Always exercise extreme caution when moving goals and allow adequate manpower to move goals of varied sizes and weights. Movable soccer goals should only be moved by authorized and trained personnel.

- Always instruct players on the safe handling of and potential dangers associated with movable soccer goals.

- Movable soccer goals should only be used on LEVEL (flat) fields.

List of Soccer Organizations

Federation of Internationale De Football Association
Hitzigweg 11, 8030
Zurich, Switzerland
Tel: 41-1-384-9595

National Federation of State High School Associations
P.O. Box 690
Indianapolis, IN 46206
Tel: 317-972-6900
Fax: 317-822-5700
Internet: http://www.nfshsa.org

National Collegiate Athletic Association
700 W. Washington Street
Indianapolis, IN 46206-6222
Tel: 317-917-6222
Fax: 317-917-6888
Internet: http://www.ncaa.org

For Further Information

For further information on soccer goal anchors and/or to obtain FREE soccer goal warning labels, safety alerts/bulletins and additional copies of this document, please contact:

The Coalition to Promote Soccer Goal Safety

c/o Soccer Industry Council of America
200 Castlewood Dr.
North Palm Beach, FL 33408
or call any of these Coalition members:
800-527-7510
800-334-4625
800-243-0533
800-531-4252

Chapter 55

Prevent Injuries to Children from Exercise Equipment

The U.S. Consumer Product Safety Commission (CPSC) estimates that each year about 8,700 children under 5 years of age are injured with exercise equipment. There are an additional 16,500 injuries per year to children ages 5 to 14. Types of equipment identified in these cases include stationary bicycles, treadmills, and stair climbers. Fractures and even amputations were reported in about 20 percent of exercise equipment related injuries.

The CPSC is concerned about the severity of injuries to children, especially because the hazard may not be obvious. Therefore, the CPSC warns parents always to keep children away from exercise equipment. Never use a bike without a chain guard, and when not using the equipment, store it or lock it so children cannot get to it.

Warning

- Children's fingers can be amputated if they touch moving parts of exercise equipment.

- Keep children away from exercise equipment.

"Prevent Injuries to Children from Exercise Equipment," an undated fact sheet produced by the Consumer Product Safety Commission, available online at http://www.cpsc.gov/cpscpub/pubs/5028.html; cited July 2001.

Part Nine

Home Maintenance Equipment

Chapter 56

Lawnmowers

Riding Lawnmowers

While homeowners generally rely on walk-behind power lawnmowers to cut small plots of grass, many suburban and country residents with large lawns have automated their grass-cutting chores out of necessity. With lots of grass needing to be cut each week, rural homeowners have come to rely on riding mowers, lawn tractors, and garden tractors as indispensable machines for maintaining the landscape. Aside from cutting large swaths of grass, some machines also accommodate a host of attachments to make quick work of otherwise cumbersome garden projects.

Although many thousands of homeowners have driven these mowers and tractors for years without mishap, others haven't been as fortunate. Hazards most often associated with riding equipment are blade contact and loss of stability. The U.S. Consumer Product Safety Commission estimates that 18,000 consumer injuries related to riding mower mishaps were treated in hospital emergency rooms in 1986. Between 1983-1986, there were an estimated 75 deaths each year related to riding mower, lawn tractors and garden tractor accidents.

"Riding Lawnmowers," an undated fact sheet produced by the Consumer Product Safety Commission, available online at http://www.cpsc.gov/cpscpub/pubs/588.html; cited July 2001; and "Power Lawnmowers," and undated fact sheet produced by the Consumer Product Safety Commission; cited August 2001.

Fatal accidents have several common patterns: the machine tips over, the victim falls under or is run over by the machine (accidents involving young children fall in this category), or the victim is thrown from or falls off the machine. The risk of an accident with a ride-on mower is almost twice the chance of a mishap with a walk-behind rotary mower.

Many new riding mowers and tractors will have new safety features not found on older machines. Under new provisions of a voluntary safety standard which took effect for units made after July, 1987, the following features have been incorporated into new equipment:

- **Operator Presence Control.** This device will stop the rotary blades if the operator leaves the control position of the riding mower or tractor without first disengaging the blade drive. This safety feature will reduce the chance of injury if the operator leaves the control position to unclog the discharge chute or perform some other activity without first stopping the mower blade(s).

- **Increased seatback height.** New machines have seatbacks of at least 4 1/2 inches to help the operator maintain a safe position on the machine.

- Dynamic turn and sudden traction performance limits have been added to improve machine stability.

If you are shopping for a new machine, a label certifying that the mower or garden tractor meets the 1986 ANSI 871.1 standard indicates that machines have these safety features.

Safe Operating Practices for Ride-On Mowers

General Operation

This cutting machine is capable of amputating hands and feet and throwing objects that are hit by the blade. Failure to observe the following safety instructions could result in serious injury or death to the operator and/or bystander.

1. Read, understand, and follow the safety and operating instructions that are in the manual and on the unit.

2. Allow only responsible adults who are familiar with the instructions and with proper operating procedures to operate the machine.

3. Clear the mowing area of objects such as rocks, toys, wire, etc., which could be picked up and thrown by the blade.

4. Be sure the area is clear of other people before mowing. Stop the mower if anyone enters the area.

5. Never carry passengers.

6. Do not mow in reverse unless absolutely necessary. Bring the machine to a full stop before shifting to reverse. Always look behind before and while operating in reverse.

7. Be aware of the discharge direction and do not point it at anyone.

8. Slow down before turning.

9. Never leave a running machine unattended. Always turn off the blades, set the parking brake, stop the engine, and remove the keys before dismounting.

10. Turn off blades and attachments when not mowing.

11. Stop the engine before removing the grass catcher or unclogging the chute.

12. Mow only in daylight or good artificial light.

13. Do not operate the machine while under the influence of alcohol or drugs.

14. Watch for traffic when operating near or crossing roadways.

Slope Operation

Slopes are a major factor related to tipover and loss of control accidents, which can result in severe injury or death. All slopes require extra caution. If you cannot back up the slope or if you feel uneasy on it, do not mow it.

DO:

- Mow up and down slopes, not across.

- Remove obstacles such as rocks, downed tree limbs, etc.

- Watch for holes, ruts or bumps. Uneven terrain could cause the mower to overturn. Tall grass can hide obstacles. Use slow speed. Shift into a lower gear before going on a slope. Choose a low enough gear so that you will not have to stop or shift while on the slope.

- Follow the manufacturer's recommendations for wheel weights or counterweights to improve stability.

- Use extra care with grass catchers or other attachments. These can change the stability of the mower.

- Empty grass catcher bags when they are only partially full.

- Keep all movement on slopes slow and gradual. Avoid sudden changes in speed and direction.

- Avoid starting or stopping on a slope. If tires lose traction, disengage the blades, and proceed slowly straight down the slope.

DO NOT:

- Do not turn on slopes unless unavoidable; then, with the blades disengaged, turn slowly and gradually downhill.

- Do not mow near dropoffs, ditches, or embankments. A wheel over the edge or an edge caving in could cause sudden overturn.

- Do not mow on wet grass. Reduced traction could cause sliding.

- Do not try to stabilize the machine by putting your foot on the ground.

- Do not use a grass catcher on steep slopes or rough terrains.

Children

Tragic accidents can occur if the operator is not alert to the presence of children. Children are often attracted to the mower and the mowing activity. Never assume that children will remain where you last saw them.

1. Keep small children out of the mowing area, preferably indoors under the watchful care of an adult other than the operator.

2. Be alert and turn the mower off if children enter the area.

3. Before and when operating in reverse, look behind and down for small children.

4. Never carry children. They may fall off and be seriously injured or interfere with safe mower operation.

5. Never allow children to operate the mower.

6. Use extra care when approaching corners, shrubs, and trees.

Service

1. Use extra care in handling gasoline. It is flammable, and the vapors are explosive.

   A. Use only an approved container.

   B. Never remove the gas cap or add fuel with the engine running. Allow the engine to cool before refueling.

   C. Never refuel the machine indoors.

   D. Never store the machine or gasoline container inside the house where there is an open flame, such as a gas water heater.

   E. Always clean up spilled gasoline.

2. Never run a machine inside a closed area without good ventilation.

3. Keep nuts and bolts, especially blade attachment bolts, tight and keep equipment in good condition.

4. Never tamper with safety devices. Check their operation regularly.

5. Keep the machine free of grass, leaves, and oil build-up to prevent fire.

6. Stop and inspect the equipment if you strike an object. Repair if necessary before restarting.

7. Never make adjustments or repairs with the engine running.

8. Grass catcher components are subject to damage and deterioration. To reduce the thrown object hazard, periodically check and replace with manufacturer's recommended parts, when necessary.

9. Mower blades are sharp and can cut. Wrap the blades or wear gloves and use extra caution when servicing them.

10. Check brake operation frequently. Adjust and service as required.

Power Lawnmowers

Even though millions of homeowners routinely use power lawnmowers every year without mishap, there is still a fairly constant parade of people into hospital emergency rooms with injuries from walk-behind powermowers. Most often, patients are treated for minor injuries and released. However, emergency surgery is sometimes required to treat severe injuries resulting from hand or foot contact with the rotating blade; toe amputations are not uncommon with homeowners cutting grass. In 1986, some 37,000 people were treated in hospital emergency rooms for mower injuries, according to recent estimates by the U.S. Consumer Product Safety Commission.

Ever since the Commission's founding in 1973, walk-behind power rotary lawnmowers have been the subject of ongoing research by engineering, human factors, economists and epidemiological personnel. Their efforts were instrumental in developing the federal safety standard for power mowers which took effect June 30, 1982. All walk behind power rotary lawnmowers manufactured since then must meet new safety requirements designed to reduce hand and foot contact with the moving blade.

For example, with most rotary mowers built before June 1982, the blade rotated as long as the engine was operating. Problems arose when wet grass clippings jammed the discharge chute. In these situations, the owner's manual emphasized that the engine should be shut down first, and that the blade should be allowed to come to a complete stop before the user reached into the discharge chute to remove the clippings.

To avoid having to restart the engine, users frequently allowed the motor to operate while they tried to remove the clippings with their hand. Many homeowners had fingers amputated by the rotating blade; others were more fortunate and only sustained severe lacerations.

The CPSC Standard

If you purchase a new walk-behind rotary lawnmower, the machine must meet the June 30, 1982 federal standard, and must be certified as complying with the regulation. Some of the safety features of the regulation include:

- *The blade brake control.* On all new mowers, an automatic brake stops the blade in three seconds when the operator releases his/her grip on the handle-mounted control bar. This feature prevents the rotary blade from operating unless the operator actuates the control. It also requires the operator to maintain continuous contact with the control to keep the blade operating, and stops the blade completely within three seconds when the operator releases the control. If the mower only has a manual start, the control must stop the blade without shutting down the engine, unless the manual starting control is located within 24 inches from the top of the handle, or the mower has a 360 degree foot shield. For user protection, the mower must also have a secondary control which must be activated before the mower can be operated.

- *Foot shield.* The area at the rear of the mower that might be reached by the foot when using the mower is subjected to a probing test using a foot-like probe. With the mower wheels on the ground, this area is probed to assure that neither the foot probe nor any part of the mower (such as a trailing shield) will enter the path of the blade. Shields at this rear area are also subjected to a strength test and an obstruction test. Shields at the rear of the mower which must be moved to attach the grass catcher or other equipment are also examined. These shields must either close automatically or prevent operation of the mower (when open) unless the grass catcher is present.

- *Labels.* New mowers must have a warning label near the discharge chute cautioning users to keep hands and feet away from the chute. The mower must also have a certification label with the inscription, "Meets CPSC blade safety requirements."

Selecting a Mower

If you are shopping for a walk-behind rotary lawnmower, consider the following factors which may affect mowing operations:

- Who will be using the machine most of the time? Will they tire quickly if they have to push the mower all the while or would a better choice be a self-propelled mower?

- Does the mower have deflectors at the discharge chute that force objects thrown from it to be ejected toward the ground rather than upward in the air?

- Does the mower start easily? Ignition systems have been improved to simplify manual starting of the mower.

- Is it easy to operate? Are controls within easy reach? Is the handle adjustable so others can use the mower without difficulty?

- Do you want to vary the cutting height of the grass during the growing season? Manufacturers use several methods to adjust the cutting height, including wheel levers and bolted wheels. Consider the ease with which you can adjust the cutting height when shopping for a mower.

- Consider your preferences for lawn care. If you don't bag grass clippings as you cut the lawn, then you will likely find the "engine kill" mower quite acceptable. With this machine, the engine will shut down and the rotary blade will stop within three seconds after you release your grip on the operator controls. With this "engine kill" mower, the pull-rope starter must be located within 24 inches of the top handle, or the protective foot shield must surround the entire mower housing.

- If you use a grass catcher to bag lawn clippings, then the mower which features the blade brake clutch should be considered. With this mower, the rotary blade stops within three seconds after you release the operator control bar, but the engine continues to operate. This allows you to empty the grass catcher frequently (the blade being stopped) without having to turn off the engine. When the catcher is returned in place, you simply engage the operator control to resume cutting grass. On these mowers, the starter cord may be found on top of the engine housing.

- Can you do some mower maintenance yourself or is the machine so complex that it must be returned to the mower shop for routine maintenance and repairs?

Using the Walk-Behind Rotary Mower

CPSC offers these suggestions for the safe use of rotary lawnmowers:

- Fill the fuel tank before starting the engine to cut the lawn. Never refuel the mower when it is running or while the engine is hot.

- Check the lawn for debris (twigs, rocks and other objects) before mowing the lawn. Objects have been struck by the mower blade and thrown out from under the mower, resulting in severe injuries and deaths.

- Don't cut the grass when it's wet. Wet clippings will probably clog the discharge chute, ultimately could jam the rotary blade and shut down the engine. When you need to remove clippings from the chute, the rotary blade must be stopped.

- Wear sturdy shoes with sure-grip soles when using the mower, never sneakers, sandals or with bare feet. Slacks rather than shorts offer better protection for the legs. Never allow young children to operate a power lawnmower.

- Children should not be allowed on or near the lawn when the rotary mower is in use. Push the mower forward, never pull it backward.

- If the lawn slopes, mow across the slope with the walk-behind rotary mower, never up and down. With a riding mower, drive up and down the slope, not across it.

- Don't remove any safety devices on the mower. Remember that the safety features were installed to help protect you against injury. Check safety features often and repair or replace if needed.

- With an electric mower, organize your work so you first cut the area nearest the electrical outlet, then gradually move away. This will minimize chances of your running over the power cord and being electrocuted.

- Read the owner's manual to become familiar with the workings of the machine. Keep the manual in a safe place so it will be handy when you need it the next time.

- Check the manual for hints on performing routine maintenance, checking engine oil levels and fluid in powered wheel drives, and performing maintenance when the mower is stored during the off-season.

Older Walk-Behind Rotary Mowers

If you cut grass with a pre-standard rotary mower, use extreme caution. Remember that the machine does not have the safety features of the new equipment, and that the problems that prompted the federal standard in the first place will still be found on your machine. For example:

- If clippings jam the discharge chute, first shut off the engine. The blade must come to a complete stop before you attempt to clear the jam. If you try to clear the chute while the blade rotates, your fingers could be amputated.

- Push the mower forward, never pull it backward.

- If you want to adjust the cutting height on any machine, do so before starting the engine. The blade should always be stationary.

- Shut down the engine if you leave the operator position for any reason. If you wish to disable the mower so no one can use it, simply remove the ignition wire from the spark plug or remove the spark plug.

Chapter 57

Weed Trimmers and Brush Cutters

Weed Trimmer Hazards

Power grass/weed trimmers can throw stones, sticks, and other objects. These objects can injure the eyes of operators and those nearby. The U.S. Consumer Product Safety Commission estimates that in 1989 there were approximately 4,600 hospital emergency room-treated injuries associated with power lawn trimmers or edgers. About one-third of the injuries were to the eye. Consumers should wear goggles to protect their eyes. Consumers also should clear the area of stones, sticks, wire, and other debris before using either a line or blade type weed trimmer.

CAUTION

- Power grass/weed trimmers can throw objects and injure eyes.

- Wear goggles to protect eyes.

- Clear away stones, sticks, and other debris before using.

Text in this chapter is from the following undated fact sheets produced by the Consumer Product Safety Commission, "Brush Cutters Require Cautious Use by Consumers," available online at http://www.cpsc.gov/cpscpub/pubs/5005.html, and "Weed Trimmers Can Throw Objects and Injure Eyes," available online at http://www.cpsc.gov/cpscpub/pubs/5108.html; both cited July 2001.

Brush Cutters Require Cautious Use by Consumers

Consumers are finding a relatively new type of power tool on the market for yard and garden work-brush cutters and combination trimmer/brush cutters. While the product is somewhat similar to the flexible string weed trimmer, it has a much greater potential for serious and disabling injury. The brush cutter uses a rigid cutting blade in place of the flexible plastic string line. The blade, made of steel or rigid plastic materials, permits the cutting of much heavier stands of brush and small diameter saplings, according to manufacturers. However, it can also cut through a hand, arm, or leg, something the flexible line trimmer will not do.

Several injury reports received by the Consumer Product Safety Commission (CPSC) indicate the blade has caused severe lacerations and near amputations. These accidents have happened even to professionals using the product.

In one case, a man was cutting brush along the bottom of a board fence. His wife, standing nearby trimming a hedge, was severely injured when he lost control and the brush cutter swung in an arc toward his wife. The blade cut into the wife's thigh and then her left hand, nearly amputating it below the wrist. In another incident, two workers were cutting brush. One held down a sapling with an axe, while the other attempted to cut through it with a brush cutter. The blade ricocheted off the sapling and into the assistant, severely cutting his right arm. In another case, a man cutting brush near a chain link fence reported that the blade threw a small piece of wire from the fence into his eye. In another case, the blade was reported to have come off the end of the shaft while it was being operated, causing a foot injury.

While only a few reports of injury have been received to date, the Commission's staff believes there may be many more injuries if extra caution is not taken in using the product. The greatest danger appears to be to bystanders or helpers. Users should read and observe safety and operating instructions in the owner's manual.

Among the safety precautions the user should take are:

- Keep all people away from the operator during use. At least one manufacturer recommends keeping people, including helpers, a minimum of 30 feet away.

- Before starting, make sure the blade is properly secured to the shaft. Replace damaged blades.

- Avoid cutting close to fences, sides of buildings, or other such obstacles that could cause the brush cutter to ricochet. Clear the work area of trash or hidden debris that could be thrown back at the operator or at a bystander.

- Use the proper cutting attachment for the job. Use the flexible string trimmer or hand tools for cutting near buildings, fences, etc., where the rigid blade may cause damage and injury.

- Wear protective clothing, including safety eye goggles.

Chapter 58

Chain Saw Hazards

Chain saw kickback can result in serious injury or death to the person operating the saw. Kickback most often occurs when the saw chain moving around the nose of the guide bar accidentally touches another object such as a log, branch or twig. Contact like this can throw the chain saw violently back toward the operator. In 1982, kickback was involved in an estimated 24,000 medically attended injuries to chain saw users.

Recent improvements in the design of saw chains have led to the production of low kickback consumer replacement chains which are capable of reducing chain saw kickback. Generally speaking, there is a low kickback replacement chain for virtually every chain saw, old and new alike. The Commission strongly recommends that you have your dealer or retailer determine whether your saw is equipped with one of these new chains. If your saw is not equipped with it, have the retailer install a new low kickback consumer replacement chain so that you enjoy the added protection every time you or someone else uses the chain saw.

If you are shopping for a new chain saw, look for the safety features found on many new chain saws:

- low kickback saw chain
- hand guard

"Chain Saw Kickback Hazard," an undated fact sheet produced by the Consumer Product Safety Commission, available online at http://www.cpsc.gov/cpscpub/pubs/5011.html; cited July 2001.

- safety tip
- chain brake
- vibration reduction system
- spark arrestor on gasoline models
- trigger or throttle lockout
- chain catcher
- bumper spikes

Chapter 59

Pressure Washers

A 53-year-old man was electrocuted recently while using an electric pressure washer to wash a truck. This incident has prompted the U.S. Consumer Product Safety Commission to reissue a consumer alert about these products.

Pressure washers are devices that are hooked up to a plumbing connection. They pump water under high pressure through a hose, sometimes mixing the water with a cleaning solution. Pressure washers may be used to wash farm equipment, motor vehicles, outdoor power equipment, porches, or houses.

The Commission warns that consumers could receive a fatal electrical shock from pressure washers if the power cord connections become wet or an internal short exists. At least 13 such fatalities have been reported to the Commission to date, including incidents in Iowa, Louisiana, Minnesota, Alabama, and Illinois.

One incident involved a 3-year-old boy who was killed when he contacted a pressure washer being used by his father.

Since pressure washers are used to spray water, the power cord, washer, and consumer are often in contact with water. This can be a fatal combination, especially if the machine is not properly grounded.

It is important not to defeat a proper ground connection. Consumers should not use "adapter plugs" to connect the three-wire plug to a two-prong household receptacle without properly grounding the

"Commission Issues Pressure Washer Warning," an undated fact sheet produced by the Consumer Product Safety Commission, available online at http://www.cpsc.gov/cpscpub/pubs/5069.html; cited July 2001.

465

adapter plug. Consumers should have three-wire receptacles checked by a competent person to assure that they are properly wired for grounding. Even when the machine is in good mechanical condition and properly grounded, care must be taken to avoid hazardous conditions. For example, power cord connections should never be allowed to lie in water.

The 1987 edition of the National Electrical Code requires that pressure washers be protected by ground fault circuit interrupters (GFCls). During the past few years the Underwriters Laboratories (UL) voluntary standard for pressure washers has undergone several changes to make the machines safer UL is in the process of adding a new provision that will require that most pressure washers be equipped with built-in GFCIs. However, it may be several years before all pressure washers subject to the UL revisions are available with GFCIs.

For electric pressure washers, without built-in GFCls, the Commission recommends that electrical circuit being using protected by either a circuit breaker type GFCI or a receptacle type GFCI. If none of the available circuits is protected by a GFCI, portable GFCIs can be purchased at some retail Outlets. Be sure to test the GFCI, before using the pressure washer.

NEVER allow children to operate a pressure washer. Keep children at a safe distance when The Commission also recommends the following precautions, particularly if no GFCI is available:

- Always plug a three-wire grounded pressure washer into a properly grounded receptacle.

- If an extension cord must be used, keep the power cord connection out of any standing water, and use a heavy duty, three-wire, properly grounded type. Keep the connection as far away as possible from the item being washed and away from any water runoff.

- Wear rubber-soled footwear that provides some insulation when operating the pressure washer.

- NEVER cut or splice the power cord or extension cords.

- NEVER remove the grounding prong from the power cord plug!

- NEVER operate the pressure washer after it has tripped a an adult is using a pressure washer.

Chapter 60

Garage Door Opener Hazards

Homeowners with automatic garage door openers that do not automatically reverse should repair or replace them with new openers which do reverse to prevent young children from being trapped and killed under closing garage doors.

According to reports received by the U.S. Consumer Product Safety Commission (CPSC), approximately 60 children between the ages of 2 and 14 have been trapped and killed under automatic garage doors since March 1982. This is approximately 4 such deaths per year. Other children have suffered brain damage or serious injuries when the closing door contacted them, and failed to stop and reverse its direction.

CPSC urges consumers to check the condition and operation of their garage door and the opener. A properly operating garage door will be "balanced." This means that the door will stay in place when stopped in any partially opened position. A severely unbalanced garage door could unexpectedly crash to the floor possibly striking someone under the open door.

To check the garage door, the garage door opener must be detached from the door while in the closed position. On most openers manufactured since 1982, a "quick-release" mechanism is provided which permits the opener to be detached from the door.

To avoid amputation or crushing injuries, homeowners should be careful when manually operating the door not to place hands or fingers

"Non Reversing Garage Door Openers A Hazard," an undated fact sheet produced by the Consumer Product Safety Commission, available online at http://www.cpsc.gov/cpscpub/pubs/523.html; cited July 2001.

between door sections or near pulleys, hinges, or springs. The door should not stick or bind when opened or closed. If doors are not "balanced," or if they bind or stick, they should be serviced by a professional.

Once the garage door is operating properly, homeowners should check to see that the garage door opener's force and limit settings are adjusted according to manufacturer's instructions. Check the garage door operator owners manual for any instructions on testing the safety features. One quick test is to place a 2x4 on the floor of the garage in the door's path. If the door does not properly reverse on striking the 2x4 then the garage door opener should be disengaged until the unit is either adjusted according to the instructions in the owners manual, repaired, or replaced with a new garage door opener. A professional garage door service should be contacted if the homeowner is not comfortable with performing these tests, repairs and adjustments.

All homeowners should disconnect all garage door openers that have not been certified as meeting the requirements of the voluntary ANSI/UL standard 325-1982.The standard calls for a number of safety features not found on earlier openers, and also subjects new openers to more stringent safety tests.

CPSC cautions consumers that not all devices that open and close the garage door are necessarily safe. Some old openers are equipped with a mechanism that only stops the closing door when it strikes an object, not reversing the door in the process. Other pre-1982 openers have a device intended to reverse the closing door when it strikes an object, but for reasons related to age, installation and maintenance, these products may not be safe enough to prevent entrapment of a child. These openers cannot be adjusted or repaired to provide the automatic reversing feature found on later devices.

The CPSC requires that all garage door operators manufactured or imported after January 1, 1993, for sale in the United States be outfitted with an external entrapment protection system. This system can be an electric eye, a door edge sensor, or any other device that provides equivalent protection. If an electric eye is used, it should be installed at a height of 4 to 6 inches above the floor.

Consumers should inspect garage doors and operation of the door opener every 30 days to verify that the system is functioning properly. Hardware and fittings should be checked to keep the door on track at all times. Should a hazard exist, homeowners should disconnect the automatic opener from the door as specified in the owner's manual, and manually open and close the garage door until needed repair/replacement is completed.

468

Lastly, homeowners should relocate the wall switch in the garage as high as practical above the floor in an effort to restrict children's use of the automatic garage door. Remote control door operating devices should be kept locked in the car and away from children. Parents should also tell their children about the potential hazard.

Part Ten

Holiday and Recreation Safety

Chapter 61

Christmas Safety

Trees

Many artificial trees are fire resistant. If you buy one, look for a statement specifying this protection.

A fresh tree will stay green longer and be less of a fire hazard than a dry tree. To check for freshness, remember:

- A fresh tree is green.

- Fresh needles are hard to pull from branches.

- When bent between your fingers, fresh needles do not break.

- The trunk butt of a fresh tree is sticky with resin.

- When the trunk of a tree is bounced on the ground, a shower of falling needles shows that tree is too dry.

Place tree away from fireplaces, radiators and other heat sources. Heated rooms dry trees out rapidly, creating fire hazards.

Cut off about two inches of the trunk to expose fresh wood for better water absorption. Trim away branches as necessary to set tree trunk in the base of a sturdy, water-holding stand with wide spread feet. Keep the stand filled with water while the tree is indoors.

"Merry Christmas with Safety," an undated fact sheet produced by the Consumer Product Safety Commission, available online at http://www.cpsc.gov/cpscpub/pubs/611.html; cited July 2001.

Place the tree out of the way of traffic and do not block doorways. Use thin guy-wires to secure a large tree to walls or ceiling. These wires are almost invisible.

"Snow"

Artificial snow sprays can irritate lungs if inhaled. To avoid injury, read container labels; follow directions carefully.

Lights

Indoors or outside, use only lights that have been tested for safety. Identify these by the label from an independent testing laboratory.

Check each set of lights, new or old, for broken or cracked sockets, frayed or bare wires, or loose connections. Discard damaged sets or repair them before using.

Fasten outdoor lights securely to trees, house, walls or other firm support to protect from wind damage.

Use no more than three standard-size sets of lights per single extension cord.

Turn off all lights on trees and other decorations when you go to bed or leave the house. Lights could short and start a fire.

Never use electric lights on a metallic tree.

The tree can become charged with electricity from faulty lights, and any person touching a branch could be electrocuted! To avoid this danger, use colored spotlights above or beside a tree, never fastened onto it!

Keep "bubbling" lights away from children. These lights with their bright colors and bubbling movement can tempt curious children to break candle-shaped glass, which can cut, and attempt to drink liquid, which contains a hazardous chemical.

Candles

Never use lighted candles on a tree or near other evergreens. Always use non-flammable holders. Keep candles away from other decorations and wrapping paper. Place candles where they cannot be knocked down or blown over.

Trimmings

Use only non-combustible or flame-resistant materials.

Wear gloves while decorating with spun glass "angel hair" to avoid irritation to eyes and skin.

Choose tinsel or artificial icicles or plastic or non-leaded metals. Leaded materials are hazardous if ingested by children.

In homes with small children, take special care to:

- Avoid decorations that are sharp or breakable.

- Keep trimmings with small removable parts out of the reach of children. Pieces could be swallowed or inhaled.

- Avoid trimmings that resemble candy or food. A child could eat them!

Fires

Before lighting any fire, remove all greens, boughs, papers, and other decorations from fireplace area. Check to see that flue is open.

Keep a screen before the fireplace all the time a fire is burning.

Use care with "fire salts" which produce colored flames when thrown on wood fires. They contain heavy metals which can cause intense gastrointestinal irritation or vomiting if eaten. Keep away from children.

Paper

When making paper decorations, look for materials labeled non-combustible or flame-resistant.

Never place trimming near open flames or electrical connections.

Remove all wrapping papers from tree and fireplace areas immediately after presents are opened.

Do not burn papers in the fireplace. A flash fire may result as wrappings ignite suddenly and burn intensely.

General Rules for Holiday Safety

- Keep matches, lighters, and candles out of the reach of children.

- Avoid smoking near flammable decorations.

- Make an emergency plan to use if a fire breaks out anywhere in the home. See that each family member knows what to do. PRACTICE THE PLAN!

- Avoid wearing loose flowing clothes—particularly long, open sleeves near open flames—such as those of a fireplace, stove, or candlelit table.

- Never burn candles near evergreens. Burning evergreens in the fireplace can also be hazardous. When dry, greens burn like tinder. Flames can flare out of control, and send sparks flying into a room, or up the chimney to ignite creosote deposits.

- Plan for safety. Remember, there is no substitute for common sense. Look for and eliminate potential danger spots near candles, fireplaces, trees, and/or electrical connections.

Chapter 62

Halloween Safety

Treats

Warn children not to eat any treats before an adult has carefully examined them for evidence of tampering.

Flame Resistant Costumes

When purchasing a costume, masks, beards, and wigs, look for the label Flame Resistant.

Although this label does not mean these items won't catch fire, it does indicate the items will resist burning and should extinguish quickly once removed from the ignition source. To minimize the risk of contact with candles or other sources of ignition, avoid costumes made with flimsy materials and outfits with big, baggy sleeves or billowing skirts.

Costume Designs

Purchase or make costumes that are light and bright enough to be clearly visible to motorists.

- For greater visibility during dusk and darkness, decorate or trim costumes with reflective tape that will glow in the beam of

"Halloween Safety," an undated fact sheet produced by the Consumer Product Safety Commission, available online at http://www.cpsc.gov/cpscpub/pubs/100.html; cited July 2001.

a car's headlights. Bags or sacks should also be light colored or decorated with reflective tape. Reflective tape is usually available in hardware, bicycle, and sporting goods stores.

- To easily see and be seen, children should also carry flashlights.

- Costumes should be short enough to prevent children from tripping and falling.

- Children should wear well-fitting, sturdy shoes. Mother' s high heels are not a good idea for safe walking.

- Hats and scarfs should be tied securely to prevent them from slipping over children's eyes.

- Apply a natural mask of cosmetics rather than have a child wear a loose-fitting mask that might restrict breathing or obscure vision. If a mask is used, however, make sure it fits securely and has eyeholes large enough to allow full vision.

- Swords, knives, and similar costume accessories should be of soft and flexible material.

Pedestrian Safety

Young children should always be accompanied by an adult or an older, responsible child. All children should WALK, not run from house to house and use the sidewalk if available, rather than walk in the street. Children should be cautioned against running out from between parked cars, or across lawns and yards where ornaments, furniture, or clotheslines present dangers.

Choosing Safe Houses

Children should go only to homes where the residents are known and have outside lights on as a sign of welcome.

- Children should not enter homes or apartments unless they are accompanied by an adult.

- People expecting trick-or-treaters should remove anything that could be an obstacle from lawns, steps and porches. Candlelit jack-o'-lanterns should be kept away from landings and doorsteps where costumes could brush against the flame. Indoor jack-o-lanterns should be kept away from curtains, decorations, and other furnishings that could be ignited.

Chapter 63

Fireworks

The American traditions of parades, cookouts, and fireworks help us celebrate the summer season. Fireworks were also a part of the many celebrations welcoming the new millennium. However, fireworks can turn a joyful celebration into a painful memory when children and adults are injured while incorrectly using fireworks.

Consumers should be aware that fireworks—even illegal fireworks—can be dangerous, causing serious burn and eye injuries. Illegal fireworks are especially dangerous and present substantial risks that can result in deaths, blindings, amputations and severe burns. The U.S Consumer Product Safety Commission strongly recommends that consumers leave fireworks to the professionals.

The following are examples of injuries from legal and illegal fireworks:

- A 7-year-old boy lost half of his left hand including the fingers when he ignited an M-80 he found hidden in a family bedroom. The M-80 exploded in the boy's hand.

- An 8-year-old girl received second and third degree burns to her leg when a spark from a sparkler she was holding ignited her dress.

"Fireworks Fact Sheet," an undated fact sheet produced by the Consumer Product Safety Commission, available online at http://www.cpsc.gov/cpscpub/pubs/012.html; and "1999 Fireworks Annual Report," produced by the Consumer Product Safety Commission; both cited July 2001.

- Two boys, ages 10 and 8, received first and second degree burns to their arms when a bottle rocket exploded in a garage at their house. The garage and a car were totally destroyed.

To help prevent incidents like these, the federal government, under the Federal Hazardous Substances Act, prohibits the sale of the most dangerous types of fireworks to consumers. These banned fireworks include large reloadable shells, cherry bombs, aerial bombs, M-80 salutes and larger firecrackers containing more than two grains of powder. Also banned are mail-order kits designed to build these fireworks.

Even legal fireworks should be used only with extreme caution. In a regulation that went into effect December 6, 1976, the U.S. CPSC lowered the permissible charge in firecrackers to no more than 50 milligrams of powder. In addition, the recently amended regulation provides performance specifications for fireworks other than firecrackers intended for consumers' use, including a requirement that fuses burn at least 3 seconds, but no longer than 9 seconds. All fireworks must carry a warning label describing necessary safety precautions and instructions for safe use.

The Commission recently issued a new performance requirement to reduce the risk of potentially dangerous tip-over of large multiple tube mine and shell devices. Tip-over of these devices has resulted in two fatalities. The new requirement went into effect on March 26, 1997.

The U.S. Consumer Product Safety Commission estimates that in 1999 about 8,500 people were treated in hospital emergency rooms for injuries associated with fireworks. Approximately 55 percent of the injuries were burns, and most of the injuries involved the hands, eyes and head. About 45 percent of the victims were under 15 years of age.

Before using fireworks, make sure they are permitted in your state or local area. Many states and local governments prohibit or limit consumer fireworks, formerly known as class C fireworks, which are the common fireworks and firecrackers sold for consumer use. Consumer fireworks include shells and mortars, multiple tube devices, Roman Candles, rockets, sparklers, firecrackers with no more than 50 milligrams of powder and novelty items such as snakes and airplanes.

Leave Fireworks to the Professionals!

But if the fireworks are legal where you live and you decide to set them off on your own, be sure to follow these important safety tips:

- Never allow children to play with or ignite fire works.

- Read and follow all warnings and instructions.

- Be sure other people are out of range before lighting fireworks.

- Only light fireworks on a smooth, flat surface away from the house, dry leaves, and flammable materials.

- Never try to relight fireworks that have not fully functioned.

- Keep a bucket of water handy in case of a malfunction or a fire.

Fireworks should be used only with extreme caution. Children should not be allowed to play with fireworks.

Parents should supervise the ordering and use of mail-order "make your own" firework kits.

State Regulations

The following is a summary of state regulations as of May 1, 1999.

I. STATES THAT ALLOW SOME OR ALL TYPES OF CONSUMER FIREWORKS (formerly known as class C fireworks), APPROVED BY ENFORCING AUTHORITY, OR AS SPECIFIED IN LAW (34 states including the District of Columbia):

Alabama	Louisiana	Oregon
Alaska	Michigan	South Carolina
Arkansas	Mississippi	South Dakota
California	Missouri	Tennessee
Colorado	Montana	Texas
District of Columbia	Nebraska	Utah
Florida	New Hampshire	Virginia
Hawaii	New Mexico	Washington
Idaho	North Carolina	West Virginia
Indiana	North Dakota	Wisconsin
Kansas	Oklahoma	Wyoming
Kentucky		

(The above states enforce the federal regulations and applicable state restrictions).

481

II. STATE HAVING NO FIREWORKS LAWS EXCEPT AT COUNTY LEVEL:

Nevada

(CPSC regulations are still applicable for this state).

III. STATES THAT ALLOW ONLY SPARKLERS AND / OR OTHER NOVELTIES (total of 6 states):

Illinois	Maine	Ohio
Iowa	Maryland	Pennsylvania

IV. STATES THAT BAN ALL CONSUMER FIREWORKS (including those which are allowed by CPSC regulations) — (total of 10 states):

Arizona	Massachusetts	New York
Connecticut	Minnesota	Rhode Island
Delaware	New Jersey	Vermont
Georgia		

Fireworks-Related Deaths, Emergency Department Treated Injuries, and Enforcement Activities

Following are the results of the U. S. Consumer Product Safety Commission (CPSC) staff analysis of 1999 data on fireworks-related injuries and deaths. The report also includes a summary of CPSC enforcement activities during 1999.

Information on fireworks deaths were obtained primarily from news clips in CPSC's Injury and Potential Injury Incident (IPII) database. More detailed analyses of injuries including the type of injury and the firework involved were based on a special study conducted between June 23 and July 23, 1999.

Highlights of the report are as follows:

- CPSC has reports of 16 deaths from fireworks in 1999. There were 13 deaths reported in 1998.

- Fireworks devices were involved in an estimated 8,500 injuries treated in U. S. hospital emergency departments during calendar year 1999. CPSC estimated the same number of injuries in 1998.

- There was no increase in injuries in 1999 despite a 20 percent increase in the dollar value of fireworks imported into the

United States. Some of the increase in imports was for the additional fireworks activity associated with millennium celebrations.

- Estimated emergency department treated injuries for the period 1997-1999 were significantly lower than the estimates for 1992 through 1994, when the average was almost 12,500 injuries per year.

- An estimated 5,700 fireworks-related injuries were treated in U. S. hospital emergency departments during the one month special study period surrounding the Fourth of July, 1999 (June 23, 1999-July 23, 1999). The highest injury estimates were for firecrackers (1,800), rockets (1,000), and sparklers (600). These were about the same levels as 1998.

- During this one-month period, as in previous years, injuries to children were a major component of fireworks-related injuries with children under 15 accounting for 45 percent of the injuries.

- About 35 percent of the injuries to children under age 15 involved firecrackers. Rockets accounted for about 20 percent of the injuries and sparklers accounted for about 15 percent of the injuries. About three times as many males were injured as females.

- Also during this period, the parts of the body most often injured were the hands (estimated 2,300 cases), eyes (1,000) and head/face (1,200). Over half the injuries involved burns. Burns were the most frequent injury to all parts of the body except the eyes, where contusions, lacerations, and foreign bodies in the eyes were the most frequent.

- A review of NEISS in-depth investigations of injuries during the special study period, showed that some serious injuries were associated with (1) fireworks explosions that were earlier or later than expected by the user, (2) rockets with errant flight patterns or (3) inappropriate use of fireworks by children.

- During 1999, CPSC has participated in multi-state fireworks investigations. As a result, several fireworks retailers and distributors of illegal fireworks were shut down and tens of thousands of illegal explosive devices were seized. Following a separate investigation, a large fireworks importer was permanently enjoined from selling violative fireworks.

- CPSC and the U.S. Customs Service have continued to sample shipments and to seize shipments that violate CPSC's mandatory safety requirements.

- During 1999, these surveillance operations were stepped-up in anticipation of increased fireworks usage and also to cover an extended sales season associated with the millennium celebrations.

- In criminal cases, five defendants pled guilty to violations of Federal explosives laws and violations of the Federal Hazardous Substances Act. The courts imposed prison sentences, fines and forfeitures.

Fireworks deaths were obtained from the CPSC Death Certificate file and the IPII (Injury or Potential Injury Incident) file. There may be up to a two-year lag between when a death occurs and when the death is reported in the Death Certificate file, so reporting for 1999 may not be complete. Data for the IPII file come from news clips, consumer complaints and reports from government agencies. Because reporting is voluntary, there may have been fireworks deaths that were not reported to any of these sources, and are not included among the deaths in this report. Therefore, the number of deaths from fireworks-related injuries might be greater than reported here.

Total estimated emergency department treated injuries for fireworks in 1999 were obtained from CPSC's National Electronic Injury Surveillance System (NEISS). NEISS is a probability sample of U. S. hospitals that have emergency departments.[1] All estimates for the number of injuries in this report were obtained using the hospital totals and the sampling weights in NEISS. These estimates reflect emergency department treated injuries for the entire country.

The detailed analysis of injuries in hospital emergency departments in this report is based on a special study of fireworks injuries treated between June 23, 1999 and July 23, 1999. This special study focused on the types of fireworks involved in these injuries. Victims were shown illustrations of fireworks at emergency departments to help them identify the device associated with the injury. The type of fireworks device was not usually recorded during other periods of the year.

Also, during the special study period, CPSC completed in-depth investigations of 38 fireworks injuries. These in-depth investigations were limited to injuries involving amputation, eye injuries, or injuries requiring admission to the hospital. There were also some investigations where it was suspected that the fireworks device was illegal or that the device was illegally purchased. In most cases, victims were telephoned and read a questionnaire. These investigations were intended to determine how the most serious injuries occurred. Victims were asked about the circumstances of the incident, where the device was obtained and future medical treatment required for the injury.

In this report, injury estimates derived from NEISS are rounded to the nearest 100 injuries and percentages are rounded to the nearest 5 percent. Estimates of less than 50 injuries are shown with an asterisk (*). Values may not add to totals because of rounding.

Although a number of different analyses are provided in this report for different categories of injuries, including the age distribution of victims and the types of fireworks involved in the injury, interpretation of these estimates should be made with caution. This is because estimates based on small sample sizes have relatively large amounts of sampling variability. For example, when comparing subsets of the data, say between injuries associated with two different types of fireworks, or between two different years, it is difficult to determine how much of the difference between estimates is associated with sampling variability and how much comes from real differences in national injury totals.

Information about enforcement activities was provided by CPSC's Office of Compliance.

Death and Injury Estimates

Fireworks-related Deaths for 1999

CPSC has reports of 16 deaths that occurred from fireworks during 1999.

- Five people in Gardendale, Alabama were killed when smoldering fireworks remains in a trash can adjacent to a house ignited. The fire spread to the house. The victims were a 43 year-old male, 41 year-old female and 3 male children, 10, 10 and 6 years old.

- A house fire that started from smoldering fireworks debris in a trash can, killed 5 people in Salem, Wisconsin. This included a 31 year-old female, a 9 year-old male, a 4 year-old male, and two female children, one 2 years old and the other 1 year old.

- Three teenagers were killed in Centerville, Arizona, when a shell exploded in a trailer that contained fireworks. The ages of

485

the victims were not disclosed in the newspaper account of this incident.

- A 5 year-old male in the San Diego area was killed from burns when sparklers ignited in his pocket.

- A 15 year-old male was killed in Kanorado, Kansas. He placed fireworks in a partially buried pipe. When he lit them, he was killed by the explosion.

- A 13 year-old male in Lake Roesiger, Washington was killed when he placed a shell inside a tube. The shell struck him in the head when it exploded.[2]

National Injury Estimates for 1999 and Comparison with Prior Years

Table 63.1 presents the estimated number of fireworks-related injuries for 1988 through 1999 treated in U. S. hospital emergency departments annually.

Table 63.1. Estimated Fireworks-Related Injuries 1988-1999

Year	Injuries
1999	8,500
1998	8,500
1997	8,300
1996	7,300
1995	10,900
1994	12,500
1993	12,000
1992	12,500
1991	10,900
1990	12,000
1989	9,600
1988	10,100

Source: NEISS, U. S. Consumer Product Safety Commission/EPHA. Estimates for 1988-1996 were revised to adjust for the new sampling frame and do not match values published in reports for 1997 or earlier.

In 1999, there were an estimated 8,500 fireworks injuries for the calendar year.[3] This was the same value as the estimate reported for 1998 and was slightly greater than the values reported for 1996 and 1997 (Greene, 1999). None of the totals for 1996-1999 were statistically significantly different from each other.[4] However, the difference between 1999 and the high value in 1994 of 12,500 injuries was significant.[5] Also, the difference between the three-year average for 1997-1999 and the three-year average for the historic high period between 1992 and 1994 was statistically significant.[6] 3 95 percent confidence interval 6,000 to 11,000.

In 1999, 75 percent of fireworks injuries occurred during the July 4th holiday period (June 23-July 23). In the last decade, about 60 to 80 percent of fireworks-related injuries occurred during this period.

There was no increase in injuries in 1999 despite an increase of about 20 percent in shipments of fireworks to the United States from 1998 to 1999, based on dollar values.[7] Some of the increase in imports was probably associated with the additional fireworks activity for the millennium celebrations.

Injury Estimates for the 1999 Special Study

The remainder of the injury analysis in this report presents the results of the 1999 special study of hospital emergency department treated fireworks injuries that occurred between June 23 and July 23, 1999. During this period, there were an estimated 5,700 fireworks-related injuries for the special study period.[8] This estimate was based on 179 emergency department cases.

Table 63.2 shows the distribution of July 1999 holiday season fireworks injuries by type of device.

As shown in Table 63.2, firecrackers accounted for about 30 percent (1,800) of all injuries that occurred during this period. Among firecrackers, illegal, large firecrackers, such as M-80's were involved in 500 estimated injuries. This was less than 10 percent of the total injuries. Among legal consumer devices, rockets (1,000 injuries), sparklers (600 injuries), and Roman candles (600 injuries) were the major contributors. Bottle rockets accounted for 700 of the 1,000 rocket-related injuries.

Although most of these fireworks-related injuries were treated at emergency departments and then released, an estimated 7 percent (400 cases) required hospital admission or transfer to another hospital for treatment. This was somewhat higher than the hospitalization and treat/transfer rate of 4.5 percent for all consumer products.

Age and Sex of Injured Persons

Less than 10 percent (400 injuries) of all fireworks-related injuries were to children under 5 years of age as shown in Table 63.3. Children in the 5 to 14 age group accounted for about 35 percent (estimated 2,100) fireworks-related injuries. Together, children under 15 experienced 45 percent of the fireworks injuries.

Table 63.2. Estimated Fireworks-Related Injuries By Type of Firework

Fireworks Type	Estimated Injuries
Total	5,700
Firecrackers	1,800
Small	100
Illegal	500
Unknown	1,200
Rockets	1,000
Bottle Rockets	700
Other, Unspecified	300
Other Consumer Devices	1,900
Sparklers	600
Fountains	*
Novelties	200
Multiple Tube and Shell	400
Roman Candles	600
Helicopters	*
Homemade/Altered	*
Public Display	100
Unknown	900

Source: NEISS, U. S. Consumer Product Safety Commission/EPHA. Based on 179 reported emergency department visits between June 23, 1999 and July 23, 1999. Cases were weighted by the NEISS sampling weights. Frequencies reported in the table were rounded to the nearest 100. Totals may not add due to rounding. Estimates of less than 50 injuries are shown as an asterisk (*). Caution is recommended in comparing estimates in this table because of the relatively small number of injuries from which each estimate was derived.

The age group 15 to 24 had 30 percent of the injuries (1,800) and the 25 to 44 age group had 20 percent of the injuries (1,100). There were no recorded fireworks-related injuries to people 65 years of age and over in the NEISS sample.

Injury rates per 100,000 population were highest among people aged 5 to 24 years. Children between 5 and 14 years of age had 5.3 injuries per 100,000 people, while young adults 15 to 24 had 4.8 injuries per 100,000 people.

In general, most injuries were to males, accounting for 4,200 incidents. About three times as many males were injured as females.

Age of the Injured Person by Type of Fireworks

Table 63.4 presents the ages of those injured by the type of fireworks device involved in the injury. Injuries to the youngest children, under 5, were associated with sparklers, firecrackers, and bottle rockets. For 5-14 year olds and for 15-24 year olds, firecrackers, other devices (including sparklers) and rockets were the source of injuries.

Table 63.3. Estimated Fireworks-Related Injuries By Age and Sex June 23-July 23, 1999

Age Group (years)	Total	Male	Female	Injuries per 100,000 people
Total	5,700	4,200	1,500	2.1
Less than 5	400	300	200	2.1
5 to 14	2,100	1,600	500	5.3
15 to 24	1,800	1,200	500	4.8
25 to 44	1,100	1,000	200	1.3
45 to 64	300	100	100	0.5

Source: NEISS, U. S. Consumer Product Safety Commission/EPHA. Notes: See Table 63.2. US population from www.census.gov/population/estimates/nation/intfile2-1.txt.

Table 63.4. Estimates Fireworks-Related Injuries By Device Type and Age Group June 23-July 23, 1999

Fireworks Type	Totals	Age Group (years)				
		<5	5-14	15-24	25-44	45-64
Total	5,700	400	2,100	1,800	1,100	300
Firecrackers	1,800	100	800	700	200	*
Small	100	*	100	*	*	*
Illegal	500	*	*	400	100	*
Unspecified	1,200	100	700	300	100	*
Rockets	1,000	100	400	200	200	*
Bottle	700	100	300	100	100	*
Other	300	*	100	100	100	*
Other Devices	1,900	300	600	400	400	100
Sparklers	600	100	300	*	100	100
Various	1,200	100	300	400	300	100
Homemade/Altered	*	*	*	*	*	*
Public Display	100	*	*	*	*	*
Unspecified	900	200	400	200	100	*

Source: NEISS, U. S. Consumer Product Safety Commission/EPHA. Notes: See Table 63.2. Various Other Devices include multiple tube devices, novelties, reloadable aerial shell devices, Roman candles, fountains, and novelties.

Injury Diagnosis and Body Part Injured

Table 63.5 presents the types of injuries sustained to specific parts of the body. Eighty percent of injuries (4,500) were to the hands, head/face, and eyes. Hands and fingers with an estimated 2,300 injuries, accounted for 40 percent of the total injuries. Injuries to the head and face at 1,200 total injuries were about 20 percent of the total.

Among diagnoses, burns with 3,200 estimated injuries and 55 percent of the total, were the most frequent. Contusions and lacerations, at 1,300 injuries and 25 percent of the total were the second most frequent. Contusions, lacerations, and foreign bodies (in other diagnoses) were the most common eye injuries. Head and facial injuries primarily involved burns and contusions or lacerations.

Type of Fireworks and Body Part Injured

Table 63.6 presents estimated injuries by the fireworks device and body part involved. Firecracker injuries occurred most frequently to the hand (900 injuries). Typically, victims sustained injuries from firecrackers while holding the device, or attempting to release it after ignition. Rockets were represented in injuries to the eye, head/face, and arm/leg region. Victims sustained injuries from erratic rocket flight patterns, or burning debris from the rocket. Sparkler injuries typically involved the hands. Sparklers burn at a high temperature.

In-depth Investigations of Fireworks Deaths and Injuries

CPSC conducted in-depth investigations of the more serious injuries associated with fireworks that occurred during the month surrounding the July 4 holiday. Injuries were selected when they involved the eye, or amputations, or when the victim was either admitted to the hospital or transferred to another facility for treatment. These injuries were selected for investigation to develop information on potential long term effects. Investigations were also conducted because the injury was suspected to result from the use of illegal fireworks.

Most of these investigations were conducted by telephone. Either the victim was the source of information or the victim's guardian, when the victim was under 18. Thirty-eight completed investigations were reviewed. Typical causes of injuries shown in these reports included the following:

Table 63.5. Estimated Fireworks-Related Injuries By Body Part and Diagnosis June 23-July 23, 1999.

Body Part	Total	Burns	Contusions/ Lacerations	Fractures/ Sprains	Other Diagnoses
Total	5,700	3,200	1,300	300	900
Hands/Fingers	2,300	1,300	500	200	300
Head/Face	1,200	600	400	*	200
Eyes	1,000	300	300	*	400
Legs	300	300	*	*	*
Trunk	200	100	*	*	100
Arms	500	400	*	100	*
Feet/Toes	100	100	*	*	*

Source: NEISS, U. S. Consumer Product Safety Commission/EPHA. Notes: See Table 63.2. Fractures and sprains also included dislocations. Other diagnoses included all other injury categories. Head/Face injuries include the NEISS codes for face, eyelid, eye area and nose, head, neck, mouth, lips, tongue, teeth and ear. The category for legs includes codes for upper leg, knee, lower leg, and ankle. Trunk includes NEISS codes for lower trunk, upper trunk (not including shoulders), and pubic region. The arms category includes lower arm, elbow, upper arm, shoulder, and wrist.

- Fireworks that exploded earlier or later than the victim expected. Often the device exploded after the victim thought it was not operating and the victim retrieved it to light it again.

- Errant flight paths for rockets and mortars, injuring bystanders. In some cases, the rocket had blown off its stand, or the flight path had been affected by the wind.

- Inappropriate usage of fireworks devices, especially by children. This includes cutting open fireworks, using them near flammable liquids, using devices indoors or in cars, burying devices in pipes, etc.

The review of the investigations showed that victims, for the most part, expected a full recovery. Some eye injuries, however, involved surgery for cornea or lens replacement. Also, some hand injuries resulted in severe burns and lacerations. One victim reported some loss of function with full recovery uncertain. A second victim had part of his thumb amputated. He reported that partial recovery was expected after prolonged physical therapy.

Enforcement Activities

As part of its focus on reducing fireworks injuries, CPSC is working to ensure that imported fireworks meet CPSC's regulations. CPSC works with the U. S. Customs Service on surveillance of fireworks imports. Surveillance operations were stepped-up in 1999 in anticipation of increased fireworks usage, and also to cover an extended sales season associated with the millennium celebrations. As part of these activities, CPSC and Customs selectively sampled 522 shipments of fireworks to ascertain the level of compliance with fireworks regulations. About 31 percent of these shipments were found to violate fireworks regulations. These shipments accounted for more than 6 million units presenting violations serious enough to warrant seizure or other actions by the U.S. Customs Service (CPSC, 2000).

Also during 1999, CPSC collected and tested more than three times as many domestic fireworks samples than in previous years.

CPSC has also initiated or participated in multi-state criminal investigations of illegal fireworks. These investigations have led to more than a dozen criminal search warrants and the seizure of tens of thousands of illegal explosive devices, tons of professional display fireworks being illegally sold or distributed to consumers, and

Table 63.6. Estimated Fireworks-Related Injuries By Type of Firework and Body Part Injured June 23-July 23, 1999

Type of Fireworks	Total	Hands/ Fingers	Head/ Face	Eyes	Arms/ Legs	Trunk
Total	5,700	2,300	1,200	1,000	900	200
Firecrackers	1,800	900	400	300	100	100
Sparklers	600	400	100	100	-	-
Rockets	1,000	100	300	300	300	-
Other Devices	2,200	900	400	300	600	100

Source: NEISS, U. S. Consumer Product Safety Commission/EPHA. Notes: See Table 63.2. The arms and legs category includes feet and toes. The other body regions are defined in the note under Table 63.5. Other devices included fountains, novelties, multiple tube and shell, Roman candles, public display, homemade/altered and unspecified.

components used to manufacture illegal fireworks. Several fireworks retailers and distributors have either been permanently or temporarily shut down. In addition, a recent CPSC investigation led to a permanent injunction in a civil case against Midwest Fireworks Manufacturing Co., Inc. of Ohio, a large fireworks importer. This order enjoined the firm from distributing and selling violative fireworks.

Also, five defendants in criminal cases pled guilty to felony violations of Federal explosives laws as well as violations of the Federal Hazardous Substances Act. Four defendants were sentenced to federal prison terms of 8 to 30 months. Fines ranging from $6,000 to $60,000 were imposed. One defendant also forfeited $300,000 in illegal proceeds to the federal government.

Discussion

The total number of estimated fireworks injuries for 1999 was the same as for 1998, 8,500. Despite a 20 percent increase in imports this year, there were no changes in the number of injuries. Also, the injuries for recent years continue to be significantly lower than the estimates for the years 1992 through 1994.

Injuries during the 1999 one-month special study period at 5,700 were higher than 1998's estimate of 5,000, but the difference was not statististically significant. For 1999, the types of fireworks associated with the injuries, the age and gender distribution, hospital dispositions and diagnoses, all were within the range of what was reported for 1998.

As in previous years, in 1999, injuries to children were a major component of fireworks-related injuries with children under 15 accounting for 45 percent of the injuries. The disproportionate involvement of children is further illustrated by the high rate of injury for the 5 to 14 age group, compared to the rate for the population as a whole. Children in this age group experienced 5.3 emergency department treated fireworks injuries per 100,000 people as compared with the general population rate of 2.1 per 100,000 people.

A review of in-depth investigations of serious fireworks injuries showed that typical causes of injuries included (1) fireworks exploding earlier or later than expected by the user, (2) errant flight paths or tipping over of rockets, and (3) inappropriate use. During 1999, CPSC's Office of Compliance increased its investigation of the sale of illegal fireworks. Compliance was involved in seizures of illegal devices, injunctions against manufacture of illegal devices and criminal cases for violation of the Federal Hazardous Substances Act.

References

Greene, M.A. (1999), *"1998 Fireworks-Related Injuries,"* U. S. Consumer Product Safety Commission, Washington, DC.

Kessler, E. and Schroeder, T. (1998), *"The NEISS Sample (Design and Implementation),"* U. S. Consumer Product Safety Commission, Washington, DC.

Marker, D., Lo, A., Brick, M. and Davis, W. (1999), *"Comparison of National Estimates from Different Samples and Different Sampling Frames of the National Electronic Injury Surveillance System (NEISS),"* Final Report prepared for the U. S. Consumer Product Safety Commission, Westat. Rockville, MD.

Schroeder, T. (2000), *"Trend Analysis of NEISS Data."* U. S. Consumer Product Safety Commission, Washington, D. C.

U.S. Consumer Product Safety Commission (2000), *"Saving Lives and Keeping Families Safe,"* 1999 Performance Report. Washington, D. C.; http://www.cpsc.gov/about/gpra/gpra.html.

Notes

1. For a description of NEISS, including the revised sampling frame, see Kessler and Schroeder (1998). Procedures used for variance and confidence interval calculations, and adjustments for the sampling frame change in 1997 are found in Marker, Lo, Brick, and Davis (1999). SAS statistical software for trend and confidence intervals is documented in Schroeder (2000).

2. This incident was also in CPSC's Death Certificate File.

3. 95 percent confidence interval 6,000 to 11,000.

4. *P-values* as follows: for 1998 and 1999, $p=0.9849$; for 1999 and 1997, $p=0.8576$.

5. $p=0.0411$, one tail.

6. $p<0.01$, one tail.

7. Data from the USITC Trade Database-Web Access. Included were U.S. imports at Customs value for HTS8 36041010 and HTS8 36041090.

8. 95 percent confidence interval: 4,000 to 7,5000.

Chapter 64

Bicycles and Bike Helmets

Bicycle Fact Sheet

The U.S. Consumer Product Safety Commission estimates that over 600,000 persons suffered bicycle-related injuries serious enough to require hospital emergency room treatment in 1994. Here are some typical cases:

> "Karen applied her hand brakes and lost control of her bicycle. She went down an embankment into a creek, and fractured her shoulder."

> "As Jimmy was riding his bicycle downhill, the front wheel of his bicycle suddenly became loose and twisted. Jimmy lost control, fracturing his knee."

> "Bob was riding a bike without a chain guard when his foot caught between the pedal and chain. He fell, suffering a concussion and skull fracture."

Text in this chapter is from the following undated fact sheets produced by the Consumer Product Safety Commission, "Bicycle Fact Sheet," available at http://www.cpsc.gov/cpscpub/pubs/346.html, "Night Bike Riders at Risk," available at http://www.cpsc.gov/cpscpub/pubs/5003.html, "CPSC Urges Bicyclists to Wear Helmets," available at http://www.cspc.gov/cpscpub/pubs/5002.html, "Kids Speak Out on Bike Helmets," available at http://www.cpsc.gov/cpscpub/pubs/345.html, and "Wear Helmets to Prevent Sports Related Head Injuries," available at http://www.cpsc.gov/cpscpub/pubs/5044.html; all cited July 2001.

"Michele was riding her bike alongside a friend's. As her friend moved his bike to the right, the two front wheels collided, causing Michele to fall. She suffered a concussion and fractured a wrist."

These case histories illustrate some major accident patterns associated with bicycles. They are:

- Collision with a car or another bicycle.

- Loss of Control—This occurs because of a number of factors, including: difficulty in braking; riding too large a bike; riding too fast; riding double; stunting; striking a rut, bump, or obstacle; and riding on slippery surfaces.

- Mechanical and Structural Problems—These include brake failure; wobbling or disengagement of the wheel or steering mechanism; difficulty in shifting gears; chain slippage; pedals falling off, or spoke breakage.

- Entanglement of a person's feet, hands, or clothing in the bicycle.

- Foot slippage from pedal.

To make bicycles safer, the U.S. Consumer Product Safety Commission developed a mandatory safety standard for bicycles to help eliminate injuries due to mechanical and structural failures.

The CPSC regulations establish strict performance and construction standards for the brakes, wheels, steering system and frame. They require reflectors on the front, back, sides and pedals to make bicycles visible at night; require elimination of uncovered sharp edges and jutting parts; and require brakes on bicycles with seat height of 22 inches or more. New bicycles are required to meet the standards.

The U.S. Consumer Product Safety Commission offers the following safety tips when shopping for a new bike or taking care of an old one:

Selecting the Bicycle

- If you're buying a bicycle for a child, choose one to fit the child's size today, not one he or she will "grow into" later.

- A bicycle should suit the rider's ability and kind of riding.

- Check hand and foot brakes for fast, easy stops without instability or jamming.

- Avoid slippery plastic pedals. Look instead for rubber-treated pedals, or metal pedals with serrated rattrap edges or with firmly attached toe clips.

Using the Bicycle

- Always wear a helmet to help prevent head injuries. CPSC is setting a new mandatory standard for bike helmets.

- Observe all traffic laws and signals, just as automobiles must do.

- Don't ride double or attempt stunts.

- Ride near the curb in the same direction as traffic.

- Find alternate routes, rather than ride through busy intersections and heavy or high-speed traffic.

- Walk—don't ride—your bicycle across busy intersections and left turn corners.

- Avoid riding in wet weather. When wet, handbrakes may require a long distance to stop.

- Avoid riding in the dark. If you do, be sure the bike is equipped with a headlight, a taillight and reflectors. Apply retro-reflective trim to clothing, or wear reflective vests and jackets.

- Avoid loose clothing or long coats that can catch in pedals or wheels. Leg clips or bands keep pants legs from tangling in the chain.

- Avoid crossing raised sewer grates.

Maintaining the Bicycle

- Regular maintenance is essential for safe riding. Refer to the owner's manual for the manufacturer's maintenance recommendations. An experienced repair technician should do complicated work.

- Align (or "true") wobbly wheels for better control. Spokes also may need adjustment.

- Replace all missing, damaged, or worn parts; for example, brake pads, chain guards, chain links, spokes, screws and bolts, handlebar grips.

- Tighten and/or adjust loose parts.

- Periodically inspect frame, fork, spindles and other components for cracking.

- Parts should be adjusted to manufacturer's torque specifications.

- Inflate tires to recommended pressure, and replace worn tires.

- Lightly oil and clean moving parts. Keep oil off rubber.

- Keep bicycle indoors when not in use—moisture may cause rust and weaken metal parts.

Night Bike Riders at Risk

To help reduce nighttime bicyclist fatalities, cyclists should always wear a good helmet, use front and rear lights and reflectors, and wear reflective clothing. Children should never ride at night, and cyclists should avoid riding on unlighted, narrow roadways.

Because of a sharp increase in the number of bicyclist fatalities resulting from car-bike collisions at night, the U.S. Consumer Product Safety Commission has issued a warning to bike riders to take necessary steps to make themselves and their bicycles more visible at night.

The number of bicyclists killed at night has increased from 304 to 372 per year. In 1975, the number of nighttime deaths accounted for 30% of the total number of bicyclists killed. By 1982 (the latest year for which complete data are available), nighttime deaths accounted for 42% of the total number of bicyclists killed. One factor contributing to fatal nighttime bicyclist accidents is that the bicycles and riders are not readily visible to motorists. Motorists involved in car/bicycle collisions report that they hit bicyclists because the bicycles and riders were not visible. Cyclists' failure to wear protective helmets may have also contributed to the severity of head injuries suffered in car-bike collisions.

Therefore, CPSC recommends the following actions to cyclists:

1. Be sure your bike has reflectors required on all new bicycles by the CPSC bicycle regulation. Each bike should have front and rear reflectors, pedal reflectors, and side rim or wheel reflectors. Use front and rear lights (as required in many

States) to help make your bicycle more noticeable to cars at night. Small battery-operated lamps strapped to your legs also help.

2. Wear reflective clothing to make yourself more visible to automobile drivers. Wear a reflective vest, reflective bands on arms and legs, and reflector tape on helmet.

3. Always wear a good helmet with a rigid (but crushable) interior material which may help absorb the force of an impact. (This is important for daytime riding, too.)

4. Never allow children to ride at night.

5. Avoid riding on dark, narrow roadways where the posted speed limit is more than 35 mph.

Bicycle Helmets

Each year about 800 bicyclists are killed and more than half a million are treated in hospital emergency rooms. In recent years, almost two-thirds of the deaths and one-third of the injuries involved head and face injury. About one-half the injuries to children under the age of 10 involved the head or face. Helmets may reduce the risk of head injury to bicyclists by as much as 85 percent. Yet, only about 50 percent of bicyclists wear helmets.

The purpose of a helmet is to absorb the energy of an impact to minimize or prevent a head injury. Crushable, expanded polystyrene foam generally is used for this purpose.

A bicycle helmet should have a snug but comfortable fit on the rider's head. Some helmets are available with several different thicknesses of internal padding to custom fit the helmet to the user. If a parent is buying a helmet for a child, the CPSC recommends that the child accompany the parent so that the helmet can be tested for a good fit.

For a helmet to provide protection during impact, it must have a chin strap and buckle that will stay securely fastened. No combination of twisting or pulling should remove the helmet from the head or loosen the buckle on the strap. Children should be instructed to always wear the helmet level on the forehead, not tilted back. The chin strap should be adjusted correctly and firmly buckled.

Helmets manufactured after March 1999, are required by federal law to meet the CPSC standard. When purchasing a helmet, consumers

501

are urged to examine the helmet and accompanying instructions and safety literature carefully. Consumers should also look for a label stating conformance with the CPSC standard.

Bicyclists should avoid riding at night. If you must ride at night, install and use front and rear lights on the bicycle and wear clothing with reflective tape or markings. These precautions are in addition to the reflectors that the CPSC requires to be on the front, rear, pedals, and wheels of bicycles.

Many bicycle-car crashes can be avoided by applying the rules of the road and by increasing attentiveness of cyclists and motorists. Bicyclists have a legal right to share the road, but they are often not noticed in traffic. Drivers should always keep an eye out for bicyclists, especially when turning, merging, changing lanes, or entering intersections.

Kids Speak out on Bike Helmets

Kids all across the country have opinions about bike helmets. Some kids wear them. Others don't. And many kids have ideas on how to get others to wear bike helmets more often.

282 kids, ages 8 to 13, from schools in Pennsylvania, Florida, Oklahoma, Ohio, New Mexico, New York, Nebraska, and Washington, were asked just what they thought about bike helmets.

Look what they had to say!

What could happen if you had a bike crash and weren't wearing a helmet?

- "You could be paralyzed, killed, or you could suffer damage."

- "You could bust your head open on the sidewalk or a rock."

- "You could go into a coma."

- "You could break your neck or crack your head."

- "You could have serious brain damage and you might have to learn all you know over again."

You may think you're a pretty good biker, but crashes happen all the time to very good riders. In fact:

- Wearing a bike helmet is the single most important thing you can do to protect your brain—and your like—when you ride your bike.

- Children between ages 5 and 14 have the highest rate of injury of all bicycle riders.

- Each year, more than 500,000 children go to hospital emergency rooms or doctors' offices due to bicycle injuries.

- More than half of these collisions happen on neighborhood streets, sidewalks, or playgrounds.

Why do you wear a bike helmets?

- "I wear a helmet because I had an accident and I was wearing a helmet and my head felt fine."

- "Because it looks cool and it keeps my head safe."

- "Because I don't want to hurt my head like my cousin (who almost died in a bike accident)."

- "I wear my helmet most of the time because there is law about helmets."

- "I wear my helmet all the time because:
  1. my parents make me and
  2. I don't want to get any head injuries."

- "You should always wear them because they keep you and your brain safe."

Nationally, only about 15 percent of all kids wear bike helmets. In this AAA survey of school children, here's how often kids wore bike helmets:

- Always or most of the time—43%

- Occasionally—11%

- Seldom or never—44%

- No answer—2%

Helmet usage of the surveyed kids is better than the national average. Even so, more than half of the children surveyed don't wear bike helmets most of the time. This means lots of these kids could be injured riding bikes.

What would get your best friend to wear a bike helmet more often?

- "You could make a commercial with a famous person wearing a helmet and kids could use them as role modes."

- "Put baseball, football and race driver numbers and names on helmets."

- "Show pros wearing helmets and being cool."

- "Put extra padding inside of it to make it more comfortable."

- "Put little compartments on the helmets."

- "Make helmets for girls with ponytails."

- "You could have a bike-a-thon to encourage kids to wear helmets."

- "If you wear one, you get a free pizza."

- "Tell them it's the law and if they don't they will have to eat spinach."

- "Have kids who wouldn't wear helmets and got in serious collisions go and talk to other kids who won't wear helmets."

- "Tell them to watch the hazards on the news of kids who don't wear a helmet."

What you can do to help save lives?

- Always wear your bike helmet—and make sure your brothers and sisters do, too.

- Make a deal with your best friend to always wear your helmets when you ride together.

- Talk to your parents or teachers to help organize projects with your school, safety patrol, Scout troop, religious organization, or other group that will encourage kids to wear bike helmets.

- Ask local businesses to sell bikes only with bike helmets or set up bike-helmet giveaway or discount-coupon programs.

Ten tips for safe bike riding:

1. Always wear a bike helmet.

2. Stop and check traffic before riding into a street.

3. Don't ride at night.

4. Obey traffic signs and signals.

5. Ride on the right-hand side of the street.

6. Check your brakes before riding.

7. Give cars and pedestrians the right-of-way.

8. Wear light or bright-colored clothing so that motorists can see you.

9. Be extra careful turning left—motorists don't expect it.

10. Avoid broken pavement, loose gravel and leaves—which can cause you to lose control of your bike.

For More Information

Contact your AAA Club Traffic Safety Office for information and availability of additional bicycle and other traffic safety materials.

Call the U.S. Consumer Product Safety Commission's toll-free hotline at 1-800-638-CPSC for information about bicycles and other consumer products.

Wear Helmets to Prevent Sports Related Head Injuries

The U.S. Consumer Product Safety Commission estimates that about 3 million head injuries related to consumer products were treated in hospital emergency rooms in 1988. About 440,000 or these were injuries such as concussions and skull fractures. Many of these accidents happened when helmets could have been worn.

The Commission's study of head injuries showed that these four products or activities had large numbers of hospital emergency room-treated head injuries related to them and high hospitalization rates for these injuries.

Many people do not wear helmets. Fewer than 1 out of 10 bicyclists wear helmets. Three-fourths of ATV drivers with head injuries were not wearing helmets.

There are several nationally-recognized voluntary safety standards for helmets. These standards require helmets to absorb the energy of an impact to lessen or prevent head injuries.

Crushable, expanded plastic foam can serve this purpose. Many helmets also have a hard outer shell to protect against collision with a sharp object.

To reduce head injuries, bicyclists, ATV riders, horseback riders, and skiers should wear the helmet appropriate for each activity.

Chapter 65

In-Line Roller Skates: Safety Alert

Each year, more than 100,000 people are treated in hospital emergency departments for injuries related to in-line skating, and nearly 40,000 seek emergency treatment for skateboarding injuries. The majority of these patients are under age 25. Many injuries can be prevented if skaters wear proper safety gear and avoid risky skating behavior.

Safety Tips

Injury Prevention Tips for In-line Skaters

To help your child avoid injuries while in-line skating, follow these safety tips from the American Academy of Pediatrics, the Centers for Disease Control and Prevention (CDC), the U.S. Consumer Product Safety Commission, and other sports and health organizations. (Note: Adult skaters should heed this advice, too.)

- Make sure your child wears all the required safety gear every time he or she skates. All skaters should wear a helmet, knee and elbow pads, and wrist guards. If your child does tricks or plays roller hockey, make sure he or she wears heavy-duty gear.

Produced by the Centers for Disease Control and Prevention (CDC), 2001; available online at http://www.cdc.gov.

- Check your child's helmet for proper fit. The helmet should be worn flat on the head, with the bottom edge parallel to the ground. It should fit snugly and should not move around in any direction when your child shakes his or her head.

- Choose in-line skates that best suits your child's ability and skating style. If your child is a novice, choose in-line skates with three or four wheels. Skates with five wheels are only for experienced skaters and people who skate long distances. Choose a skateboard designed for your child's type of riding-slalom, freestyle, or speed. Some boards are rated for the weight of the rider.

- Find a smooth skating surface for your child; good choices are skating trails and driveways without much slope (but be careful about children skating into traffic). Check for holes, bumps, and debris that could make your child fall. Novice in-line skaters should start out in a skating rink where the surface is smooth and flat and where speed is controlled.

- Don't let your child skate in areas with high pedestrian or vehicle traffic. Children should not skate in the street or on vehicle parking ramps.

- Tell your child never to skitch. Skitching is the practice of holding on to a moving vehicle in order to skate very fast. People have died while skitching.

- If your child is new to in-line skating, lessons from an instructor certified by the International In-line Skating Association may be helpful. These lessons show proper form and teach how to stop. Check with your local parks and recreation department to find a qualified instructor.

- If your child gets injured while skating, see your doctor. Follow all the doctor's instructions for your child's recovery, and get the doctor's OK before your child starts skating again.

Who Is Affected?

Millions of people in the U.S.—the majority of them under age 25—take part in in-line skating and skateboarding as a form of recreation and exercise. But these sports can be dangerous, especially when safety precautions are ignored. Each year, more than 100,000 skaters are injured seriously enough to need medical care in hospital emergency departments, doctors' offices, clinics, and outpatient centers. Most of these injuries occur when skaters lose control, skate over an obstacle, skate too fast, or perform a trick.

While most skating injuries are minor or require only outpatient care, 36 fatalities have been reported since 1992. Thirty-one of those skating deaths were from collisions with motor vehicles.

Among all age groups, 63 percent of skating injuries are fractures, dislocations, sprains, strains, and avulsions (tears). More than one-third of skating injuries are to the wrist area, with two-thirds of these injuries being fractures and dislocations. Approximately 5 percent are head injuries.

Safety gear has been shown to be highly effective in preventing injuries among skaters. Pads can reduce wrist and elbow injuries by about 85 percent and knee injuries by 32 percent. Although studies have not determined the degree to which helmets reduce head injuries among skaters, helmets have been shown to be highly protective among bicyclists.

Despite the proven safety benefits and relative low cost of helmets and pads, many skaters don't wear them. Nearly two-thirds of injured in-line skaters and skateboarders were not wearing safety gear when they crashed. One study found that one-third of skaters wear no safety gear, and another one-third use only some of the recommended safety equipment. Teens are least likely to wear all the safety gear. Nine out of ten beginning skaters wear all the safety gear, but studies have shown that many skaters shed the helmet and pads as they gain experience.

On-Line Safety Resources

American Academy of Pediatrics
Internet: http://www.aap.org

American Academy of Orthopaedic Surgeons
Internet: http://www.aaos.org

Brain Injury Association
Internet: http://www.biausa.org

U.S. Consumer Product Safety Commission
Internet: http://www.cpsc.gov/kids/skate.html

National Pediatric Trauma Registry
Internet: http://www.nemc.org

National SAFE KIDS Campaign
Internet: http://www.safekids.org

National Youth Sports Safety Foundation
Internet: http://www.nyssf.org

Chapter 66

Skateboards and Scooter Safety

Skateboards

According to the U.S. Consumer Product Safety Commission, approximately 26,000 persons are treated in hospital emergency rooms each year with skateboard related injuries. Sprains, fractures, contusions and abrasions are the most common types of injuries. Deaths due to collisions with cars and from falls also are reported.

Several factors—lack of protective equipment, poor board maintenance and irregular riding surfaces—are involved in these accidents. Skateboard riding requires good balance and body control, yet many young skateboarders have not developed the necessary balance and do not react quickly enough to prevent injury.

Who Gets Injured

Six out of every 10 skateboard injuries are to children under 15 years of age. Skateboarders who have been skating for less than a week suffer one-third of the injuries; riders with a year or more of experience have the next highest number of injuries.

Injuries to first-time skateboarders are, for the most part, due to falls. Experienced riders mainly suffer injuries when they fall after their skateboards strike rocks and other irregularities in the riding surface or when they attempt difficult stunts.

The text in this chapter is from the following undated fact sheets produced by the Consumer Product Safety, "Skateboards," CPSC publication number 93, and "Scooter Sales Skyrocket"; both cited July 2001.

511

Environmental Hazards

Irregular riding surfaces account for over half the skateboarding injuries due to falls. Before riding, skateboarders should screen the area where they will be riding by checking for holes, bumps, rocks and any debris. Areas set aside especially for skateboarding generally have smoother riding surfaces.

Skateboarding in the street can result in collisions with cars causing serious injury and even death.

The Skateboard

There are boards with varying characteristics for different types of riding (i.e., slalom, freestyle, or speed). Some boards are rated as to the weight of the intended user. Before using their boards, riders should check them for hazards, such as loose, broken, or cracked parts; sharp edges on metal boards; slippery top surface; and wheels with nicks and cracks. Serious defects should be corrected by a qualified repairman.

Protective Gear

Protective gear, such as closed, slip resistant shoes, helmets, and specially designed padding, may not fully protect skateboarders from fractures, but its use is recommended as such gear that can reduce the number and severity of injuries.

Padded jackets and shorts are available, as well as padding for hips, knees, elbows, wrist braces and special skateboarding gloves. All of this protective gear will help absorb the impact of a fall. With protective gear, it is important to look for comfort, design, and function. The gear should not interfere with the skater's movement, vision, or hearing.

The protective gear currently on the market is not subject to Federal performance standards, and, therefore, careful selection is necessary. In a helmet, for example, look for proper fit and a chin strap; make sure the helmet does not block the rider's vision and hearing. Body padding should fit comfortably. If padding is too tight, it could restrict circulation and reduce the skater's ability to move freely. Loose fitting padding, on the other hand, could slip off or slide out of position.

Tips for Using a Skateboard

The U.S. Consumer Product Safety Commission offers the following suggestions for safe skateboarding:

- Never ride in the street.

- Don't take chances.

  Complicated tricks require careful practice and a specially designed area.

  Only one person per skateboard.

  Never hitch a ride from a car, bus, truck, bicycle, etc.

- Learning how to fall in case of an accident may help reduce your chances of being seriously injured.

- If you are losing your balance, crouch down on the skateboard so that you will not have so far to fall.

- In a fall, try to land on the fleshy parts of your body.

- If you fall, try to roll rather than absorb the force with your arms.

- Even though it may be difficult, during a fall try to relax your body, rather than stiffen.

Scooters

The U.S. Consumer Product Safety Commission (CPSC) reports that emergency room-treated injuries related to popular lightweight scooters have increased sixteen-fold from May to September 2000. CPSC data show that there were more than 8,000 scooter related injuries treated in hospital emergency rooms in September alone. There have been 40,500 emergency room-treated injuries reported for 2000, and 5 deaths have occurred so far in 2000-2001. About 85 percent of the injuries are to children under 15 years of age.

CPSC recommends that riders, especially children, wear proper safety gear including a helmet and knee and elbow pads to help prevent injuries. CPSC estimates that more than 60 percent of injuries could be prevented or reduced in severity if protective gear had been worn.

The scooters, which first went on the market in the United States in 1999, are new versions of the foot propelled scooters first popular in the 1950s. They are made of lightweight metal such as aluminum and have small low-friction wheels similar to those on inline skates. They usually cost between $50 and $120 and typically weigh less than 10 pounds. They can be folded for easy portability.

Most injuries resulted when riders fell from the scooter. Fractures and dislocations accounted for about one-quarter of the injuries. Most of the fractures and dislocations were to arms and hands.

The best investment against injury is protective gear which can cost less than $30. CPSC recommends the following safety guidelines:

- Wear a helmet that meets CPSC's bike helmet standard, along with knee and elbow pads.

- Make sure both handle bars and the steering column are securely locked in place before riding.

- Routinely check all nuts and bolts to be sure they are secure.

- Ride the scooters on smooth, paved surfaces without any motor vehicle traffic. Avoid streets, or surfaces with water, sand, gravel or dirt.

- Do not ride the scooter at night.

Chapter 67

Caution for Three- and Four-Wheeled All-Terrain Vehicles

The U.S. Consumer Product Safety Commission warns consumers of the potential operator risks associated with three- and four-wheeled all-terrain vehicles. All-terrain motorized cycles with three or four large, soft tires and are designed for off-road use. Most units are sold for recreational use. In recent years, their popularity and sales have soared.

The average risk of injury from ATV riding is high. Over its estimated seven-year life, the average ATV has a one-in-three chance of being involved in an accident resulting in injury. The majority of accidents occurred when the ATV overturned after hitting a terrain irregularity or obstacle, or while turning or traversing a slope.

- *Children under 12 years of age should not operate any ATV.*

  This is because typically they lack adequate physical size and strength, cognitive abilities, motor skills and perception to operate a motor vehicle safety. ATVs are difficult to ride and require constant attention to avoid accidents.

- *Children between the ages of 12 and 15 should not operate adult-size (greater than 90 cc) ATVs.*

  The risk of injury for 12-15 year old drivers of adults ATVs is one and one-half to two times the average risk of injury on

"CPSC Urges Caution for Three- and Four-Wheeled All-Terrain Vehicles," an undated fact sheet produced by the Consumer Product Safety Commission, available online at http://www.cpsc.gov/cpscpub/pubs/540.html; cited July 2001.

ATVs. CPSC has received reports of 168 deaths to children between 12 and 15 years of age. Most deaths have occurred on adult-size ATVs.

- *A hands-on training course is necessary for all ATV operators.*

  Inexperienced drivers in their first month of using an ATV have 13 times the average risk of injury. Beginning drivers should receive a training course from certified instructors, and basic maneuvers taught in training should be practiced regularly on safe terrain.

- *Children should ride only under close adult supervision.*

  The CPSC injury survey showed that almost half of the drivers had less than a year's experience, and one-fourth had less than one month's experience.

- *Helmets could have saved the lives of approximately 25 percent of the people who died from head injuries in ATV accidents.*

  In the CPSC injury survey, three-fourths of the drivers with head injuries were not wearing an approved helmet. Without the protection of a helmet, the risk of head injury was twice as high as when the injured person wore a helmet. Over half of the injured persons had worn no protective equipment, such as helmets, gloves and heavy boots.

- *Do not ride double.*

  ATVs are designed for one driver and no passengers and have unique handling characteristics. The presence of a passenger seriously impairs the driver's ability to shift weight in order to steer and control the ATV. In the CPSC injury survey 31 percent of the drivers carried passengers on the ATV, and 20 percent of the injured people were passengers.

- *Almost 10 percent of the injuries and over 25 percent of the deaths occurred while operating the ATV on paved roads.*

  These accidents occur because of collisions with other vehicles and because ATVs are difficult to control on pavement. In 30 percent of all fatal ATV accidents, some alcohol use was mentioned.

CPSC also offers these safety tips for ATV riders:

- Before you ride an ATV, always read the owner's instruction manual and follow the manufacturer's guidance for use, maintenance, and pre-use checks.

- Drive carefully and use good judgment when using your ATV.

- Observe local laws or regulations and any regulations which have been established for public recreational areas where ATV use is permitted.

- Although the stability of all ATVs is low, the stability of four wheeled ATVs is better than the stability of three-wheeled ATVs. The risk of an accident on a three-wheeled ATV is about one and one-half to two times the risk oil a four-wheeled ATV.

- CPSC engineering tests show that the handling performance of a fully-suspended ATV is significantly better than that of front-only or tire-only suspended ATVs.

Chapter 68

Snowmobile Hazards

The U.S. Consumer Product Safety Commission estimates that each year about 110 people die while riding snowmobiles. The Commission estimates that about 13,400 hospital emergency room-treated injuries occur each year with snowmobiles. Approximately two-fifths or 40 percent of the reported deaths resulted from colliding with trees, wires, bridges, and other vehicles. Some deaths occurred when the snowmobile rolled to the side in a ditch or stream and pinned the operator under the vehicle. Deaths also have occurred when the snowmobile entered water, mostly when it was operating on ice and fell through.

The following safe snowmobiling rules are recommended for recreational snowmobiling:

1. Never drive your snowmobile alone or on unfamiliar ground Have someone ride along with you, so you can help each other in case of breakdown or accident.

2. Drive only on established and marked trails or in specified use areas.

3. Avoid waterways. Frozen lakes and rivers can be fatal. It is almost impossible to judge adequate ice coverage or depth.

"Safety Commission Warns About Snowmobile Hazards," an undated fact sheet produced by the Consumer Product Safety Commission, available online at http://www.cpsc.gov/cpscpub/pubs/541.html; cited July 2001.

4. Avoid driving in bad weather. Check warnings for snow, ice, and wind chill conditions before starting.

5. Watch the path ahead to avoid rocks, trees, fences (particularly barbed wire), ditches, and other obstacles.

6. Slow down at the top of a hill A cliff, snowbank, or other unforeseen hazard could be on the other side.

7. Don't hurdle snowbanks You have control only when your skis are on the ground.

8. Learn the snowmobile traffic laws and regulations for the area. Many states prohibit using snowmobiles on public roads Some states have mini-mum age requirements for drivers.

9. Be sensible about stopping at roads or railroad tracks. Signal your turns to other drivers Avoid tailgating Control speed according to conditions.

10. Use extra caution if driving at night, because un-seen obstacles could be fatal. Do not drive faster than your headlights will allow you to see. Do not open new trails after dark.

11. Never drink while driving your snowmobile. Drinking and driving can prove fatal.

12. Be sure the snowmobile is properly maintained in good operating condition. Some cases report that the throttle sticks, leading to loss of control. Snowmobiles manufactured before 1983 may not have a "throttle interruption device" designed to shut off the snowmobile in the event the throttle sticks.

Part Eleven

Additional Help and Information

Chapter 69

Terms You Should Know

A

Acid Aerosol: Acidic liquid or solid particles that are small enough to become airborne. High concentrations of acid aerosols can be irritating to the lungs and have been associated with some respiratory diseases, such as asthma.

Active Ingredient: In any pesticide product, the component that kills, or otherwise controls, target pests. Pesticides are regulated primarily on the basis of active ingredients.

Acute Exposure: A single exposure to a toxic substance which may result in severe biological harm or death. Acute exposures are usually characterized as lasting no longer than a day, as compared to longer, continuing exposure over a period of time.

Acute Toxicity: The ability of a substance to cause severe biological harm or death soon after a single exposure or dose. Also, any poisonous effect resulting from a single short-term exposure to a toxic substance.

Excerpted from "Terms of Environment," produced by the United States Environment Protection Agency (EPA), 1998; and "A Guide to Indoor Air Quality," an undated fact sheet produced by the Consumer Product Safety Commission, available online at http://www.cpsc.gov/cpscpub/pubs/450.html; cited July 2001.

Adsorption: Removal of a pollutant from air or water by collecting the pollutant on the surface of a solid material; e.g., an advanced method of treating waste in which activated carbon removes organic matter from waste water.

Adverse Effects Data: FIFRA requires a pesticide registrant to submit data to EPA on any studies or other information regarding unreasonable adverse effects of a pesticide at any time after its registration.

Aerosol: 1. Small droplets or particles suspended in the atmosphere, typically containing sulfur. They are usually emitted naturally (e.g., in volcanic eruptions) and as the result of anthropogenic (human) activities such as burning fossil fuels. 2. The pressurized gas used to propel substances out of a container.

Air Cleaning: Indoor-air quality-control strategy to remove various airborne particulates and/or gases from the air. Most common methods are particulate filtration, electrostatic precipitation, and gas sorption.

Air Pollutant: Any substance in air that could, in high enough concentration, harm man, other animals, vegetation, or material. Pollutants may include almost any natural or artificial composition of airborne matter capable of being airborne. They may be in the form of solid particles, liquid droplets, gases, or in combination thereof. Generally, they fall into two main groups: (1) those emitted directly from identifiable sources and (2) those produced in the air by interaction between two or more primary pollutants, or by reaction with normal atmospheric constituents, with or without photoactivation.

Exclusive of pollen, fog, and dust, which are of natural origin, about 100 contaminants have been identified. Air pollutants are often grouped in categories for ease in classification; some of he categories are: solids, sulfur compounds, volatile organic chemicals, particulate matter, nitrogen compounds, oxygen compounds, halogen compounds, radioactive compound, and odors.

Air Pollution: The presence of contaminants or pollutant substances in the air that interfere with human health or welfare, or produce other harmful environmental effects.

Air Pollution Control Device: Mechanism or equipment that cleans emissions generated by a source (e.g., an incinerator, industrial smokestack, or an automobile exhaust system) by removing pollutants that would otherwise be released to the atmosphere.

Air Quality Standards: The level of pollutants prescribed by regulations that are not be exceeded during a given time in a defined area.

Airborne Particulates: Total suspended particulate matter found in the atmosphere as solid particles or liquid droplets. Chemical composition of particulates varies widely, depending on location and time of year.

Allergen: A substance that causes an allergic reaction in individuals sensitive to it.

Allergic Rhinitis: Inflammation of the mucous membranes in the nose that is caused by an allergic reaction.

Animal Dander: Tiny scales of animal skin.

Asbestos: A mineral fiber that can pollute air or water and cause cancer or asbestosis when inhaled. EPA has banned or severely restricted its use in manufacturing and construction.

Asbestos Abatement: Procedures to control fiber release from asbestos-containing materials in a building or to remove them entirely, including removal, encapsulation, repair, enclosure, encasement, and operations and maintenance programs.

Asbestos Assessment: In the asbestos-in-schools program, the evaluation of the physical condition and potential for damage of all friable asbestos containing materials and thermal insulation systems.

Asbestos Program Manager: A building owner or designated representative who supervises all aspects of the facility asbestos management and control program.

Asbestos-Containing Waste Materials (ACWM): Mill tailings or any waste that contains commercial asbestos and is generated by a source covered by the Clean Air Act Asbestos NESHAPS.

Asbestosis: A disease associated with inhalation of asbestos fibers. The disease makes breathing progressively more difficult and can be fatal.

B

Bacteria: (Singular: bacterium) Microscopic living organisms that can aid in pollution control by metabolizing organic matter in sewage, oil spills or other pollutants. However, bacteria in soil, water or air can also cause human, animal and plant health problems.

Bioaccumulants: Substances that increase in concentration in living organisms as they take in contaminated air, water, or food because the substances are very slowly metabolized or excreted.

Biological Contaminants: Living organisms or derivates (e.g., viruses, bacteria, fungi, and mammal and bird antigens that can cause harmful health effects when inhaled, swallowed, or otherwise taken into the body.

Biological Treatment: A treatment technology that uses bacteria to consume organic waste.

Botanical Pesticide: A pesticide whose active ingredient is a plant-produced chemical such as nicotine or strychnine. Also called a plant-derived pesticide.

Building-Related Illness: A discrete, identifiable disease or illness that can be traced to a specific pollutant or source within a building. (Contrast with "Sick building syndrome").

C

Carbon Monoxide (CO): A colorless, odorless, poisonous gas produced by incomplete fossil fuel combustion.

Carcinogen: Any substance that can cause or aggravate cancer.

Chemical Sensitization: Evidence suggests that some people may develop health problems characterized by effects such as dizziness, eye and throat irritation, chest tightness, and nasal congestion that appear whenever they are exposed to certain chemicals. People may react to even trace amounts of chemicals to which they have become "sensitized."

Child-Resistant Packaging (CRP): Packaging that protects children or adults from injury or illness resulting from accidental contact with or ingestion of residential pesticides that meet or exceed specific toxicity levels. Required by Federal Insecticide, Fungicide, and Rodenticide Act (FIFRA) regulations. Term is also used for protective packaging of medicines.

Chlorinated Hydrocarbons: 1. Chemicals containing only chlorine, carbon, and hydrogen. These include a class of persistent, broad-spectrum insecticides that linger in the environment and accumulate in the food chain. Among them are DDT, aldrin, dieldrin, heptachlor, chlordane, lindane, endrin, Mirex, hexachloride, and toxaphene. Other examples include TCE, used as an industrial solvent. 2. Any chlorinated organic compounds including chlorinated solvents such as dichloromethane, trichloromethylene, chloroform.

Chlorofluorocarbons (CFCs): A family of inert, nontoxic, and easily liquefied chemicals used in refrigeration, air conditioning, packaging, insulation, or as solvents and aerosol propellants. Because CFCs are not destroyed in the lower atmosphere they drift into the upper atmosphere where their chlorine components destroy ozone.

Chronic Exposure: Multiple exposures occurring over an extended period of time or over a significant fraction of an animal's or human's lifetime (usually seven years to a lifetime).

Concentration: The relative amount of a substance mixed with another substance. An example is five ppm of carbon monoxide in air or 1 mg/l of iron in water.

Contact Pesticide: A chemical that kills pests when it touches them, instead of by ingestion. Also, soil that contains the minute skeletons of certain algae that scratch and dehydrate waxy-coated insects.

Contaminant: Any physical, chemical, biological, or radiological substance or matter that has an adverse effect on air, water, or soil.

Contamination: Introduction into water, air, and soil of microorganisms, chemicals, toxic substances, wastes, or wastewater in a concentration that makes the medium unfit for its next intended use. Also applies to surfaces of objects, buildings, and various household and agricultural use products.

D

DDT: The first chlorinated hydrocarbon insecticide chemical name: Dichloro-Diphenyl-Trichloroethane). It has a half-life of 15 years and can collect in fatty tissues of certain animals. EPA banned registration and interstate sale of DDT for virtually all but emergency uses in the United States in 1972 because of its persistence in the environment and accumulation in the food chain.

Decontamination: Removal of harmful substances such as noxious chemicals, harmful bacteria or other organisms, or radioactive material from exposed individuals, rooms and furnishings in buildings, or the exterior environment.

Dermal Toxicity: The ability of a pesticide or toxic chemical to poison people or animals by contact with the skin.

Disinfectant: A chemical or physical process that kills pathogenic organisms in water, air, or on surfaces. Chlorine is often used to disinfect sewage treatment effluent, water supplies, wells, and swimming pools.

E

Emission: Pollution discharged into the atmosphere from smokestacks, other vents, and surface areas of commercial or industrial facilities; from residential chimneys; and from motor vehicle, locomotive, or aircraft exhausts.

Environmental/Ecological Risk: The potential for adverse effects on living organisms associated with pollution of the environment by effluents, emissions, wastes, or accidental chemical releases; energy use; or the depletion of natural resources.

Environmental Exposure: Human exposure to pollutants originating from facility emissions. Threshold levels are not necessarily surpassed, but low-level chronic pollutant exposure is one of the most common forms of environmental exposure.

Environmental Tobacco Smoke: Mixture of smoke from the burning end of a cigarette, pipe, or cigar and smoke exhaled by the smoker.

F

Filtration: A treatment process, under the control of qualified operators, for removing solid (particulate) matter from water by means of porous media such as sand or a man-made filter; often used to remove particles that contain pathogens.

Flammable: Any material that ignites easily and will burn rapidly.

Formaldehyde: A colorless, pungent, and irritating gas, CH_2O, used chiefly as a disinfectant and preservative and in synthesizing other compounds like resins.

Friable Asbestos: Any material containing more than one-percent asbestos, and that can be crumbled or reduced to powder by hand pressure. (May include previously non-friable material which becomes broken or damaged by mechanical force.

Fungus (Fungi): Molds, mildews, yeasts, mushrooms, and puffballs, a group of organisms lacking in chlorophyll (i.e., are not photosynthetic) and which are usually non-mobile, filamentous, and multicellular. Some grow in soil, others attach themselves to decaying trees and other plants whence they obtain nutrients. Some are pathogens, others stabilize sewage and digest composted waste.

G

Germicide: Any compound that kills disease-causing microorganisms.

Grasscycling: Source reduction activities in which grass clippings are left on the lawn after mowing.

H

Hazard: 1. Potential for radiation, a chemical or other pollutant to cause human illness or injury. 2. In the pesticide program, the inherent toxicity of a compound. Hazard identification of a given substances is an informed judgment based on verifiable toxicity data from animal models or human studies.

Hazard Assessment: Evaluating the effects of a stressor or determining a margin of safety for an organism by comparing the concentration which causes toxic effects with an estimate of exposure to the organism.

Hazardous Air Pollutants: Air pollutants which are not covered by ambient air quality standards but which, as defined in the Clean Air Act, may present a threat of adverse human health effects or adverse environmental effects. Such pollutants include asbestos, beryllium, mercury, benzene, coke oven emissions, radionuclides, and vinyl chloride.

Hazardous Chemical: An EPA designation for any hazardous material requiring an MSDS under OSHA's Hazard Communication Standard. Such substances are capable of producing fires and explosions or adverse health effects like cancer and dermatitis. Hazardous chemicals are distinct from hazardous waste.

Hazardous Substance: 1. Any material that poses a threat to human health and/or the environment. Typical hazardous substances are toxic, corrosive, ignitable, explosive, or chemically reactive. 2. Any substance designated by EPA to be reported if a designated quantity of the substance is spilled in the waters of the United States or is otherwise released into the environment.

Hazardous Waste: By-products of society that can pose a substantial or potential hazard to human health or the environment when improperly managed. Possesses at least one of four characteristics (ignitability, corrosivity, reactivity, or toxicity), or appears on special EPA lists.

Herbicide: A chemical pesticide designed to control or destroy plants, weeds, or grasses.

Household Hazardous Waste: Hazardous products used and disposed of by residential as opposed to industrial consumers. Includes paints, stains, varnishes, solvents, pesticides, and other materials or products containing volatile chemicals that can catch fire, react or explode, or that are corrosive or toxic.

Humidifier Fever: A respiratory illness caused by exposure to toxins from microorganisms found in wet or moist areas in humidifiers and air conditioners. Also called air conditioner or ventilation fever.

Hypersensitivity Pneumonitis: A group of respiratory diseases that cause inflammation of the lung (specifically granulomatous cells). Most forms of hypersensitivity pneumonitis are caused by the inhalation of organic dusts, including molds.

I

Ignitable: Capable of burning or causing a fire.

Imminent Hazard: One that would likely result in unreasonable adverse effects on humans or the environment or risk unreasonable hazard to an endangered species during the time required for a pesticide registration cancellation proceeding.

Impermeable: Not easily penetrated. The property of a material or soil that does not allow, or allows only with great difficulty, the movement or passage of water.

In-Line Filtration: Pre-treatment method in which chemicals are mixed by the flowing water; commonly used in pressure filtration installations. Eliminates need for flocculation and sedimentation.

Indoor Air: The breathable air inside a habitable structure or conveyance.

Indoor Air Pollution: Chemical, physical, or biological contaminants in indoor air.

Infectious Agent: Any organism, such as a pathogenic virus, parasite, or bacterium, that is capable of invading body tissues, multiplying, and causing disease.

Infectious Waste: Hazardous waste capable of causing infections in humans, including: contaminated animal waste; human blood and blood products; isolation waste, pathological waste; and discarded sharps (needles, scalpels or broken medical instruments).

Infiltration: 1. The penetration of water through the ground surface into sub-surface soil or the penetration of water from the soil into sewer or other pipes through defective joints, connections, or manhole walls. 2. The technique of applying large volumes of waste water to land to penetrate the surface and percolate through the underlying soil.

Inhalable Particles: All dust capable of entering the human respiratory tract.

Insecticide: A pesticide compound specifically used to kill or prevent the growth of insects.

Irritant: A substance that can cause irritation of the skin, eyes, or respiratory system. Effects may be acute from a single high level exposure, or chronic from repeated low-level exposures to such compounds as chlorine, nitrogen dioxide, and nitric acid.

L

Land Disposal Restrictions: Rules that require hazardous wastes to be treated before disposal on land to destroy or immobilize hazardous constituents that might migrate into soil and ground water.

Lifetime Exposure: Total amount of exposure to a substance that a human would receive in a lifetime (usually assumed to be 70 years).

M

Material Safety Data Sheet (MSDS): A compilation of information required under the OSHA Communication Standard on the identity of hazardous chemicals, health, and physical hazards, exposure limits, and precautions. Section 311 of SARA requires facilities to submit MSDSs under certain circumstances.

Mercury (Hg): Heavy metal that can accumulate in the environment and is highly toxic if breathed or swallowed.

Methane: A colorless, nonpoisonous, flammable gas created by anaerobic decomposition of organic compounds. A major component of natural gas used in the home.

Methanol: An alcohol that can be used as an alternative fuel or as a gasoline additive. It is less volatile than gasoline; when blended with gasoline it lowers the carbon monoxide emissions but increases hydrocarbon emissions. Used as pure fuel, its emissions are less ozone-forming than those from gasoline. Poisonous to humans and animals if ingested.

Mulch: A layer of material (wood chips, straw, leaves, etc.) placed around plants to hold moisture, prevent weed growth, and enrich or sterilize the soil.

N

Nitrogen Dioxide (NO2): The result of nitric oxide combining with oxygen in the atmosphere; major component of photochemical smog.

No Observable Adverse Effect Level (NOAEL): An exposure level at which thee are no statistically or biologically significant increases in the frequency or severity of adverse effects between the exposed population and its appropriate control; some effects may be produced at this level, but they are not considered as adverse, or as precurors to adverse effects. In an experiment with several NOAELs, the regulatory focus is primarily on the highest one, leading to the common usage of the term NOAEL as the highest exposure without adverse effective.

O

Operation and Maintenance: 1. Activities conducted after a Superfund site action is completed to ensure that the action is effective.

2. Actions taken after construction to ensure that facilities constructed to treat waste water will be properly operated and maintained to achieve normative efficiency levels and prescribed effluent limitations in an optimum manner. 3. On-going asbestos management plan in a school or other public building, including regular inspections, various methods of maintaining asbestos in place, and removal when necessary.

Organic Compounds: Chemicals that contain carbon. Volatile organic compounds vaporize at room temperature and pressure. They are found in many indoor sources, including many common household products and building materials.

Ozonation/Ozonator: Application of ozone to water for disinfection or for taste and odor control. The ozonator is the device that does this. Ozone (O3): Found in two layers of the atmosphere, the stratosphere and the troposphere. In the stratosphere (the atmospheric layer 7 to 10 miles or more above the earth's surface) ozone is a natural form of oxygen that provides a protective layer shielding the earth from ultraviolet radiation. In the troposphere (the layer extending up 7 to 10 miles from the earth's surface), ozone is a chemical oxidant and major component of photochemical smog. It can seriously impair the respiratory system and is one of the most wide- spread of all the criteria pollutants for which the Clean Air Act required EPA to set standards. Ozone in the troposphere is produced through complex chemical reactions of nitrogen oxides, which are among the primary pollutants emitted by combustion sources; hydrocarbons, released into the atmosphere through the combustion, handling and processing of petroleum products; and sunlight.

P

Packaging: The assembly of one or more containers and any other components necessary to ensure minimum compliance with a program's storage and shipment packaging requirements. Also, the containers, etc., involved.

Particle Count: Results of a microscopic examination of treated water with a special "particle counter" that classifies suspended particles by number and size.

Particulates: 1. Fine liquid or solid particles such as dust, smoke, mist, fumes, or smog, found in air or emissions. 2. Very small solids suspended in water; they can vary in size, shape, density and electrical charge and can be gathered together by coagulation and flocculation.

Passive Smoking/Secondhand Smoke: Inhalation of others' tobacco smoke.

Pathogens: Microorganisms (.g., bacteria, viruses, or parasites) that can cause disease in humans, animals and plants.

Personal Protective Equipment: Clothing and equipment worn by pesticide mixers, loaders and applicators and re-entry workers, hazmat emergency responders, workers cleaning up Superfund sites, et al, which is worn to reduce their exposure to potentially hazardous chemicals and other pollutants.

Pesticide: Substances or mixture there of intended for preventing, destroying, repelling, or mitigating any pest. Also, any substance or mixture intended for use as a plant regulator, defoliant, or desiccant.

Pesticide Tolerance: The amount of pesticide residue allowed by law to remain in or on a harvested crop. EPA sets these levels well below the point where the compounds might be harmful to consumers. PETE (Polyethylene Terepthalate): Thermoplastic material used in plastic soft drink and rigid containers. PETE (Polyethylene Terepthalate): Thermoplastic material used in plastic soft drink and rigid containers.

Picocurie (pCi): A unit for measuring radioactivity, often expressed as picocuries per liter (pCi/L) of air.

Pollen: The fertilizing element of flowering plants; background air pollutant.

Pollutant: Generally, any substance introduced into the environment that adversely affects the usefulness of a resource or the health of humans, animals, or ecosystems.

Pollutant Pathways: Avenues for distribution of pollutants. In most buildings, for example, HVAC systems are the primary pathways although all building components can interact to affect how air movement distributes pollutants.

Pollutant Standard Index (PSI): Indicator of one or more pollutants that may be used to inform the public about the potential for adverse health effects from air pollution in major cities.

Pollution: Generally, the presence of a substance in the environment that because of its chemical composition or quantity prevents the functioning of natural processes and produces undesirable environmental and health effects. Under the Clean Water Act, for example, the term has been defined as the man-made or man-induced alteration of the physical, biological, chemical, and radiological integrity of water and other media.

Q

Quality Assurance/Quality Control: A system of procedures, checks, audits, and corrective actions to ensure that all EPA research design and performance, environmental monitoring and sampling, and other technical and reporting activities are of the highest achievable quality.

R

Radon (Rn) and Radon Decay Products: Radon is a radioactive gas formed in the decay of uranium. The radon decay products (also called radon daughters or progeny) can be breathed into the lung where they continue to release radiation as they further decay.

Reverse Osmosis: A treatment process used in water systems by adding pressure to force water through a semi-permeable membrane. Reverse osmosis removes most drinking water contaminants. Also used in wastewater treatment. Large-scale reverse osmosis plants are being developed.

S

Safe: Condition of exposure under which there is a practical certainty that no harm will result to exposed individuals.

Safe Water: Water that does not contain harmful bacteria, toxic materials, or chemicals, and is considered safe for drinking even if it may have taste, odor, color, and certain mineral problems.

Sand Filters: Devices that remove some suspended solids from sewage. Air and bacteria decompose additional wastes filtering through the sand so that cleaner water drains from the bed.

Sediments: Soil, sand, and minerals washed from land into water, usually after rain. They pile up in reservoirs, rivers and harbors, destroying fish and wildlife habitat, and clouding the water so that sunlight cannot reach aquatic plants. Careless farming, mining, and building activities will expose sediment materials, allowing them to wash off the land after rainfall.

Sick Building Syndrome: Building whose occupants experience acute health and/or comfort effects that appear to be linked to time spent therein, but where no specific illness or cause can be identified. Complaints may be localized in a particular room or zone, or may spread throughout the building.

Stagnation: Lack of motion in a mass of air or water that holds pollutants in place.

Sterilization: The removal or destruction of all microorganisms, including pathogenic and other bacteria, vegetative forms, and spores.

Sterilizer: One of three groups of anti-microbials registered by EPA for public health uses. EPA considers an antimicrobial to be a sterilizer when it destroys or eliminates all forms of bacteria, viruses, and fungi and their spores. Because spores are considered the most difficult form of microorganism to destroy, EPA considers the term sporicide to be synonymous with sterilizer.

T

Toxic Dose: The dose level at which a substance produces a toxic effect.

Toxic Substance: A chemical or mixture that may present an unreasonable risk of injury to health or the environment.

Toxic Waste: A waste that can produce injury if inhaled, swallowed, or absorbed through the skin.

Toxicity: The degree to which a substance or mixture of substances can harm humans or animals. Acute toxicity involves harmful effects in an organism through a single or short-term exposure. Chronic toxicity is the ability of a substance or mixture of substances to cause harmful effects over an extended period, usually upon repeated or continuous exposure sometimes lasting for the entire life of the exposed organism. Subchronic toxicity is the ability of the substance to cause effects for more than one year but less than the lifetime of the exposed organism.

Treatment: (1) Any method, technique, or process designed to remove solids and/or pollutants from solid waste, waste-streams, effluents, and air emissions. (2) Methods used to change the biological character or composition of any regulated medical waste so as to substantially reduce or eliminate its potential for causing disease.

U

Ultraviolet Rays: Radiation from the sun that can be useful or potentially harmful. UV rays from one part of the spectrum (UV-A) enhance plant life. UV rays from other parts of the spectrum (UV-B) can cause skin cancer or other tissue damage. The ozone layer in the atmosphere partly shields us from ultraviolet rays reaching the earth's surface.

V

Ventilation Rate: The rate at which indoor air enters and leaves a building. Expressed as the number of changes of outdoor air per unit of time (air changes per hour (ACH), or the rate at which a volume of outdoor air enters in cubic feet per minute (CFM).

Volatile Liquids: Liquids which easily vaporize or evaporate at room temperature.

W

Waste: 1. Unwanted materials left over from a manufacturing process. 2. Refuse from places of human or animal habitation.

Water Quality Standards: State-adopted and EPA-approved ambient standards for water bodies. The standards prescribe the use of the water body and establish the water quality criteria that must be met to protect designated uses.

Waterborne Disease Outbreak: The significant occurrence of acute illness associated with drinking water from a public water system that is deficient in treatment, as determined by appropriate local or state agencies.

Y

Yard Waste: The part of solid waste composed of grass clippings, leaves, twigs, branches, and other garden refuse.

Chapter 70

Guide to CPSC Internet, Fax-on-Demand and Hotline Services

The U.S. Consumer Product Safety Commission (CPSC) is an independent regulatory agency of the United States Government established to protect the public against unreasonable risks of injuries and deaths associated with consumer products. The CPSC has jurisdiction over approximately 15,000 types of consumer products from coffee makers, to toys, to lawn mowers, to fireworks. Information on CPSC activities can be obtained in a number of ways including the agency's Internet, fax-on-demand and toll-free Hotline services.

Access through the Internet

CPSC news releases, public calendar and other information can be obtained via the Internet from the agency's Web Site:

Internet: http://www.cpsc.gov

E-Mail: info@cpsc.gov

If you know the name of the CPSC staff person to whom the message should be directed, please include the name at the beginning of your message.

"Guide to CPSC Internet, Fax-on-Demand and Hotline Services," an undated fact sheet produced by the Consumer Product Safety Commission, available online at http://www.cpsc.gov/cpscpub/pubs/181.html; cited July 2001.

Internet E-Mail Subscription Service

List Server

Copies of product recall and product safety information can be sent to you automatically via Internet e-mail, as they are released by CPSC. To subscribe to this service send an e-mail message to:

E-Mail: listproc@cpsc.gov

In the message area, enter: "join CPSCINFO-L"

You will receive an acknowledgment of your subscription.

To unsubscribe from the list, again send a message to listproc@cpsc.gov and enter the following in the message area: "leave CPSCINFO-L"

You will receive an acknowledgment that you have unsubscribed.

Fax-on-Demand

CPSC news releases and certain other information can be obtained by fax 24 hours each day, 7 days a week, 365 days a year, from the agency's Fax-On-Demand Service (FODS). Dial the number below from the handset of your fax machine and follow the instructions to place an order or receive a catalog of available information.

Fax-on-Demand

301-504-0051

From the handset of a fax machine, and, when asked to enter a 3-digit number, press 456 for free access to CPSC's fax-on-demand service.

Hotline

The CPSC's telephone Consumer Hotline can be dialed 24 hours each day, 7 days a week, 365 days a year. CPSC Hotline staff are available to assist you between the hours of 8:30 am to 5:00 pm, Eastern time, weekdays (excluding Federal holidays). Prerecorded information on product recalls and product safety is available 24 hours a day when calling from a "touchtone" telephone.

Toll Free Hotline

800-638-2772; 800-638-8270 (Hearing and Speech Impaired)

Our Hotline Services

You can call our toll-free Hotline to:

- report an unsafe product;

- report a product-related injury;

- find out whether a product has been recalled;

- learn how to return a recall product or arrange for its repair;

- get information on what to look for when buying a consumer product;

- get information on how to use a consumer product safely; and

- receive information about ordering CPSC safety publications. (For a list of publications, send a postcard to Publications List, CPSC, Washington, DC 20207).

If you have a product complaint or want to report a product- related injury, you will speak directly to a Hotline operator. The Hotline staff is available between 8:30 AM and 5:00 PM Eastern time, Monday through Friday, except holidays.

Our Hotline also has a TTY number for the hearing-or speech impaired (1-800-638-8270).

We have Hotline staff who speak both English and Spanish. In addition, arrangements can be made for callers to speak with someone in any of the following other languages: Arabic, Burmese, Cambodian, Cantonese Chinese, French, German, Greek, Hindi, Italian, Korean, Japanese, Punjabi, Ukrainian, Urdu, Vietnamese and Yiddish.

Recorded Recall and Safety Information

Our Hotline has a wide variety of recorded messages on product recall, consumer products and product safety. The messages below are accessible with a touch-tone telephone 24 hours a day, seven days a week by pushing the three-digit number shown below after you have called our main Hotline number 1-800-638-2772.

Toys (including crayons)—211

Bunk beds, toddler beds—212

Children's furniture, indoor equipment—213

Hotline Standards

When you call our Hotline, you can expect the following:

- to be given easy-to-follow instructions on how to use the hotline;

- to hear the most up-to-date and easy-to-understand recorded information on product safety recalls and consumer products, seven days a weeks, 24 hours a day;

542

- to be given courteous service;

- to have your complaint of an unsafe product or product-related injury taken accurately and a copy of the report sent to you so that you can confirm the information recorded by our Hotline staff; and

- to have your message left at night, weekends or holidays returned the next business day, or, if you do not want a return call, to receive a letter confirming receipt of your product-complaint message.

CPSC Wants to Hear from You

We want to provide you with the best Hotline service possible and are always interested in learning how we can improve. If you have any comments or suggestions, we would like to hear from you. Simply ask to speak with the Hotline manager when you call:

800-638-CPSC
800-638-2772
800-638-8270 (TTY)

Or write us at:

CPSC Hotline
Washington, D.C. 20207

The U.S. Consumer Product Safety Commission protects the public from the unreasonable risk of injury or death from 15,000 types of consumer products under the agency's jurisdiction. To report a dangerous product or a product-related injury, you can go to CPSC's forms page and use the first on-line form on that page. Or, you can call CPSC's hotline at 800-638-2772 or CPSC's teletypewriter at 800-638-8270, or send the information to info@cpsc.gov. Consumers can obtain this publication and additional publication information from the Publications section of CPSC's web site or by sending your publication request to publications@cpsc.gov. If you would like to receive CPSC's recall notices, subscribing to the email list will send all press releases to you the day they are issued.

Chapter 71

Environmental Protection Agency Hotlines

Acid Rain Hotline
US EPA
Clean Air Markets Division
1200 Pennsylvania Avenue, NW
Mail Code 6204N
Washington, DC 20460
Tel: 202-564-9620

Aerometric Information Retrieval System (AIRS)— Air Quality Subsystem (AQS)—Hotline
Toll Free: 800-334-2405
Internet: http://www.epa.gov/air/data

Aerometric Information Retrieval System (AIRS)— AIRS Facility Subsystem (AFS)—Helpline
Toll Free: 800-367-1044
Internet: http://www.epa.gov/airs/afs.html

Air Risk Information Center Hotline (Air RISC)
Office of Air Quality Planning and Standards
MD-15
Research Triangle Park, NC 27711
Tel: 919-541-0888
Fax: 919-541-1818

Asbestos Abatement/ Management Ombudsman
401 M Street, SW
Mail Code 1230C
Washington, DC 20460
Toll Free: 800-368-5888
Tel: 703-305-5938
Fax: 703-305-6462

United States Environmental Protection Agency (EPA), 2000. Contact information verified and updated in August 2001.

Center for Exposure Assessment Modeling (CEAM) Help Desk

National Exposure Research Laboratory—Ecosystems Research Division
Office of Research and Development(ORD)
960 College Station Road
Athens, GA 30605-2700
Tel: 706-355-8400
Fax: 706-355-8302
Internet: http://www.epa.gov/ceampubl/ceamhome.htm
E-mail: ceam@epamail.epa.gov

Clean Air Technology Center (CATC) Infoline

(formerly Control Technology Center)
Clean Air Technology Center (MD-12)
Research Triangle Park, NC 27711
Toll-Free from Mexico: 800-304-1115 (Spanish)
Tel: 919-541-0800 (English) or 919-541-1800 (Spanish)
Fax: 919-541-0242
Internet: http://www.epa.gov/ttn/catc
E-mail: catcmail@epamail.epa.gov

Clearinghouse for Inventories and Emission Factors (CHIEF) Help Desk

Emission Factor and Inventory Group (MD-14)
Research Triangle Park, NC 27711
Tel: 919-541-5285
Fax: 919-541-5680
Internet: http://www.epa.gov/ttn/chief
E-mail:
info.chief@epamail.epa.gov

Emergency Planning and Community Right-To-Know Act (EPCRA) hotline

Toll Free: 800-424-9346
Tel: 703-412-9810
TDD: 800-553-7672 or 703-412-3323
Internet: http://www.epa.gov/epaoswer/hotline

Endangered Species Hotline

401 M Street SW
Washington, DC 20469
Toll Free: 800-447-3813
Internet: http://www.epa.gov/oppfead1/endanger

Energy Star Hotline

Toll Free: 888-STAR-YES (888-782-7937)
Internet: http://www.energystar.gov
E-Mail: info@energystar.gov

Environmental Financing Information Network (EFIN)

Tel: 202-564-4994
Fax: 202-565-2587
Internet: http://www.epa.gov/efinpage/efinserve.htm
E-Mail: efin@epa.gov

Environmental Justice Hotline

Toll Free: 800-962-6215
E-Mail: environmental-justice-epa@epa.gov

EPA Enforcement Economic Models Helpline

Toll Free: 888-ECONSPT (888-326-6778)

EPA Grants and Fellowships Hotline (NCERQA Hotline)
Toll Free: 800-490-9194

Federal Facilities Docket Hotline
Toll Free: 800-548-1016

Indoor Air Quality Information Clearinghouse (IAQINFO)
P.O. Box 37133
Washington, D.C. 20013-7133
Toll Free: 800-438-4318
Tel: 703-356-4020
Internet: http://www.epa.gov/iaq
E-Mail: iaqinfo@aol.com

Inspector General Hotline
Environmental Protection Agency
1200 Pennsylvania Avenue, NW
Washington, D.C. 20460
Toll Free: 888-546-8740
Internet: http://www.epa.gov/oigearth/hotline

Local Government Reimbursement Program Helpline
Toll Free: 800-431-9209

Methods Information Communication Exchange Service (MICE)
Tel: 703-821-4690
Fax: 703-903-1373
Internet: http://www.epa.gov/SW-846/mice.htm
E-Mail: mice@cpmx.saic.com

Mexico Border Hotline
Toll Free: 800-334-0741 (English/Spanish)
Internet: http://www.epa.gov/usmexicoborder
E-Mail: border.team@epa.gov

National Antimicrobial Information Network
Toll Free: 800-447-6349
Internet: http://www.ace.ace.orst.edu
E-Mail: nain@ace.orst.edu

National Service Center for Environmental Publications (NSCEP, formerly NCEPI)
P.O. Box 42419
Cincinnati, Ohio 45242-4219
Toll Free: 800-490-9198
Tel: 513-489-8190
Fax: 513-489-8695
Internet: http://www.epa.gov/ncepihome
E-Mail: ncepi.mail@epa.gov

National Hispanic Indoor Air Quality Hotline
Toll Free: 800-SALUD-12 (800-725-8312) (Spanish/English)
Tel: 202-265-6388

National Lead Information Center Hotline
8601 Georgia Ave, Suite 503
Silver Spring, MD 20910
800-424-LEAD (800-424-5323)
Fax: 301-585-7976
Internet: http://www.epa.gov/opptintr/lead/nlic.htm
E-Mail: leadctr@epa.gov

National Pesticide Telecommunications Network

Oregon State University
333 Weniger
Corvallis, OR 97331-6502
Toll Free: 800-858-7378
Internet: http://
wwwace.ace.orst.edu/info/nptn
E-Mail: nptn@ace.orst.edu

National Radon Hotline

1025 Connecticut Avenue, NW
Suite 1200
Washington, DC 20036
Toll Free: 800-SOS-RADON (800-767-7236)
Tel: 202-293-2270
Fax: 202-293-0032
Internet: http://www.nsc.org/ehc/radon.htm
E-Mail: airqual@nsc.org

National Response Center Hotline

Toll Free: 800-424-8802

National Small Flows Clearinghouse Hotline

P.O. box 6064
West Virginia University
Morgantown, WV 26506-6064
Toll Free: 800-624-8301
Tel: 304-293-4191
Fax: 304-293-3161
Internet: http://
www.nesc.wvu.edu/nsfc/
nsfc_homepage.html

Ozone Protection Hotline

Toll Free: 800-296-1996
Tel: 301-614-3396

Pay-As-You-Throw (PAYT) Helpline

Toll Free: 888-EPA-PAYT (1-888-372-7298)
Internet: http://www.epa.gov/payt

Pollution Prevention Information Clearinghouse (PPIC)

Rm. NEB606 (Mailcode 7407)
401 M Street, SW
Washington, DC 20460
Hotline: 202-260-1023
Fax: 202-260-4659
E-Mail: ppic@epa.gov

RCRA, Superfund and EPCRA Hotline

Hotline: 800-424-9346
Tel: 703-412-9810
TDD: 800-553-7672 or 703-412-3323

Safe Drinking Water Hotline

Hotline: 800-426-4791
E-Mail: hotline-sdwa@epa.gov

Small Business Ombudsman Hotline

Ariel Rios Building, 1808
1200 Pennsylvania Avenue, NW
Washington, DC 20460
Hotline: 800-368-5888
Tel: 202-260-0490
Fax: 202-401-2303
Internet: http://www.epa.gov/sbo

Storet Water Quality System Hotline

Hotline:800-424-9067
Internet: http://www.epa.gov/storet
E-mail: storet@epa.gov

Toxic Release Inventory— User Support Service

401 M Street, SW
Washington, DC 20460
Tel: 202-260-1531
Fax: 202-401-2347
E-Mail: tri.us@epamail.epa.gov

Toxic Release Inventory— Community Right To Know—EPCRA Hotline

Hotline: 800-535-0202
Internet: http://www.epa.gov/tri
E-Mail: tri.us@epa.gov

Toxic Substances Control Act (TSCA) Hotline

401 M. Street, SW
Mail Code 7408
Washington, DC 20460
Tel: 202-554-1404
Fax: 202-554-5603
TDD: 202-554-0551
E-Mail: tsca-hotline@epamail.epa.gov

WasteWise Helpline

WasteWise Program (5306W)
Ariel Rios Building
1200 Pennsylvania Avenue, NW
Washington, DC 20460
Toll Free: 800-EPA-WISE (800-372-9473)
E-Mail: ww@cais.net

Wetlands Information Helpline

6858 Old Dominion Drive
Suite 301
McLean, VA 22101
Toll Free: 800-832-7828
Fax: 703-748-1308
Internet: http://www.epa.gov/OWOW/wetlands/wetline.html
E-Mail: wetlands-hotline@epa.gov

Chapter 72

America's Poison Centers Hotline

More than three million times a year, U.S. residents call their poison centers for emergency treatment advice and poison prevention information. Poison centers provide expert, cost-effective services to the residents of every state. By calling 1-800-222-1222 from anywhere in the country, people are automatically connected to the closest poison center. Most calls can be managed entirely over the telephone.

Poison center staff includes physicians who are board-certified in medical toxicology; board-certified clinical toxicologists; nurses, pharmacists, and physicians certified as specialists in poison information; and educators. Each poison center has extensive on-site resources and a network of specialty consultants. Services include: 24-hour emergency treatment advice; telephone follow-up; referral to medical facilities if needed; poison prevention advice, literature, and outreach education; education for health care providers in the causes, recognition and treatment of poisoning; research; and data collection.

Poison centers are members of the American Association of Poison Control Centers (AAPCC). This not-for-profit professional organization analyzes and publishes the AAPCC Toxic Exposure Surveillance System (TESS), the only national data collection system for poison exposures in the United States. AAPCC coordinates the nationwide toll-free poison emergency number and an accompanying national outreach education effort. It also certifies poison centers, certifies specialists in poison information, and works with public and private entities and regulatory agencies to prevent poisonings.

Most fatalities due to poisoning are in adults, because of suicides, drug abuse, and chemical exposures on the job. Most poisoning fatalities are due to pain relievers; antidepressants; sedative, hypnotic, and antipsychotic drugs; stimulants and street drugs; cardiovascular drugs; alcohols; anticonvulsants; muscle relaxants; gases and fumes; and chemicals.

About half of all poison exposures are in children aged five and under, and most of these occur at home. The most common calls to poison centers about poison exposures in this age group are to cosmetics and personal care products; cleaning substances; pain relievers; foreign bodies; plants; medicines intended for external use; cough and cold preparations; pesticides; vitamins; and gastrointestinal preparations. These are not necessarily the most dangerous potential poisons, but reflect the fact that children reach, climb, imitate adult behaviors, and put into their mouths whatever is most readily available.

Every adult who spends time with children has a part to play in poison prevention. Store products and medicines in their original child-resistant packaging. Lock poisons high, out of sight and reach of children. Take medicine so that children can't watch, because children imitate adults.

Poison prevention for all ages includes reading labels before taking medicine, giving medicine, and using products; following product labels for correct use instructions; storing products and medicines in their original packaging, not transferring them into other containers, e.g. food containers; and turning on the lights and putting on glasses when needed.

First aid for a poison emergency is straightforward:

- *Poison in the eye:* Flush with running water for at least 15 minutes and call the poison center.

- *Poison on the skin:* Flush with running water for at least 15 minutes while removing contaminated clothing and call the poison center.

- *Inhaled poison:* Get to fresh air immediately. Call the poison center.

- *Swallowed the wrong medicine or too much medicine:* Call the poison center immediately.

- *Swallowed something that isn't medicine or food:* Drink a small amount of water or milk. Call the poison center immediately.

Chapter 73

National Electronic Injury Surveillance System

For nearly 30 years the U.S. Consumer Product Safety Commission (CPSC) has operated a statistically valid injury surveillance and follow-back system known as the National Electronic Injury Surveillance System (NEISS). The primary purpose of NEISS has been to provide timely data on consumer product-related injuries occurring in the U.S. In the year 2000, CPSC initiated an expansion of the system to collect data on all injuries. With the expansion, NEISS becomes an important public health research tool, not just for CPSC, but for users throughout the U.S. and around the world.

What Is the Source of the Data?

NEISS injury data are gathered from the emergency departments of 100 hospitals selected as a probability sample of all 5,300+ U.S. hospitals with emergency departments. The system's foundation rests on emergency department surveillance data, but the system also has the flexibility to gather additional data at either the surveillance or the investigation level.

Surveillance data enable CPSC analysts to make timely national estimates of the number of injuries associated with (not necessarily caused by) specific consumer products. These data also provide evidence of the need for further study of particular products. Subsequent

"National Electronic Injury Surveillance System," an undated fact sheet produced by the Consumer Product Safety Commission; cited July 2001.

follow-back studies yield important clues to the cause and likely prevention of injuries.

Information gathered from NEISS, together with data from other CPSC sources, not only guides the Commission in setting priorities for further study, but also may provide the Commission with evidence of the need for:

- a product recall,
- a public awareness campaign,
- a product safety standard.

How Does NEISS Work?

The data collection process begins when a patient is admitted to the emergency department (ED) of a NEISS hospital. An ED staff member elicits critical information as to how the injury occurred and enters that information in the patient's medical record.

At the end of each day, a NEISS hospital coordinator reviews all ED records for the day, selecting those that meet the (current) criteria for inclusion in NEISS. The NEISS coordinator abstracts pertinent data from the selected ED record and transcribes it in coded form to a NEISS coding sheet using rules described in a NEISS Coding Manual.

Identifying the consumer product(s) related to the injury is crucial for CPSC. The NEISS coordinator assigns a product code from an alphabetical listing of hundreds of products and recreational activities, being as specific as the data allow. For example, if a lawn mower were involved in an injury, the coordinator would use a different product code for a walk-behind mower than for a riding mower. If the ED record contains additional product detail, the coordinator includes that in a line or two of narrative text (e.g., gasoline-powered rotary mower made by XYZ Company).

The victim's age, gender, injury diagnosis, body parts affected and incident locale are among other data variables coded. A brief narrative description of the incident is also included.

Once the abstracting and coding are completed, the NEISS coordinator enters the data for the day's NEISS injury cases into a personal computer provided by CPSC. As the coordinator keys in data, CPSC-designed software interactively edits the data, requiring that all fields be filled and allowing only acceptable entries.

Following completion of data entry at the hospital, the PC modem is set to receive a telephone call. During the early morning hours, a

PC in the CPSC Washington office polls each NEISS hospital, and collects the newly entered data over telephone lines. After undergoing a second computer editing process, acceptable cases are automatically incorporated into the Commission's permanent NEISS database. The data are available immediately for further review.

The CPSC analytical process begins on the same morning the data are collected. Analysts in the Directorate for Epidemiology read each case, not only checking items for quality control, but also screening each case for a potential emerging hazard.

Follow-Back Investigations

For some incidents identified at the NEISS surveillance level, follow-back investigations are conducted through telephone and on-site interviews with the patient or the patient's relative. Investigation reports provide important information about the likely causes of the incident, including the interaction among person, product and environment. Commission staff uses this information:

- to classify incidents by hazard pattern,
- to provide insight into the type of actions needed to reduce or eliminate the hazards,
- to identify defective products and
- to evaluate the effectiveness of safety standards.

Sample Updates

The NEISS is periodically redesigned to update and improve the sample and thereby maintain the validity of injury estimates. This is necessary because, over time, new hospital emergency departments open, others close, while still others change significantly in size (as measured by the number of ED visits).

NEISS sampling statisticians have provided a systematic means for updating the sample of hospitals while retaining the basic sampling plan. In order to minimize the statistical variance while ensuring an adequate geographic distribution, the sampling frame (a list of hospitals meeting the necessary criteria) has been stratified by hospital size and ordered by geographic location.

At each redesign to date, operational improvements in procedures have helped NEISS managers to improve and upgrade the system. Over time this has led to decreases in coding errors and in the amount of underreporting.

The first major redesign occurred in 1978. Several updates have occurred since then:

- In 1990, CPSC again updated the NEISS sample to accommodate changes in the universe of U.S. hospitals with emergency departments.

- In 1991, CPSC increased the size of the NEISS sample of hospitals from 65 to 91 while retaining the sample design. The increase in hospitals provided approximately 40 percent more injury cases per year. This increase in cases not only allowed for the faster completion of special studies, but also provided for modest improvement in measures of statistical confidence.

- In 1997, CPSC again updated the NEISS sample to reflect the current distribution of U.S. hospitals with emergency departments. The current NEISS sample includes 100 hospitals grouped into five strata, four representing hospital emergency departments of differing sizes and a fifth representing emergency departments from children's hospitals.

Other System Milestones

In addition to updating the sample, over time CPSC managers have altered NEISS operational collection and coding rules to accommodate the needs of other agencies and the differing interpretations of which products fall under the Commission's jurisdiction.

Over time, CPSC managers also have modified the definitions of the NEISS variables collected. For example, product codes have been added, deleted, combined or split into two or more codes.

The year 2000 initiative to expand NEISS to collect all injuries necessitated several important operational revisions. The expanded system includes:

- injuries where no product is mentioned (e.g. fell on ground),

- injuries related to products not currently collected (e.g. motor vehicles), and

- intentional injuries such as assaults or suicide attempts.

Data users should carefully consider the likely impact of system updates and modifications, especially when comparing estimated injuries over time.

NEISS Serves Others, Too!

Since 1978, CPSC has assisted other Federal agencies by collecting data of special interest through NEISS. This has allowed other organizations to quickly and easily gather critically needed, statistically-valid national data without the investment in personnel, time and dollars that designing, implementing and executing an independent special survey would require.

In serving the needs of other agencies the scope of NEISS has been broadened to include incidents outside the jurisdiction of CPSC, such as occupational or intentional injuries. The usefulness of these data has been enhanced by adding to the NEISS record a limited number of additional variables, such as the injured worker's occupation. To date other agencies have used NEISS to study injuries associated with motor vehicles, firearms, medical devices, mobile homes, pesticides, acts of violence, and occupation.

With the advent of the expanded all injury NEISS initiated in the year 2000, more Federal agencies may find NEISS a powerful and useful tool to identify and track the public health problems associated with injuries.

For further information on how your organization can benefit by sharing the NEISS, contact:

Division of Hazard and Injury Data Systems
U.S. Consumer Product Safety Commission
Washington, D.C. 20207
Tel: 301-504-0539, extension 1249
Fax: 301-504-0038
Internet: http://www.cpsc.gov

Availability of NEISS Data

The Consumer Product Safety Act requires the maintenance of a National Injury Information Clearinghouse "to collect, investigate, analyze and disseminate injury data and information relating to the causes and prevention of death, injury and illness associated with consumer products..." (CPSA, Section 5(a) (1)).

NEISS surveillance data are available to the public in various computer formats. Certain standard reports may be requested from the National Injury Information Clearinghouse. Custom reports are also available at rates specified in the Freedom of Information Act.

Follow-back investigation data are available as computer printouts, special reports, and hazard analyses.

Each year the Clearinghouse responds to about 6,000 requests for information. Most requests are answered without charge within 10 working days.

To request injury information, write or call:

National Injury Information Clearinghouse
U.S. Consumer Product Safety Commission
4330 East West Highway, Room 504
Washington, D.C. 20207
Tel: 301-504-0424
Internet: http://www.cpsc.gov
E-Mail: clearinghouse@cpsc.gov

Chapter 74

State Pesticide Agencies

Environmental Protection Agency EPA Addresses

U.S. Environmental Protection Agency
Office of Pesticide Programs 7506C
401 M Street, SW
Washington, DC 20460
Tel: 703-305-5017
Fax: 703-305-5558
Internet: http://www.epa.gov

U.S. EPA, Region 1
Air, Pesticides and Toxic Management Division
State Assistance Office ASO
1 Congress Street
Boston, MA 02114
Tel: 888-372-7341 (New England States)
Tel: 617-918-1111 (Outside New England)
Internet: http://www.epa.gov/region01

U.S. EPA, Region 2
Building 10 MS-105
Pesticides and Toxics Branch
2890 Woodbridge Avenue
Edison, NJ 08837-3679
Tel: 732-321-6765
Fax: 732-321-6788
Internet: http://www.epa.gov/region02

U.S. EPA, Region 3
Toxics and Pesticides Branch
1650 Arch Street
Philadelphia, PA 19103
Tel: 215-814-2300
Fax: 215 597-3156
Internet: http://www.epa.gov/region03

Excerpted from *"Citizen's Guide to Pest Control and Pesticide Safety,"* United States Environmental Protection Agency EPA, EPA 730-K-95-001, September 1995. Contact information verified and updated in August 2001.

U.S. EPA, Region 4

Pesticides and Toxics Branch
4-APT-MD
61 Forsyth Street, NW
Atlanta, GA 30303
Tel: 404-562-9077
Fax: 404-562-8174
Internet: http://www.epa.gov/region4

U.S. EPA, Region 5

Pesticides and Toxics Branch SP-14J
77 West Jackson Boulevard
Chicago, IL 60604
Toll Free: 800-621-8431
Tel: 312-353-2000
Internet: http://www.epa.gov/region5

U.S. EPA, Region 6

Pesticides and Toxics Branch
6PD-P
1445 Ross Avenue, Suite 1200
Dallas, TX 75202
Toll Free: 800-877-6063
Tel: 214-665-6444
Internet: http://www.epa.gov/region6

U.S. EPA, Region 7

Water, Wetlands and Pesticides
Division
726 Minnesota Avenue
Kansas City, KS 66101
Toll Free: 800-223-0425
Tel: 913-551-7003
Internet: http://www.epa.gov/region7

U.S. EPA, Region 8

Air, Radiation and Toxics Division
8ART
999 18th Street, Suite 300
Denver, CO 80202-2466
Toll Free: 800-227-8917
Tel: 303-293-6312
Internet: http://www.epa.gov/region8

U.S. EPA, Region 9

Pesticides and Toxics Branch A-4
75 Hawthorne Street
San Francisco, CA 94105
Tel: 415-744-1500
Internet: http://www.epa.gov/region9

U.S. EPA, Region 10

Pesticides and Toxics Branch AT-083
1200 Sixth Avenue
Seattle, WA 98101
Toll Free: 800-424-4EPA
Tel: 206-553-1200
Internet: http://www.epa.gov/region10
E-Mail: epa-seattle@epa.gov

State Pesticide Agencies

Region 1

Connecticut
Pesticide Management Division
Department of Environmental
Protection
79 Elm Street
Hartford, CT 06106
Tel: 860-424-3369
Internet: http://dep.state.ct.us

Maine
Board of Pesticide Control
Maine Department of Agriculture
State House Station #28
Augusta, ME 04333
Tel: 207-287-7548
Internet://www.state.me.us/agri-
culture

Massachusetts
Pesticides Bureau
Massachusetts Department of
Food and Agriculture
251 Causeway Street, Suite 500
Boston, MA 02114
Tel: 617-727-1700
Fax: 617-626-1850
Internet: http://www.massdfa.org/
pesticides

New Hampshire
Division of Pesticide Control
New Hampshire Department of
Agriculture, Markets and Food
P.O. Box 2042
Concord, NH 03302-2042
Tel: 603-271-3551
Fax: 603-271-1109
Internet: http://www.state.nh.us/
agric

Rhode Island
Division of Agriculture
Rhode Island Department of En-
vironmental Management
235 Promenade Street
Providence, RI 02908
Tel: 401-222-6800
After Hours Emergencies: 401-
222-3070
TDD: 401-222-4462
Internet: http://www.state.ri.us/
dem

Vermont
Plant Industry, Laboratory and
Standards Division
Vermont Department of Agriculture
116 State Street
Montpelier, VT 05602
Tel: 802-828-2416
Fax: 802-828-3813
Internet: http://www.state.vt.us/
agric

Region 2

New Jersey
Pesticide Control Program
New Jersey Department of Envi-
ronmental Protection
401 E. State Street
7th Floor, East Wing
Trenton, NJ 08625-0402
Tel: 609-292-2885
Fax: 609-292-7695
Internet: http://www.state.nj.us/
dep

New York
Bureau of Pesticides and Radiation
Division of Solid and Hazardous
Materials Regulation
New York Department of Environ-
mental Conservation
625 Broadway
Albany, NY 12233
Tel: 518-457-7482
Internet: http://
www.dec.state.ny.us

Puerto Rico
Analysis and Registration of Agri-
cultural Materials
Puerto Rico Department of Agri-
culture
Agrological Laboratory
P.O. Box 10163
San Juan, PR 00908
Tel: 787-724-5158
Fax: 787-722-0320

Virgin Islands
Pesticide Program Director
8000 Nisky Center, Suite 231
Estate Nisky, Charlotte Amalie
St. Thomas, US VI 00802
Tel: 809-774-3320, ext. 135

Region 3

Delaware
Delaware Department of Agricul-
ture
Division of Consumer Protection
2320 South DuPont Highway
Dover, DE 19901
Toll Free: 800-282-8685 (DE only)
Tel: 302 739-4811
Fax: 302-697-6287
Internet: http://www.state.du.us/
deptagri

District of Columbia
Pesticide Hazardous Waste and
Underground Storage Tank Divi-
sion
Environmental Regulation Ad-
ministration
Department of Consumer and
Regulatory Affairs
441 4th Street, Nw
Washington, DC 20001
Tel: 202-727-1000
Internet: http://www.dcra.org

Maryland
Pesticide Regulation Section
Office of Plant Industries and
Pest Management
Maryland Department of Agricul-
ture
50 Harry S. Truman Parkway
Annapolis, MD 21401-7080
Tel: 410-841-5700
http://www.mda.state.md.us

Pennsylvania
Agronomic Services Division
Bureau of Plant Industry
Pennsylvania Department of Agri-
culture
2301 North Cameron Street
Harrisburg, PA 17110-9408
Tel: 717-787-4737
Internet: http://
www.pda.state.pa.us

Virginia
Office of Pesticide Services
Virginia Department of Agricul-
ture and Consumer Service
1100 Bank Street
Richmond, VA 23219
Tel: 804-786-2373
Internet: http://
www.vdacs.state.va.us

West Virginia
Pesticide Division
West Virginia Department of Agriculture
1900 Kanawha Boulevard, East
Charleston, WV 25305-0170
Tel: 304-558-2201
Fax: 304-558-2203
http://www.state.wv.us/agriculture

Region 4

Alabama
Division of Plant Protection and
Pesticide Management
Alabama Department of Agriculture and Industries
P.O. Box 3336
Montgomery, AL 36109-0336
Tel: 334-240-7100
Fax: 334-240-7190
Internet: http://
www.agi.state.al.us

Florida
Division of Agricultural
Environmental Services
Department of Agriculture and
Consumer Services
3125 Conner Boulevard
Tallahassee, FL 32399-1650
Tel: 850-488-3022
Internet: http://doacs.state.fl.us

Georgia
Plant Industry Division
Georgia Department of Agriculture
19 Martin Luther King Drive, SW
Atlanta, GA 30334
Tel: 404-656-3685
Fax: 404-651-7957
Internet: http://
www.agr.state.ga.us

Kentucky
Division of Pesticides
Kentucky Department of Agriculture
Capitol Annex
Room 188
Frankfort, KY 40601
Tel: 502-564-5126
Fax: 502-564-5016
Internet: http://www.kyagr.com

Mississippi
Bureau of Plant Industry
Mississippi Department of Agriculture and Commerce
121 North Jefferson Street
Jackson, MS 39201
Tel: 601-359-1100
Fax: 601-354-6290
Internet: http://
www.mdac.state.ms.us

North Carolina
Assistant Pesticide Administrator
Food and Drug Protection Division
North Carolina Department of Agriculture
2 West Edenton Street
Raleigh, NC 27601
Tel: 919-733-7125
Internet: http://www.ncagr.com

South Carolina
Department of Pesticide Regulation
511 Westinghouse Road
Pendleton, SC 29670
Tel: 864-646-2120
Fax: 864-646-2179
Internet: http://
www.drpsp.clemson.edu

Tennessee
Plant Industries Division
Tennessee Department of Agriculture
P.O. Box 40627
Nashville, TN 37204
Tel: 615-837-5103
Fax: 615-837-5333
Internet: http://www.state.tn.us/agriculture

Region 5

Illinois
Bureau of Environmental Programs
Illinois Department of Agriculture
P.O. Box 19281
Springfield, IL 62794-9281
Toll Free: 800-273-4763
Tel: 217-785-2172
Internet: http://www.agr.state.il.us

Indiana
Pesticide Administrator
Office of the Indiana State Chemist
1154 Biochemistry Building
Purdue University
West Lafayette, IN 47907-1154
Tel: 765-494-1492
Fax: 765-494-4331
Internet: http://www.isco.purdue.edu

Michigan
Pesticide and Plant
Management Division
Michigan Department of Agriculture
611 W. Ottawa
Lansing, MI 48909
Toll Free: 800-292-9393
Tel: 517-373-1104
Fax: 517-335-7071
Internet: http://www.mda.state.us

Minnesota
Division of Agronomy Services
Minnesota Department of Agriculture
90 West Plato Boulevard
St. Paul, MN 55107
Toll Free: 800-967-2472
Tel: 651-287-2200
Internet: http://www.mda.state.mn.us

Ohio
Specialist in Charge of Pesticide Regulation
Division of Plant Industry
Ohio Department of Agriculture
8995 East Main Street
Reynoldsburg, OH 43068
Tel: 614-728-6200
Fax: 614-466-6124
Internet: http://www.state.oh.us/agr

Wisconsin
Agricultural Resources
Management Division
Wisconsin Department of Agriculture, Trade and Consumer Protection
Trade and Consumer Protection
2811 Agriculture Drive
Madison, WI 53708
Toll Free: 800-422-7128
Tel: 608-224-4525
Internet: http://datcp.state.wi.us

Region 6

Louisiana
Pesticide and Environmental Programs
Louisiana Department of Agriculture and Forestry
P.O. Box 3596
Baton Rouge, LA 70821-3596
Tel: 225-922-1234
Fax: 225-922-1253
Internet: http://www.ldaf.state.la.us

Oklahoma
Department of Environmental Quality
Plant Industry and Consumer Services
Oklahoma Department of Agriculture
Post Office Box 528804
Oklahoma City, OK 73152
Tel: 405-271-3864
Internet: http://www.state.ok.us

Texas
Assistant Commissioner for Pesticides
Texas Department of Agriculture
P.O. Box 12847
Austin, TX 78711
Tel: 512-463-7476
Fax: 512-463-1104
Internet: http://www.agr.state.tx.us

Region 7

Iowa
Pesticide Bureau
Iowa Department of Agriculture
Henry A. Wallace Building
East 9th Street and Grand Avenue
Des Moines, IA 50319
Tel: 515-281-5321
Internet: http://www2.state.ia.us/agriculture

Kansas
Plant Health Division
Kansas Department of Agriculture
901 S Kansas Ave., 7th Floor
Topeka, KS 66612-1281
Tel: 785-296-3556
Internet: http://www.ink.org/public/kda/phealth/phealth.html

Missouri
Bureau of Pesticide Control
Missouri Department of Agriculture
P.O. Box 630
Jefferson City, MO 65102
Tel: 573-751-4211
Internet: http://www.mda.state.mo.us/d.htm

Nebraska
Bureau of Plant Industry
Nebraska Department of Agriculture
301 Centennial Mall
P.O. Box 94756
Lincoln, NE 68509
Tel: 402-471-2394
Fax: 402-471-6892
Internet: http://www.agr.state.ne.us

Region 8

Colorado
Division of Plant Industry
Colorado Department of Agriculture
700 Kipling Street, Suite 4000
Lakewood, CO 80215-5894
Tel: 303-239-4125
Internet: http://
www.ag.state.co.us

Montana
Agricultural Sciences Division
Montana Department of Agriculture
P.O. Box 200201
Helena, MT 59620-0201
Tel: 406-444-3144
Fax: 406-444-4687
Internet: http://
www.agr.state.mt.us

North Dakota
Pesticide Division
North Dakota Department of Agriculture
State Capitol, 600 East Boulevard, Dept. 602
Bismarck, ND 58505-0020
Toll Free: 800-242-7535
Tel: 701-328-2231
Fax: 701-328-4567
Internet: http://
www.agdepartment.com

South Dakota
Office of Agronomy Services
Agricultural Services
South Dakota Department of Agriculture
Foss Building
523 E. Capitol
Pierre, SD 57501-3182
Toll Free: 800-228-5254
Tel: 605-773-3375
Fax: 605-773-3481
Internet: http://www.state.sd.us/
doa/doa.html

Utah
Division of Plant Industry
Utah Department of Agriculture
and Food
350 N. Redwood Road
Salt Lake City, UT 84114-6500
Tel: 801-538-7100
Internet: http://
www.ag.state.ut.us

Wyoming
Technical Services
Wyoming Department of Agriculture
2219 Carey Avenue
Cheyenne, WY 82002-0100
Tel: 307-777-7321
Fax: 307-777-6593
Internet: http://
wyagric.state.wy.us

Region 9

Arizona
Environmental Services Division
Arizona Department of Agriculture
1688 West Adams
Phoenix, AZ 85007
Tel: 602-542-4373
Internet: http://
www.agriculture.state.az.us

California
California Department of Pesticide Regulation
1001 I Street
Sacramento, CA 95812-4015
Tel: 916-445-4300
Fax: 916-324-1452
Internet: http://www.cdpr.ca.gov

Hawaii
Pesticide Programs
Hawaii Department of Agriculture
1428 South King Street
Honolulu, HI 96814
Tel: 808-973-9401
Internet: http://www.haiaii.gov/icsd/doa/doa.html

Nevada
Bureau of Plant Industry
Nevada Division of Agriculture
350 Capitol Hill Avenue
Reno, NV 89520
Tel: 775-688-1180
Fax: 775-688-1178
Internet: http://agri.state.nv.us

Guam
Pesticide Program Director
Guam Environmental Protection Agency
P.O. Box 22439-GMF
Barrigada, GU 96921
Tel: 671-475-1658
Fax: 671-477-9402
Internet: http://www.gepa.gov.gu

American Samoa EPA
Office of the Governor
American Samoa Government
P.O. Box 2609
Pago Pago, American Samoa 97699
Tel: 684-633-2304
Internet: http://www.government.as

Commonwealth of the Northern Mariana Islands
Department of Public Works
Division of Environmental Quality
Commonwealth of the Northern Mariana Islands CNMI
P.O. Box 1304
Saipan, Mariana Islands 96950
Tel: 670-234-1011
Fax: 670-234-1003

Region 10

Idaho
Division of Agricultural Technology
Idaho Department of Agriculture
2270 Old Penitentiary Road
Boise, ID 83712
Tel: 208-332-8500
Fax: 208-334-2170
Internet: http://www.agri.state.id.us

Oregon
Plant Division
Oregon Department of Agriculture
635 Capitol Street, NE
Salem, OR 97310-0110
Tel: 503-986-4550
Internet: http://www.oda.state.or.us

Washington
Pesticide Management Division
Washington State Department of
Agriculture
1111 Washington Street, S.E.
Olympia, WA 98504-2560
Tel: 360-902-1800
TDD: 360-902-1996
Internet: http://www.wa.gov/agr

Alaska
Division of Environmental Health
Alaska Department of Environ-
mental Conservation
410 Willoughby Avenue, Room 107
Juneau, AK 99801-1795
Tel: 907-465-5010
Fax: 907-465-5097
TDD/TTY: 907-465-5040
Internet: http://www.state ak.us/
local/akpages/env.conserv/
home.htm

Index

Index

Page numbers followed by 'n' indicate a footnote. Page numbers in *italics* indicate a table or illustration.

A

AAPCC *see* American Association of Poison Control Centers
acetone 369
acid aerosol, defined 523
Acid Rain Hotline, contact information 545
active ingredient, defined 523
acute exposure, defined 523
acute toxicity, defined 523, 536
ACWM *see* asbestos-containing waste materials
adhesive removers 365
adsorption, defined 524
adverse effects, data defined 524
Aerometric Information Retrieval System (AIRS), contact information 545
aerosol, defined 524
AFCI *see* arc fault circuit interrupter
airborne particulates, defined 525
air cleaners 299–300
air cleaning, defined 524

air conditioners
  biological pollutants 374, 377–78, 380
  formaldehyde emissions 313
air exchange rate 295
air pollutants
  defined 524
  pesticides 138–39
  see also pollutants
air pollution, defined 524
  see also indoor air pollution
air pollution control device, defined 524
air quality standards, defined 525
  see also indoor air quality
Air Risk Information Center Hotline, contact information 545
AIRS *see* Aerometric Information Retrieval System
Alabama
  drowning statistics *232*
  firework regulations 481
  pesticide agency 563
Alaska
  drowning statistics *232*
  fireworks regulations 481
  pesticide agency 568
alcohol use, drownings 233–34
aldehydes 333, 336
aldrin 527

571

Health Reference Series

COMPLETE CATALOG

AIDS Sourcebook, 1st Edition

Basic Information about AIDS and HIV Infection, Featuring Historical and Statistical Data, Current Research, Prevention, and Other Special Topics of Interest for Persons Living with AIDS

Along with Source Listings for Further Assistance

Edited by Karen Bellenir and Peter D. Dresser. 831 pages. 1995. 0-7808-0031-1. $78.

"One strength of this book is its practical emphasis. The intended audience is the lay reader . . . useful as an educational tool for health care providers who work with AIDS patients. Recommended for public libraries as well as hospital or academic libraries that collect consumer materials."
— *Bulletin of the Medical Library Association, Jan '96*

"This is the most comprehensive volume of its kind on an important medical topic. Highly recommended for all libraries." — *Reference Book Review, '96*

"Very useful reference for all libraries."
— *Choice, Association of College and Research Libraries, Oct '95*

"There is a wealth of information here that can provide much educational assistance. It is a must book for all libraries and should be on the desk of each and every congressional leader. Highly recommended."
— *AIDS Book Review Journal, Aug '95*

"Recommended for most collections."
— *Library Journal, Jul '95*

AIDS Sourcebook, 2nd Edition

Basic Consumer Health Information about Acquired Immune Deficiency Syndrome (AIDS) and Human Immunodeficiency Virus (HIV) Infection, Featuring Updated Statistical Data, Reports on Recent Research and Prevention Initiatives, and Other Special Topics of Interest for Persons Living with AIDS, Including New Antiretroviral Treatment Options, Strategies for Combating Opportunistic Infections, Information about Clinical Trials, and More

Along with a Glossary of Important Terms and Resource Listings for Further Help and Information

Edited by Karen Bellenir. 751 pages. 1999. 0-7808-0225-X. $78.

"Highly recommended."
— *American Reference Books Annual, 2000*

"Excellent sourcebook. This continues to be a highly recommended book. There is no other book that provides as much information as this book provides."
— *AIDS Book Review Journal, Dec-Jan 2000*

"Recommended reference source."
— *Booklist, American Library Association, Dec '99*

"A solid text for college-level health libraries."
— *The Bookwatch, Aug '99*

Cited in *Reference Sources for Small and Medium-Sized Libraries, American Library Association, 1999*

Alcoholism Sourcebook

Basic Consumer Health Information about the Physical and Mental Consequences of Alcohol Abuse, Including Liver Disease, Pancreatitis, Wernicke-Korsakoff Syndrome (Alcoholic Dementia), Fetal Alcohol Syndrome, Heart Disease, Kidney Disorders, Gastrointestinal Problems, and Immune System Compromise and Featuring Facts about Addiction, Detoxification, Alcohol Withdrawal, Recovery, and the Maintenance of Sobriety

Along with a Glossary and Directories of Resources for Further Help and Information

Edited by Karen Bellenir. 613 pages. 2000. 0-7808-0325-6. $78.

"This title is one of the few reference works on alcoholism for general readers. For some readers this will be a welcome complement to the many self-help books on the market. Recommended for collections serving general readers and consumer health collections."
— *E-Streams, Mar '01*

"This book is an excellent choice for public and academic libraries."
— *American Reference Books Annual, 2001*

"Recommended reference source."
— *Booklist, American Library Association, Dec '00*

"Presents a wealth of information on alcohol use and abuse and its effects on the body and mind, treatment, and prevention." — *SciTech Book News, Dec '00*

"Important new health guide which packs in the latest consumer information about the problems of alcoholism." — *Reviewer's Bookwatch, Nov '00*

SEE ALSO Drug Abuse Sourcebook, Substance Abuse Sourcebook

Allergies Sourcebook, 1st Edition

Basic Information about Major Forms and Mechanisms of Common Allergic Reactions, Sensitivities, and Intolerances, Including Anaphylaxis, Asthma, Hives and Other Dermatologic Symptoms, Rhinitis, and Sinusitis

Along with Their Usual Triggers Like Animal Fur, Chemicals, Drugs, Dust, Foods, Insects, Latex, Pollen, and Poison Ivy, Oak, and Sumac; Plus Information on Prevention, Identification, and Treatment

Edited by Allan R. Cook. 611 pages. 1997. 0-7808-0036-2. $78.

Allergies Sourcebook, 2nd Edition

Basic Consumer Health Information about Allergic Disorders, Triggers, Reactions, and Related Symptoms, Including Anaphylaxis, Rhinitis, Sinusitis, Asthma, Dermatitis, Conjunctivitis, and Multiple Chemical Sensitivity

Along with Tips on Diagnosis, Prevention, and Treatment, Statistical Data, a Glossary, and a Directory of Sources for Further Help and Information

Edited by Annemarie S. Muth. 600 pages. 2001. 0-7808-0376-0. $78.

■

Alternative Medicine Sourcebook

Basic Consumer Health Information about Alternatives to Conventional Medicine, Including Acupressure, Acupuncture, Aromatherapy, Ayurveda, Bioelectromagnetics, Environmental Medicine, Essence Therapy, Food and Nutrition Therapy, Herbal Therapy, Homeopathy, Imaging, Massage, Naturopathy, Reflexology, Relaxation and Meditation, Sound Therapy, Vitamin and Mineral Therapy, and Yoga, and More

Edited by Allan R. Cook. 737 pages. 1999. 0-7808-0200-4. $78.

"Recommended reference source."
—*Booklist, American Library Association, Feb '00*

"A great addition to the reference collection of every type of library." —*American Reference Books Annual, 2000*

■

Alzheimer's, Stroke & 29 Other Neurological Disorders Sourcebook, 1st Edition

Basic Information for the Layperson on 31 Diseases or Disorders Affecting the Brain and Nervous System, First Describing the Illness, Then Listing Symptoms, Diagnostic Methods, and Treatment Options, and Including Statistics on Incidences and Causes

Edited by Frank E. Bair. 579 pages. 1993. 1-55888-748-2. $78.

"Nontechnical reference book that provides reader-friendly information."
—*Family Caregiver Alliance Update, Winter '96*

"Should be included in any library's patient education section." —*American Reference Books Annual, 1994*

"Written in an approachable and accessible style. Recommended for patient education and consumer health collections in health science center and public libraries." —*Academic Library Book Review, Dec '93*

"It is very handy to have information on more than thirty neurological disorders under one cover, and there is no recent source like it." —*Reference Quarterly, American Library Association, Fall '93*

SEE ALSO *Brain Disorders Sourcebook*

Alzheimer's Disease Sourcebook, 2nd Edition

Basic Consumer Health Information about Alzheimer's Disease, Related Disorders, and Other Dementias, Including Multi-Infarct Dementia, AIDS-Related Dementia, Alcoholic Dementia, Huntington's Disease, Delirium, and Confusional States

Along with Reports Detailing Current Research Efforts in Prevention and Treatment, Long-Term Care Issues, and Listings of Sources for Additional Help and Information

Edited by Karen Bellenir. 524 pages. 1999. 0-7808-0223-3. $78.

"Provides a wealth of useful information not otherwise available in one place. This resource is recommended for all types of libraries."
—*American Reference Books Annual, 2000*

"Recommended reference source."
—*Booklist, American Library Association, Oct '99*

■

Arthritis Sourcebook

Basic Consumer Health Information about Specific Forms of Arthritis and Related Disorders, Including Rheumatoid Arthritis, Osteoarthritis, Gout, Polymyalgia Rheumatica, Psoriatic Arthritis, Spondyloarthropathies, Juvenile Rheumatoid Arthritis, and Juvenile Ankylosing Spondylitis

Along with Information about Medical, Surgical, and Alternative Treatment Options, and Including Strategies for Coping with Pain, Fatigue, and Stress

Edited by Allan R. Cook. 550 pages. 1998. 0-7808-0201-2. $78.

". . . accessible to the layperson."
—*Reference and Research Book News, Feb '99*

■

Asthma Sourcebook

Basic Consumer Health Information about Asthma, Including Symptoms, Traditional and Nontraditional Remedies, Treatment Advances, Quality-of-Life Aids, Medical Research Updates, and the Role of Allergies, Exercise, Age, the Environment, and Genetics in the Development of Asthma

Along with Statistical Data, a Glossary, and Directories of Support Groups, and Other Resources for Further Information

Edited by Annemarie S. Muth. 628 pages. 2000. 0-7808-0381-7. $78.

"A worthwhile reference acquisition for public libraries and academic medical libraries whose readers desire a quick introduction to the wide range of asthma information." —*Choice, Association of College and Research Libraries, Jun '01*

"Recommended reference source."
—*Booklist, American Library Association, Feb '01*

"Highly recommended." — *The Bookwatch, Jan '01*

"There is much good information for patients and their families who deal with asthma daily."
— American Medical Writers Association Journal, Winter '01

"This informative text is recommended for consumer health collections in public, secondary school, and community college libraries and the libraries of universities with a large undergraduate population."
— American Reference Books Annual, 2001

■

Back & Neck Disorders Sourcebook

Basic Information about Disorders and Injuries of the Spinal Cord and Vertebrae, Including Facts on Chiropractic Treatment, Surgical Interventions, Paralysis, and Rehabilitation

Along with Advice for Preventing Back Trouble

Edited by Karen Bellenir. 548 pages. 1997. 0-7808-0202-0. $78.

"The strength of this work is its basic, easy-to-read format. Recommended."
— Reference and User Services Quarterly, American Library Association, Winter '97

■

Blood & Circulatory Disorders Sourcebook

Basic Information about Blood and Its Components, Anemias, Leukemias, Bleeding Disorders, and Circulatory Disorders, Including Aplastic Anemia, Thalassemia, Sickle-Cell Disease, Hemochromatosis, Hemophilia, Von Willebrand Disease, and Vascular Diseases

Along with a Special Section on Blood Transfusions and Blood Supply Safety, a Glossary, and Source Listings for Further Help and Information

Edited by Karen Bellenir and Linda M. Shin. 554 pages. 1998. 0-7808-0203-9. $78.

"Recommended reference source."
—Booklist, American Library Association, Feb '99

"An important reference sourcebook written in simple language for everyday, non-technical users. "
— Reviewer's Bookwatch, Jan '99

■

Brain Disorders Sourcebook

Basic Consumer Health Information about Strokes, Epilepsy, Amyotrophic Lateral Sclerosis (ALS/Lou Gehrig's Disease), Parkinson's Disease, Brain Tumors, Cerebral Palsy, Headache, Tourette Syndrome, and More

Along with Statistical Data, Treatment and Rehabilitation Options, Coping Strategies, Reports on Current

Research Initiatives, a Glossary, and Resource Listings for Additional Help and Information

Edited by Karen Bellenir. 481 pages. 1999. 0-7808-0229-2. $78.

"Belongs on the shelves of any library with a consumer health collection." *— E-Streams, Mar '00*

"Recommended reference source."
— Booklist, American Library Association, Oct '99

SEE ALSO *Alzheimer's, Stroke & 29 Other Neurological Disorders Sourcebook, 1st Edition*

■

Breast Cancer Sourcebook

Basic Consumer Health Information about Breast Cancer, Including Diagnostic Methods, Treatment Options, Alternative Therapies, Self-Help Information, Related Health Concerns, Statistical and Demographic Data, and Facts for Men with Breast Cancer

Along with Reports on Current Research Initiatives, a Glossary of Related Medical Terms, and a Directory of Sources for Further Help and Information

Edited by Edward J. Prucha and Karen Bellenir. 580 pages. 2001. 0-7808-0244-6. $78.

SEE ALSO *Cancer Sourcebook for Women, 1st and 2nd Editions, Women's Health Concerns Sourcebook*

■

Breastfeeding Sourcebook

Basic Consumer Health Information about the Benefits of Breastmilk, Preparing to Breastfeed, Breastfeeding as a Baby Grows, Nutrition, and More, Including Information on Special Situations and Concerns, Such as Mastitis, Illness, Medications, Allergies, Multiple Births, Prematurity, Special Needs, and Adoption

Along with a Glossary and Resources for Additional Help and Information

Edited by Jenni Lynn Colson. 350 pages. 2001. 0-7808-0332-9. $48.

SEE ALSO *Pregnancy & Birth Sourcebook*

■

Burns Sourcebook

Basic Consumer Health Information about Various Types of Burns and Scalds, Including Flame, Heat, Cold, Electrical, Chemical, and Sun Burns

Along with Information on Short-Term and Long-Term Treatments, Tissue Reconstruction, Plastic Surgery, Prevention Suggestions, and First Aid

Edited by Allan R. Cook. 604 pages. 1999. 0-7808-0204-7. $78.

"This key reference guide is an invaluable addition to all health care and public libraries in confronting this ongoing health issue."
—American Reference Books Annual, 2000

Cancer Sourcebook, 1st Edition

Basic Information on Cancer Types, Symptoms, Diagnostic Methods, and Treatments, Including Statistics on Cancer Occurrences Worldwide and the Risks Associated with Known Carcinogens and Activities

Edited by Frank E. Bair. 932 pages. 1990. 1-55888-888-8. $78.

New Cancer Sourcebook, 2nd Edition

Basic Information about Major Forms and Stages of Cancer, Featuring Facts about Primary and Secondary Tumors of the Respiratory, Nervous, Lymphatic, Circulatory, Skeletal, and Gastrointestinal Systems, and Specific Organs; Statistical and Demographic Data; Treatment Options; and Strategies for Coping

Edited by Allan R. Cook. 1,313 pages. 1996. 0-7808-0041-9. $78.

Cancer Sourcebook, 3rd Edition

Basic Consumer Health Information about Major Forms and Stages of Cancer, Featuring Facts about Primary and Secondary Tumors of the Respiratory, Nervous, Lymphatic, Circulatory, Skeletal, and Gastrointestinal Systems, and Specific Organs

Along with Statistical and Demographic Data, Treatment Options, Strategies for Coping, a Glossary, and a Directory of Sources for Additional Help and Information

Edited by Edward J. Prucha. 1,069 pages. 2000. 0-7808-0227-6. $78.

Cancer Sourcebook for Women, 1st Edition

Basic Information about Specific Forms of Cancer That Affect Women, Featuring Facts about Breast Cancer, Cervical Cancer, Ovarian Cancer, Cancer of the Uterus and Uterine Sarcoma, Cancer of the Vagina, and Cancer of the Vulva; Statistical and Demographic Data; Treatments, Self-Help Management Suggestions, and Current Research Initiatives

Edited by Allan R. Cook and Peter D. Dresser. 524 pages. 1996. 0-7808-0076-1. $78.

"Presents a comprehensive knowledge base for general readers. Men and women both benefit from the gold mine of information nestled between the two covers of this book. Recommended."
— *Academic Library Book Review, Summer '96*

"This timely book is highly recommended for consumer health and patient education collections in all libraries." — *Library Journal, Apr '96*

SEE ALSO *Breast Cancer Sourcebook, Women's Health Concerns Sourcebook*

Cancer Sourcebook for Women, 2nd Edition

Basic Consumer Health Information about Specific Forms of Cancer That Affect Women, Including Cervical Cancer, Ovarian Cancer, Endometrial Cancer, Uterine Sarcoma, Vaginal Cancer, Vulvar Cancer, and Gestational Trophoblastic Tumor; and Featuring Statistical Information, Facts about Tests and Treatments, a Glossary of Cancer Terms, and an Extensive List of Additional Resources

Edited by Karen Bellenir. 600 pages. 2001. 0-7808-0226-8. $78.

SEE ALSO *Breast Cancer Sourcebook, Women's Health Concerns Sourcebook*

Cardiovascular Diseases & Disorders Sourcebook, 1st Edition

Basic Information about Cardiovascular Diseases and Disorders, Featuring Facts about the Cardiovascular System, Demographic and Statistical Data, Descriptions of Pharmacological and Surgical Interventions, Lifestyle Modifications, and a Special Section Focusing on Heart Disorders in Children

Edited by Karen Bellenir and Peter D. Dresser. 683 pages. 1995. 0-7808-0032-X. $78.

". . . comprehensive format provides an extensive overview on this subject."
— *Choice, Association of College and Research Libraries, Jun '96*

". . . an easily understood, complete, up-to-date resource. This well executed public health tool will make valuable information available to those that need it most, patients and their families. The typeface, sturdy non-reflective paper, and library binding add a feel of quality found wanting in other publications. Highly recommended for academic and general libraries. "
— *Academic Library Book Review, Summer '96*

SEE ALSO *Healthy Heart Sourcebook for Women, Heart Diseases & Disorders Sourcebook, 2nd Edition*

Caregiving Sourcebook

Basic Consumer Health Information for Caregivers, Including a Profile of Caregivers, Caregiving Responsibilities and Concerns, Tips for Specific Conditions, Care Environments, and the Effects of Caregiving

Along with Facts about Legal Issues, Financial Information, and Future Planning, a Glossary, and a Listing of Additional Resources

Edited by Joyce Brennfleck Shannon. 600 pages. 2001. 0-7808-0331-0. $78.

Colds, Flu & Other Common Ailments Sourcebook

Basic Consumer Health Information about Common Ailments and Injuries, Including Colds, Coughs, the Flu, Sinus Problems, Headaches, Fever, Nausea and Vomiting, Menstrual Cramps, Diarrhea, Constipation, Hemorrhoids, Back Pain, Dandruff, Dry and Itchy Skin, Cuts, Scrapes, Sprains, Bruises, and More

Along with Information about Prevention, Self-Care, Choosing a Doctor, Over-the-Counter Medications, Folk Remedies, and Alternative Therapies, and Including a Glossary of Important Terms and a Directory of Resources for Further Help and Information

Edited by Chad T. Kimball. 638 pages. 2001. 0-7808-0435-X. $78.

Communication Disorders Sourcebook

Basic Information about Deafness and Hearing Loss, Speech and Language Disorders, Voice Disorders, Balance and Vestibular Disorders, and Disorders of Smell, Taste, and Touch

Edited by Linda M. Ross. 533 pages. 1996. 0-7808-0077-X. $78.

"This is skillfully edited and is a welcome resource for the layperson. It should be found in every public and medical library." — *Booklist Health Sciences Supplement, American Library Association, Oct '97*

Congenital Disorders Sourcebook

Basic Information about Disorders Acquired during Gestation, Including Spina Bifida, Hydrocephalus, Cerebral Palsy, Heart Defects, Craniofacial Abnormalities, Fetal Alcohol Syndrome, and More

Along with Current Treatment Options and Statistical Data

Edited by Karen Bellenir. 607 pages. 1997. 0-7808-0205-5. $78.

"Recommended reference source."
— *Booklist, American Library Association, Oct '97*

SEE ALSO *Pregnancy & Birth Sourcebook*

Consumer Issues in Health Care Sourcebook

Basic Information about Health Care Fundamentals and Related Consumer Issues, Including Exams and Screening Tests, Physician Specialties, Choosing a Doctor, Using Prescription and Over-the-Counter Medications Safely, Avoiding Health Scams, Managing Common Health Risks in the Home, Care Options for Chronically or Terminally Ill Patients, and a List of Resources for Obtaining Help and Further Information

Edited by Karen Bellenir. 618 pages. 1998. 0-7808-0221-7. $78.

"Both public and academic libraries will want to have a copy in their collection for readers who are interested in self-education on health issues."
— American Reference Books Annual, 2000

"The editor has researched the literature from government agencies and others, saving readers the time and effort of having to do the research themselves. Recommended for public libraries."
— Reference and User Services Quarterly, American Library Association, Spring '99

"Recommended reference source."
— Booklist, American Library Association, Dec '98

∎

Contagious & Non-Contagious Infectious Diseases Sourcebook

Basic Information about Contagious Diseases like Measles, Polio, Hepatitis B, and Infectious Mononucleosis, and Non-Contagious Infectious Diseases like Tetanus and Toxic Shock Syndrome, and Diseases Occurring as Secondary Infections Such as Shingles and Reye Syndrome

Along with Vaccination, Prevention, and Treatment Information, and a Section Describing Emerging Infectious Disease Threats

Edited by Karen Bellenir and Peter D. Dresser. 566 pages. 1996. 0-7808-0075-3. $78.

∎

Death & Dying Sourcebook

Basic Consumer Health Information for the Layperson about End-of-Life Care and Related Ethical and Legal Issues, Including Chief Causes of Death, Autopsies, Pain Management for the Terminally Ill, Life Support Systems, Insurance, Euthanasia, Assisted Suicide, Hospice Programs, Living Wills, Funeral Planning, Counseling, Mourning, Organ Donation, and Physician Training

Along with Statistical Data, a Glossary, and Listings of Sources for Further Help and Information

Edited by Annemarie S. Muth. 641 pages. 1999. 0-7808-0230-6. $78.

"Public libraries, medical libraries, and academic libraries will all find this sourcebook a useful addition to their collections."
— American Reference Books Annual, 2001

"An extremely useful resource for those concerned with death and dying in the United States."
— Respiratory Care, Nov '00

"Recommended reference source."
— Booklist, American Library Association, Aug '00

"This book is a definite must for all those involved in end-of-life care." — Doody's Review Service, 2000

∎

Diabetes Sourcebook, 1st Edition

Basic Information about Insulin-Dependent and Non-insulin-Dependent Diabetes Mellitus, Gestational Diabetes, and Diabetic Complications, Symptoms, Treatment, and Research Results, Including Statistics on Prevalence, Morbidity, and Mortality

Along with Source Listings for Further Help and Information

Edited by Karen Bellenir and Peter D. Dresser. 827 pages. 1994. 1-55888-751-2. $78.

". . . very informative and understandable for the layperson without being simplistic. It provides a comprehensive overview for laypersons who want a general understanding of the disease or who want to focus on various aspects of the disease."
— Bulletin of the Medical Library Association, Jan '96

∎

Diabetes Sourcebook, 2nd Edition

Basic Consumer Health Information about Type 1 Diabetes (Insulin-Dependent or Juvenile-Onset Diabetes), Type 2 (Noninsulin-Dependent or Adult-Onset Diabetes), Gestational Diabetes, and Related Disorders, Including Diabetes Prevalence Data, Management Issues, the Role of Diet and Exercise in Controlling Diabetes, Insulin and Other Diabetes Medicines, and Complications of Diabetes Such as Eye Diseases, Periodontal Disease, Amputation, and End-Stage Renal Disease

Along with Reports on Current Research Initiatives, a Glossary, and Resource Listings for Further Help and Information

Edited by Karen Bellenir. 688 pages. 1998. 0-7808-0224-1. $78.

"This comprehensive book is an excellent addition for high school, academic, medical, and public libraries. This volume is highly recommended."
— American Reference Books Annual, 2000

"An invaluable reference." — Library Journal, May '00

Selected as one of the 250 "Best Health Sciences Books of 1999." — Doody's Rating Service, Mar-Apr 2000

"Recommended reference source."
— Booklist, American Library Association, Feb '99

". . . provides reliable mainstream medical information . . . belongs on the shelves of any library with a consumer health collection." — E-Streams, Sep '99

"Provides useful information for the general public."
— Healthlines, University of Michigan Health Management Research Center, Sep/Oct '99

Diet & Nutrition Sourcebook, 1st Edition

Basic Information about Nutrition, Including the Dietary Guidelines for Americans, the Food Guide Pyramid, and Their Applications in Daily Diet, Nutritional Advice for Specific Age Groups, Current Nutritional Issues and Controversies, the New Food Label and How to Use It to Promote Healthy Eating, and Recent Developments in Nutritional Research

Edited by Dan R. Harris. 662 pages. 1996. 0-7808-0084-2. $78.

"Useful reference as a food and nutrition sourcebook for the general consumer." — *Booklist Health Sciences Supplement, American Library Association, Oct '97*

"Recommended for public libraries and medical libraries that receive general information requests on nutrition. It is readable and will appeal to those interested in learning more about healthy dietary practices." — *Medical Reference Services Quarterly, Fall '97*

"An abundance of medical and social statistics is translated into readable information geared toward the general reader." — *Bookwatch, Mar '97*

"With dozens of questionable diet books on the market, it is so refreshing to find a reliable and factual reference book. Recommended to aspiring professionals, librarians, and others seeking and giving reliable dietary advice. An excellent compilation." — *Choice, Association of College and Research Libraries, Feb '97*

SEE ALSO *Digestive Diseases & Disorders Sourcebook, Gastrointestinal Diseases & Disorders Sourcebook*

Diet & Nutrition Sourcebook, 2nd Edition

Basic Consumer Health Information about Dietary Guidelines, Recommended Daily Intake Values, Vitamins, Minerals, Fiber, Fat, Weight Control, Dietary Supplements, and Food Additives

Along with Special Sections on Nutrition Needs throughout Life and Nutrition for People with Such Specific Medical Concerns as Allergies, High Blood Cholesterol, Hypertension, Diabetes, Celiac Disease, Seizure Disorders, Phenylketonuria (PKU), Cancer, and Eating Disorders, and Including Reports on Current Nutrition Research and Source Listings for Additional Help and Information

Edited by Karen Bellenir. 650 pages. 1999. 0-7808-0228-4. $78.

"This book is an excellent source of basic diet and nutrition information." — *Booklist Health Sciences Supplement, American Library Association, Dec '00*

"This reference document should be in any public library, but it would be a very good guide for beginning students in the health sciences. If the other books in this publisher's series are as good as this, they should all be in the health sciences collections." — *American Reference Books Annual, 2000*

"This book is an excellent general nutrition reference for consumers who desire to take an active role in their health care for prevention. Consumers of all ages who select this book can feel confident they are receiving current and accurate information." — *Journal of Nutrition for the Elderly, Vol. 19, No. 4, '00*

"Recommended reference source." — *Booklist, American Library Association, Dec '99*

SEE ALSO *Digestive Diseases & Disorders Sourcebook, Gastrointestinal Diseases & Disorders Sourcebook*

Digestive Diseases & Disorders Sourcebook

Basic Consumer Health Information about Diseases and Disorders that Impact the Upper and Lower Digestive System, Including Celiac Disease, Constipation, Crohn's Disease, Cyclic Vomiting Syndrome, Diarrhea, Diverticulosis and Diverticulitis, Gallstones, Heartburn, Hemorrhoids, Hernias, Indigestion (Dyspepsia), Irritable Bowel Syndrome, Lactose Intolerance, Ulcers, and More

Along with Information about Medications and Other Treatments, Tips for Maintaining a Healthy Digestive Tract, a Glossary, and Directory of Digestive Diseases Organizations

Edited by Karen Bellenir. 335 pages. 1999. 0-7808-0327-2. $48.

"This title would be an excellent addition to all public or patient-research libraries." — *American Reference Books Annual, 2001*

"This title is recommended for public, hospital, and health sciences libraries with consumer health collections." — *E-Streams, Jul-Aug '00*

"Recommended reference source." — *Booklist, American Library Association, May '00*

SEE ALSO *Diet & Nutrition Sourcebook, 1st and 2nd Editions, Gastrointestinal Diseases & Disorders Sourcebook*

Disabilities Sourcebook

Basic Consumer Health Information about Physical and Psychiatric Disabilities, Including Descriptions of Major Causes of Disability, Assistive and Adaptive Aids, Workplace Issues, and Accessibility Concerns

Along with Information about the Americans with Disabilities Act, a Glossary, and Resources for Additional Help and Information

Edited by Dawn D. Matthews. 616 pages. 2000. 0-7808-0389-2. $78.

"A much needed addition to the Omnigraphics *Health Reference Series*. A current reference work to provide people with disabilities, their families, caregivers or those who work with them, a broad range of information in one volume, has not been available until now. . . . It is recommended for all public and academic library reference collections." — *E-Streams, May '01*

"An excellent source book in easy-to-read format covering many current topics; highly recommended for all libraries." — *Choice, Association of College and Research Libraries, Jan '01*

"Recommended reference source." —*Booklist, American Library Association, Jul '00*

"An involving, invaluable handbook." — *The Bookwatch, May '00*

■

Domestic Violence & Child Abuse Sourcebook

Basic Consumer Health Information about Spousal/ Partner, Child, Sibling, Parent, and Elder Abuse, Covering Physical, Emotional, and Sexual Abuse, Teen Dating Violence, and Stalking; Includes Information about Hotlines, Safe Houses, Safety Plans, and Other Resources for Support and Assistance, Community Initiatives, and Reports on Current Directions in Research and Treatment

Along with a Glossary, Sources for Further Reading, and Governmental and Non-Governmental Organizations Contact Information

Edited by Helene Henderson. 1,064 pages. 2000. 0-7808-0235-7. $78.

"Recommended reference source." — *Booklist, American Library Association, Apr '01*

"Important pick for college-level health reference libraries." — *The Bookwatch, Mar '01*

"Because this problem is so widespread and because this book includes a lot of issues within one volume, this work is recommended for all public libraries." — *American Reference Books Annual, 2001*

■

Drug Abuse Sourcebook

Basic Consumer Health Information about Illicit Substances of Abuse and the Diversion of Prescription Medications, Including Depressants, Hallucinogens, Inhalants, Marijuana, Narcotics, Stimulants, and Anabolic Steroids

Along with Facts about Related Health Risks, Treatment Issues, and Substance Abuse Prevention Programs, a Glossary of Terms, Statistical Data, and Directories of Hotline Services, Self-Help Groups, and Organizations Able to Provide Further Information

Edited by Karen Bellenir. 629 pages. 2000. 0-7808-0242-X. $78.

"Containing a wealth of information, this book will be useful to the college student just beginning to explore the topic of substance abuse. This resource belongs in libraries that serve a lower-division undergraduate or community college clientele as well as the general public." — *Choice, Association of College and Research Libraries, Jun '01*

"Recommended reference source." — *Booklist, American Library Association, Feb '01*

"Highly recommended." — *The Bookwatch, Jan '01*

"Even though there is a plethora of books on drug abuse, this volume is recommended for school, public, and college libraries." —*American Reference Books Annual, 2001*

SEE ALSO Alcoholism Sourcebook, Substance Abuse Sourcebook

■

Ear, Nose & Throat Disorders Sourcebook

Basic Information about Disorders of the Ears, Nose, Sinus Cavities, Pharynx, and Larynx, Including Ear Infections, Tinnitus, Vestibular Disorders, Allergic and Non-Allergic Rhinitis, Sore Throats, Tonsillitis, and Cancers That Affect the Ears, Nose, Sinuses, and Throat

Along with Reports on Current Research Initiatives, a Glossary of Related Medical Terms, and a Directory of Sources for Further Help and Information

Edited by Karen Bellenir and Linda M. Shin. 576 pages. 1998. 0-7808-0206-3. $78.

"Overall, this sourcebook is helpful for the consumer seeking information on ENT issues. It is recommended for public libraries." —*American Reference Books Annual, 1999*

"Recommended reference source." —*Booklist, American Library Association, Dec '98*

■

Eating Disorders Sourcebook

Basic Consumer Health Information about Eating Disorders, Including Information about Anorexia Nervosa, Bulimia Nervosa, Binge Eating, Body Dysmorphic Disorder, Pica, Laxative Abuse, and Night Eating Syndrome

Along with Information about Causes, Adverse Effects, and Treatment and Prevention Issues, and Featuring a Section on Concerns Specific to Children and Adolescents, a Glossary, and Resources for Further Help and Information

Edited by Dawn D. Matthews. 322 pages. 2001. 0-7808-0335-3. $78.

■

Endocrine & Metabolic Disorders Sourcebook

Basic Information for the Layperson about Pancreatic and Insulin-Related Disorders Such as Pancreatitis, Diabetes, and Hypoglycemia; Adrenal Gland Disorders Such as Cushing's Syndrome, Addison's Disease, and Congenital Adrenal Hyperplasia; Pituitary Gland Disorders Such as Growth Hormone Deficiency, Acromegaly, and Pituitary Tumors; Thyroid Disorders Such as Hypothyroidism, Graves' Disease, Hashimoto's Disease, and Goiter; Hyperparathyroidism; and Other Diseases and Syndromes of Hormone Imbalance or Metabolic Dysfunction

Along with Reports on Current Research Initiatives

Edited by Linda M. Shin. 574 pages. 1998. 0-7808-0207-1. $78.

"Omnigraphics has produced another needed resource for health information consumers."
—*American Reference Books Annual, 2000*

"Recommended reference source."
—*Booklist, American Library Association, Dec '98*

Environmentally Induced Disorders Sourcebook

Basic Information about Diseases and Syndromes Linked to Exposure to Pollutants and Other Substances in Outdoor and Indoor Environments Such as Lead, Asbestos, Formaldehyde, Mercury, Emissions, Noise, and More

Edited by Allan R. Cook. 620 pages. 1997. 0-7808-0083-4. $78.

"Recommended reference source."
—*Booklist, American Library Association, Sep '98*

"This book will be a useful addition to anyone's library." —*Choice Health Sciences Supplement, Association of College and Research Libraries, May '98*

". . . a good survey of numerous environmentally induced physical disorders . . . a useful addition to anyone's library."
—*Doody's Health Sciences Book Reviews, Jan '98*

". . . provide[s] introductory information from the best authorities around. Since this volume covers topics that potentially affect everyone, it will surely be one of the most frequently consulted volumes in the *Health Reference Series*." —*Rettig on Reference, Nov '97*

Ethnic Diseases Sourcebook

Basic Consumer Health Information for Ethnic and Racial Minority Groups in the United States, Including General Health Indicators and Behaviors, Ethnic Diseases, Genetic Testing, the Impact of Chronic Diseases, Women's Health, Mental Health Issues, and Preventive Health Care Services

Along with a Glossary and a Listing of Additional Resources

Edited by Joyce Brennfleck Shannon. 664 pages. 2001. 0-7808-0336-1. $78.

Family Planning Sourcebook

Basic Consumer Health Information about Planning for Pregnancy and Contraception, Including Traditional Methods, Barrier Methods, Hormonal Methods, Permanent Methods, Future Methods, Emergency Contraception, and Birth Control Choices for Women at Each Stage of Life

Along with Statistics, a Glossary, and Sources of Additional Information

Edited by Amy Marcaccio Keyzer. 520 pages. 2001. 0-7808-0379-5. $78.

SEE ALSO *Pregnancy & Birth Sourcebook*

Fitness & Exercise Sourcebook, 1st Edition

Basic Information on Fitness and Exercise, Including Fitness Activities for Specific Age Groups, Exercise for People with Specific Medical Conditions, How to Begin a Fitness Program in Running, Walking, Swimming, Cycling, and Other Athletic Activities, and Recent Research in Fitness and Exercise

Edited by Dan R. Harris. 663 pages. 1996. 0-7808-0186-5. $78.

"A good resource for general readers."
—*Choice, Association of College and Research Libraries, Nov '97*

"The perennial popularity of the topic . . . make this an appealing selection for public libraries."
—*Rettig on Reference, Jun/Jul '97*

Fitness & Exercise Sourcebook, 2nd Edition

Basic Consumer Health Information about the Fundamentals of Fitness and Exercise, Including How to Begin and Maintain a Fitness Program, Fitness as a Lifestyle, the Link between Fitness and Diet, Advice for Specific Groups of People, Exercise as It Relates to Specific Medical Conditions, and Recent Research in Fitness and Exercise

Along with a Glossary of Important Terms and Resources for Additional Help and Information

Edited by Kristen M. Gledhill. 646 pages. 2001. 0-7808-0334-5. $78.

Food & Animal Borne Diseases Sourcebook

Basic Information about Diseases That Can Be Spread to Humans through the Ingestion of Contaminated Food or Water or by Contact with Infected Animals and Insects, Such as Botulism, E. Coli, Hepatitis A, Trichinosis, Lyme Disease, and Rabies

Along with Information Regarding Prevention and Treatment Methods, and Including a Special Section for International Travelers Describing Diseases Such as Cholera, Malaria, Travelers' Diarrhea, and Yellow Fever, and Offering Recommendations for Avoiding Illness

Edited by Karen Bellenir and Peter D. Dresser. 535 pages. 1995. 0-7808-0033-8. $78.

"Targeting general readers and providing them with a single, comprehensive source of information on selected topics, this book continues, with the excellent caliber of its predecessors, to catalog topical information on health matters of general interest. Readable and thorough, this valuable resource is highly recommended for all libraries."
—*Academic Library Book Review, Summer '96*

"A comprehensive collection of authoritative information." —*Emergency Medical Services, Oct '95*

Food Safety Sourcebook

Basic Consumer Health Information about the Safe Handling of Meat, Poultry, Seafood, Eggs, Fruit Juices, and Other Food Items, and Facts about Pesticides, Drinking Water, Food Safety Overseas, and the Onset, Duration, and Symptoms of Foodborne Illnesses, Including Types of Pathogenic Bacteria, Parasitic Protozoa, Worms, Viruses, and Natural Toxins

Along with the Role of the Consumer, the Food Handler, and the Government in Food Safety; a Glossary, and Resources for Additional Help and Information

Edited by Dawn D. Matthews. 339 pages. 1999. 0-7808-0326-4. $48.

"**This book is recommended for public libraries and universities with home economic and food science programs.**"
— *E-Streams, Nov '00*

"**This book takes the complex issues of food safety and foodborne pathogens and presents them in an easily understood manner. [It does] an excellent job of covering a large and often confusing topic.**"
— *American Reference Books Annual, 2000*

"**Recommended reference source.**"
— *Booklist, American Library Association, May '00*

Forensic Medicine Sourcebook

Basic Consumer Information for the Layperson about Forensic Medicine, Including Crime Scene Investigation, Evidence Collection and Analysis, Expert Testimony, Computer-Aided Criminal Identification, Digital Imaging in the Courtroom, DNA Profiling, Accident Reconstruction, Autopsies, Ballistics, Drugs and Explosives Detection, Latent Fingerprints, Product Tampering, and Questioned Document Examination

Along with Statistical Data, a Glossary of Forensics Terminology, and Listings of Sources for Further Help and Information

Edited by Annemarie S. Muth. 574 pages. 1999. 0-7808-0232-2. $78.

"**Given the expected widespread interest in its content and its easy to read style, this book is recommended for most public and all college and university libraries.**"
— *E-Streams, Feb '01*

"**There are several items that make this book attractive to consumers who are seeking certain forensic data. . . . This is a useful current source for those seeking general forensic medical answers.**"
— *American Reference Books Annual, 2000*

"**Recommended for public libraries.**"
— *Reference & User Services Quarterly, American Library Association, Spring 2000*

"**Recommended reference source.**"
— *Booklist, American Library Association, Feb '00*

"**A wealth of information, useful statistics, references are up-to-date and extremely complete. This wonderful collection of data will help students who are interested in a career in any type of forensic field. It is a great**

resource for attorneys who need information about types of expert witnesses needed in a particular case. It also offers useful information for fiction and nonfiction writers whose work involves a crime. A fascinating compilation. All levels.**"
— *Choice, Association of College and Research Libraries, Jan 2000*

Gastrointestinal Diseases & Disorders Sourcebook

Basic Information about Gastroesophageal Reflux Disease (Heartburn), Ulcers, Diverticulosis, Irritable Bowel Syndrome, Crohn's Disease, Ulcerative Colitis, Diarrhea, Constipation, Lactose Intolerance, Hemorrhoids, Hepatitis, Cirrhosis, and Other Digestive Problems, Featuring Statistics, Descriptions of Symptoms, and Current Treatment Methods of Interest for Persons Living with Upper and Lower Gastrointestinal Maladies

Edited by Linda M. Ross. 413 pages. 1996. 0-7808-0078-8. $78.

"**. . . very readable form. The successful editorial work that brought this material together into a useful and understandable reference makes accessible to all readers information that can help them more effectively understand and obtain help for digestive tract problems.**"
— *Choice, Association of College and Research Libraries, Feb '97*

SEE ALSO *Diet & Nutrition Sourcebook, 1st and 2nd Editions, Digestive Diseases & Disorders Sourcebook*

Genetic Disorders Sourcebook, 1st Edition

Basic Information about Heritable Diseases and Disorders Such as Down Syndrome, PKU, Hemophilia, Von Willebrand Disease, Gaucher Disease, Tay-Sachs Disease, and Sickle-Cell Disease, Along with Information about Genetic Screening, Gene Therapy, Home Care, and Including Source Listings for Further Help and Information on More Than 300 Disorders

Edited by Karen Bellenir. 642 pages. 1996. 0-7808-0034-6. $78.

"**Recommended for undergraduate libraries or libraries that serve the public.**"
— *Science & Technology Libraries, Vol. 18, No. 1, '99*

"**Provides essential medical information to both the general public and those diagnosed with a serious or fatal genetic disease or disorder.**"
— *Choice, Association of College and Research Libraries, Jan '97*

"**Geared toward the lay public. It would be well placed in all public libraries and in those hospital and medical libraries in which access to genetic references is limited.**" — *Doody's Health Sciences Book Review, Oct '96*

598

Genetic Disorders Sourcebook, 2nd Edition

Basic Consumer Health Information about Hereditary Diseases and Disorders, Including Cystic Fibrosis, Down Syndrome, Hemophilia, Huntington's Disease, Sickle Cell Anemia, and More; Facts about Genes, Gene Research and Therapy, Genetic Screening, Ethics of Gene Testing, Genetic Counseling, and Advice on Coping and Caring

Along with a Glossary of Genetic Terminology and a Resource List for Help, Support, and Further Information

Edited by Kathy Massimini. 768 pages. 2001. 0-7808-0241-1. $78.

"Recommended for public libraries and medical and hospital libraries with consumer health collections."
— *E-Streams, May '01*

"Recommended reference source."
— *Booklist, American Library Association, Apr '01*

"Important pick for college-level health reference libraries." — *The Bookwatch, Mar '01*

Head Trauma Sourcebook

Basic Information for the Layperson about Open-Head and Closed-Head Injuries, Treatment Advances, Recovery, and Rehabilitation

Along with Reports on Current Research Initiatives

Edited by Karen Bellenir. 414 pages. 1997. 0-7808-0208-X. $78.

Health Insurance Sourcebook

Basic Information about Managed Care Organizations, Traditional Fee-for-Service Insurance, Insurance Portability and Pre-Existing Conditions Clauses, Medicare, Medicaid, Social Security, and Military Health Care

Along with Information about Insurance Fraud

Edited by Wendy Wilcox. 530 pages. 1997. 0-7808-0222-5. $78.

"Particularly useful because it brings much of this information together in one volume. This book will be a handy reference source in the health sciences library, hospital library, college and university library, and medium to large public library."
— *Medical Reference Services Quarterly, Fall '98*

Awarded "Books of the Year Award"
— *American Journal of Nursing, 1997*

"The layout of the book is particularly helpful as it provides easy access to reference material. A most useful addition to the vast amount of information about health insurance. The use of data from U.S. government agencies is most commendable. Useful in a library or learning center for healthcare professional students."
— *Doody's Health Sciences Book Reviews, Nov '97*

Health Reference Series Cumulative Index 1999

A Comprehensive Index to the Individual Volumes of the Health Reference Series, Including a Subject Index, Name Index, Organization Index, and Publication Index

Along with a Master List of Acronyms and Abbreviations

Edited by Edward J. Prucha, Anne Holmes, and Robert Rudnick. 990 pages. 2000. 0-7808-0382-5. $78.

"This volume will be most helpful in libraries that have a relatively complete collection of the Health Reference Series."
— *American Reference Books Annual, 2001*

"Essential for collections that hold any of the numerous *Health Reference Series* titles."
— *Choice, Association of College and Research Libraries, Nov '00*

Healthy Aging Sourcebook

Basic Consumer Health Information about Maintaining Health through the Aging Process, Including Advice on Nutrition, Exercise, and Sleep, Help in Making Decisions about Midlife Issues and Retirement, and Guidance Concerning Practical and Informed Choices in Health Consumerism

Along with Data Concerning the Theories of Aging, Different Experiences in Aging by Minority Groups, and Facts about Aging Now and Aging in the Future; and Featuring a Glossary, a Guide to Consumer Help, Additional Suggested Reading, and Practical Resource Directory

Edited by Jenifer Swanson. 536 pages. 1999. 0-7808-0390-6. $78.

"Recommended reference source."
— *Booklist, American Library Association, Feb '00*

SEE ALSO *Physical & Mental Issues in Aging Sourcebook*

Healthy Heart Sourcebook for Women

Basic Consumer Health Information about Cardiac Issues Specific to Women, Including Facts about Major Risk Factors and Prevention, Treatment and Control Strategies, and Important Dietary Issues

Along with a Special Section Regarding the Pros and Cons of Hormone Replacement Therapy and Its Impact on Heart Health, and Additional Help, Including Recipes, a Glossary, and a Directory of Resources

Edited by Dawn D. Matthews. 336 pages. 2000. 0-7808-0329-9. $48.

"A good reference source and recommended for all public, academic, medical, and hospital libraries."
— *Medical Reference Services Quarterly, Summer '01*

599

"Because of the lack of information specific to women on this topic, this book is recommended for public libraries and consumer libraries."
—*American Reference Books Annual, 2001*

"Contains very important information about coronary artery disease that all women should know. The information is current and presented in an easy-to-read format. The book will make a good addition to any library." — *American Medical Writers Association Journal, Summer '00*

"Important, basic reference."
—*Reviewer's Bookwatch, Jul '00*

SEE ALSO *Cardiovascular Diseases & Disorders Sourcebook, 1st Edition, Heart Diseases & Disorders Sourcebook, 2nd Edition, Women's Health Concerns Sourcebook*

Heart Diseases & Disorders Sourcebook, 2nd Edition

Basic Consumer Health Information about Heart Attacks, Angina, Rhythm Disorders, Heart Failure, Valve Disease, Congenital Heart Disorders, and More, Including Descriptions of Surgical Procedures and Other Interventions, Medications, Cardiac Rehabilitation, Risk Identification, and Prevention Tips

Along with Statistical Data, Reports on Current Research Initiatives, a Glossary of Cardiovascular Terms, and Resource Directory

Edited by Karen Bellenir. 612 pages. 2000. 0-7808-0238-1. $78.

"This work stands out as an imminently accessible resource for the general public. It is recommended for the reference and circulating shelves of school, public, and academic libraries."
—*American Reference Books Annual, 2001*

"Recommended reference source."
—*Booklist, American Library Association, Dec '00*

"Provides comprehensive coverage of matters related to the heart. This title is recommended for health sciences and public libraries with consumer health collections."
—*E-Streams, Oct '00*

SEE ALSO *Cardiovascular Diseases & Disorders Sourcebook, 1st Edition, Healthy Heart Sourcebook for Women*

Household Safety Sourcebook

Basic Consumer Health Information about Household Safety, Including Information about Poisons, Chemicals, Fire, and Water Hazards in the Home

Along with Advice about the Safe Use of Home Maintenance Equipment, Choosing Toys and Nursery Furniture, Holiday and Recreation Safety, a Glossary, and Resources for Further Help and Information

Edited by Dawn D. Matthews. 606 pages. 2001. 0-7808-0338-8. $78.

Immune System Disorders Sourcebook

Basic Information about Lupus, Multiple Sclerosis, Guillain-Barré Syndrome, Chronic Granulomatous Disease, and More

Along with Statistical and Demographic Data and Reports on Current Research Initiatives

Edited by Allan R. Cook. 608 pages. 1997. 0-7808-0209-8. $78.

Infant & Toddler Health Sourcebook

Basic Consumer Health Information about the Physical and Mental Development of Newborns, Infants, and Toddlers, Including Neonatal Concerns, Nutrition Recommendations, Immunization Schedules, Common Pediatric Disorders, Assessments and Milestones, Safety Tips, and Advice for Parents and Other Caregivers

Along with a Glossary of Terms and Resource Listings for Additional Help

Edited by Jenifer Swanson. 585 pages. 2000. 0-7808-0246-2. $78.

"As a reference for the general public, this would be useful in any library." —*E-Streams, May '01*

"Recommended reference source."
—*Booklist, American Library Association, Feb '01*

"This is a good source for general use."
—*American Reference Books Annual, 2001*

Kidney & Urinary Tract Diseases & Disorders Sourcebook

Basic Information about Kidney Stones, Urinary Incontinence, Bladder Disease, End Stage Renal Disease, Dialysis, and More

Along with Statistical and Demographic Data and Reports on Current Research Initiatives

Edited by Linda M. Ross. 602 pages. 1997. 0-7808-0079-6. $78.

Learning Disabilities Sourcebook

Basic Information about Disorders Such as Dyslexia, Visual and Auditory Processing Deficits, Attention Deficit/Hyperactivity Disorder, and Autism

Along with Statistical and Demographic Data, Reports on Current Research Initiatives, an Explanation of the Assessment Process, and a Special Section for Adults with Learning Disabilities

Edited by Linda M. Shin. 579 pages. 1998. 0-7808-0210-1. $78.

Liver Disorders Sourcebook

Basic Consumer Health Information about the Liver and How It Works; Liver Diseases, Including Cancer, Cirrhosis, Hepatitis, and Toxic and Drug Related Diseases; Tips for Maintaining a Healthy Liver; Laboratory Tests, Radiology Tests, and Facts about Liver Transplantation

Along with a Section on Support Groups, a Glossary, and Resource Listings

Edited by Joyce Brennfleck Shannon. 591 pages. 2000. 0-7808-0383-3. $78.

Medical Tests Sourcebook

Basic Consumer Health Information about Medical Tests, Including Periodic Health Exams, General Screening Tests, Tests You Can Do at Home, Findings of the U.S. Preventive Services Task Force, X-ray and Radiology Tests, Electrical Tests, Tests of Blood and Other Body Fluids and Tissues, Scope Tests, Lung Tests, Genetic Tests, Pregnancy Tests, Newborn Screening Tests, Sexually Transmitted Disease Tests, and Computer Aided Diagnoses

Along with a Section on Paying for Medical Tests, a Glossary, and Resource Listings

Edited by Joyce Brennfleck Shannon. 691 pages. 1999. 0-7808-0243-8. $78.

Men's Health Concerns Sourcebook

Basic Information about Health Issues That Affect Men, Featuring Facts about the Top Causes of Death in Men, Including Heart Disease, Stroke, Cancers, Prostate Disorders, Chronic Obstructive Pulmonary Disease, Pneumonia and Influenza, Human Immunodeficiency Virus and Acquired Immune Deficiency Syndrome, Diabetes Mellitus, Stress, Suicide, Accidents and Homicides; and Facts about Common Concerns for Men, Including Impotence, Contraception, Circumcision, Sleep Disorders, Snoring, Hair Loss, Diet, Nutrition, Exercise, Kidney and Urological Disorders, and Backaches

Edited by Allan R. Cook. 738 pages. 1998. 0-7808-0212-8. $78.

Mental Health Disorders Sourcebook, 1st Edition

Basic Information about Schizophrenia, Depression, Bipolar Disorder, Panic Disorder, Obsessive-Compulsive Disorder, Phobias and Other Anxiety Disorders, Paranoia and Other Personality Disorders, Eating Disorders, and Sleep Disorders

Along with Information about Treatment and Therapies

Edited by Karen Bellenir. 548 pages. 1995. 0-7808-0040-0. $78.

Mental Health Disorders Sourcebook, 2nd Edition

Basic Consumer Health Information about Anxiety Disorders, Depression and Other Mood Disorders, Eating Disorders, Personality Disorders, Schizophrenia, and More, Including Disease Descriptions, Treatment Options, and Reports on Current Research Initiatives

Along with Statistical Data, Tips for Maintaining Mental Health, a Glossary, and Directory of Sources for Additional Help and Information

Edited by Karen Bellenir. 605 pages. 2000. 0-7808-0240-3. $78.

Mental Retardation Sourcebook

Basic Consumer Health Information about Mental Retardation and Its Causes, Including Down Syndrome, Fetal Alcohol Syndrome, Fragile X Syndrome, Genetic Conditions, Injury, and Environmental Sources

Along with Preventive Strategies, Parenting Issues, Educational Implications, Health Care Needs, Employment and Economic Matters, Legal Issues, a Glossary, and a Resource Listing for Additional Help and Information

Edited by Joyce Brennfleck Shannon. 642 pages. 2000. 0-7808-0377-9. $78.

Obesity Sourcebook

Basic Consumer Health Information about Diseases and Other Problems Associated with Obesity, and Including Facts about Risk Factors, Prevention Issues, and Management Approaches

Along with Statistical and Demographic Data, Information about Special Populations, Research Updates, a Glossary, and Source Listings for Further Help and Information

Edited by Wilma Caldwell and Chad T. Kimball. 376 pages. 2001. 0-7808-0333-7. $48.

Ophthalmic Disorders Sourcebook

Basic Information about Glaucoma, Cataracts, Macular Degeneration, Strabismus, Refractive Disorders, and More

Along with Statistical and Demographic Data and Reports on Current Research Initiatives

Edited by Linda M. Ross. 631 pages. 1996. 0-7808-0081-8. $78.

Oral Health Sourcebook

Basic Information about Diseases and Conditions Affecting Oral Health, Including Cavities, Gum Disease, Dry Mouth, Oral Cancers, Fever Blisters, Canker Sores, Oral Thrush, Bad Breath, Temporomandibular Disorders, and other Craniofacial Syndromes

Along with Statistical Data on the Oral Health of Americans, Oral Hygiene, Emergency First Aid, Information on Treatment Procedures and Methods of Replacing Lost Teeth

Edited by Allan R. Cook. 558 pages. 1997. 0-7808-0082-6. $78.

Osteoporosis Sourcebook

Basic Consumer Health Information about Primary and Secondary Osteoporosis and Juvenile Osteoporosis and Related Conditions, Including Fibrous Dysplasia, Gaucher Disease, Hyperthyroidism, Hypophosphatasia, Myeloma, Osteopetrosis, Osteogenesis Imperfecta, and Paget's Disease

Along with Information about Risk Factors, Treatments, Traditional and Non-Traditional Pain Management, a Glossary of Related Terms, and a Directory of Resources

Edited by Allan R. Cook. 584 pages. 2001. 0-7808-0239-X. $78.

SEE ALSO Women's Health Concerns Sourcebook

■

Pain Sourcebook

Basic Information about Specific Forms of Acute and Chronic Pain, Including Headaches, Back Pain, Muscular Pain, Neuralgia, Surgical Pain, and Cancer Pain

Along with Pain Relief Options Such as Analgesics, Narcotics, Nerve Blocks, Transcutaneous Nerve Stimulation, and Alternative Forms of Pain Control, Including Biofeedback, Imaging, Behavior Modification, and Relaxation Techniques

Edited by Allan R. Cook. 667 pages. 1997. 0-7808-0213-6. $78.

"The text is readable, easily understood, and well indexed. This excellent volume belongs in all patient education libraries, consumer health sections of public libraries, and many personal collections."
— *American Reference Books Annual, 1999*

"A beneficial reference." — *Booklist Health Sciences Supplement, American Library Association, Oct '98*

"The information is basic in terms of scholarship and is appropriate for general readers. Written in journalistic style . . . intended for non-professionals. Quite thorough in its coverage of different pain conditions and summarizes the latest clinical information regarding pain treatment." — *Choice, Association of College and Research Libraries, Jun '98*

"Recommended reference source."
— *Booklist, American Library Association, Mar '98*

■

diatric Cancer Sourcebook

*Consumer Health Information about Leuke-
Brain Tumors, Sarcomas, Lymphomas, and
ncers in Infants, Children, and Adolescents,
Descriptions of Cancers, Treatments, and
tegies*

*uggestions for Parents, Caregivers, and
atives, a Glossary of Cancer Terms, and*

J. Prucha. 587 pages. 1999. 0-7808-

*to all libraries specializing in
y public libraries."
eference Books Annual, 2000*

*urce."
rary Association, Feb '00*

*tion. Recommended for
ce libraries with con-
— E-Streams, Jun '00*

Physical & Mental Issues in Aging Sourcebook

Basic Consumer Health Information on Physical and Mental Disorders Associated with the Aging Process, Including Concerns about Cardiovascular Disease, Pulmonary Disease, Oral Health, Digestive Disorders, Musculoskeletal and Skin Disorders, Metabolic Changes, Sexual and Reproductive Issues, and Changes in Vision, Hearing, and Other Senses

Along with Data about Longevity and Causes of Death, Information on Acute and Chronic Pain, Descriptions of Mental Concerns, a Glossary of Terms, and Resource Listings for Additional Help

Edited by Jenifer Swanson. 660 pages. 1999. 0-7808-0233-0. $78.

"Recommended for public libraries."
— *American Reference Books Annual, 2000*

"This is a treasure of health information for the layperson." — *Choice Health Sciences Supplement, Association of College & Research Libraries, May 2000*

"Recommended reference source."
— *Booklist, American Library Association, Oct '99*

SEE ALSO Healthy Aging Sourcebook

■

Podiatry Sourcebook

Basic Consumer Health Information about Foot Conditions, Diseases, and Injuries, Including Bunions, Corns, Calluses, Athlete's Foot, Plantar Warts, Hammertoes and Clawtoes, Clubfoot, Heel Pain, Gout, and More

Along with Facts about Foot Care, Disease Prevention, Foot Safety, Choosing a Foot Care Specialist, a Glossary of Terms, and Resource Listings for Additional Information

Edited by M. Lisa Weatherford. 380 pages. 2001. 0-7808-0215-2. $78.

■

Pregnancy & Birth Sourcebook

Basic Information about Planning for Pregnancy, Maternal Health, Fetal Growth and Development, Labor and Delivery, Postpartum and Perinatal Care, Pregnancy in Mothers with Special Concerns, and Disorders of Pregnancy, Including Genetic Counseling, Nutrition and Exercise, Obstetrical Tests, Pregnancy Discomfort, Multiple Births, Cesarean Sections, Medical Testing of Newborns, Breastfeeding, Gestational Diabetes, and Ectopic Pregnancy

Edited by Heather E. Aldred. 737 pages. 1997. 0-7808-0216-0. $78.

"A well-organized handbook. Recommended."
— *Choice, Association of College and Research Libraries, Apr '98*

"Recommended reference source."
— *Booklist, American Library Association, Mar '98*

SEE ALSO *Congenital Disorders Sourcebook, Family Planning Sourcebook*

Prostate Cancer Sourcebook

Basic Consumer Health Information about Prostate Cancer, Including Information about the Associated Risk Factors, Detection, Diagnosis, and Treatment of Prostate Cancer

Along with Information on Non-Malignant Prostate Conditions, and Featuring a Section Listing Support and Treatment Centers and a Glossary of Related Terms

Edited by Dawn D. Matthews. 358 pages. 2001. 0-7808-0324-8. $78.

Public Health Sourcebook

Basic Information about Government Health Agencies, Including National Health Statistics and Trends, Healthy People 2000 Program Goals and Objectives, the Centers for Disease Control and Prevention, the Food and Drug Administration, and the National Institutes of Health

Along with Full Contact Information for Each Agency

Edited by Wendy Wilcox. 698 pages. 1998. 0-7808-0220-9. $78.

Reconstructive & Cosmetic Surgery Sourcebook

Basic Consumer Health Information on Cosmetic and Reconstructive Plastic Surgery, Including Statistical Information about Different Surgical Procedures, Things to Consider Prior to Surgery, Plastic Surgery Techniques and Tools, Emotional and Psychological Considerations, and Procedure-Specific Information

Along with a Glossary of Terms and a Listing Resources for Additional Help and Information

Edited by M. Lisa Weatherford. 374 pages. 2001. 0214-4. $48.

Rehabilitation Sourcebook

*Basic Consumer Health Information about Rehabilitation for People Recovering from Heart Surgery, Spinal Cord Injury, Stroke, Orthopedic Impairments, Amputation, Pulmonary Impairments, Traumatic In-*jury, and More, Including Physical Therapy, Occupational Therapy, Speech/ Language Therapy, Massage Therapy, Dance Therapy, Art Therapy, and Recreational Therapy

Along with Information on Assistive and Adaptive Devices, a Glossary, and Resources for Additional Help and Information

Edited by Dawn D. Matthews. 531 pages. 1999. 0-7808-0236-5. $78.

Respiratory Diseases & Disorders Sourcebook

Basic Information about Respiratory Diseases and Disorders, Including Asthma, Cystic Fibrosis, Pneumonia, the Common Cold, Influenza, and Others, Featuring Facts about the Respiratory System, Statistical and Demographic Data, Treatments, Self-Help Management Suggestions, and Current Research Initiatives

Edited by Allan R. Cook and Peter D. Dresser. 771 pages. 1995. 0-7808-0037-0. $78.

Sexually Transmitted Diseases Sourcebook, 2nd Edition

Basic Consumer Health Information about Sexually Transmitted Diseases, Including Information on the Diagnosis and Treatment of Chlamydia, Gonorrhea, Hepatitis, Herpes, HIV, Mononucleosis, Syphilis, and Others

Along with Information on Prevention, Such as Condom Use, Vaccines, and STD Education; And Featuring a Section on Issues Related to Youth and Adolescents, a Glossary, and Resources for Additional Help and Information

Edited by Dawn D. Matthews. 538 pages. 2001. 0-7808-0249-7. $78.

"Recommended pick both for specialty health library collections and any general consumer health reference collection." — *The Bookwatch, Apr '01*

"Recommended reference source."
— *Booklist, American Library Association, Apr '01*

Skin Disorders Sourcebook

Basic Information about Common Skin and Scalp Conditions Caused by Aging, Allergies, Immune Reactions, Sun Exposure, Infectious Organisms, Parasites, Cosmetics, and Skin Traumas, Including Abrasions, Cuts, and Pressure Sores

Along with Information on Prevention and Treatment

Edited by Allan R. Cook. 647 pages. 1997. 0-7808-0080-X. $78.

". . . comprehensive, easily read reference book."
— *Doody's Health Sciences Book Reviews, Oct '97*

***SEE ALSO** Burns Sourcebook*

Sleep Disorders Sourcebook

Basic Consumer Health Information about Sleep and Its Disorders, Including Insomnia, Sleepwalking, Sleep Apnea, Restless Leg Syndrome, and Narcolepsy

Along with Data about Shiftwork and Its Effects, Information on the Societal Costs of Sleep Deprivation, Descriptions of Treatment Options, a Glossary of Terms, and Resource Listings for Additional Help

Edited by Jenifer Swanson. 439 pages. 1998. 0-7808-0234-9. $78.

"This text will complement any home or medical library. It is user-friendly and ideal for the adult reader."
— *American Reference Books Annual, 2000*

"Recommended reference source."
— *Booklist, American Library Association, Feb '99*

"A useful resource that provides accurate, relevant, and accessible information on sleep to the general public. Health care providers who deal with sleep disorders patients may also find it helpful in being prepared to answer some of the questions patients ask."
— *Respiratory Care, Jul '99*

Sports Injuries Sourcebook

Basic Consumer Health Information about Common Sports Injuries, Prevention of Injury in Specific Sports, Tips for Training, and Rehabilitation from Injury

Along with Information about Special Concerns for Children, Young Girls in Athletic Training Programs, Senior Athletes, and Women Athletes, and a Directory of Resources for Further Help and Information

Edited by Heather E. Aldred. 624 pages. 1999. 0-7808-0218-7. $78.

"Public libraries and undergraduate academic libraries will find this book useful for its nontechnical language." — *American Reference Books Annual, 2000*

"While this easy-to-read book is recommended for all libraries, it should prove to be especially useful for public, high school, and academic libraries; certainly it should be on the bookshelf of every school gymnasium." — *E-Streams, Mar '00*

Substance Abuse Sourcebook

Basic Health-Related Information about the Abuse of Legal and Illegal Substances Such as Alcohol, Tobacco, Prescription Drugs, Marijuana, Cocaine, and Heroin; and Including Facts about Substance Abuse Prevention Strategies, Intervention Methods, Treatment and Recovery Programs, and a Section Addressing the Special Problems Related to Substance Abuse during Pregnancy

Edited by Karen Bellenir. 573 pages. 1996. 0-7808-0038-9. $78.

"A valuable addition to any health reference section. Highly recommended."
— *The Book Report, Mar/Apr '97*

". . . a comprehensive collection of substance abuse information that's both highly readable and compact. Families and caregivers of substance abusers will find the information enlightening and helpful, while teachers, social workers and journalists should benefit from the concise format. Recommended."
— *Drug Abuse Update, Winter '96/'97*

***SEE ALSO** Alcoholism Sourcebook, Drug Abuse Sourcebook*

Transplantation Sourcebook

Basic Consumer Health Information about Organ and Tissue Transplantation, Including Physical and Financial Preparations, Procedures and Issues Relating to Specific Solid Organ and Tissue Transplants, Rehabilitation, Pediatric Transplant Information, the Future of Transplantation, and Organ and Tissue Donation

Along with a Glossary and Listings of Additional Resources

Edited by Joyce Brennfleck Shannon. 600 pages. 2001. 0-7808-0322-1. $78.

Traveler's Health Sourcebook

Basic Consumer Health Information for Travelers, Including Physical and Medical Preparations, Transportation Health and Safety, Essential Information about Food and Water, Sun Exposure, Insect and Snake Bites, Camping and Wilderness Medicine, and Travel with Physical or Medical Disabilities

Along with International Travel Tips, Vaccination Recommendations, Geographical Health Issues, Disease Risks, a Glossary, and a Listing of Additional Resources

Edited by Joyce Brennfleck Shannon. 613 pages. 2000. 0-7808-0384-1. $78.

"Recommended reference source."
— *Booklist, American Library Association, Feb '01*

"This book is recommended for any public library, any travel collection, and especially any collection for the physically disabled."
— *American Reference Books Annual, 2001*

■

Women's Health Concerns Sourcebook

Basic Information about Health Issues That Affect Women, Featuring Facts about Menstruation and Other Gynecological Concerns, Including Endometriosis, Fibroids, Menopause, and Vaginitis; Reproductive Concerns, Including Birth Control, Infertility, and Abortion; and Facts about Additional Physical, Emotional, and Mental Health Concerns Prevalent among Women Such as Osteoporosis, Urinary Tract Disorders, Eating Disorders, and Depression

Along with Tips for Maintaining a Healthy Lifestyle

Edited by Heather E. Aldred. 567 pages. 1997. 0-7808-0219-5. $78.

"Handy compilation. There is an impressive range of diseases, devices, disorders, procedures, and other physical and emotional issues covered . . . well organized, illustrated, and indexed." — *Choice, Association of College and Research Libraries, Jan '98*

SEE ALSO *Breast Cancer Sourcebook, Cancer Sourcebook for Women, 1st and 2nd Editions, Healthy Heart Sourcebook for Women, Osteoporosis Sourcebook*

Workplace Health & Safety Sourcebook

Basic Consumer Health Information about Workplace Health and Safety, Including the Effect of Workplace Hazards on the Lungs, Skin, Heart, Ears, Eyes, Brain, Reproductive Organs, Musculoskeletal System, and Other Organs and Body Parts

Along with Information about Occupational Cancer, Personal Protective Equipment, Toxic and Hazardous Chemicals, Child Labor, Stress, and Workplace Violence

Edited by Chad T. Kimball. 626 pages. 2000. 0-7808-0231-4. $78.

"Provides helpful information for primary care physicians and other caregivers interested in occupational medicine. . . . General readers; professionals."
— *Choice, Association of College and Research Libraries, May '01*

"Recommended reference source."
— *Booklist, American Library Association, Feb '01*

"Highly recommended." —*The Bookwatch, Jan '01*

■

Worldwide Health Sourcebook

Basic Information about Global Health Issues, Including Malnutrition, Reproductive Health, Disease Dispersion and Prevention, Emerging Diseases, Risky Health Behaviors, and the Leading Causes of Death

Along with Global Health Concerns for Children, Women, and the Elderly, Mental Health Issues, Research and Technology Advancements, and Economic, Environmental, and Political Health Implications, a Glossary, and a Resource Listing for Additional Help and Information

Edited by Joyce Brennfleck Shannon. 614 pages. 2001. 0-7808-0330-2. $78.